W9-DAU-395

Leadership's 4th Evolution

Leadership's 4th Evolution:

COLLABORATION FOR THE 21ST CENTURY

First Edition

Edward M. Marshall, Ph.D.

Duke University

SAN DIEGO

Bassim Hamadeh, CEO and Publisher
Kaela Martin, Project Editor
Christian Berk, Production Editor
Emely Villavicencio, Senior Graphic Designer
Alexa Lucido, Licensing Manager
Natalie Piccotti, Director of Marketing
Kassie Graves, Vice President of Editorial
Jamie Giganti, Director of Academic Publishing

cognella® | ACADEMIC PUBLISHING
3970 Sorrento Valley Blvd., Ste. 500, San Diego, CA 92121

Endorsements

ACADEMICS

This book is a remarkable combination of principles, historical analysis, review of major theories of organization development, and detailed prescriptions for the kind of leadership and collaborative group work that will be necessary to save our planet and the kind of civil society that we all value. By reviewing the work of many academic theorists, successful consultants, and analysts of leadership, group, and cultural dynamics, the author extracts the important insights, principles, and practices necessary to cope with the evermore complex challenges that our world presents us with. This book is, in effect, a manifesto to move from an egocentric "I and me" society to a collaborative "We" society.

Edgar H. Schein, Ph.D.
Professor Emeritus, MIT Sloan School of Management
Author with Peter Schein of *Organizational Culture and Leadership* (2017), *Humble Leadership* (2018), and *The Corporate Culture Survival Guide*, 3d ed. (2019)

A thorough, thoughtful, and actionable look at what's required in the 21st Century to lead yourself as well as your team and organization. Complete with advice about steps to take and pitfalls to avoid.

Barry Z. Posner, Ph.D.
Accoiti Professor of Leadership and Former Dean of the Leavey School of Business, Santa Clara University Co-author with James M. Kouzes of *The Leadership Challenge*, 6th ed. (2017)

While halfway through the first chapter of *Leadership's 4th Evolution: Collaboration for the 21st Century*, I couldn't help thinking that this was the book I needed a few years back for my MBA Management and Organization Development class. Though I'm not teaching any longer, I still need this book—for colleagues (leaders as well as consultants) who request readings to help them *really* understand organizations, initiate and implement development plans, and help those around them to do the same.

This book is a fantastic treatise on leadership and, given its title, will be visible and attractive to many readers interested in the topic. It is important to add, however, that the chapters are equally relevant to and informative for those interested in *organizational culture*. Over the past 40 years, organizational culture has evolved from a rarely used and somewhat misunderstood construct to one that is overly used yet still frequently misunderstood. From the very first chapter, Edward Marshall clarifies the construct, provides in-depth insights into the types of cultures that enable organizations to be effective today, and discusses viable levers for moving cultures in a more constructive and collaborative direction. In the process, he provides a great list of references and makes it easy for the reader to track down both classic and contemporary writings on organizational culture and leadership.

Robert A. Cooke, Ph.D.
Associate Professor Emeritus of Management at the University of Illinois at Chicago
Author of the *Organizational Culture Inventory*, with Janet L. Szumal, 1994
Coauthor with Janet L. Szumal, *Creating Constructive Cultures* (2019)
CEO, Human Synergistics International

Edward Marshall's book lays bare the urgent leadership imperative for all of us, in this generation, at this time, to take on complex issues like climate change collectively. He maps out the path of *collaborative leadership* so we can meet our responsibilities in our time. He recognizes that any change, any progress, ultimately happens through people. His great insight is that collaborative leadership has the potential to do something that power-based leadership could never do—transform people involved in the collaboration for effective, sustained change. This is infinitely more desirable a goal that transactional, short-term "wins" that the power model of leadership might attain at best.

Ravi V. Bellamkonda, Ph.D.
Dean, The Pratt School of Engineering, Duke University
Fellow, American Association for the Advancement of Science

An excellent process for defining and refocusing the roles of leaders and managers in the turbulent years ahead.

Warren E. Baunach, Ph.D.
Professor and Former Associate Dean for Executive Education, Kenan-Flagler Business School, University of North Carolina at Chapel Hill

The relationship-based, networked organization will be the dominant structure in the 21st Century. Edward Marshall has put forth a very insightful and challenging discussion on the need for trust and integrity to be the cornerstones of successful organizations of this type. Business leaders struggling with change should read this book.

John Burbridge, Ph.D.
Former Dean, The Martha and Spencer Love School of Business, Elon University

BUSINESS LEADERS

I have seen the collaborative approach described in this book build trust and produce outstanding results. It should be considered by every business leader.

J. W. Marriott, Jr.
Chairman and CEO, Marriott International

Having worked with Dr. Marshall's framework and approach to leadership in multiple organizations, I can attest to the power and the practicality of this approach to leadership in a modern organization. It was essential to our organizational and team development at Microsoft, and later at VMware. This is an essential guide to managing in a world that has transformed nearly every organization.

Tony Scott
Former CIO of Microsoft, VMware and Disney
Former Federal CIO for President Barack Obama
CEO, Tony Scott & Company

The business community must redefine its covenant with employees. This approach builds value and ownership and delivers extraordinary results.

Ann Dore McLaughlin
Former US Secretary of Labor

If we are to address the challenges of speed in today's marketplace, we must strengthen the trust in our relationships with our people, customers, shareholders, and other partners. Dr. Marshall's practical framework for change enables businesses to achieve high performance, speed, and trust.

William Shaw
Former President, Marriott International

We are now entering a new renaissance; an era where "business as usual" is dead (or dying) and where human relationships will once again matter more than technology. Edward's book is showing us a solid path towards this exponentially different future, redefining the very definition of leadership and describing how hyper-collaboration trumps hyper-competition. Read this book and get future-ready!

Gerd Leonhard
European Futurist & Humanist, Zurich
Author of *Technology vs. Humanity*, 2016
CEO, The Futures Agency

Dr. Marshall has found the key to managing and motivating knowledge workers in the new workplace.

Pierce A. Quinlan
Former President, Loral Learning Systems

Edward Marshall has rightly pointed to the importance of character, will, and discipline—but most of all, *trust*—as the cornerstones for successful change. His Collaborative Method is a very effective way to ensure that the principles of owner-ship, accountability, and integrity become the foundation for increasing productivity and speed.

David Russo
Former Vice President for Human Resources, SAS Institute, Inc.

The reader takes an enlightening journey through organizational changes that remove barriers and result in improved leadership, increased trust, enhanced integrity, and a shared commitment to manage change.

Komei Arai
Former Vice President and Plant Manager, Ajinomoto, USA

Our organization delivered results never before achieved—and we did it largely through improved organizational unity and trust across geographically distributed groups. The principles, methods, and tools described by Edward Marshall have helped us create a shared organizational view of who we are and who we want to be.

Steven T. Miller
Information Systems Manager, E.I. DuPont de Nemours & Co., Inc.
Initial Sponsor and Mentor for the Collaborative Method, 1989–2000

Contents

A Note About the Cover
Lessons From Geese

Leadership's 4th Evolution: Collaboration for the 21st Century
Edward M. Marshall, Ph.D.

In case you are wondering why there are four geese on the cover of this book. How geese work and live together is a metaphor for the central focus of this book—collaborative leadership. We have a lot to learn from our flying friends, so I turned to the work Dr. Robert McNeish, who in 1972, wrote:

LESSONS FROM GEESE[1]

As each goose flaps its wings, it creates an "uplift" for the bird following. By flying in a "V" formation, the whole flock adds 71% more flying range than if each bird flew alone.

> *Lesson: People who share a common direction and sense of community can get where they are going quicker and easier because they are traveling on the thrust of one another.*

Whenever a goose falls out of formation, it suddenly feels the drag and resistance of trying to fly alone, and quickly gets back into formation to take advantage of the "lifting power" of the bird immediately in front.

> *Lesson: If we have as much sense as a goose, we will join in formations with those who are headed where we want to go.*

When the lead goose gets tired, it rotates back into the formation and another goose flies at the point position.

> *Lesson: It pays to take turns doing the hard tasks and sharing leadership—with people, as with geese, interdependent with one other.*

The geese in formation honk from behind to encourage those up front to keep up their speed.

> *Lesson: We need to make sure our honking from behind is encouraging—not something less helpful.*

When a goose gets sick or wounded or shot down, two geese drop out of formation and follow their fellow member down to help provide protection. They stay with this member of the flock until he or she is either able to fly again or dies. Then they launch out on their own, with another formation, or catch up with their own flock.

> *Lesson: If we have as much sense as the geese, we'll stand by each other like that.*

ENDNOTE

1   *Lessons from the Geese* was written in 1972 by Dr. Robert McNeish of Baltimore. Dr. McNeish, was, for many years a science teacher before he became involved in school administration. He had always been intrigued with observing geese for years and first wrote this piece for a sermon he delivered in his church; https://transformation-center.org/wp-content/uploads/2015/03/Lessons_From_The_Geese1.pdf

Preface

WE ARE AT THE DAWN of a new age of collaboration, the 4th Evolution of Leadership. Gone are the days of the Industrial Revolution when Frederick Winslow Taylor's approach to leadership focused on power and control, motivating the workforce by fear. Even though the power and politics of organizational hierarchy are still prevalent today, the anomalies of the 20th Century's Power Paradigm were so serious that in 1960 Douglas McGregor gave us the 2nd Evolution of leadership, Theory Y, or the People Paradigm. McGregor helped us understand that human beings are social creatures, liked working in groups/teams, and were motivated by appreciation and respect. McGregor's prescient vision of the future predicted that someday, collaboration would be the way we work. That day is today!

By 1990 the 3rd Evolution of leadership emerged with Stephen Covey's focus on principles and the understanding that human beings are moral, ethical creatures. He argued that immutable truths govern how we behave. Leadership, to Covey, comes from the inside out, a journey that is grounded in these truths and self-awareness.

Since 1989 the 4th Evolution of Leadership, the Collaboration Paradigm, took shape as my clients taught me people naturally want to collaborate with each other, want to own their work and the workplace, and are motivated by trust and mutual respect. In 1995, my first book on collaborative leadership, *Transforming the Way We Work: The Power of the Collaborative Workplace,* spelled out the basic argument for how a collaborative work ethic, a set of principles, should govern how leaders, and organizations are led and managed.[1] In 2000, after five years of disastrous results from radical re-engineering, I wrote my second book on collaborative leadership, *Building Trust at the Speed of Change,* which argued that there could be lasting collaborative change if leadership demonstrated character, will, and discipline.[2] By 2010 the *Collaborative Method's* focus on *how* to implement collaborative principles and behaviors at the individual, team and organizational levels, resulted in tools and processes that had been designed, tested, implemented, and strengthened to solve client challenges. Today, with *Leadership's 4th Evolution,* McGregor's prediction has come true. Collaboration, based on the principles of psychological safety, ownership, and trust, is the new predicate for how to lead organizations in the Digital Age, where Millennials and GenZers are two-thirds of the world's population. It is a complete replacement for hierarchy's power, control, and fear-based leadership. We have quite a way to go, though, which is one of the main reasons for this book—it is a road map and handbook for leaders to transform themselves, their teams, and organizations from power to collaboration and to bring collaborative leadership to the solution of global crises like global pandemics, hunger and income inequality, and climate change.

WHY I WROTE THIS BOOK

I wrote this book because our world is at an inflection point, and the choices we make in the next decade will determine the future of our planet and humanity. Our planet is on fire, with carbon-fueled global warming, which threatens our very existence as a human race. Covid-19 has invaded every country on Earth, with devastating consequences for millions and millions of people. Other than the United Nations, global leadership largely remains incapable of working collaboratively to address these clear and present dangers to the people of this planet. Instead, denial, selfish interests, greed, and petty politics are sealing our fate. There are also challenges to our humanity from the accelerated rate of technological change, which require us to have a new theory of how we work with each other in the Digital Age. The continued prevalence of hierarchical leadership also puts our future at risk, a future that requires agility, trust, workforce ownership, psychological safety, and the ability to work across the boundaries of time, culture, regional differences, and language. Companies can no longer afford to go up and down the chain of command to get a decision that may be wrong.

The Collaboration Paradigm, and its implementation mechanism, the *Collaborative Method*, offer us a way forward. It is time for a fundamental transformation and realignment of how we lead. It is time for a national and international conversation among leaders, managers, and workers about the future of the global workplace. It is time for a conversation among students who are our future leaders, about how they choose to work with others in a highly volatile, complex, uncertain, and interdependent world. It is time for a conversation about how we will transform leadership mindsets, behaviors, and structures from hierarchy, power, control and fear, to collaboration, psychological safety, ownership and trust. This book not only provides a new theory of Collaboration, but also the practical implementation tools and processes for its implementation.

When I started working at DuPont in 1989, my sponsor, mentor, and friend, Stephen T. Miller, a senior leader at DuPont, challenged me and my criticism of hierarchical leadership with a simple question: "What will you put in its place?" I wish Steve were here today so that he could read the answer to his question. *Leadership's 4th Evolution: Collaboration for the 21st Century* is the stem-to-stern replacement for hierarchy. My deepest appreciation to Steve for his wisdom, foresight, and challenge to make this happen.

I believe in a different leadership culture than the one based on power, a culture where every individual is honored for the gifts they bring and is empowered to be the best version of themselves. Where every team is empowered to do their best work and produce superior results. Where the organization's culture is fit for the human spirt. Where the peoples of this planet can have economic and social justice, have their dignity and human rights protected, and where the deep inequalities in wealth and power between rich and poor nations are reduced or eliminated. And where global leaders set aside their national self-interest, corporate greed, and short-term political posturing, to collaborate to get to net zero carbon emissions by 2030.

I believe, based on more than 40 years of research and applied work in leadership and organizational culture change, that collaboration is our last best hope. We have failed up to now. It is insane to think that we can keep doing the same things we've been doing for over 100 years and expect a different result. It is time for the fundamental transformation of how we lead ourselves, our teams and organizations, and lead globally.

I am also writing this book because, after returning to academia from 40 years in business, I am amazed at the type of leadership being taught. As we will learn, the Power Paradigm of leadership is apparently embedded in the pedagogical systems of universities and leadership development programs, at precisely the time that transformational, collaborative leadership is needed. My hope is that this book can serve as an inspiration to the Millennial and GenZ generations of future leaders.

ORIGINS: THE POWER OF CULTURE

As I write this, it is 50 years since I arrived in New Delhi, India, to work at the Ford Foundation as part of my Master's Degree in International Public Administration at the Maxwell School, Syracuse University. My first professional goal was to work in international economic development, helping what were then called "developing nations" become self-sufficient and able to care for their people. It was an extraordinary 18 months. I was overwhelmed almost immediately by the desperation that comes with the deep poverty of what is now over a billion people. I was also inspired by the sparkle in people's eyes, their fierce resolve to live, and their struggle to be free. I came to better understand the depth of their culture, their nearly 30,000 years of history, their 200 years of colonial rule under the British, and the untidiness of their struggling new democracy. This was the land of Gandhi, Nehru, Ambedkar, Bose, and Patel. It is a land of immense pride and dignity. What India taught me is the power of culture as a driver for human behavior.

Returning to the United States, I continued to explore the role culture plays in organization development and human behavior, my chosen field. I worked in the Civil Rights movement, with community action agencies, community-based economic development corporations, and community advocacy organizations in the African-American and Latino communities. I again witnessed the power of their cultures, norms, and values, born in the struggle for freedom, and how these influenced their behavior. A pattern was emerging. So I educated myself about organizational culture, learning from the best, Edgar Schein, whose book *Organizational Culture and Leadership*, not only defined organizational culture as DNA, but also helped me understand the full impact that it has on shaping human behavior.[3]

I was also immensely influenced by Talcott Parsons and his book *The Social System*,[4] where he spells out the relationship between content and process in an organization—*what* an organization does and *how* it does it. This became the basis for my early years as a consultant. We would do executive retreats away from the office, and the participants would have major revelations about why their relationships were broken and would make commitments to fix them. But when they returned to the office, it was only a matter of hours or days before they were right back to behaving badly. I was curious why this was the case and began looking for the root cause.

It did not take long to realize that what was missing was a deep appreciation of the culture of an organization, and the behavioral patterns of the people working there. It became clear that their relationships were shaped by the values, beliefs, assumptions, and expectations of the workforce, and how those values and beliefs shaped their behavior. But culture was missing from Parsons' model of content and process. So, in 1989, I added the culture circle to the process and content circles making it a Venn diagram, with the culture circle on top. This became known as the Collaboration Systems Model, which is central to the new theory of Collaboration.

In 1989, I was hired by DuPont to work with its Information Systems group in one of the major business units. I began working with a leadership team in East Texas, a group that was experiencing severe competition. They were mandated by headquarters to work together differently so they could beat their competitor. I had no idea how to do this, so at our first meeting I asked them what they needed to work together effectively as a team. The result was the *Collaborative Team Governance Process*. Several hundred teams later, I can say that this process was perfected to the point that it is an incredibly powerful tool that builds high trust through ownership of their governance process and transforms their relationships. By turning their shared values and beliefs into agreed-upon behavior, I had threaded the Parsons/Schein needle—I had connected Culture to Process through a structured relationship-building process. Each team's front-loaded governance process was always tied to the solution of a critical organizational issue. They did not have to go away on a retreat, go to training, or do a ropes course. They did this work in their workplace, focused on solving their high-value issue, but doing it Culture-First, resulting in the development of permanent high-trust relationships that transformed the workplace. This team development process, along with the individual collaborative leadership journey, and the process for transformative organizational change were codified in my first book, *Transforming the Way We Work*.

But something was missing. The reengineering craze, which by the late 1990s was beginning to crater, really shined a light on it. It was the need for leadership to demonstrate their character, will, and discipline in building sustainable high-trust relationships and workplace cultures and to not be distracted by "bright shiny objects" like the fad of the day. So I wrote my second book *Building Trust at the Speed of Change*. Leadership was finally realizing the power of trust in how people worked together in a global, highly interdependent, digital world.

Still, something was missing in this evolving theory of collaboration. Over the next 20 years, I came to realize that with all the changes that organizations were going through, and with over 70% of them failing, there was something fundamental needed. When I worked with the US Air Force on a major information technology transformation, it finally dawned on me that what was missing was the critical ingredient of ownership of the change process by those who were directly impacted by it and who must live with its consequences. I went to work on developing an ownership strategy for implementing organizational change, applied it in a number of change processes, and had an 80% success rate. It seemed like a simple solution, but it took a lot of trial and error to get to this point. The realization was that we get work done through people, that leaders need to honor and respect them, trust their professionalism and judgment, and give them a stake in the process. If they own their jobs, their working relationships, and the organization's mission, vision, and values, they will take care of them. It was from these experiences that I came to the saying: "People take care of what they own—they don't wash rented cars."

When I was invited by Cognella Academic Publishing to write this textbook, I welcomed the opportunity to articulate a new and complete theory of Collaboration, with all of its many applications. *Leadership's 4th Evolution: Collaboration for the 21st Century* has been an extraordinary journey, fueled by my passion for the transformation of power-based leadership to collaborative leadership, by my commitment to empowering the workforce, giving them a substantial voice in their work life, and by my deep concern that unless we start to make this shift very now, we may very well not have organizations or a planet to lead.

WHO SHOULD READ THIS BOOK?

There are two primary audiences. First, after working with business leaders on collaborative change implementations of many kinds throughout my career, I have come to believe this work must start with the leaders of tomorrow, in the classrooms of our universities, community colleges, and high schools. It needs to be a required part of the curriculum for schools of engineering, business, public administration, health care, public policy, education, and social work. It needs to be part of the curriculum of both public and private high schools. These are the leaders who will be faced with the consequences of actions taken in the past century. They are the ones who will guide us all through the crises of the next century.

Second, this book is written for the leaders of today, whether in for-profit corporations, public sector organizations, executive education programs, corporate universities, foundations, non-profits, and nongovernmental organizations (NGOs). We must begin this transformation today and create workplaces that will not only empower today's workforce, but also welcome the leaders and workers of tomorrow. The world in which these organizations now exist is being driven by forces beyond our individual control. Digitization of everything, artificial intelligence, robotization of work, global volatility, uncertainty, complexity, and ambiguity, along with existential threats from global pandemics and climate change, combined create an environment of great concern, even fear. At the same time, Collaboration is a leadership philosophy and way of working which is grounded in principle, which empower us to be our best selves and do our best work, and to act collectively to transform our workplaces. It is also a value system that honors our humanity, respects our dignity, believes in redemption, and gives us a framework, and the tools and processes that can fundamentally shift the trajectory of our lives as we know it, for the better.

This is a vision of hope. This is a journey of discovery. This is a concrete way to express our collective will for the good of all. Welcome to the journey.

Edward M. Marshall, Ph.D., PCC
Chapel Hill, North Carolina
July, 2020
edward.marshall@duke.edu
edward@marshallgroup.com
https://www.linkedin.com/in/
edward-m-marshall-ph-d-pcc-
a84209b/

ENDNOTES

1 Edward M. Marshall, *Transforming the Way We Work: The Power of the Collaborative Workplace* (New York: AMACOM Books, 1995).
2 Edward M. Marshall, *Building Trust at the Speed of Change: The Power of the Relationship-Based Corporation* (New York: AMACOM Books, 2000).
3 Edgar H. Schein, *Organizational Culture and Leadership*, 5th ed. (Hoboken, NJ: Wiley, 2017).
4 Talcott Parsons, *The Social System* (London: Routledge & Kegan Paul, 1951).

Author's Biography

Edward M. Marshall, Ph.D., PCC
Adjunct Professor in Management, Fuqua School
of Business & Pratt School of Engineering
Duke University
edward.marshall@duke.edu (919) 265-9616

EDWARD MARSHALL'S CAREER has focused on leadership and team development, collaborative organizational change, executive coaching, and helping corporations transform their leadership cultures. In 2016, after 40 years in business, he joined the faculty of the Fuqua School of Business and the Pratt School of Engineering at Duke University, where he teaches leadership courses. He is Founder and Managing Partner of The Marshall Group, LLC, a collaborative leadership, team development, and change consulting firm, based in Chapel Hill, N.C. He has worked with C-suite executives at Fortune 500 companies like Microsoft, DuPont, Marriott, IBM, and Philips, as well as entrepreneurial and mid-sized firms. In his many engagements, he has served as an executive coach, culture and organizational change strategist, team developer, and facilitator. His work has taken him beyond clients in North America to South Asia, Africa, Latin America, and Europe. He has facilitated more than 100 change initiatives in technology, healthcare, and manufacturing companies, ranging from strategic alliances and business process redesigns, to mergers, IT integrations, and cultural transformations. As an ICF-certified executive coach, Dr. Marshall has helped many senior executives reach their professional goals.

Edward is best known for developing the best-practice *Collaborative Method(sm)*, a suite of services that enable organizations to create a collaborative leadership culture at the organization, team, and individual levels. This methodology won the *Excellence in Organization Development* Award from the Association for Talent Development. In 2015, he was recognized by Trust Across America with a *Lifetime Achievement Award as a Top 15 Trust Thought Leader.*

As a pioneer and leader in the field of collaborative leadership, team development, and cultural transformation, Edward has authored two Knight-Ridder best-selling business books, *Transforming the Way We Work: The Power of the Collaborative*

Workplace, and *Building Trust at the Speed of Change,* and has been a contributing author to four other books on trust and culture change. Since 1997, he has been a nationally syndicated columnist writing *In the Workplace* column for American Cities *Business Journals.* His latest book, *Leadership's 4th Evolution: Collaboration for the 21st Century (2020),* is the third in a series of books on collaborative leadership. He also holds three service marks for his work in developing collaborative leadership and change processes.

Professor Marshall holds a Ph.D. from the University of North Carolina at Chapel Hill, a Masters from Syracuse University and a BA from Claremont McKenna College. He holds coaching certificates from Duke University and the International Coach Federation. He is also certified in a range of 360 assessment instruments.

Edward is married to Julie, a nationally certified teacher who has retired from the Duke School for Children in Durham, N.C. He has three grown sons who are engaged in hospital administration, Habitat for Humanity, and public interest law. Edward's interests include spending time with family, the beach, travel, swimming, writing, jazz piano, and cooking for his family.

Acknowledgments

W RITING THIS BOOK has been a journey that would never have been possible had I not had the loving support of my wife, Julie. She has been a saint throughout the year and a half it took to research and write this work. She gave up weekends, evenings, and a good part of a summer, and she did so because she knows how important this work is, not only for me but for future generations of leaders. Julie's optimism, loving heart, and appreciative approach to life also inspired me to be hopeful in the face of the challenges this book explores. Her insights and challenging questions throughout the writing process also helped make the writing better and more coherent. To my best friend, you have my deepest respect, appreciation, and love.

I have also written this book for my sons, Jonathan and David, both Millennials and leaders in their own right, that they may live in a world that is substantially more collaborative than it is today and in a world where peace, trust, mutual respect, and a just and sustainable way of life is possible for all. It was Jonathan, in fact, who first challenged me to deal with the climate emergency when he was 13 years old and who, in his work with Habitat for Humanity, helped me understand the importance of serving others and addressing the enormous income inequalities in our country and around the world. David helped me understand, in his volunteer work as a first responder and his professional life as a health care provider, how important self-sacrifice and hard work are if we are to save each other and the planet.

To my hundreds of students at Duke University's Pratt School of Engineering, you inspired me to be the best version of myself, to be a better professor, and to articulate the frameworks, concepts, and skills needed for leaders of all kinds to become more collaborative. You are from South Asia, East Asia, Europe, Africa, Latin America, the Middle East, and the United States and have helped me better understand that collaboration is the way people around the world want to work. You are the next generation of leaders who will face the challenges of global pandemics and the climate emergency. Now you have a coherent theory of collaboration and its practical tools and processes to empower you so that you can be your best selves and do your best work while giving to the peoples of the planet. Another special appreciation goes to our 11 year old rescue English lab, Katie, for keeping me company for the last 18 months, camped out by my side and providing support.

To all of my clients, who since 1989 co-created this body of work with me, trusted me to be your guide, and embraced the quest for high trust, to you I owe a deep debt of gratitude. You made this work come alive. A special note of appreciation is needed here for my friend and colleague, my original sponsor in this work, Stephen T. Miller of DuPont, may he rest in peace. In 1989 he supported the early stages of the development of the *Collaborative Method* in project after project at DuPont and Conoco over five years. He challenged my mind and my heart, enriched my spirit, and showed me what a truly humble collaborative leader was like. Unlike most information systems organizations at the time, Steve's was one that people lined up to get into.

To my former client, colleague, and friend Tony Scott, former CIO of Disney, Microsoft, and VMware, and former President Barack Obama's Federal CIO, thank you for believing in me and for your commitment to transforming leadership cultures from Power to Collaboration. Your authentic, humble, and visionary leadership inspired me to see the full potential of collaborative leadership and how it could transform the planet.

To my dear friend and brother in South Africa, Morare Manaka, a deep appreciation for your efforts to bring collaborative leadership to the leadership of Limpopo Province, to departments of the South African government, and to the business community. Our many Skype conversations over the past five years provided me with a deep insight into the power of *Ubuntu*, the Zulu philosophy that means, "I am because we are."

This book has also given me the opportunity to "meet" António Guterres, Secretary-General of the United Nations, who has led the global effort to stop global warming before it is too late. He represents the type of global collaborative leadership required to address this emergency before 2030. Without his humility, grace, passion, and collaborative spirit, we would not have the same level of understanding of what we must do to save our planet.

To the peoples of the planet, especially those who live in the Sahel, Sub-Saharan and East Africa, the Middle East, South Asia, East Asia, and the island nations in the Indian and South Pacific Oceans, my hope and prayer is that leaders of organizations and governments around the world may be inspired by this work, that they will make a conscious choice to put your human rights, economic justice, and climate equity before their national self-interest, corporate profits, and short-term political posturing in order to solve the climate emergency. Your desperate life circumstances, pain and suffering, migration for survival, and deep inequality have given me the passion to put forth collaborative leadership as the fastest way to redress these injustices.

To my intellectual mentors, and their deep understanding of the human condition, I extend my deepest appreciation and gratitude. Without you, this book would have been about tools and processes, rather than culture, systems, and leadership. First and foremost, to Douglas McGregor and Chris Argyris, who helped us understand the human side of enterprise, human motivation, and the dynamics of group behavior. The beginnings of the human potential movement and the conceptual and theoretical foundations of this theory of collaboration are rooted in your groundbreaking work. To Edgar Schein, whose work in organizational culture and leadership I first used in my graduate Public Administration Master's degree classes at Northeastern University in 1976, I extend my deepest respect and appreciation. It was an honor to finally meet and work with him forty years later in a weeklong seminar with Dr. Robert Cooke of Human Synergistics International. The work you both have done in cultural DNA and leadership culture paradigms has provided the theoretical and statistically validated foundation for this theory of collaboration. James Kouzes and Barry Posner wrote one of the most influential leadership books of all time, which provided a clear 21st Century articulation of the responsibilities of emotionally intelligent leaders to those who work with them. Peter Senge's work provided a profound and deep understanding of what a learning organization is and how critical it is for 21st Century leaders to make this an integral part of their leadership cultures. Daniel Goleman's work in emotional intelligence helped me understand the central role of self-awareness and empathy in collaborative leaders. Patrick Lencioni's work in team development cemented my belief that without trust, collaboration is not possible.

There are, of course, many other authors with whom I became great friends while writing this book, not the least of whom was Lao Tzu, 6th Century BCE, and the father of collaborative leadership. There was Talcott Parsons, Gerd Leonhard, Jeffrey Sachs, Jeff Nesbit, David Wallace-Wells, Andrew Leigh, Jacque Ellul, Viktor Frankl, Virginia Satir, James Tamm, and Ronald Luyet—to all of you, my deep appreciation for the gifts you have given me and to millions of leaders around the world.

A special thank you to Swati Jain, Yansen Geng, Shagun Sharma, and Maria Kuriachan, all Masters of Engineering Management graduates from the Pratt School of Engineering at Duke University, for their inspiration while they were my students and for their insights as they reviewed a number of early chapters in the book. You have made this book better and more focused for the students who come after you.

Finally, I wish to recognize my Project Editor at Cognella Publishing, Kaela Martin, who has been the model of patience, support, and effectiveness in our publishing journey together.

Introduction

What We Have Inherited

It was the best of times, it was the worst of times, it was the age of wisdom, it was the age of foolishness, it was the epoch of belief, it was the epoch of incredulity, it was the season of light, it was the season of darkness, it was the spring of hope, it was the winter of despair.
—Charles Dickens, *A Tale of Two Cities*

GLOBALLY, WE ARE at both the beginning of a mass extinction event for the peoples of the planet[1] and the dawn of a new era, when the leaders of the world can decide whether they will finally work together collaboratively to ensure peace, security, and sustainability for all nations. Global leaders are, however, like Nero, fiddling while the planet burns. Failure is truly not an option. As President Barack Obama said in 2015, "There is no Plan B."[2]

Organizations are in the midst of a technological revolution, where the accelerated speed of change is outpacing our human capacity to adapt. At the same time, the rise of the technologically savvy Millennials and Gen Zers offer organizations their best hope for the cultural transformation needed to enable that adaptation. They have grown up digital and collaborative, and this is how they want to work.

Teams still exist in leadership cultures that are predominantly hierarchical, where power, control, and motivation by fear prevent the building of high-trust relationships. At the same time, collaboration is how people naturally want to work. To do so, they need workplace cultures that build trust, respect, and ownership.

Individual leadership is also on the edge between the more traditional command-and-control leadership paradigm of the 20th Century Industrial Age and the emerging collaborative, principle-based paradigm of the 21st Century Digital Age. Traditional leadership styles no longer apply. Hierarchy is out of step with the realities of our times, which call for a flatter, globally networked, team-based collaborative leadership culture based on trust and respect. And yet we still have hierarchy. As Marshall Goldsmith reminds us, "What got you here won't get you there."[3]

Thomas Kuhn would argue that it is time for a paradigmatic revolution.[4] If we are to survive beyond 2100 on this planet as we now know it, we urgently need to transform how we think about and teach leadership in terms of principles, beliefs, assumptions, skills, behaviors, and work practices. To survive, we must learn how to lead collaboratively at every level of our society—globally, in our communities, our organizations, and teams. To do so requires a new theory of collaborative leadership that reflects the realities of the world we now live in, how leadership cultures shape the relationships between people and their work, and how we can create work cultures that empower the human spirit.

This is *Leadership's 4th Evolution*—from hierarchy, power, control, and fear to collaboration, psychological safety, trust, and ownership. This evolution is about creating leadership cultures that empower people to be their best selves so they can do their best work and create superior results. This evolution is about developing a generation of leaders who are principled, ethical above reproach, self-aware, emotionally intelligent, and have developed a range of collaborative skills that enable them to empower others. This 4th Evolution means that teams of all kinds have collaborative governance processes that result in high trust and ownership so that the members can accelerate their effectiveness. For global leadership, the 4th Evolution means putting the welfare and needs of the peoples of the planet above national self-interest, corporate profits, and short-term political posturing.

In this book, we will go on a journey, a journey of hope and opportunity in the face of seemingly insurmountable challenges. It is a journey about rediscovering our humanity as individuals and our power as we work collaboratively and collectively to meet these challenges head on. It is a journey based on our faith in ourselves and each other, of optimism, and a belief that anything is possible, including saving the planet.

Let's get started.

21ST CENTURY LEADERSHIP CHALLENGES

Leaders face an extraordinary set of challenges as the 21st Century unfolds. These challenges are happening on three levels: (1) External realities that are shaping our world and lives; (2) 20th Century vs. 21st Century leadership assumptions, values, and beliefs that shape leadership behavior in organizations; and (3) Identity factors that shape our leadership. It is the confluence of these three levels that shape this leadership journey. How will you navigate and manage these challenges? What will they mean for your leadership? As we begin, keep an open mind and see what opportunities there are for you to become a masterful 21st-Century collaborative leader.

External Realities Shaping Our World and Lives

As we start our journey in the third decade of the 21st Century, there are a number of major forces shaping our world, as well as how we think about our leadership. These are forces that are beyond our control, and yet they define the contours of our lives.

- **Political Turmoil:** For the first time since World War II, we see the rise of nationalism and authoritarianism in countries around the world, from China and India to Hungary and Brazil, and, for the first time, in the United States. This nationalism has been fueled by hate and racism against people of color, antipathy toward "the other," and public policies that exclude immigrants, whether this is in Europe, China, India, the Democratic Republic of Congo, or the United States. Brexit, "America First," trade wars, and other isolationist attitudes have created new levels of tension and conflict. The Middle East remains a tinderbox, and there are demonstrations for democratic rights and against police brutality and discrimination around the world, from Hong Kong to Lebanon to Minneapolis, Minnesota to Bolivia. We see the rise of "fake news," increased cyberwarfare, and an extreme level of divisiveness in nations around the world. Terrorist groups still threaten the global order on almost every continent. It is an overwhelming complexity of disruptions to peace, freedom, and security.

- **VUCA:** Leaders also face a world being shaped by market VUCA—volatility, uncertainty, complexity, and ambiguity. In 2016 the Strategic Agility Institute™ issued its first *VUCA Report* defining these terms:[5]

  - **Volatility:** An increase in the pace or rate of change
  - **Uncertainty:** Unpredictability about the future
  - **Complexity:** Having interconnected parts or variables
  - **Ambiguity:** Lack of clarity about the meaning or trends of events

  The Institute surveyed close to 300 business leaders across a range of industries in terms of the speed at which VUCA was impacting them, and found that on a scale of 0 to 100, their VUCA Index was 69.57 for these respondents, in terms of the expected level of future turbulence.[6]

- **Velocity of Change:** The acceleration of technological advancement over the next 30 years is almost beyond comprehension. The Emerging Future organization predicts that by the early 2040's:[7]

  > *... rapid pace of improved changes will be hundreds of millions of times faster than today. ... The only way humans will be able to keep up. ... will be with virtual assistants and computers inside us, and around us. Evolutions will bring about artificial general intelligence ... in the form of intelligent machines that have the ability to create and improve its own software and hardware. ...*[8]

The question we must all consider is whether human beings have the capacity to adapt to all of this change. What will be its impact on our organizations, leadership cultures, and our relationships with each other? How will we, as human beings, cope with and absorb all of this change? We're way beyond the concept of being agile. We need a comprehensive systems approach to understanding how our organizations function and we how we need to lead in a way that respects the abilities of all human beings and that empowers us to respond to these inevitable disruptions.

- **The Transformation of Industry:** As a consequence of all this technological transformation, industries are also being transformed. Alec Ross, in *The Industries of the Future,* helps us understand how technological changes like artificial intelligence, big data, and robots are shaping the future of business and markets, let alone our organizations and the people who work there. He points to the following changes:[9]

  - Cutting-edge advances in robotics, artificial intelligence, and machine learning
  - The uneven distribution of economic returns from robotics and life sciences, leaving those who are behind today even further behind
  - The code-ification of money, markets, and trust
  - The weaponization of code by bad actors causing damage to the international economy
  - The expansion of big data as it becomes an instrument with profound applications in both industry and solving social problems

How will we lead and manage in this transformed environment? What will be the relationship between management and the workforce, between people and machines, between our humanity and what we must do to ensure the effectiveness of our organizations?

- **The Rise of Millennials and GenZers:** Close to 2 billion Millennials and 2 billion GenZers around the world represent a very potent force for change in our organizations. Millennials now dominate the global workforce, and they expect more collaborative leadership cultures. According to the Pew Research Center, as of 2017 in the United States, 56% of the workforce are Millennials.[10] In the global workforce, by 2020 fully 75% will be Millennials.[11] They have very specific expectations about the type of workplace they want to be in, but at the same time they remain increasingly skeptical about business, leadership, and their own futures. They want more collaboration in the workplace and substantially more flexibility, independence, and autonomy.[12] Will leadership be able to meet these needs?

- **Ethical Lapses:** In almost every sphere of public and private sector life, there are significant ethical lapses among leadership in both the private and public sectors: financial or sexual impropriety; fraud and abuse; racial, gender, and religious discrimination; public and private sector corruption; and a range of acts that have deleterious impacts on other human beings. There are scandals in almost every industry, the public sector, and in civil society. Even the President of the United States, for only the third time in history, has been impeached for public corruption. There are unethical decisions being made that impact the very existence of the planet, as well as decisions that compromise the existence of entire cultures, or the well-being, health, and happiness of certain populations. Ethical principles and conduct are a cornerstone of collaborative leadership, especially honor, integrity, responsibility, and accountability; they provide the guardrails for collaborative decisions or actions taken by individual leaders, teams, or organizations. How will we restore ethical behavior that is above reproach?

- **Global Warming and the Threat of Extinction:** On December 2, 2019, the Secretary-General of the United Nations, António Guterres, gave the world a warning: *"The point of no return is no longer over the horizon. It is in sight and hurtling towards us."*[13] In November, 2018, the United Nation's scientific panel of global climate scientists, known as the Intergovernmental Panel on Climate Change (IPCC), issued a very stark warning to all of us—it gave world leaders until 2030 to reverse the trajectory of carbon dioxide (CO_2) levels in the atmosphere to keep global warming below $1.5°$ Celsius of pre-industrial levels or face catastrophic consequences as we pass the "tipping point" from which there is no return.[14] In late 2019, 11,000 climate scientists gave us another warning that the peoples of the world are now in a "climate emergency," and that our lifestyles were going to have to dramatically change if we are to survive.[15] The track record for global leadership on reducing carbon emissions is dismal. In fact, emissions have gone up in the past few years. It is time for a new kind of leadership, leaders who will put the interests of the peoples of the world over self-interest, profit, or national interest, and collaborate to get to net-zero carbon emissions by 2030.

20th vs. 21st Century Leadership Assumptions, Values, and Beliefs

21st Century leaders also face a second level of contextual challenge, which involves a range of assumptions, values, and beliefs that are embedded in the cultures of the organizations in which they work. The dichotomous nature of these assumptions, values, and beliefs represents a critical choice for leaders, between a 20th Century Industrial Age view of leadership based on power, control, and fear, and a 21st-Century Digital Age view based on principle, ownership, and trust.

- **Power vs. Principle:** As we will see in the ensuing chapters, 20th Century leadership was grounded in what will be called the Power Paradigm, the belief that leadership had a right to control the workforce, incentivize or punish them, and terminate their employment if necessary. The workers in the Industrial Revolution of the early 1900s were considered to be lazy and indolent, and those in power believed the workers had to be pushed, threatened, or incented to perform. Hierarchical structures and command-and-control management struck fear into the hearts of the workforce. Compliance was the order of the day. By the mid- to late 20th Century, researchers and theorists found that people were responsible, hard-working, and trustworthy; that they needed to be encouraged, supported, and nurtured. By the early 21st Century, flatter, more team-based organizations began to emerge, as people became more valued by management. But still, the Power Paradigm was and is the predominant leadership culture. In the 21st Century, with the realities of globalization, digitization, and a highly interdependent world, there is a need for leadership that is based on principle, is emotionally intelligent, empowers the workforce, and builds high levels of trust.

- **Individualistic vs. Collectivist:** A second set of assumptions, values, and beliefs is the distinction between individualism and collectivism. There are leaders who believe that the primary unit for getting work done is the individual and that individual effort is the only effort to be evaluated and rewarded. This 20th Century view is the fundamental assumption of most human resources departments, evaluation systems, and reward/recognition programs. There is an increased recognition that work in the 21st Century is done in teams of all kinds, and that this team effort is what needs to be recognized and rewarded. 20th Century leaders focus on "Me," while 21st Century 4th Evolution leaders focus on "We." Some leaders have tried to bridge the divide by creating hybrid systems that reward both team and individual performance, but the predominant mode of operating remains individualistic.

- **Competitive vs. Collaborative:** A third set of assumptions, values, and beliefs is about how best to motivate the workforce. The 20th Century belief is that people are best motivated when they compete against each other. In some companies it is called "friendly competition" in an effort to take the edge of the adversarial or oppositional nature for the assumption. Often this view is justified by talking about team sports, where "the best performance" comes when they compete against each other. People in silos are pitted against each other, often leading to dysfunctional behavior that hurts the company's bottom line. In the 21st Century, the belief is that people fundamentally want to collaborate with each other to get the job done. They want community, connectedness, and the ability to compete externally rather than internally. Leaders with this belief system work to create cross-functional collaboration, share information, and take down the silo walls.

- **Boss vs. Coach:** A fourth set of assumptions, values, and beliefs is about the nature of the relationship between management and the workforce. In the 20th Century approach, leaders are "bosses" and "supervisors," people who control the work, performance reviews, bonuses, and futures of the workforce. It is a compliant, dependent relationship, which lines up with the assumptions and values of hierarchy, individualism, and competition. The 21st Century approach is that leaders serve and support the workforce, empower and facilitate them in the completion of their work, and are coaches when it comes to performance. Professionals are recognized as being competent, innovative, and hardworking, whose managers are emotionally intelligent, self-aware, and effective at giving them feedback.

- **Closed vs. Transparent:** A fifth set of assumptions, values, and beliefs is that in the 20th Century organization, management has a right to keep corporate information closely held, to be opaque when it comes to the operations of the business. Much of this view is tied up in the capitalist notion that ownership of capital controls the information flow, and the workforce does not have the "right to know" or the "need to know." Information flows are one-way, and if the organization goes into bankruptcy, and the workforce is laid off, the workers are simply are out of luck. In the 21st Century organization, there is the expectation of transparency, that the workforce has a right and need to know how the organization operates, that there is at least a two-way flow of information, and that if the organization gets into trouble, everyone will know and be part of the solution. This is a partnership, and if the workforce is laid off, there is a planned and fair approach to do so that protects their futures.

- **Extrinsic vs. Intrinsic Motivation:** A sixth set of assumptions, values, and beliefs is about how best to motivate the workforce. 20th Century leaders believe that people are driven by extrinsic rewards such as salary/hourly rate, benefits, and even the workplace. Some companies try to incent their workforce with foosball tables, beanbag chairs, car washes, massages, and 24-hour free food. While people clearly need to make a salary with benefits, 21st Century leaders know that the workforce is primarily motivated by intrinsic rewards such as meaningful work, a clear organizational purpose and vision, making a difference, and contributing to the solution of societal problems.

- **Control vs. Ownership:** A seventh set of assumptions, values, and beliefs is about who "owns" the work and the workplace. 20th Century leaders believes they do and that they have a right to control the workforce and use their position and authority to do so. What they don't realize is that they don't control anyone. The only way leaders today can get their work done is through influence, based on their credibility, empathy, and support of their workforce. The 21st Century leader has no illusion about "control," has no need for it, uses a facilitative style, and works to give the workforce ownership of their work and the workplace. It's not about authority. It's about empowering the workforce to get the work done.

- **Productivity vs. Productive Energy:** The eighth and final set of assumptions, values, and beliefs is the focus on productivity vs. productive energy. The 20th

Century leader focuses almost exclusively on output, results, and the bottom line. The entire approach to managing others is about driving results, sometimes at great cost to the workforce or ethical conduct. Often an "ends justifies the means" rationale is used, and workers become mere cogs in the wheel. The 21st Century leader understands that the only difference between company A and company B is the "productive energy" of the workforce—which is defined as *what workers are willing to give of themselves to the enterprise. It reflects their pride in the organization, their self-esteem, how they are treated by leadership, their level of engagement, the degree of trust and ownership in the culture, and the extent to which they feel respected, appreciated, and acknowledged for their contributions.*[16] High productive energy organizations have collaborative leadership cultures.

Identity Factors That Shape Our Leadership

There is yet a third, and deeper, level of context for each and every leader—one's identity. Who am I? Who do I want to be as a leader? How will I deal with all of the complexity and turmoil I see in the world? As we will discover in Chapter 5, "Becoming a Collaborative Leader," our self-awareness, ability to reflect, and ability to adapt will depend on understanding the identity that defines where we came from, and the identity we choose to create for ourselves. We each start this journey with an existing identity, in effect a worldview, shaped by many factors, including the following:

- Family, culture, religion, education, life experiences, and travel
- Gender, ethnicity, and sexual identity
- Values, beliefs, and assumptions about human behavior, and the relationship between people, work, and technology
- Leadership style as manifested by any number of personality style assessments
- The communities we belong to—social, demographic, and geographic
- Personal mission, vision, and legacy—why we think we've been put on this planet and the impact we would like to make

We begin this journey thinking we know who we are as leaders. And then we come up against the realities of global warming, VUCA, and technological acceleration. We see leaders still in hierarchies and see the impact it has on people we work with. Who am I now? How will I cope with the stress, tension, and fear that is resulting from forces beyond my control? Where do I go inside of me to find out how to cope, to determine how I will respond?

Leadership in the 21st Century is much more complex than it was in the 20th Century. Not only is there a myriad of external forces over which you have no control and yet must be responsive to, but you are also entering or already working in leadership cultures that are still in transition from the 20th Century Industrial Age culture of compliance to the 21st Century Digital Age of collaboration. Navigating external forces as well as organizational culture variables is a daunting task. The key to your success will be the ground you stand on—what your values and assumptions are, what you believe about how to motivate and work with the others, and your own identity and sense of self. You are the key to your own success, and the conscious choices you make about which path to follow will determine whether you achieve your mission, purpose, and legacy. This is the journey we are on in this book. I invite you to leave all of your assumptions about leadership at the door. Embrace this journey and discover your new self as you explore *Leadership's 4th Evolution*.

INTENTIONS OF THIS BOOK

This book has three primary intentions:

- *To articulate a coherent and comprehensive theory of collaboration that can be practiced at the individual, team, organization, and global levels and that can replace 20th Century hierarchy and the Power Paradigm as the predominant leadership culture for 21st Century organizations*
- *To empower you, the reader, to discover or strengthen your collaborative leadership with new understandings, insights, and self-awareness so that you can create, nurture, and sustain a collaborative leadership culture that empowers people to be their best selves, do their best work, and deliver superior results*
- *To provide you with specific, concrete ways in which you can implement this theory of collaboration in your teams, in organizational change, and at the global level in terms of the greatest threat to our existence, global warming*

For over a century, leadership has been defined by the predominant paradigm, the Power Paradigm, which focuses on the importance of top-down authority, the centralization of power, specialization of labor, and a hierarchical structure to control the workforce and keep them focused on results. In the early 20th Century, this paradigm's view of the workforce was that they were lazy and irresponsible and needed to be prodded or punished to do their jobs and keep the assembly lines moving. The Power Paradigm kept them in a dependent, compliant mode. It was not long before industrial enterprises in the United States began to see the rise of organized labor, strikes, and even substantial violence against workers.

In the 1930s, however, researchers found that people are social beings, like to be appreciated, and given attention. The birth of the human potential movement was at hand, with Douglas McGregor, author of *The Human Side of Enterprise*, as its leader.[17] The anomalies in the Power Paradigm were exposed, and the primacy of people began its ascendency. By the time we reached the dawn of the 21st Century, however, hierarchy still prevailed as organizations tried different approaches to leadership and the management-worker relationship. Even Stephen Covey's approach, Principle-Centered Leadership,[18] was unable to dissuade our graduate educational institutions from teaching yet another generation of leaders the primacy of authority and control.

With the birth of the internet, the gradual explosion of high technology, globalization, increased diversity in the workforce, and increasingly rapid change in the marketplace, cracks began to show up in the hierarchical facade. Experiments that empowered teams, opened up communications, engaged workers, and made early efforts at greater collaboration began, along with substantial research on the human side of enterprise, all combined to increase general awareness and confidence that a more coherent approach to collaboration and collaborative leadership was possible. I toiled in these fields beginning in 1969, and by 1990 had developed not only the beginnings of a coherent systems theory of collaboration, but was having substantial success implementing it at the team and project level. When *Transforming the Way We Work: The Power of the Collaborative Workplace* was published in 1995,[19] this theory of collaboration focused on its application to individual leadership journeys, teams, and organizational change. By 2000, when rapid organizational change was an annual phenomenon, *Building Trust at the Speed of Change* talked about the critical importance of leaders building trust-based relationships, and demonstrating their character, will, and discipline to ensure that teams and organizations could adapt to and withstand rapid change, and to do so collaboratively.[20]

It is now 20 years later, and the predominant leadership paradigm remains hierarchy, power, and control and is still, even in the face of the external forces mentioned earlier, being taught in our graduate schools to yet another generation of graduate, executive education, and corporate university students. But hierarchy's time has come and gone. In the VUCA, globalized, digital world we live in, one that is at risk of mass extinction, hierarchical approaches to leadership are out of step with the times. But as one of my mentors asked me over 40 years ago, "What will you replace it with?" The answer is: *Leadership's 4th Evolution: Collaboration for the 21st Century*. Now we have a coherent, documented, theoretically grounded systems theory of collaboration, *and* there is 40 years of practical implementation of this methodology in every aspect of organizations, from individual leaders to teams to organizational change and transformation. Lessons were learned and the methodology was refined, so that in 2020 I can say without hesitation that there is now a complete replacement for hierarchy, control, power, and fear.

Insanity is defined as continuing to do the same thing over and over again but expecting different results. By this definition, the persistent use of the Power Paradigm is insane. It is time for business, nonprofit, and public sector organizations to move beyond their love affair with command and control. There are many reasons for doing so, not the least of which is that we cannot save the planet without global collaborative leadership. It is also time for graduate education in our schools of business, engineering, public administration, health care, policy, education, and social work to teach that collaborative leadership is *the* most effective and relevant way to address the many complex challenges of the 21st Century. It is time for us to put a premium on building trust and mutual respect, creating ownership opportunities for the workforce of their own jobs and of organizational change. It is time to transform the traditional industrial power paradigm to a transformational, people-centric, collaborative approach to leadership.

Organizations are living, breathing organisms made up of people. The only way work gets done, even in the era of emerging artificial intelligence, is through people. The only way organizational change gets implemented is by people. And the only way we will save the planet is by empowering the people to do so. It's the people! McGregor said it this way in 1960:

Fads will come and go. The fundamental fact of man's capacity to collaborate with his fellows in the face-to-face group will survive the fads and one day be recognized. Then, and only then, will management discover how seriously it has underestimated the true potential of human resources.[21]

That day is today!

LEADERSHIP'S 4TH EVOLUTION: COLLABORATION

This book's ten chapters are organized in five parts, each of which will be reviewed in more detail. Part I is focused on leadership cultures and paradigms, and the 4th Evolution—collaboration. Part II is focused on what collaborative leadership is, how you become a collaborative leader, and the skills you need to be successful. Part III is about collaborative teams and the specific process for creating a high-trust, high-ownership collaborative team. Part IV focuses on organizational change, its human impacts, and the emergence of the 4th Evolution of change, the *Collaborative Method*. Finally, Part V addresses the global threat of climate change and what collaborative leaders can do to address it.

Part I: The Evolution of Leadership Cultures
Part I focuses on how our thinking about leadership has evolved over time, but also it is a story of how the predominant approach to leadership, hierarchy, which was born in the 20th Century Industrial Age, is still the predominant leadership style in the 21st Century Digital Age. It is a story about the power of leadership cultures as drivers of how people work with each other. It is a story about how economic, political, organizational, and technological realities, combined with human needs, have resulted in the need for a complete replacement of this power and control-based leadership paradigm with a collaborative leadership paradigm. It is also a story about how the Collaboration Paradigm evolved over 40 years to become a comprehensive, systems-based replacement for hierarchy, for how to lead and manage in the Digital Age.

In **Chapter 1, "The Journey Begins,"** we will explore how we got to where we are today in terms of the evolutionary chain of leadership and leadership cultures since 1900, from the Industrial Revolution to today in the Digital Age. We will learn what a *paradigm* is, as well as a *systems model,* which gives us a common framework for comparing and contrasting four different leadership paradigms. We start with the Industrial Revolution and the Power Paradigm's approach to leadership, which was based on hierarchy, power, control, and fear (Theory X). We will learn that researchers in the 1930s and 1940s discovered the importance of human motivation and behavior in how work gets done, leading to a set of *anomalies* in the Power Paradigm. This in turn led to the articulation of the People Paradigm of leadership in 1960 and the dawn of the human potential movement (Theory Y). For the next 40 years, leadership was in a transition period when there was a lot of experimentation, but the predominant leadership culture was still the Power Paradigm. The Principle Paradigm, which emerged at the end of the 20th Century, shifted the leadership conversation from power to principle. Both the People and Principle Paradigms provided the conceptual and practical foundations for the Collaboration Paradigm of leadership, which emerged in the mid-1990s, but was fully formed by 2000, signaling the *dawn of a new age of collaboration.*

Our journey continues in **Chapter 2, "The Power of Leadership Cultures,"** where we will explore the critical role that a leadership culture plays in any organization. First, we will consider what an organization's *leadership culture* is, building on the groundbreaking work of Edgar Schein, who for more than 45 years has defined the field of organizational culture as cultural DNA—the beliefs, artifacts, and underlying assumptions of any organization.[22] By understanding the power of culture as a driver for individual, team, and organizational behavior, we then explore three basic types of leadership cultures, as defined by Dr. Robert Cooke of Human Synergistics International, and their related behaviors—passive/defensive, passive/aggressive, and constructive/collaborative. He discovered that no matter what culture you are from, nearly everyone prefers working in a constructive/collaborative culture.[23] This leads us to an articulation of the third paradigm of leadership, the Principle Paradigm, which is based on the work of Stephen Covey and helped frame the principles foundation of leadership's 4th Evolution, the Collaboration Paradigm. We will take a deeper look into what a collaborative leadership culture is, its beliefs and assumptions about human behavior, and its 8 guiding ethical principles, with a specific focus on two core principles, Ownership and Trust, and how they show up in how people work with each other.

It took 60 years to fully realize the anomalies of the Power Paradigm, and McGregor gave us the foundations for the People Paradigm. It then took another 30 years to get us to the understanding that leadership should be principle-based, and Covey gave us the foundations for the Principle Paradigm. It took us another 10–15 years to get to the realization we needed to evolve to the next level, the next paradigm—and the Collaboration Paradigm came into existence, the essence of which is this:

The fundamental assumption and belief of collaboration is that people want to be honored for who they are as human beings, as well as professionals, and want to be empowered by the leadership culture so they can be their best selves and to do their best work.

In **Chapter 3, "The 4th Evolution of Leadership: Collaboration,"** we build on the work of Schein and Cooke, as well as the work of six additional thought leaders, to articulate the elements of the 4th Evolution of leadership, a theory of collaborative leadership that will help us explain why the Collaboration Paradigm needs to replace the Power Paradigm if we are to survive the 21st Century and beyond. We will learn about the espoused beliefs about people, the principles of collaborative leadership, and how they are manifested in the culture, processes, and structure of an organization.

From its early beginnings in the late 20th Century, *collaboration* has represented what I have called the 4th Evolution of leadership. First considered a buzzword and fad, it was then considered to be a tool or a process. We did not fully understand, at that time (1995), the incredible power that collaboration holds for our ability to transform ourselves, our teams, our workplaces, and the planet.

Collaboration is about people, about optimism for the human race, about how to realize our full potential as human beings, teams, and organizations. It is about a principle-based foundation, the rudder of a huge vessel, that will guide us through the stormy waters of our volatile world. Collaborative leadership holds out our best hope as the human race to survive this next century and beyond.

Part II: Collaborative Leadership

So, what is a collaborative leader, how do you become one, and what skills do you need to have? This is the focus of Part II, where we go in depth into what it truly means to be a collaborative leader in terms of attributes, behaviors, and roles and responsibilities. You become a collaborative leader by going on an inside-out journey, discovering your values and beliefs, mission and legacy, and what makes you unique as a human being and professional. You make a conscious choice to explore and understand yourself and build your foundation so that you are agile in a volatile world.

In **Chapter 4, "The Collaborative Leader,"** we learn that collaborative leadership is not a function, title, or position. Anyone can be a collaborative leader and may also happen to have a title. It may happen in a meeting, a team, a business unit, or department that the situation calls for an individual to step up and provide direction, focus, or alternative solutions. Everyone can be of service to others. Everyone can foster trust and ownership and can nurture and support each other.

Collaborative leaders have these attributes: ethical above reproach, principle-based, clear purpose, credible and trustworthy, collaborative mindset, emotionally intelligent, facilitative, optimistic and inspiring, and have leadership will and discipline. These attributes are not intended to exclude or discourage people from the journey but to give a framework that is grounded in theory, practice, and principle, that can be used as a developmental guide to which leaders can aspire.

We learn that collaborative leaders also exhibit behaviors that are quite different from the power-oriented or ego-driven leader. They start from the inside, with a focus on self-awareness, reflection, feedback, and self-accountability. In working with others, their behaviors involve building high-trust relationships through connecting, engaging, facilitating, and nurturing. At the organizational level, collaborative leaders are all about building ownership, trust and credibility, alignment and inspiration, systems thinking, and adaptation. They ensure that a collaborative leadership culture is developed and sustained.

Underlying this entire conversation is the recognition that work gets done through people, who usually work in teams and conduct their work in meetings of one kind or another. In this culture, the glue that holds all of these relationships together is trust, not fear. Trust is built through ownership of meetings, teams, projects, processes, and organizational change. Ownership is created by leaders trained in the art of facilitation, protected by leaders who are sponsors and Chief Cultural Officers, guided by leaders who are ethical above reproach, and supported by leaders who nurture, appreciate, and acknowledge the gifts, hard work, intellect, and enormous contributions that every member of the organization makes.

Chapter 5, "Becoming a Collaborative Leader," begins with a provocative question: Do you really want to become a collaborative leader? Right out of the starting gate, it is important to say that collaborative leadership is not for everyone. Some leaders are so tied to the past, to their power and ego, to the need for control that they are unable to make the shift. Some leaders, however, have experienced a *significant personal emotional event* like a heart attack, a failed business, a lost child, a divorce, or other traumatic event that causes them to evaluate what is important in their lives. Still others are up-and-coming managers and leaders who will find what is discussed here as being obvious and natural. To those who choose to become collaborative leaders or to deepen their collaborative skills, there is a journey to go on, a series of steps that will help you discover who you truly are and strengthen the foundations of your ability to collaborate.

The journey to become a collaborative leader is about revealing who you are as a human being, your core values, your reason for being on this planet, your assumptions and beliefs about those you work with, your ethics, behaviors, skills, life experiences, style, and all the things that go into making you who you are. It is designed to help you create and validate who you are and what you stand for. When you have solid ground to stand on, you can not only withstand the turbulence that awaits you but can also empower others you work with to be their best selves and do their best work.

Collaborative leadership is not about power and control, telling people what to do, and then delegating tasks and holding people accountable. In **Chapter 6, "Collaborative**

Leadership Skills," we will learn that collaborative leadership is about building trust-based relationships, giving people ownership over the vision, mission, values, and work processes of a team or organization. It is about influencing, facilitating, and empowering them, forming and developing teams, and creating a workplace that empowers the human spirit so that people can be their best selves, do their best work, and be productive. To this end, we will look at a set of core skills collaborative leaders need to be successful: self-awareness, envisioning, alignment, modeling the way, building ownership, teaming, facilitation, people problem-solving, communications, nurturing the workforce, and change leadership. Collaborative leadership skills need to be learned, practiced, and perfected so that the workforce of today and tomorrow will be engaged and motivated.

The organizational terrain for collaborative leaders is incredibly challenging. The predominant leadership culture is still the Power Paradigm, which is based on power, control, and compliance. To begin practicing collaborative skills in this environment can be challenging, but even in this hostile climate, it is possible to make collaborative gains. To help you navigate the power-based terrain, a number of strategies are suggested to help you manage these organizational challenges.

Part III: Collaborative Teams

In the 20th Century there was always group-based work in organizations, but the Power Paradigm of leadership prevailed as the way in which they were organized, led, and managed. Whether it was a group, committee, or "team," it was a top-down process where power was used to control, delegate, often micro-manage, and hold members accountable. The "rules" for how the team operated were the boss' rules. Everyone on the team had to agree or face the consequences. It was a compliance culture. In the 21st Century, this approach is no longer effective. There is a need to have an approach to teams that builds trust, ownership, full responsibility, and accountability. 21st Century teams work across boundaries of all kinds—cultural, language, demographic, geographic, and organizational. They need a new way to manage themselves, which is the 4th Evolution of teams, called *Collaborative Teams*.

In **Chapter 7, "Collaborative Teams: The Drivers of Transformation,"** we learn that the history of teams is littered with failed efforts of people trying to figure out how best to work with each other so that they can be their most productive. For decades, and even to this day, the approaches to teaming that companies tried were implemented within the predominant Power Paradigm of leadership. Teams were power-based and task driven, with leaders who told the members to produce specific outcomes within a specific time frame and budget. Some business leaders began to experiment with self-directed teams, autonomous teams, and team-based management. Many companies and organizations adopted the approach known as "forming-storming-norming-performing," which was never empirically tested. In real life it didn't work. Typically, the team process ended up more like "forming-storming-

storming-non-performing," and then the team would become dysfunctional, collapse, or fade away. Members became disillusioned because they ended up positioning themselves for power or control of the team or arguing with each other about the task. They ended up wasting their energy and the company's time and money, all because they didn't know how to work together. It makes no sense to continue using this 20ᵗʰ Century approach when there is a more successful alternative—Collaborative teams.

Collaborative teams have a different starting point. They first go on an inside-out journey as they shift from Power to Collaboration. They move from a culture of "I" to a culture of "We," where the well-being of the team is more important than the individual, and yet where individuals' needs and differences are respected, nurtured, and revered. To become a "We," members build high levels of trust and mutual respect, through ownership of what is called the Collaborative Team Governance Process, a culture-first, principle-based, and front-loaded process that ensures all team members are playing by the same rules. What is unique to Collaborative Teams is the power of 100% true consensus, no reservations, the gold standard of collaborative team decision-making. This ensures that every member of the team owns the decision, and that they have worked *through* their differences.

Collaborative teams are about "We," not "Me":

> *They require individuals to put the good of the team ahead of their own interests so that the team can empower each member to be their best self and do their best work. This is done by giving team members ownership of how they will work together, ownership based on true consensus decision-making, which in turn builds high levels of trust, responsibility, and accountability.*

Part IV: Collaborative Organizational Change

A tsunami of change has been and will continue to impact our global institutions, business organizations, and economies. Among these major forces that are shaping how organizations respond are the velocity of technological change, the fundamental transformation of industry through artificial intelligence and robots, the increased volatility, uncertainty, complexity and ambiguity in markets (VUCA), globalization, and global warming.

How organizations adapt will determine whether they survive and thrive. The ways in which most organizations have adapted is by implementing change processes, left over from the 20ᵗʰ Century, methodologies that are top-down and do not engage the workforce. As a result, more than 70% of them fail. In Part IV, we will explore these traditional approaches to change and will discover that organizational change is an intensely human endeavor that involves the hopes, dreams, and aspirations of the workforce. The workforce not only must live with the consequences of the changes made, but must also implement them. The failure of leadership to fully engage them, let alone give them ownership over the change initiatives, has led to significant human impacts.

A 21st Century alternative, the 4th Evolution of organizational change—the *Collaborative Method*—is then explored to see how it gives the workforce ownership of change initiatives. Based on 40 years of development and implementation in over 100 change processes, the *Collaborative Method* has a more than 80% success rate, in large part due to ownership by the workforce. Each of the phases of the Collaborative Method's approach will be detailed, along with its leadership requirements and how leaders can address the inevitable breakdowns that occur in any change initiative.

In **Chapter 8, "The Human Side of Organizational Change,"** we learn that since the 1970s, more than 70% of change processes have failed, due largely to two critical reasons: (1) The failure of leadership to persist rather than follow the next bright shiny object and (2) The failure to give the workforce ownership of the change process. Our central focus is on the *human side of organizational change*:

> *Organizational changes and transformations are intensely human endeavors. It is not just about structure or process, value generation, efficiency, or "headcount reduction." Organizational change is about the hopes and aspirations of the workforce, their professional careers, their families, and their communities. It's about the people.*

Organizational change is not just about strategy, tactics, or the consulting firm brought in to implement the change. It's about the impacts that this change will have on these human beings in the organization. It's about the people. We will explore how a number of key thinkers have helped frame the organizational change conversation, and then the three traditional approaches most organizations have used to implement their organizational change initiatives. Our major finding is that they forgot the people! The result is resistance to change, withholding information, noncooperation, and sometimes even sabotage. Traditional leadership's failure to trust the workforce with ownership of the change initiative largely results in failure.

Chapter 9, "The 4th Evolution of Organizational Change: The Collaborative Method," however, offers a decidedly different approach. In the Collaborative Method, the workforce is front and center in every aspect of the change initiative, from direct involvement in decision-making at the senior-most level to strategy, communications, engagement, and implementation. We define what the Collaborative Method is, explain the kind of leadership infrastructure needed for it to be implemented successfully, and provide guidelines for implementation. Each of the phases of the implementation process are described, with a step-by-step guide so that organization development professionals can implement it. Finally, we explore the human dynamics of collaborative organizational change, and in particular several types of challenges collaborative change leaders may encounter and how to address them.

Organizational change initiatives are intensely human endeavors, and they require direct involvement of the people who will be most directly impacted by the changes. Their involvement, however, must be substantive and direct, from decision-making to implementation, and based on this author's practical experience, this will result in a substantially high probability of success for the organization.

Part V: Global Collaborative Leadership

In **Chapter 10, "Collaborative Leadership in a World at Risk,"** we tackle global leadership's responsibility for dealing with the most significant global issue facing the peoples of the planet—global warming. The scientific data leave no doubt that unless superhuman, collaborative *actions* are taken *now*, the human race is likely to face the 6th mass extinction at some point in the next century. Life as we have known it to this point will evaporate in the heat of a warming planet within the next several decades. As the CO_2 emissions continue to increase, the water continues to warm, the glaciers continue to melt, and plant, animal, fish, and sea creatures continue to go extinct, the human consequences will be horrific. Those who are already poor, hungry, diseased, or suffering regular drought or floods—mostly in the Southern Hemisphere—are the first to suffer now, and this suffering will only increase exponentially as we pass the "point of no return," when global warming is irreversible. The United Nations has been given leaders until 2030 to keep the planet's temperature at 1.5°C above preindustrial levels. In 2020 we are at 1.2°.

It is up to the leaders of the world in governments, businesses, civil society, and international organizations to transform our economic, social, and political systems so that greed, corruption, national self-interest, and political short-sightedness are no longer the drivers of the future. To date, even with the formidable efforts of the United Nations, these leaders have failed us. At the glacial rate at which they are moving, mostly backward, it is now crystal clear that there is not yet the will to take the actions required to save the planet and the peoples who live here.

The question, then, is what are each of our responsibilities as a collaborative leader to confront this existential threat? We cannot wait for the global leaders who have failed to solve the problem. We must take concrete actions. Each one of us is challenged to consider our own ethics, our morality, and our sense of responsibility to others on the planet to take decisive action so that all can survive and thrive.

BON VOYAGE

I wish each and every one of you an amazing journey as you explore what it means to be a collaborative leader. You are the 21st Century vanguard, a new generation of leader who understands that Leadership's 4th Evolution is Collaboration. My hope is that you will find this journey to be helpful to you, to your colleagues and teammates in your workplace, and to your teams and organizations, and that you will join me in positive, constructive, collaborative action to help spare the peoples of the planet from global warming.

Edward M. Marshall, Ph.D.
Chapel Hill, North Carolina, USA
July, 2020

ENDNOTES

1. United Nations Intergovernmental Panel on Climate Change, *Global warming of 1.5°C, Summary for Policymakers*, 2018.
2. "Remarks by the President in Announcing the Clean Power Plan," The White House, Washington, D.C. August 3, 2015.
3. Marshall Goldsmith, *What Got You Here Won't Get You There* (London: Profile Books, 2008).
4. Thomas Kuhn, *The Structure of Scientific Revolutions*, 50th Anniversary Edition (Chicago, IL: University of Chicago Press, 2012).
5. Strategic Agility Institute, "The VUCA Report™," March 2016, 5, https://static1.squarespace. com/static/5579c941e4b00a23147233ce/t/56eff7f420c6474a7cd617ab/1458567164889/The_ VUCA_Report_1.1_March_2016.pdf
6. Ibid., 6.
7. "The Speed of Change," http://theemergingfuture.com/speed-of-change.htm; see also Gerd Leonard, *Technology vs. Humanity: The Coming Class between Man and Machine* (Zurich: Futures Agency, 2016), for a detailed look at the ten technological megashifts shaping our planet and what they mean for humanity.
8. Ibid.
9. Alec Ross, *The Industries of the Future* (New York: Simon & Schuster, 2016, pp. 12–14).
10. Richard Fry, "Millennials Are the Largest Generation in the U.S. Labor Force," Pew Research Center, April 11, 2018; https://www.pewresearch.org/fact-tank/2018/04/11/ millennials-largest-generation-us-labor-force/
11. Peter Economy, "The (Millennial) Workplace of the Future Is Almost Here—These 3 Things Are About to Change Big Time," *Inc.* Magazine, January, 15, 2019.
12. Ibid.
13. Andy Gregory, "COP25: Climate Change Close to 'Point of No Return,' UN Secretary General Warns Ahead of Key International Talks," *Independent* (London), December 2, 2019, https://www.independent.co.uk/environment/cop25-climate-change-un-greta-thunberg-antonio-guterres-madrid-a9228851.html
14. IPCC, Intergovernmental Panel on Climate Change, "Global Warming of 1.5°C, Summary for Policymakers," United Nations, October, 6, 2018.

15 William J. Ripple, Christopher Wolf, Thomas M. Newsome, Phoebe Barnard, William R. Moomaw, "World Scientists' Warning of a Climate Emergency," *Bio Science* Vol. XX, No. X, (November 5, 2019): 1–5.

16 This definition of *productive energy* was developed by Dr. Edward M. Marshall based on his work with a number of companies implementing collaborative organizational change. Over two years, he worked with leaders at DuPont to develop a way to measure the "intangibles" of workforce empowerment. The result was the *Collaborative Interdependence Index*, which is used before and after a change process.

17 Douglas McGregor, *The Human Side of Enterprise* (New York: McGraw-Hill, 2006).

18 Stephen R. Covey, *Principle-Centered Leadership* (New York: Free Press, 1990).

19 Edward M. Marshall, *Transforming the Way We Work: The Power of the Collaborative Workplace* (New York: American Management Association, 1995).

20 Edward M. Marshall, *Building Trust at the Speed of Change* (New York: American Management Association, 2000).

21 Douglas McGregor, *The Human Side of Enterprise* (New York: McGraw-Hill Companies, 2006).

22 Edgar Schein, *Organizational Culture and Leadership,* 5th ed. (Hoboken, NJ: Wiley, 2017).

23 Robert A. Cooke and Janet L. Szumal, "Using the Organizational Culture Inventory® to Understand the Operating Cultures of Organizations," Human Synergistics International, 2013; reprinted from R. A. Cooke and J. L. Szumal, *Handbook of Organizational Culture and Climate* (Thousand Oaks, CA: Sage, 2000), 147–162.

PART I

The Evolution of
Leadership Cultures

CHAPTER ONE

The Journey Begins

*W*HEN THE *Learning Team for the leadership class got their first assignment—to agree on the best way for leaders to motivate an organization's work-force—they quickly realized they had very different points of view, shaped by their different cultures and experiences. All five were Millennials with high expectations that this course would help them succeed once they graduated. Priyanka, from India, and Hanyue, from China, both come from cultures where authority and power come from the top and workers do what they are told. Morare, from South Africa, grew up in Zulu culture, which is more egalitarian and collaborative. Ana, from Brazil, is from a culture where building trust in relationships comes before focusing on task. Linda is from the United States, where the culture of individualism and competition conflicts with the need for more collective action.*

As their conversation continued, they concluded they needed a lot more information to help them come to an agreement. They realized that they were just beginning their leadership journey, that this was, as their professor had told them, an inside-out journey of self-awareness, self-discovery, and reflection. It was much more than learning a set of tools or techniques, casework, or team exercises. It was about discovering their own leadership brand, core values, mission, vision, and purpose on this planet. It was about learning how to work with teammates, solve challenging people problems, and be resilient in the face of rapid change. It was about learning what motivates people in the workplace, communications, emotional intelligence, and ethics. It was also about how they were going to lead in a world facing existential threats like global warming, hunger, mass migrations, and nuclear proliferation.

In the team, the members shared both their concerns and trepidation about their futures, but also their optimism and hopes that what they were going to learn would help them meet these challenges head-on. As they looked at each other, there was a realization that while this journey wasn't going to be easy, it

3

was well worth taking. It was time to get to work. They opened up their first assignment to find these questions:

- *As you start this journey, how do you define "leadership"?*
- *What is a leadership "paradigm," and what are "anomalies" that cause a shift to another paradigm?*
- *How can a systems model help us better understand how organizations work and the role of leadership?*
- *What assumptions about the workforce are represented by Theory X and Theory Y?*

LEARNING OBJECTIVES

By the end of this chapter, you will:

- Learn what a leadership *paradigm* is and how leadership paradigms, or theories, have evolved over time as *anomalies* emerge that the theories cannot explain
- Learn that a *systems model* can help you understand how organizations work and how leaders can lead; four key variables will be considered: culture, leadership, process, and organization design/structure
- Learn that there are 3 primary leadership paradigms that represent how workers and management have related to each other since the early 1900s in the United States: Power, People, and Principle
- Discover the origins, assumptions, and implementation of the Power Paradigm (Theory X) and the People Paradigm (Theory Y) and how Theory Y has reshaped our thinking about leadership
- Understand the Transitional Period of leadership in the latter half of the 20th Century, when leaders tried a number of different approaches to motivating the workforce
- Understand that even now, in the 21st Century, the Power Paradigm remains the predominant way in which organizations are led, due in part to how leaders have been educated

THE MAIN POINT OF THIS CHAPTER

In this chapter, we will explore the Power and People leadership paradigms which dominated how people were led and managed during the 20th Century, from the Industrial Revolution to the dawn of the Digital Age. We will start with the Power Paradigm, which took root in the early 1900s during the Industrial Revolution, in what Frederick

Winslow Taylor called *Scientific Management*, with its focus on power, control, fear, hierarchy, and efficiency. Within several decades, research revealed significant anomalies in the Power Paradigm that led to the emergence of the People Paradigm, as documented in Douglas McGregor's 1960 seminal work, *The Human Side of Enterprise*. During the next three decades, both Power and People approaches to leadership were implemented. It was during *the* Transitional Period, 1960–1990, that business leaders, management experts, researchers, and consultants tried to understand how best to motivate the workforce in the context of dramatic changes in the economy.

We will see that even as we entered the 21st Century Digital Age, the Power Paradigm remained the predominant way in which organizations were led and managed, even though by 1990 there was a fuller recognition of the importance of engaging the intellect, hearts, talents, and productive energy of the workforce to ensure innovation and productivity.

We will also see that graduate and executive education programs in the United States continue to teach the Power Paradigm in their leadership curriculum, even though the anomalies in the digital economy point to the need for a new paradigm.

In the 21st Century, leaders have a choice of paradigms—Power, People, Principle, or Collaboration. The economic, technological, demographic, and global realities of the 21st Century, however, require a new collective approach to leadership, which is about principle not power, about "We" not "Me," and is humanistic not mechanistic in how leaders approach motivation. We have evolved as people, teams, and organizations. The time for collaborative leadership has arrived.

FOUNDATIONAL CONCEPTS: LEADERSHIP PARADIGMS AND SYSTEMS THINKING

Critical for our journey are two concepts, leadership paradigms and systems thinking. They will help us understand how our thinking about leadership has evolved over time and why, as well as how to understand the complexity of organizational systems leaders must navigate.

The Structure of Leadership Evolution

Approaches to leadership have evolved largely in response to economic, political, technological, historical, and cultural forces. To help us understand this evolution, we turn to Thomas Kuhn, a philosopher of science who, in his seminal work *The Structure of Scientific Revolutions*, introduced the concept of a *paradigm*—which is a way of looking at reality, a theory that helps us understand how things work or are supposed to work.[1] The dictionary defines a paradigm as a model or a worldview underlying the theories and methodology of a particular scientific subject.[2]

Kuhn studied the scientific revolutions that resulted from discoveries by Copernicus, Newton, Lavoisier, and Einstein. He discovered that what he called *normal science* was based on the assumption that the scientific community, at any given point in time, knows what the world is like and is willing to defend that assumption. Sometimes it can't because there are problems that cannot be explained by that science: "... *normal research fails to perform in the anticipated manner, revealing an anomaly that cannot, despite repeated effort, be aligned with professional expectation.*"[3]

An *anomaly* is something that deviates from what is normal or expected.[4] Kuhn helps us understand that when there are anomalies that cannot be explained by "normal science," *breakdowns* occur in the prevailing theory, or in our case, the leadership paradigm. At this point, there is a *crisis* and the beginning of what he calls a *paradigm shift,* or in our case, a "leadership paradigm evolution." Kuhn helps us understand this shift:

> *The transition from a paradigm in crisis to a new one ... is a reconstruction of the field from new fundamentals, a reconstruction that changes some of the field's most elementary theoretical generalizations as well as many of its ... methods and applications. ... When it is complete, the profession will have changed its view of the field, its methods, and its goals.*[5]

In the context of our leadership journey, think of a paradigm shift as going from analogue to digital, from no internet to the internet, or from PC to Mac. It's a different operating system, based on different assumptions, that better explains the realities of a given point in time. In this chapter, we will see this in the paradigm shift from the Power approach to leadership to the People approach.

A Systems Model for Organizations

As we continue our journey to understand human motivation and leadership in organizations, it is helpful to have a model that can help us understand how they work. Our purpose here is to provide a systems perspective on the core elements of any organization: Culture, Leadership, Process, and Organization Design/Structure as a way to help us compare and contrast the leadership paradigms discussed in this book.[6]

These four elements were selected after an analysis of a number of sociologists and organization theorists. Rensis Likert, an American social psychologist, is known for his "Management Systems 1–4," in which he identified 20 variables to compare types of leadership.[7] Keith Davis, an organization theorist, along with the legendary Abraham Maslow, developed another matrix with 28 variables used to evaluate behaviors at various levels of hierarchical organizations.[8] Another noted sociologist, Talcott Parsons, in his book *Structure and Process in Modern Societies,* posited that human dynamics in organizations are divided into two basic areas, structure/content and process.[9]

For years, many management and organization development consultants used Parsons' model of looking at organizations as the basis for their interventions with leadership or management teams, or other parts of the organization to address behavioral or organizational performance issues. Interventions to create new behavior ranged from training or team development at retreats to process changes, only to learn that when the engagement ended, the individuals and teams in the organization reverted back to their old behavior. As powerful as Parsons' model was, something was missing when it came to organizational behavior, leadership, and change.

In my work in India with the Ford Foundation, I learned from observation and research into the history, beliefs, values, and traditions of the Indian people that culture was the fundamental driver for human behavior and that if we want to shift the ways in which people, teams, and organizations behave, interventions must start with the culture. Edgar Schein, the world-renowned organization development and culture expert, helped us understand the power of culture in his seminal work *Organizational Culture and Leadership,* in which he defines culture as artifacts, or visible phenomena, espoused beliefs and values, and assumptions people have that are taken for granted.[10] We will get into Schein's model in more detail in Chapter 2.

The point here is that what was missing in Parsons' Structure-Process model was the organization's culture. In order for us to fully understand leadership, workforce behavior, relationships, and psychological dynamics inside an organization, we must first understand the organization's culture and how it impacts the organization. As a result, I added Culture to the Content-Process model, and all 3 elements were organized into a Venn diagram (See Figure 1.1) to represent their critical interrelationships. Leadership was placed in the center of the Venn diagram to represent the central role and responsibility leadership has in understanding and orchestrating the relationships between the culture, process, and organization design/structure.

Each leadership paradigm will be evaluated in terms of these four variables. Each variable has a number of indicators that will help us understand them. The solid-line

FIGURE 1.1   Organizational Systems Model.

circle around the outside of the four elements represents the external boundary of the organization.

- **Culture—What Shapes Behavior in Organizations:** Assumptions about what motivates the workforce; values, principles, and ethics; espoused beliefs; artifacts such as customs, history, and language; the productive energy of the workforce
- **Leadership—How Leadership Manifests the Culture in Their Behavior:** Direction—vision, mission, and goals; power and authority, including decision-making style; workforce relationships
- **Process—How Work Gets Done:**

  o **People Processes:** Cultural drivers for behavior like fear or trust, individualistic or team based, workforce engagement and ownership, communications, how conflicts are handled, accountability
  o **Business Processes:** Marketing and sales, information flows, research and development, production, supply chain, customers

- **Organization Design/Structure—How the Organization is Designed and What it Does:** Organization design and structure, what the organization does, supporting systems like finance, human resources, and information technology

As we begin our journey through the paradigms, put yourself in the shoes of someone who works in an organization that is run by leaders who hold the beliefs, values, or assumptions that the school of thought represents. Ask yourself these questions:

- What are the core assumptions about people and the work they do to make a living?
- How are power and authority used, and what is the impact on people and results?
- What is the "contract" that exists between the workers and the organization?
- How do leaders treat the workforce?
- What motivates the workers?

As we explore these questions and more, we are going to see an evolution of leadership thought across more than a century, an evolution that will bring us to the present day—collaborative leadership.

THE POWER PARADIGM OF LEADERSHIP

It's October 17, 1913, and Henry Ford has just launched the first moving assembly line for the Model T Ford at the Highland Park Ford motor plant in Michigan.[11] Ford would revolutionize manufacturing forever, and with it the leader-workforce relationship. The next year, World War I broke out and did not end until 1918, the same year as the Spanish Flu. Woodrow Wilson was President. A law was passed that you couldn't produce alcohol, but you could drink it. Children were working in the factories under brutal conditions. There was no workers' compensation insurance, so if you got injured, it was viewed as your fault and you had to pay for it yourself.[12] It was survival of the fittest.

People were moving from their farms and a predominately agrarian economy to the cities, where there were more new industrial jobs with higher wages. But the titans of the Industrial Revolution held views about the workers that were straight out of a Charles Dickens novel: "The American labor force became dehumanized as modern technology experts analyzed the science of worker efficiency."[13] One of the results of the poor treatment of workers—long hours, poor working conditions, and low wages—was the rise of the trade union movement and organized labor. Workers struck for better working conditions, benefits, and wages.

Women won the right to vote in 1920, the Model T Ford cost $260 in 1924, the Ku Klux Klan was on the move, hanging and terrorizing African Americans, there was an anti-Communist scare resulting from the Russian Revolution in 1917, and anti-immigrant fever was the order of the day. In 1929, after 15 years of rapidly growing incomes, the US stock market crashed, putting 25% of the workforce on the streets all across the country.[14] It was in this context that Scientific Management was born, leading to the development of the Power Paradigm of leadership, where power, control, and hierarchy were how work got done.

The Power Paradigm of Leadership: The Rise of Scientific Management

Here a question arises: whether it is better to be loved than feared. ... The answer is, of course, that it would be best to be both loved and feared. But since the two rarely come together, anyone compelled to choose will find greater security in being feared than loved.
—Niccolo Machiavelli, 1513[15]

In the early 1900s the Industrial Revolution was well underway, and new manufacturing enterprises were starting up all across the country. These industrial enterprises grew so rapidly to meet increased consumer demand that they had to become more efficient. Enter Frederick Winslow Taylor (1856–1915), a mechanical engineer and one of the first management consultants, who was dedicated to improving industrial efficiency. His leadership theory was called *Scientific Management*, which rested on the beliefs that workers are inherently lazy, avoid responsibility, have to be incentivized or punished to produce, and that leadership must direct and control them to ensure sufficient output. Time and motion studies were used to increase worker efficiency and speeding up assembly lines. Taylor believed there was "one best way" to do any task and that he could figure that out scientifically. In the process, workers were dehumanized and treated like cogs in the machines they operated. Their psychological and physical well-being were not top of mind for these leaders. Nonetheless, Taylor was very successful, and within a short period of time, he claimed that most types of industries were using Scientific Management successfully.[16]

The Power Paradigm of leadership found its beginnings in Taylor's work, which was built around these assumptions, values, and beliefs about the inherent nature of people in the workforce. Using our systems model, let's take a closer look at Taylor's approach to leadership. Note that the references Taylor makes to "men" reflect the lack of social and equality awareness of the times:

- The average man is by nature indolent and works as little as possible
- Lacks ambition, dislikes responsibility, prefers to be led
- Is inherently self-centered, indifferent to organizational needs
- By nature resists change
- Is gullible and the ready dupe of the charlatan and the demagogue[17]

The assumptions Taylor made about the nature of the typical worker during the late 1800s and early 1900s are, by today's standards, quite backward—for example, Taylor's view on the work ethic of the labor force: *"They firmly believe that it is for their interest to give as little work in return for the money that they get as is practical."*[18] As a result of these assumptions, and the idea that all people want is security, Taylor saw the role of leaders as providing direction and controlling the workforce:

- Management is responsible for organizing the money, materials, equipment, and people of the enterprise in the interest of economic ends
- With respect to people, this is a process of directing their efforts, motivating them, controlling their actions, modifying their behavior with rewards or punishments to fit the needs of the organization, because they would be passive and resistant[19]

Taylor considered Scientific Management to be a "mental revolution" in how employers, and what he called "workmen," view their contract—that both can "win" if there is more surplus and they stop fighting each other. Here are three key principles to Taylor's view of what employers and workmen needed to buy into: 1) Time and motion studies to measure worker performance and efficiency; 2) The scientific selection of workmen who were trained; and 3) The division of labor between management and the workers where conflict was anticipated.[20]

To implement time and motion studies, for example, Taylor would use a stopwatch and a clipboard to calculate time intervals for each function in the production process. Then the data would be used to reduce that time interval, thereby increasing production, regardless of the impact on the workers. The same process is being used today in Amazon distribution centers, only robots are doing the calculations.

The idea that workers were inherently lazy and would avoid work if they could, fed into the Power Paradigm's view of leadership: leadership is about power, control, and the application of authority through a strict hierarchical system. Leadership has a narrow span of control (1:5), used some rewards and punishments to motivate workers, and closely supervised them.[21]

Channeling Machiavelli, the basis for leading an industrial enterprise was power and fear. People were told what to do, since they were too lazy and unmotivated to figure it out themselves. If they didn't do what they were told, they would be fired or replaced by a machine. You can see why workers organized into unions, which Taylor saw as "brutal, dominating, and selfish."[22] This attitude led to a continuation of labor-management conflict and even violence from the late 19th Century into the 20th Century. The Power Paradigm in this era demonstrated near utter contempt for the worker.

The Role of Formal Organization and Power

Scientific Management was the foundation or the Power Paradigm of leadership. Taylor's embrace of an individualistic approach to workers, the creation of a hierarchical structure with top-down decision-making, opposition to organized labor, and the subordination of human endeavor to more efficient machines, all laid the predicate for what came next—formal organization, which survives to this day. There are three key elements to it:

<u>Mechanistic Systems:</u> In 1961 Burns and Stalker talked about how the mechanistic framework for an organization was rational because it was "deliberately created and maintained to exploit the human resources of a concern in the most efficient manner feasible."[23] Here is an explicit reference to the idea that people are to be "exploited" by the organization to achieve efficiency, the same efficiency that Taylor talked about nearly 50 years earlier. The authors go on to provide the following select attributes of a mechanistic formal organization: Hierarchical structure of control, authority, and communication; decisions are made at the top; specialization of labor; insistence on loyalty and obedience to superiors as a condition of employment.[24]

<u>Power and Bureaucracy:</u> The noted German sociologist Max Weber is known as the "Father of Bureaucracy." Often associated with how public sector organizations are structured, the same elements apply to private sector and nonprofit organizations. At the center of his bureaucratic construct is the role of power, which Weber says *"is the probability that one actor within a social relationship will be in a position to carry out his own will, despite resistance."*[25] Other attributes of power-based leadership include the following:

- The principle of hierarchy and of levels of graded authority, with a firmly ordered system of super- and subordination
- A principle of fixed and official jurisdictional areas, where are ordered by rules, by laws, or administrative regulations

- The management of the modern office [1946] is based on written documents which are preserved in their original form; there is a "bureau" where they are kept
- Knowledge of the files is essential to one's success
- The management of the office follows general rules which can be learned[26]

Sources of Power: In 1961, Amitai Etzioni, another famous sociologist, wrote about power in his book *A Comparative Analysis of Complex Organizations*, where he said that power derived from a person's office, what could be called positional power, and that it may be "coercive ... remunerative ... or normative. ..."[27] He also made these observations about power:

- Formal leaders occupy organizational offices with power over their subordinates
- Informal leaders have personal power but not official power over "lower participants"
- Formal leaders are considered organizational elites
- Leaders succeed, whether formal or informal, when they maintain compliance of others[28]

Most organizations make the distinction between formal and informal leadership, which you will see disappears when we move into the Principle Paradigm of leadership. What matters is not the office or control but influence, service to others, engagement, and facilitation.

Anomalies in the Power Paradigm of Leadership

The Power Paradigm resulted in significant anomalies, or breakdowns and dysfunctions in organizations, ranging from worker resistance to the compliance function, sabotage, union organizing, and strikes. Given the assumptions Scientific Management made about the workforce, leadership, power, and work practices, the Power Paradigm was unable to address these breakdowns. By the middle of the 20th Century, it was time for a new leadership paradigm, a more humanistic approach—the People Paradigm.

But first let's review what Chris Argyris, a world-renowned business theorist, and Professor Emeritus at Harvard Business School, had to say about Scientific Management in his work on the relationships between individuals and organizations. In 1957 he summarized five core elements of the formal hierarchy and pointed us toward the anomalies that exist in the Power Paradigm that led us toward the first evolution of leadership theory in the 20th Century.[29]

- **Formal Organizations as Rational Organizations:** The underlying assumption is that people will act rationally, as formal plans require them to act for the organization to work effectively.
    - **Anomaly:** "Resistance to scientific management occurs because human beings 'are what they are' or 'because it's human nature.' ... Perhaps there is

something inherent in the principles [of formal organization] which cases human resistance."[30]

- **Specialization of Work:** The assumptions behind the idea that specialization of labor should increase production are that humans will behave more efficiently with specialization, that there is "one best way" to increase speed, and that individual differences can be ignored by transferring more skill to machines.

   ○ **Anomaly:** The culture begins to reward the more superficial or materialistic characteristics of the worker.

- **Chain of Command:** Taylor argued for the creation of a management function, separate from the labor function, whose primary responsibility was to control, direct, and coordinate their work, and that efficiency would be increased with a hierarchy of authority.

   ○ **Anomalies:**

      ○ People are made dependent, passive, and submissive, with little control over their work lives; rewards are given by the bosses, meaning individuals feel paid off, or paid to be unhappy with their jobs. The assumption is that people are only working to make money, rather than for any intrinsic reward.
      ○ Second, the assumption is that leaders are technically competent, objective, rational and loyal; leadership becomes emotionally detached; they lose the respect of their subordinates because they only care about the workers for what they can do—they are objectified.
      ○ The workers are expected to compete with each other, increasing conflict.[31]

- **Unity of Direction:** The leader controls everything—the goal people are working toward, how they're going to get there, and how to address any obstacles in the way.

   ○ **Anomalies:**

      ○ Everyone has an ego; this function of leadership creates psychological failure.
      ○ Psychological success is achieved when people can define and reach their own goals.

- **Span of Control:** This element increases administrative efficiency; a leader's span of control is 5-6 subordinates.

   ○ **Anomalies:** It creates administrative distance between individuals, increases red tape, wastes time, and increases the dependence of subordinates.

Argyris closes his analysis of formal organization and hierarchy with this set of conclusions:

- There is a lack of congruence between the needs of healthy individuals and the demands of the formal organization for dependent, passive people.
- As a result, there is frustration, conflict, and failure.
- Formal organization principles cause subordinates to experience competition, rivalry, and hostility.[32]

Clearly, Argyris is telling us that the formal organization model, which is at the heart of Scientific Management and the Power Paradigm, has serious people deficiencies that undermine the credibility and legitimacy of the hierarchical approach to leadership. Time for a paradigm shift.

THE PEOPLE PARADIGM OF LEADERSHIP: THE HUMANISTIC MOVEMENT IN ORGANIZATIONS

It's 1941, with the United States and the world still recovering from the Great Depression (1929–39). President Franklin Delano Roosevelt's New Deal had put people back to work and created some level of economic security for most Americans during the 1930s. The Federal government's role was instrumental in the recovery and its power dramatically increased, as did the power of trade unions as they fought for better working conditions, salaries, and benefits. Then, on December 7, 1941, the Japanese attacked Pearl Harbor in Hawaii, sinking the US Pacific fleet. America entered World War II against both the Japanese and the German Nazis in Europe.[33] As men went off to war, one of the biggest demographic developments in business was the dramatic increase in the role of women, both in the military and civilian workforce. During the war, 350,000 women were in the military, though fully 70% of them were in traditional "female" jobs such as typists, clerks, and mail sorters.[34] In the workplace, the percentage of women workers increased to 37% in 1945. Rosie the Riveter made famous the role of women in the aircraft industry, where they were 65% of the workforce. By the end of World War II in 1945, which concluded with two atom bombs being dropped on Japan, 25% of all married women in the country worked outside the home.[35]

It was time to come home and build a new life. With the 1950s came a significant increase in the standard of living for many Americans. There was another "hot war" in Korea, 1950–53, and a "cold war" with the Soviet Union, as the arms race began in earnest. The Soviets launched the first satellite, *Sputnik*, in 1957, followed by President John Kennedy committing the United States to landing on the moon by 1970. The landing happened in 1969.[36]

Economically, small businesses grew, corporations merged, and they needed skilled labor. More and more workers joined labor unions, which negotiated with management for better wages, benefits, and working conditions. Workers started making enough money on one salary to be able to buy a home and a car.[37] Almost 40% of women were in the workforce in 1950, which later increased to 60% by 1999.[38]

It was a new world, a new era, and with all of these changes came new approaches to leading and managing the workforce, what is called the People Paradigm of leadership.

Defining the People Paradigm of Leadership

Our technological development in the past hundred years has been tremendous. Our methods of handling people are still archaic. If this civilization is to survive, we must obtain a new understanding of human motivation and behavior in business organizations.
—Fritz J. Roethlisberger, 1941[−]

In the post—World War II era, the People Paradigm of leadership represented a new understanding of human motivation—that when enterprises produce things, it is people who produce them, and that people want to work hard, are responsible, and contribute to improved performance. The negative stereotypes of the first 40 years of the century gave way to a recognition, thanks to Roethlisberger and Mayo, that people are social creatures, that we actually do better when we work in groups. Douglas McGregor's seminal work, *The Human Side of Enterprise,* took those findings and developed them into a new theory of human motivation, known as Theory Y, contrasting itself with Taylor's Theory X. McGregor's work was grounded in a belief in the inherent goodness of people, assumptions about the value and dignity of the workforce, and a deep understanding of the integration of the individual, group, and organization as the cornerstones for understanding the role of leadership. Leadership was about creating the conditions for people to do their best and to work with each other effectively. Leadership was considered situational rather than positional. What is of particular interest is that both Roethlisberger and McGregor predicted the future development of what is now known as Collaborative Leadership.

The Hawthorne Effect
Let's return again to the 1920s and 1930s, when Elton Mayo and Fritz Roethlisberger conducted a series of experiments at the Hawthorne plant of Western Electric in a Chicago suburb. These experiments were a watershed moment in the history of our understanding about industrial organization, human motivation, and what it meant for leadership. Where Taylor focused on the individual's performance, the Hawthorne experiments focused on groups and how individual behavior is impacted by their social interactions with others. Elton Mayo, an Australian-born sociologist, along with Fritz Roethlisberger, a social scientist and management theorist at Harvard, conducted a series of experiments to determine the effects that physical or environmental conditions had on group productivity.[39]

There were three different experiments:[40]

- **Illumination:** In this experiment, there was a test group and a control group. As the lighting in the control group's room remained unchanged, the lighting in the test group's room was decreased. The test group's productivity actually went up. The researchers realized this was because people were paying attention to the workers.
- **Relay Assembly Test Room:** In 1928 these experiments focused on employee attitudes; researchers tested a new tool called "interviewing," in which they asked questions and listened to the answers of the participants. What they learned is that the behavior of workers could not be understood apart from their feelings.
- **Bank Wiring Observation Room:** In this experiment, the workers were in three different groups with four different sets of norms or rules. The researchers found that changes in output could only be explained by the feelings people had and their position in the informal organization.

Mayo and Roethlisberger were stunned to discover the results of their experiments, that people are motivated by more than money, but by being an accepted member of the group; they discovered an "informal organization." And, as if to predict what was to come more than 75 years later, Roethlisberger said this about collaboration:

> Too often we think of collaboration as something which can be logically or legally contrived. The Western Electric studies indicate that it is far more a matter of sentiment than a matter of logic. Workers are not isolated, unrelated individuals; they are social animals and should be treated as such.[41]

What we need to take away from the Hawthorne experiments are three things: 1) The importance of the group over the individual in terms of social interaction, motivation, and productivity; 2) Formal organizations generate the "informal organization," where influence, respect, and comradery result in a collaborative spirit; and 3) People are motivated by more than money—they are also motivated by their relationships.

Maslow's Hierarchy of Needs

Abraham Maslow was an American psychologist who formulated a positive theory of human motivation in 1943 called the *Hierarchy of Needs,* which built on the work of Freud, Adler, and gestalt psychology. He suggested that there are five levels of motivation for human behavior (see figure 1.2):

- **Physiological Needs:** Food, water, shelter, and sexual reproduction
- **Safety Needs:** Economic security, health and wellness, routine, physical safety, and family stability
- **Love Needs:** Love, affection, and belongingness

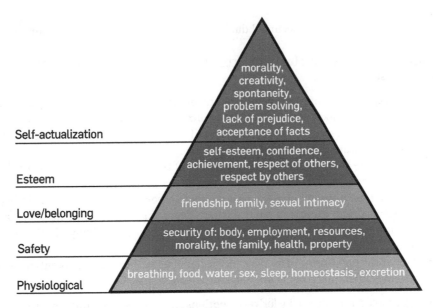

FIGURE 1.2 Maslow's Hierarchy of Needs.

- **Esteem Needs:** Self-respect, self-esteem, the esteem of others, self-confidence, strength, capability, and adequacy
- **Self-Actualization Needs:** Fulfilling one's potential and utilizing one's talents; doing what one was meant to do[42]

Maslow argued that these needs are arranged in a hierarchy, not in the sense of power and authority, but in the sense that people's motivations start at the physiological level first; once those needs are met, the individual moves to the next level, and so on. At the apex of human motivation is the ability to self-actualize.

Theory Y and the People Paradigm of Leadership

Douglas McGregor was a Professor of Management at the Sloan School of Management at the Massachusetts Institute of Technology (MIT), whose groundbreaking book *The Human Side of Enterprise,* published in 1960, was a paradigm shift. It changed how we think about the relationship between individuals and organizations, motivation, and the role of leadership.[43] The Academy of Management voted it the fourth most influential management book of the 20th century.[44] McGregor built on the work of Roethlisberger as he codified the distinctions between Taylor's work in Scientific Management, which he called *Theory X*, and his work in humanistic psychology, known as *Theory Y.* While his work came well after the end of World War II, his work on human motivation and leadership occurred during the 1950s. Here are five core components of Theory Y:

Assumptions About Human Motivation: In Theory Y, McGregor articulates these six assumptions:[45]

- The expenditure of physical and mental effort in work is natural; people do not inherently dislike work; in fact it may provide satisfaction.
- People will exercise self-direction and self-control in the service of objectives to which they are committed.
- Commitment to an objective is a function of the rewards associated with their achievement, the most significant of which is self-actualization.
- The average human being learns not only to accept but to seek responsibility.
- The capacity to exercise a relatively high degree of imagination, ingenuity, and creativity in the solution of organizational problems is widely distributed in the population.
- Under the conditions of modern industrial life, the intellectual potentialities of the average human being are only partially actualized.

McGregor took direct aim at Taylor's assumptions and beliefs about human nature and provided us with an optimistic, constructive perspective on the workforce, which is manifest in how Theory Y gets applied to organizations and leadership. There are two central principles to Theory Y.

The Principle of Integration: McGregor contrasts the Theory X principle of direction and control through the use of the leader's authority with Theory Y's central principle of integration: *"the creation of conditions such that the members of the organization can achieve their own goals best by directing their efforts toward the success of the enterprise."*[46] This principle refers not only to the formal employment agreement and general management practices, but more importantly to what has become known as the *psychological contract*, which articulates the quid pro quo in the relationship between the individual and the organization. Armstrong defines the psychological contract as a *"system of beliefs that encompasses the activities employees believe are expected of them and what response they expect in return from their employer, and, reciprocally, the actions employers believe are expected of them and what response they expect in return from their employees."*[47]

For workers, the psychological contract means security of employment; treatment that is fair, equitable and consistent; involvement and influence; career and developmental opportunities; and trust that management will keep their promises. For the employers it means the workforce is competent, will work hard, is committed and loyal, and compliant.[48]

McGregor goes on to say that in terms of the psychological contract, the integrative solution is when the needs of both the individual and the organization are met, and that if that doesn't happen, the organization will suffer because workers will not be optimally motivated.[49] He contrasts this more human approach to management-worker relationships with Theory X's approach, which involves control, rewards, fear, and punishment.

The Principle of Self-Control: Here the focus of leadership is to *"create a situation in which a subordinate can achieve his (or her) own goals best by directing his (or her) efforts toward the objectives of the enterprise."*[50] McGregor builds on his belief that people want to work hard by saying that workers need to be given more control over their future. He suggests a four-point management strategy: 1) Clarify the broad objectives of the job, 2) Establish specific targets for a given time frame, 3) Have a management process during the target period, and 4) Complete a performance appraisal.[51] He has established some of the core components of the modern human resources system by giving the workforce some control over their own development and future and their ability to self-actualize.

Theory Y's Approach to Leadership: In McGregor's view, leadership is a relationship that involves the characteristics of the leader; the attitudes, needs, and other personal characteristics of the followers; the characteristics of the organization, such as purpose and the work to be done; and the social, economic, and political context.[52] He is saying that "leadership is not a property of the individual, but a complex relationship among these variables." There are five implications of his research for leadership:

- To fill the jobs available
- To develop the entire workforce, not just at the top
- To develop the unique abilities of each person
- To promote from within
- To view leadership as a function and situational, vs. being a position[53]

McGregor's major contribution to our understanding of leadership is that in *situational leadership*, anyone can be a leader and does not need to be part of the formal hierarchy. This was truly a revolutionary conclusion in the 1950s and was the polar opposite of Theory X. He even made the prediction that *"it is probable that one day we shall begin to draw organization charts as a series of linked groups rather than as a hierarchical structure of individual 'reporting relationships.'"*[54]

Management Teamwork: McGregor's focus on the group inevitably led him to explore the dynamics of teams, both healthy and unhealthy. While we will explore team dynamics more fully in Chapter 5, it is important to note in Theory Y that healthy teamwork is viewed as part of the leadership function. He has identified 11 characteristics of effective management teamwork that can also be applied to other teams:[55]

- The team environment is informal, relaxed, where people are engaged and interested.
- Virtually everyone participates, and conversations are kept on purpose.
- Everyone understands the team's objective to which members are committed.
- Members listen to each other and are not afraid to put forth creative thoughts.

- There are disagreements, which are discussed and resolved; there is no conflict avoidance.
- Most decisions are reached by *"a kind of consensus in which it is clear that everybody is in general agreement and willing to go along."*
- Criticism is frequent, frank, and relatively comfortable.
- People are open in expressing their feelings on problems being discussed and team operations.
- Assignments are clear and accepted.
- Team leadership may shift from issue to issue.
- The group is self-aware about its own operations.

McGregor is defining many of the characteristics of a collaborative team. Of particular note is the comment about how decisions are made. What McGregor has defined is called a "can live with" consensus, where most team members agree, and the others "go along" with the decision, even though they disagree.

The Scanlon Plan: Implementing Theory Y

Joseph N. Scanlon (1899–1956) was a steelworker, accountant, professional boxer, a union leader, researcher, and eventually a lecturer at MIT, where he worked with Douglas McGregor. Scanlon is credited with a collaborative strategy to help unions and management work better together, called the Scanlon Plan. This plan is not a formula, program, or set of procedures—it is "a way of industrial life—a philosophy of management—which rests on assumptions consistent with Theory Y."[56]

There were two main features of the Scanlon Plan:

- **Cost-Reduction Sharing:** Economic gains from improvements in organizational performance are shared; if performance improves, the workers benefit.
- **Participation:** Everyone has a chance to participate in and contribute to organizational effectiveness; there are committees to receive, discuss, and evaluate proposals to improve performance.[57]

The Scanlon Plan recognized how important collaboration was between workers and managers, representing both the integration and self-control principles of Theory Y. The workforce moved from the dependence of compliant, authority-based Theory X systems to the interdependence of a more collaborative Theory Y system.

THE TRANSITIONAL PERIOD OF LEADERSHIP

Nothing in life goes in a straight line, and that is especially true when it comes to the evolution of approaches to leadership. Sometimes you have to go backwards before you can go forward, which is exactly what we did from 1960 to 1990—we entered what is called a *Transitional Period*, when a wide range of leadership methods were in play.

From the time that McGregor published *The Human Side of Enterprise* in 1960, until just before the dawn of the new century in 1990, were volatile and chaotic years. With the election of John F. Kennedy as President in 1960, there was new energy in the United States, punctuated by a commitment to go to the Moon by the end of the decade. Neil Armstrong set foot on the Moon in 1969. President Kennedy was assassinated in 1963, the same year that the Rev. Martin Luther King, Jr. gave his famous "I Have a Dream" speech at the Lincoln Memorial to punctuate the need for equal rights for African-Americans. In 1968 he too was assassinated, followed that same year by the murder of Robert F. Kennedy, then a candidate for President. The United States got embroiled in the Vietnam War, committing a half million troops. There were race riots in the streets, and hundreds of thousands of anti-war demonstrators protested the Vietnam War, which was lost in 1975. The US economy was beginning a transformation from farming and manufacturing to high technology and digital business, labor unions were growing, and more and more women were entering the workforce, because it was harder to make a living on just one salary.[58]

By the early 1970s there was more uncertainty as President Richard Nixon resigned under threat of impeachment for illegal acts taken by him during the 1972 election. Global competition increased to undermine the preeminence of the US auto market, and there was an oil embargo and severe gasoline shortages during the decade. In a sign of things to come, a few new tech start-ups called Microsoft and Apple were setting the stage for the digital era. By the 1980s unemployment reached its highest level since the Great Depression, business bankruptcies rose by 50%, and the steel industry was in a steep decline due to international competition. The US economy was in full-scale deindustrialization mode as the globalization of business became a new trend. Inequality in wealth also increased fairly dramatically as President Ronald Reagan passed tax cuts for the wealthy on the theory that the benefits would "trickle down" to the less fortunate.[59] They didn't. In fact, the cuts began an era where the gap between the richest 1% and the rest of the country grew, significantly widening income inequality.

The 1990s ushered in a new world order as the World Wide Web was launched in August 1991. All of a sudden, business began to be conducted in a new medium, the internet. New businesses sprang up, information became a commodity, and businesses had to rethink how they were organized and led.[60]

All of this chaos, violence, and revolutionary change meant that the traditional ways of leading were being questioned by some business leaders as well as theorists, analysts, and consultants. Thanks to the internet, hierarchies could not respond fast enough to meet the needs of global customers. Top-down leadership was replaced by distributed leadership and self-directed teams. With the globe being considerably "flatter," businesses started operating around the world on a 24/7/365 basis.

Global enterprises became the order of the day, and people had to learn how to work with each other across boundaries of all kinds: time zones, cultures, languages, and genders. Companies were not sure which leadership approach to use. It was unclear where leadership and human motivation were headed. It was a time of *transition*. No longer was anything predictable, except the certainty that everything was unpredictable.

Understanding the Transitional Period of Leadership

As we continue our leadership journey, the period 1960–90 was a time of great change for leadership, when a veritable smorgasbord of approaches was available to business leaders as they worked to address rapid changes in markets and technology. Everything felt like it was "up for grabs" as leadership gurus sprang up everywhere to promote their own brands. In fact, at DuPont, where I consulted for five years, this phenomenon was known as the "program-of-the-month" culture, as they tried to find the "one right answer" to fit their highly competitive global market. They had leaders across the entire spectrum: traditional hierarchy, participative management, transactional or cooperative leadership, and the early years of collaboration. It was all happening at the same time. Leadership was very much in transition, between generations, between centuries, and between the Industrial Age and the Digital Age.

Even though the Power Paradigm remained the predominant leadership approach, there were significant "cracks," or anomalies, in its facade as advancements in human behavior, social psychology, interpersonal relations, and group dynamics began to take hold in new styles of leadership and a younger generation. Cracks also resulted from the globalization of business, the rise of new technologies, the speed of change, and workforce demographics. Cracks began to show up in significant ways in the Power Paradigm, without a clear direction on where leadership was headed next.

Old habits and behaviors, however, die hard. Human beings and institutions inherently resist change. They crave stability. Their resistance becomes inertia. Not only were organizations and their leaders resisting change, but the graduate programs that educated them did as well. They continued to teach 20th Century leadership frameworks to those leaders. There was no incentive to do otherwise.[61]

Let's take a look at a sample of the approaches leadership experts, theorists, and consultants promoted during this transitional period.

Blake and Mouton's Managerial Grid: In 1964 Robert Blake and Jane Mouton argued that leadership approaches are in a "Managerial Grid," a set of five different management styles grounded in the Power Paradigm (see Figure 1.3 below). Using a four-cell grid that juxtaposes a concern for people against a concern for results, each on a 1–10 scale, the five styles might suggest that they represent a continuum of core values from high to low people concern and high to low results concern. Instead, while all of these management styles represent different levels of emphasis on people or results, they all exist within the same value set of power and hierarchy. Blake and

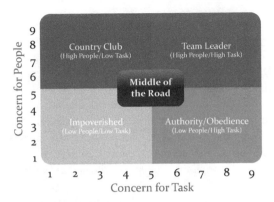

FIGURE 1.3 The Managerial Grid.

Mouton themselves said: *"It should be emphasized that the manner in which these two concerns are linked together by a manager defines how he uses hierarchy."*[62]

Paul Hersey had a similar set of distinctions in terms of leadership style, with four types based on concern for task or concern for relationship that was called "situational leadership." Hersey saw leadership as an effort to influence another individual or group and believed that *"power is influence potential—the resource that enables a leader to gain compliance or commitment from others."*[63] Even in 2001, it was as if they had not even encountered McGregor's work.

Herzberg's Hygiene and Motivating Factors: Echoing Taylor's proclamations in 1913 about human nature, in 1968 Frederick Herzberg argued in the *Harvard Business Review* that people have two needs: one stems from our "animal nature" to avoid pain and seek pleasure, and the other relates to psychological growth. His theory was that the two sources for motivation in the workplace were *hygiene factors*—namely salary, status, security, and supervision—and *motivator factors,* which he saw as achievement, growth, development, and recognition. He saw "job enrichment" as leveraging the motivator factors, but they were embedded in a power-based set of assumptions:[64]

- "If you have employees on a job use them. ... If you can't use them or get rid of them, you will have a motivation problem."
- In terms of engagement, Herzberg said: "Avoid direct participation by the employees whose jobs are to be enriched ... their direct involvement contaminates the process with human relations ... and gives them only a sense of making a contribution."

This arrogance toward the workforce indicates that the idea of job enrichment and the use of any motivational factors was driven not only by contempt for the intellect and capabilities of the workforce, but also a preeminent focus on production.

Rousseau's Psychological Contract: In 1994 Denise Rousseau built on the work of Argyris and McGregor in her analysis of the *psychological contract,*[65] which represents the assumptions, expectations, promises, and mutual obligations of the manager and the worker. D.E. Guest suggested in 1996 that there were six elements of the employment relationship that were covered by the psychological contract from the workers' point of view: how they are treated in terms of fairness, job security, ability to demonstrate competence, the opportunity to develop skills, involvement, and trust that leadership will keep their promises.[66] From leadership's perspective, their expectations and assumptions are that the workers are competent, will work hard, and will be committed, loyal, and compliant. The key to the success of the contract is that the needs of both parties are met.

Bennis on Leadership: Warren Bennis (1925–2014) was called the "Father of Leadership Development" by *Forbes* magazine after he passed away.[67] He was a prolific author, a university provost and president, and an advisor to leaders in business and politics. He was clearly in the People School of leadership, as articulated in his 1989 book, *On Becoming a Leader,* where he said there are five key ingredients to leadership:

- A guiding vision and the strength to persist in the face of setbacks and failures
- Passion for the promises of life, for a profession, and a course of action
- Integrity, which consists of self-knowledge, candor, and maturity
- Trust, which is grounded in one's integrity and must be earned
- Curiosity and daring, because leaders wonder about everything[68]

Drucker's Effective Executive: Peter Drucker (1909–2005) was an Austrian-born American management consultant, whom the November 28, 2005, cover of *Businessweek* claimed was the "Man Who Invented Management."[69] He wrote 39 books on all aspects of management, as distinct from leadership. Drucker believed that managers get things done through people, so in that sense he reflects the People Paradigm, while at the same time believed in the authority and power of managers to control and act, reflecting the premises of the Power School. He straddled both during this time of transition.

Even at 95 years of age, Drucker helped us understand the four core practices necessary for an executive to be effective: 1) Do what's right for the enterprise, 2) Take responsibility for decisions, 3) Run productive meetings, and 4) Think and say "We", not "I."[70]

Marshall on Transactional Leadership: In my work as a consultant on collaborative leadership and organizational change, I found that during the 1960–90 Transitional Period, cooperation was a way leaders straddled the fence between the Power Paradigm's hierarchy and authority, and the People Paradigm's appreciation of the human factor, emotions, and group dynamics. In my book *Building Trust at the Speed of Change,* published in 2000, I made the distinction between the transactional organization and the relationship-based corporation. In the transactional organization, leadership "cooperates" with the workforce by being open to their input into decisions, but the power to make them still resides with the hierarchy. The following excerpts are intended to help us understand this approach to leadership in more detail.[71]

Merriam-Webster defines *transaction* as an exchange or a "communicative action or activity involving two parties or things that reciprocally affect or influence each other."[72] To put this in a business context: we will define a transaction-based organization as *a system whose leadership, workforce, culture, structure, and processes are driven by the immediacy of the transaction, the task, or the result, and the authority of the leader.*

In a transaction-based organization, power resides at the top. Leadership makes the ultimate decisions. The workforce is focused on the exchange of information and the completion of tasks or projects, not necessarily on the quality, character, or impact of those tasks on work relationships. It is an organization that cares more about individual performance than that of groups or teams. It is dedicated primarily to output and shareholder value. The people side of the business, such as teamwork and skills development, are usually viewed as a means to an end, a transaction rather than a relationship.

Here are four key elements of transactional leadership, what is in effect "power paradigm-lite":

- **Core Values:** There are four core values—people cooperate with each other, power is still vested in top leadership, the focus is on efficient production and on bottom line results.
- **Culture:** Behind all the slogans of participation, teams, and empowerment lies the real driver of human behavior in a transactional organization—fear of job loss, being written up, retribution, or not meeting the expectations of superiors. Outliers may be ostracized. Candor is not rewarded. This is a culture that is "nice and kind, but not honest."
- **Leadership:** Transactional leaders retain power and control, have strong egos, focus on results, and may listen to their subordinates and ask for their input. Leadership is "hub and spoke," with the transactional leader as the hub.
- **The Psychological Contract:** The value of workers to the organization is measured by their ability to do what leadership wants them to do and their capacity to grow. Workers receive wages, benefits, and the chance for advancement.

THE ANOMALY OF GRADUATE AND EXECUTIVE LEADERSHIP EDUCATION

As a society we are facing existential threats to the survival of the planet: global warming and sea level rise, the disappearance of animal species, global pandemics, nuclear proliferation, mass migrations, and severe inequality of wealth between the few and the rest of the world. Businesses are confronting unrelenting change in a volatile, uncertain, complex, ambiguous, and interconnected world. Technological advances are outstripping the human capacity to absorb them. There are major demographic changes, specifically the increasing dominance of the Millennial generation in the workplace and their expectations for a more collaborative work culture. So why does the Power Paradigm remain embedded in graduate leadership curricula as the dominant way to lead and manage, even in the face of these realities? This is an anomaly in graduate education in business, engineering, public administration, social work, healthcare administration, and education, as well as in undergraduate education in the social sciences. Our educational system is out of step with the realities that leaders and the people of the world now face.

One reason is that business schools, in particular, focus on the science of management rather than the realities leaders actually face in business. In 2005 Warren Bennis and James O'Toole critiqued how business schools were out of touch with the reality of business when they concluded that they:

- Are too focused on "scientific" research
- Hire professors with limited real-world experience
- Graduate students who are ill equipped to wrangle with complex, unquantifiable issues
- Fail to educate students on questions of judgment, ethics, and messy people issues[73]

A second reason is that there are entrenched interests and inertia in these schools that prevent the shift in what is being taught about leadership. Steve Denning, in a 2018 article in *Forbes* provocatively entitled "Why Today's Business Schools Teach Yesterday's Expertise," notes that during this time of the "Fourth Industrial Revolution," business schools are still teaching 20ᵗʰ Century management principles: "Despite individual thought-leaders in business schools, there has been little change in the core curricula of business school teaching as a whole." Denning reinforces Bennis' central finding and points to these reasons for the inertia preventing a shift to 21ˢᵗ Century thinking:

- Executives are seeking recruits who are learning what they learned about profit maximization and "controlism"
- Professors usually have no management experience in 20ᵗʰ Century management, let alone in firms implementing a 21ˢᵗ Century paradigm
- Careers in business school depend more on research than teaching
- The accreditation process for business schools is glacial; it can take years to make minor changes in curricula
- Business schools are often a cash cow for universities; they attract wealthy students from overseas, and the schools don't want to lose that income stream[74]

Even in executive education programs that focus on the practicing business leader, the curricula do not adequately prepare them for 21ˢᵗ Century business challenges.

Moldoveanu and Narayandas point out in their article "The Future of Leadership Development" that:

> Companies are seeking the communicative, interpretive, affective, and perceptual skills needed to lead coherent, proactive collaboration. But most executive education programs—designed as extensions of or substitutes for MBA programs—focus on discipline-based skill sets, such as strategy development and financial analysis.[75]

Our graduate and executive leadership development programs are failing to educate the next generation of business leaders in the frameworks and skills they need to survive and succeed. They remain deeply rooted in the 20th Century, and their institutional inertia prevents them from making the dramatic changes needed to address current realities. Businesses, nonprofits, and nongovernmental organizations need leaders who are self-aware, emotionally intelligent, know how to engage and motivate the workforce, and can collaborate with their workers to solve problems and meet the challenges of the 21st Century head-on.

CONCLUSION: THE PARADIGM MUST SHIFT

> It seems to me unlikely that the transition will be rapid from the conception of an organization as a pattern of individual relationships to one of a pattern of relationships among groups. We have too much to learn, and too many prejudices to overcome. I do believe, however, that such a transition is inevitable in the long run. We cannot hope much longer to operate the complex, interdependent, collaborative enterprise which is the modern industrial company on the completely unrealistic premise that it consists of individual relationships.
>
> —Douglas McGregor, 1960[76]

McGregor's prescient observation anticipated what has needed to happen in the evolution of leadership paradigms for some time. The primacy of humanity over machine, of interpersonal effectiveness over machine efficiency, of the group over the individual, of interdependence over dependence—all are suggestive of the need for a radical shift in the predominant leadership paradigm—Power. External realities all reinforce the reality that the Power Paradigm's time has passed. And yet die-hard advocates for hierarchy persist, even to the present day. Harold Leavitt claims that hierarchy and the Power Paradigm thrive because they are "intrinsic to the complexity of the natural world".[77]

Entrenched interests are clinging to the deck chairs of the *Titanic* as it sinks.

There are *push* and *pull* factors that lead us to the conclusion that the Power Paradigm must now be "overthrown" and replaced by the Collaboration Paradigm. The *push factors* include the Hawthorne experiments at Western Electric, McGregor's ground-breaking work on human motivation, Maslow's work on human needs, and

Argyris' work on the individual and organization. The evidence is overwhelming that human beings have needs for connection, interaction, engagement, communication, and appreciation which the machine model of Scientific Management does not recognize. The push factors include the many anomalies that Argyris found in the principles of Scientific Management which lead us to the conclusion that the Power Paradigm cannot explain why people resist compliance, why there is dysfunction in organizations, why there are informal social networks, or why people are motivated to produce when they are recognized for their achievements.

The *pull factors* for overthrowing the Power Paradigm center on the external realities of the work world in the 21st Century, externalities that power, control, and authority are incapable of effectively addressing. Command-and-control leaders who use force, fear, and foreboding are at a competitive disadvantage in accessing or leveraging the intellect, innovation, or talent of their workforce. Global leaders cannot force other leaders to comply with agreements like the Paris Climate Agreement of 2015 to lower carbon emissions to save the planet from warming. They must influence, engage, and collaborate with others so they can problem solve.

There is a choice to be made. Leaders can cling to the past in the hopes that 20th Century leadership practices can solve 21st Century problems, or they can embrace the new paradigm of principle-based collaboration and learn about how leadership culture shapes the relationship between leaders and workers, how culture is the fundamental driver for human behavior, and how a principle-based culture can transform how we address the challenges of the 21st Century.

Before we turn to leadership culture in Chapter 2, let's review what we've learned about two leadership paradigms of the 20th Century (see Figure 1.4).

PARADIGM/ SYSTEM ELEMENTS	POWER	PEOPLE
CULTURE	Dependence; individualistic; mechanistic; workers are lazy, irresponsible; fear-based; security-based rewards & punishments; competition	Interdependence; social group-oriented; humanistic; workers work hard, are responsible; have feelings; integration of individual and organization
LEADERSHIP	Compliance; command-and-control; top-down; positional; makes all decisions; supervises	Cooperation/participatory management; relationship-based; psychological contract; situational; gets input for decisions; hub-and-spoke
PROCESS	Efficiency; machine model; specialization; time and motion studies; one best way	Effectiveness; teamwork; Scanlon Plan incentives; group-based improvements
ORGANIZATION DESIGN/STRUCTURE	Pyramid hierarchy; formal organization; 1:5 span of control	Hierarchy with teamwork; formal and informal organization

FIGURE 1.4   Leadership Paradigms Summary: Power and People.

CHAPTER REVIEW AND REFLECTIONS

Learning Objectives

Let's reflect on the learning objectives for the Chapter and summarize what we have learned:

- You learned what a leadership *paradigm* is and how leadership paradigms, or theories, have evolved over time as *anomalies* emerge that the theories cannot explain.
- You learned about a *systems model* that can help you understand how organizations work and how leaders can lead in terms of culture, leadership, process, and organization design/structure.
- You learned in detail about the two primary leadership paradigms of the 20th Century, Power (Theory X) and People (Theory Y), which describe leadership-workforce relationships.
- You now understand the Transitional Period of Leadership, from 1960 to 1990, when leaders tried many different approaches to motivating the workforce; there was no one paradigm.
- You understand that even now, in the 21st Century Digital Age, the Power Paradigm persists as the predominant way in which organizations are led, due in part to graduate education's inertia.
- Also, there are push and pull factors that suggest the need for a paradigm shift, an evolution in leadership, replacing the Power Paradigm with a paradigm that is more in step with the external realities of this century, Collaborative Leadership.

Initial Questions Revisited, and For Reflection:

- *Now that you have started this journey, how you define "leadership"?*
- *What are the anomalies in the Power Paradigm that resulted in the People Paradigm of leadership?*
- *How would you apply the systems model to help you be a better leader?*
- *If you found yourself in a Theory X organization, what would you do? How could you bring the beliefs and values of Theory Y into your workspace?*

ADDITIONAL READINGS

- Argyris, Chris. *Integrating the Individual and the Organization.* New York: Wiley, 1964.
- Bennis, Warren. *On Becoming a Leader.* Philadelphia, PA: Basic Books, 1989.

- Maslow, Abraham. *Motivation and Personality.* New York: Harper, 1954.
- McGregor, Douglas. *The Human Side of Enterprise.* New York: McGraw-Hill, 1960.

ENDNOTES

1. Thomas Kuhn, *The of Scientific Revolutions,* 3rd ed. (Chicago, IL: University of Chicago Press, Chicago, IL, 1962, 1970 1996).
2. https://www.google.com/search?source=hp&ei=p_HJXIW8LfCMggeqxYKoCA&q=definition+of+paradigm&btnK=Google+Search&oq=definition+of+paradigm&gs_l=psy-ab.3..ol10.2379.5724..6485...0.0..1.135.1508.21j3......0....1..gws-wiz.....0..oi131j0i70i249j0i10.CdHfvSXbVnU
3. Kuhn, op. cit., pp. 5–6.
4. https://www.google.com/search?source=hp&ei=avPJXJefGcHN_wSQwpOIBA&q=definition+of+anomaly&btnK=Google+Search&oq=definition+of+anomaly&gs_l=psy-ab.3..0i70i249j0l6j0i22i30l3.2253.5583..6392...0.0..1.132.2359.12j11......0....1..gws-wiz.....0..oi131j0i10.59skNV-EMHM
5. Kuhn, op.cit., pp. 52–65, 84–85, 97.
6. Peter Senge, *The Fifth Discipline* (New York: Penguin Random House, 2006); on p. 12, Senge argues that systems thinking is an integrator, enables the forming of a coherent theory and practice, prevents the thinking from being considered a fad, and increases understanding of how organizations work.
7. Rensis Likert, "Management Systems 1–4," in *The Human Organization: It's Management and Value* (New York: McGraw-Hill, 1967), pp. 3–12.
8. Keith Davis, *Human Relations at Work,* 3rd ed. (New York: McGraw-Hill, 1969), p. 480; plus comments by Abraham Maslow.
9. Talcott Parsons, *Structure and Process in Modern Societies* (New York: Free Press, 1960).
10. Edgar H. Schein with Peter Schein, *Organizational Culture and Leadership,* 5th ed. (Hoboken, NJ: Wiley, 2017).
11. https://www.history.com/this-day-in-history/fords-assembly-line-starts-rolling
12. Encyclopedia.com, "The 1910s Government, Politics, and Law: Overview," April 21, 2019, https://www.encyclopedia.com/social-sciences/culture-magazines/1910s-government-politics-and-law-overview
13. Encyclopedia.com, "The 1910s Business and the Economy."
14. https://www.history.com/topics/roaring-twenties/roaring-twenties-history
15. Niccolo Machiavelli, *The Prince* (Bantam Classics, 1984), Chapter 17, "Concerning Cruelty: Whether It Is Better to be Loved Than to Be Feared, or the Reverse," London, pp. 65–67.
16. Frederick Winslow Taylor, "The Principles of Scientific Management," in Walter Natemeyer, Paul Hersey, eds., *Classics of Organizational Behavior,* 4th ed., eds. Walter Natemeyer and Paul Hersey (Long Grove, IL: Waveland Press, 2011), p. 6.

17 Douglas M. McGregor, "The Human Side of Enterprise," Chapter 5 in *Classics in Organizational Behavior,* 4th ed., eds. Walter Natemeyer and Paul Hersey (Long Grove, IL: Waveland Press, 2011), p. 64.

18 Ibid., p. 3.

19 Douglas McGregor, *The Human Side of Enterprise, Annotated Edition "Theory X: The Traditional View of Direction and Control,"* Chapter 3, pp. 45–57, (New York: McGraw-Hill, 2006), pp. 45–46.

20 Taylor, loc. cit., pp. 9–11.

21 Dr. Vidya Hattangadi et al., *International Journal of Recent Research Aspects* ISSN: 2349–7688, Vol. 2, Issue no. 4, (December, 2015): p. 20.

22 Taylor, op. cit., pp. 5.

23 Tom Burns and G. M. Stalker, "Mechanistic and Organic Systems," in *The Management of Innovation* (Oxford University Press, London, 1961), p. 119.

24 Ibid., pp. 119–120.

25 James MacGregor Burns, "The Power of Leadership," in *Leadership* (New York: Harper Collins, 1978), p. 10.

26 Max Weber, *Essays in Sociology* (New York: Oxford University Press, 1946, 1958), pp. 196–204.

27 Amitai Etzioni, "Position Power and Personal Power," adapted from *A Comparative Analysis of Complex Organizations* (Glencoe, IL: Free Press, 1961), 153–155.

28 Ibid., 154–155.

29 This section is based on Chris Argyris, "The Individual and the Organization," *Administrative Science Quarterly,* Vol. 2, No. 1 (June, 1957): pp. 1–24.

30 *Ibid.*

31 For this point only, M. Deutsch, "An Experimental Study of the Effects of Cooperation and Competition Upon Group Process," *Human Relations* Vol. 2 (1949): pp. 199–231.

32 Argyris, "The Individual and the Organization." pp. 1–24.

33 Encyclopedia.com, "'The 1950s Government, Politics, and Law.': Overview." U*X*L American Decades. *Encyclopedia.com.* (April 19, 2019).

34 https://libguides.mnhs.org/wwii_women; Women in the Military—WWII: Overview, Minnesota History Center, Gale Family Library.

35 https://www.history.com/topics/world-war-ii/american-women-in-world-war-ii-1

36 "The 1950s Government, Politics, and Law: Overview." U*X*L American Decades. *Encyclopedia.com.* (April 19, 2019) Encyclopedia.com, "The 1950s Government, Politics, and Law."

37 "The 1940s Business and the Economy: Overview." U*X*L American Decades. *Encyclopedia.com.* (May 6, 2019) Encyclopedia.com, "The 1950s Government, Politics, and Law."

38

39 "The Hawthorne Effect," *The Economist,* November 3, 2008. https://www.economist.com/news/2008/11/03/the-hawthorne-effect

40 Roethlisberger, loc. cit.

41 Roethlisberger, ibid.

42 Abraham H. Maslow, "A Theory of Human Motivation", *Psychological Review*, vol. 50 (July 1943): pp. 370–396.

43 McGregor, *The Human Side of Enterprise, Annotated Edition*, McGraw-Hill Companies, Inc., New York, 2006; first published in 1960.

44 Bedeian, Arthur G., Wren, Daniel A. *(Winter 2001)*. ""Most Influential Management Books of the 20th Century" Most Influential Management Books of the 20th Century," *Organizational Dynamics* 29, no. 3 (Winter 2001): 221–225, https://doi:10.1016/S0090-2616(01)00022-5

45 This set of assumptions comes from McGregor, op. cit., pp. 65–66.

46 McGregor, ibid., pp. 67–68.

47 Michael Armstrong, *A Handbook of Human Resource Management Practice*, 10th ed. (New York: Chapter 16, "The Psychological Contract," Kogan Page, 2006), p. 277.

48 Ibid., p. 279.

49 McGregor, loc. cit., p. 71.

50 McGregor, ibid., p. 85.

51 McGregor, ibid., p. 85.

52 This section is based on ibid., pp. 250–253.

53 McGregor, ibid., pp. 253–257.

54 McGregor, ibid., p. 214.

55 The following points are found in McGregor, ibid., pp. 314–317.

56 McGregor, ibid., p. 149.

57 McGregor, Ibid., pp. 149–156.

58 Encyclopedia.com, ""The 1960s Business and the Economy: Overview."" U*X*L American Decades, *Encyclopedia.com*. (May 11, 2019).

59 Steven Beschloss, "Economic Trends across the Decades," December 12, 2008, http://www.entrepreneur.com

60 Ibid.

61 Steve Denning, "Why Today's Business Schools Teach Yesterday's Expertise," *Forbes*, May 27, 2018, https://www.forbes.com/sites/stevedenning/2018/05/27/why-todays-business-schools-teach-yesterdays-expertise/#73671095488b

62 Robert Blake and Jane Mouton, *The Managerial Grid: The Key to Leadership Excellence* (Houston, TX: Gulf, 1964), quoted in Walter Natemeyer and Paul Hersey, eds., *Classics of Organizational Behavior*, 4th ed. (Long Grove, IL: Waveland Press, 2011), 309.

63 Paul Hersey and Walter Natemeyer, *Situational Leadership and Power*, in *Classics of Organizational Behavior*, 4th ed., eds. Walter Natemeyer and Paul Hersey (Long Grove, IL: Waveland Press, 2011), 440.

64 This section is based on Frederick Herzberg, "One More Time, How Do You Motivate Employees?" *Harvard Business Review*, January 2003), p. 12, and p. 10.

65 Denise Rousseau, *Psychological Contracts in Organizations: Understanding Written and Unwritten Agreements* (Thousand Oaks, CA: Sage, 1994).

66 Michael Armstrong, Chapter 16, "The Psychological Contract," chap. 16 in *A Handbook of Human Resource Management Practice*, 10th ed. (London: Kogan Page, 2006), pp. 279.

67 Kevin Cashman, "Remembering Warren Bennis: The Father of Leadership Development," *Forbes*, August 5, 2014, https://www.forbes.com/sites/kevincashman/2014/08/05/350/#3382d9cf300d

68 Warren Bennis, *On Becoming a Leader* (Philadelphia, PA: Basic Books, 1989), pp. 33–35.

69 "The Man Who Invented Management, Peter Drucker, Why His Ideas Matter," *Businessweek*, November 28, 2005. https://www.bloomberg.com/news/articles/2005-11-27/the-man-who-invented-management

70 Peter Drucker, "What Makes an Effective Executive," *Harvard Business Review*, June 2004, pp. 2–14.

71 The rest of this section is based on Edward M. Marshall, *Building Trust at the Speed of Change: The Power of the Relationship-Based Corporation* (New York: AMACOM Books, 2000).

72 *Merriam-Webster*, s.v. "transaction (*n.*)," https://www.merriam-webster.com/dictionary/transaction

73 Warren Bennis and James O'Toole, "How Business Schools Lost Their Way," *Harvard Business Review*, May 2005, https://hbr.org/2005/05/how-business-schools-lost-their-way

74 Steve Denning, "Why Today's Business Schools Teach Yesterday's Expertise," *Forbes*, May 27, 2018.

75 Mihnea Moldoveanu and Das Narayandas, "The Future of Leadership Development," *Harvard Business Review*, March–April 2019, 5.

76 Douglas McGregor, *The Human Side of Enterprise* (New York: McGraw-Hill, 1960), p. 324.

77 Harold J. Leavitt, "Why Hierarchies Thrive," *Harvard Business Review*, (March 2003), pp. 4–7.

Figure Credits

CHAPTER TWO

The Power of Leadership Cultures

*T*HE LEARNING *team had gotten their coffee and settled into their early morning meeting in the library conference room to discuss their next assignment on leadership culture. No one really knew what it was or why the professor wanted them to focus on it. Linda realized organizational culture was the next step of the journey, but Hanyue and Priyanka wanted to talk more about the differences between the Power and People Paradigms and what this meant for their own leadership styles. They both realized the importance of leaders motivating the workforce to be their best selves and to do their best work. They now understood that coming from the values of power and control would not achieve that result. They had done values work as part of their own leadership journeys, which helped them see the connection between a leader's values and how they treated those with whom they work. They found that they were aligned more with the People Paradigm but wanted to find out more about the Principle Paradigm of leadership, what this "culture thing" is, and why it is so important: What does it have to do with leadership? What is the Principle Paradigm? How does it relate to the Collaboration Paradigm of leadership?*

Morare was responsible for facilitating the session, so he first appreciated the inquiry that Hanyue and Priyanka were engaged in, because he knew this work may be challenging the leadership assumptions in their cultures. He acknowledged that his own perspective on leadership paradigms had deepened as a result of learning about the Power and People Paradigms, and saw the need for the shift to a more principle-based approach. He suggested that their next assignment on leadership culture might help them all get a deeper understanding of how to be a principle-based, collaborative leader. The exercise the professor had asked them to reflect on was to think about a place they had recently worked and answer these four questions:

1. *What was it like to work there? How were people treated by leadership?*
2. *How would you describe the culture? Was it fear based or trust based; compliant, cooperative, or collaborative?*

35

3. *Given those observations, what leadership values or beliefs do you think were behind each culture?*
4. *Finally, what do you believe were the underlying assumptions leadership had about the workforce that led them to create this kind of workplace?*

The team members were excited about this assignment because it would make this idea of "culture" and "leadership culture" more concrete and specific. They got to work.

LEARNING OBJECTIVES

By the end of this chapter, you will:

- Understand what the *culture* of an organization is and how it shapes the ways people work together
- Understand what a *leadership culture* is and how it shapes the organizational system; how leadership's assumptions beliefs, and values affect how the organization actually works
- Be introduced to a typology of three types of leadership cultures present in most organizations: passive/defensive, aggressive/defensive, and constructive/collaborative
- Learn about Stephen Covey's *principle-centered leadership* and the Principle Paradigm of leadership
- Learn about the cultural dimension of the Collaboration Paradigm of leadership—its assumptions, beliefs, and principles

THE MAIN POINT OF THIS CHAPTER

Culture eats strategy, finance, and operational excellence for breakfast, lunch, and dinner. An organization's culture is the most important thing any leader can focus on, because culture drives the behavior of its workforce. If you get the culture right, the organization will work effectively and efficiently. The culture of any organization, however, is determined in large part by the values, beliefs, assumptions, and behavior of its leadership. Leadership cultures also reflect Schein's cultural DNA of the organization—its artifacts, espoused values and beliefs, and underlying assumptions that help us understand how the organization works.

We've already discovered the cultural DNA of the power and People Paradigms. We will now see how they are reflected in Cooke's typology of leadership cultures—passive/defensive, aggressive/defensive, and constructive/collaborative. The first two are Power

Paradigm cultures; the latter is constructive collaborative, which represents the DNA of people, principle, and Collaboration Paradigms.

As we explore Stephen Covey's work articulating the Principle Paradigm of leadership, we will see the foundations of Leadership's 4th Evolution—collaboration. The bottom line of this 4th Evolution is that in a collaborative leadership culture:

> *People want to be trusted, respected, and honored for who they are as responsible and accountable human beings, want to be safe, and to own their jobs and the workplace so that they can be their best selves and do their best work.*

THE CRITICAL ROLE OF CULTURE IN ORGANIZATIONS

> *Until I came to IBM, I probably would have told you that culture was just one among several important elements in any organization's makeup and success—along with vision, strategy, marketing, financials, and the like. ... I came to see, in my time at IBM, that culture isn't just one aspect of the game, it* is *the game.*

—Lou Gerstner, CEO of IBM, 1993–2002[1]

In 1993 Gerstner began a cultural transformation to pull IBM out of a steep decline in which the company was losing billions of dollars. IBM had been extraordinarily successful in the 1960s and 1970s, powered by its sales culture. Like many organizations that are more than 20 years old, it developed inertia, which impeded its growth, and its 300,000 employees around the world slowly began to witness the company's decline. Gerstner saw his job as tackling the culture of the company. He realized that the employees needed to integrate as a team, move beyond just strategy as a way to transform, and use culture and processes to regain advantage.[2] Gerstner came to see the power of culture as a primary driver for human behavior, that it *is* the "game." He also saw the fallacy, that is still being taught in business schools today, that strategy, finance, and marketing are what drive the organization. To emphasize this point, Peter Drucker, a world-famous management expert, was credited as having said, "Culture eats strategy for breakfast"[3] (Figure 2.1). In my work with companies, I have found that culture eats strategy, finance, marketing, and operations for breakfast, lunch, and dinner.

FIGURE 2.1 Culture Eats Strategy for Breakfast.

Culture has primacy. It has agency. As a columnist in the *Financial Times* said:

> *Culture, real and unnoticed is the air we breathe, is the web of unspoken, mutual understandings that frame what people expect from others and this is what is expected of them.*[4]

The power of culture is also seen on companies' bottom line. John Kotter of Harvard Business School conducted a study on the role of culture in terms of financial results over an 11-year period. He found that the companies that focused on culture increased revenues by an average of 682% compared to 166% for the companies that did not.[5]

But what *is* culture? Often the term is derided by leaders and managers who call it "fluffy," "touchy-feely," or "that soft stuff" because they don't understand what it is or the power that it has in their organizations. They see the "hard stuff" of operations, strategy, marketing, finance, or technology as much easier to understand. But not culture. It's "invisible," or as the *Financial Times* put it, it's like the air we breathe. Understanding culture and the power it has to shape an organization is the essential work of leadership.

Defining Culture as Cultural DNA

The world's leading expert on organizational culture is Dr. Edgar Schein, Professor Emeritus at the Sloan School of Management at MIT. Schein is one of the original architects of our understanding of what culture is, as well as organization development and process consultation. In a paper he prepared at the Organizational Culture and Leadership Institute in 2016, he defined culture as "a pattern or system of beliefs, values, and behavioral norms that come to be taken for granted as basic assumptions and eventually drop out of awareness."[6] Culture comes from shared experience, a shared sense of identity and mission, shared structures and procedures, and shared norms of how to work together.[7]

In his seminal book, *Organizational Culture and Leadership,*[8] Schein gives us a three-level model to help us understand what *culture* is, often referred to as the "iceberg model" (see Figure 2.2). Schein defines the first level, *artifacts,* as what you can see and feel, as well as observed behavior, which are above the water. The second level, *espoused beliefs and values,* which are just below the waterline, e.g. ideals, goals, values, aspirations, ideologies, and rationalizations. The third level of culture, the deepest part of the iceberg, *basic underlying assumptions,* is the unconscious or taken-for-granted beliefs and values that determine behavior, perception, thoughts, and feelings.[9]

Schein argues that an organization's cultural DNA is what people have learned in their work life that often becomes tacit, or automatic as to how people think, talk, feel, and behave, or "the way we do things around here." Cultural DNA internally represents the organization's current reality. It is why people do what they do, how boundaries are defined, how power is distributed, how relationships are defined, and how rewards and punishments are allocated. In effect, it represents the deeper assumptions that ultimately

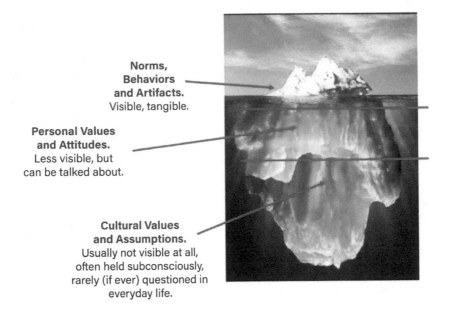

Norms, Behaviors and Artifacts.
Visible, tangible.

Personal Values and Attitudes.
Less visible, but can be talked about.

Cultural Values and Assumptions.
Usually not visible at all, often held subconsciously, rarely (if ever) questioned in everyday life.

FIGURE 2.2   Edgar Schein's Iceberg Model of Culture.

drive human behavior and define an organization's "truth." Externally, cultural DNA represents the organization's purpose, structures, processes, and a sense of identity.[10]

Other Definitions of Culture

In 1960 McGregor saw culture as "managerial climate," the product of "day-to-day behavior of the immediate superior and other significant people in the managerial organization," but he also recognized that it is a result of people's observations of managerial behavior, what Schein called "underlying assumptions."[11] Recalling Theory X, McGregor points to the underlying assumption that people must be controlled if they are to be productive, while in Theory Y there was a focus on relationships and creating an environment that encourages worker commitment to organizational goals.[12]

Leigh built on Schein's cultural DNA model, but centered his definition of culture all around values. He argues that "culture is the personality of the organization ... where values reveal themselves through people's behaviors, attitudes, and decisions."[13] The variables surrounding an organization's values that help us understand an organization's culture include self-image, character, attitudes, metaphors and symbols, stories and myths, skills and know-how, ethos, feelings, shared language, traditions, customs and rituals, purpose, beliefs, identity, behaviors, physical space, management practices, and meaning.[14]

A third definition of culture comes from Groysberg: "Culture is the tacit social order of an organization: it shapes attitudes and behaviors in wide-ranging and durable ways. Cultural norms define what is encouraged, discouraged, accepted, or rejected within a group."[5] Groysberg suggests four key characteristics of culture that are aligned with Schein's definition:[6]

- **Shared:** Behaviors, values, assumptions, and unwritten rules.
- **Pervasive:** Shows up in collective behaviors, group rituals, mind-sets, motivations, and unspoken assumptions.
- **Enduring:** Develops through collective learning by the group, becomes self-reinforcing.
- **Implicit:** People are hardwired to recognize and respond to the culture instinctively.

Finally, Hofstede's work on cross-national cultures defined it as "mental software," patterns of thinking, feeling, and acting that have been learned through life. It is learned, not innate in us:[7]

> Culture is always a collective phenomenon, because it is at least partly shared with people who live or lived within the same social environment, which is where it was learned. Culture consists of unwritten rules of the social game. It is the collective programming of the mind that distinguishes members of one group or category of people from others.

Hofstede goes on to say *organizational culture* is a fad, that there is no standard definition, but he believes most agree that it is: holistic, historically determined, rituals and symbols, socially constructed, "soft," and difficult to change.[8] I take issue with Hofstede's view that organizational culture is a fad. It is not, as we shall see later in this chapter when we discuss Robert Cooke's work on leadership cultures. It is, however, important to see the diversity of thinking about what *culture* is, and that while there is no one agreed-upon definition, we now have a better idea of the key elements that will help us understand it in the context of our leadership work.

Working Definitions of *Organizational Culture* and *Productive Energy*

In Chapter 1 a systems model was proposed for how to understand the complexity of organizations, with "culture" at the top of the Venn diagram to represent that it drives human behavior, work processes, and organization's design, and leadership in the center of the system. For purposes of this discussion, we will define *organizational culture* as follows:

> The shared assumptions and beliefs, principles, values and ethics, the history, language and customs in the organization, all of which shape and drive the behaviors of people in the workforce, the workplace environment, work processes, and how the organization is designed and organized to produce results.

An important distinction here is that organizations have a *predominant culture* that is pervasive in how leadership behaves and treats the workforce. They also have a range of *subcultures* at the business unit or team level.

When I worked at Marriott with a collaborative information technology (IT) transformation team, it was viewed by the predominant culture of the lodging business unit as a renegade subculture that ended up ostracized by others in the unit because of their great success. Often subcultures are stamped out because they may present a threat to the predominant culture. When I worked at a Fortune 100 company in the IT group, the change process was so successful that corporate human resources apparently felt threatened and sought to discredit the business unit's collaboration work. Subcultures always exist, and whether they are a threat or not, they serve an important function of giving workers a way to cope with the predominant culture.

All things considered, the key differentiator between one business and another is the *productive energy* of the workforce, whether it is individuals, teams, departments, or business units. Productive energy is defined as follows:

> *What workers are willing to give of themselves to the enterprise, which reflects their pride in the organization, self-esteem, how they are treated by leadership, their level of engagement, the degree of trust and ownership in the culture, their willingness to take risks and go the extra mile, and the degree to which they feel respected, appreciated and acknowledged for their contributions.*[19]

Given our definitions of an organization's culture and of productive energy, let's look at the role that leadership plays in shaping that culture. How responsible are they for the *predominant* organizational culture? What if they want to change that culture?

LEADERSHIP DRIVES CULTURE

At Marriott, members of senior leadership measured their relative importance by how "close" they were to Bill Marriott Jr., the CEO and chair of the board. Oftentimes one would hear, "When I was in a meeting with Bill the other day," or "I was talking with Bill about this yesterday." Marriott is what Schein would consider a "mature" culture[20] but was still in the founder's family. Mr. Marriott's assumptions and beliefs about the workforce were very evident in how employees talked about the company: "If you take care of the employees, they will take care of the customer." Once, I went to lunch with him in the company cafeteria. As we walked in, he stopped by a number of tables, calling each person by their name and asking them questions about their families and their work. This leadership culture, while hierarchical, treated its people with dignity and respect. Mr. Marriott's principles and values were equally present in how the executive team functioned. He trusted them to run their business units and used the budget process, along with quarterly reviews, to hold them accountable. Clearly, the respect which everyone in the company had for him was a direct result of the respect and reverence he had for the workforce. Marriott's leadership culture was that of a "family," which was led by the assumptions, beliefs, principles, values, and behaviors of its CEO.

On the other hand, at a start-up manufacturing company, the leadership culture reflected a different set of assumptions, beliefs, principles, values, and behaviors. Their product was definitely a hit in the market, but their internal dynamics were toxic. The CEO, straight out of graduate school, had no experience leading people. She hired her friends, gave them a lot of responsibility, and then when things did not go the way she expected, got angry and pitted them against each other. Within a matter of months senior leaders were leaving, and the venture capital funders on the board were raising serious questions about the company's viability. The company survived because board members took control of the business. The leadership culture was based on the Power Paradigm and also reflected the lack of leadership maturity of the CEO.

There are many examples of the critical role that senior leadership has in shaping the cultures of their organizations, with very different outcomes. In fact, in my consulting work I have come to appreciate the strength of the one-to-one relationship between the beliefs, principles, and values of senior leadership and the behavior of the workforce in the rest of the organization. If there is a power-based leadership culture, there will be internal competition, conflict, withholding of information, politics, and even backstabbing to gain influence. In power-based leadership cultures, their *productive energy* tends to be in the 30–40% range, and then drops to 0–10% if there is a process or structural change. Fear tends to be the driver for behavior, and people are "nice and kind but not honest" with each other. If, on the other hand, the leadership culture is more people- and principle-based, information is shared, there is more transparency, trust is the driving force, leadership is situational, and the focus is on cooperation and shared problem solving. Productive energy in this type of leadership culture tends to be 40–60%.

A Definition of Leadership Culture

Edgar Schein tells us that leaders create culture when they "impose their own values and assumptions on a group."[21] Jim Whitehurst, who is CEO of Red Hat and is also on the board of directors for United Airlines, once said that culture happens when leaders model the behavior they want to see in the organization.[22] Giberson and Resick found in their assessment of 32 CEOs of organizations that there was a direct relationship between the CEO's values and personality and the cultures that emerged in these organizations.[23] Pennington found that in 15 teams[24] in which the five leadership practices identified by Kouzes and Posner[25] were applied, there was a strong relationship between the leader's values and the culture of new organizations, but less so if the leader came to the organization from the outside.

Leadership assumptions and beliefs, principles and values, and behavior have a direct influence on the predominant culture of an organization, for better or for worse. In effect, the CEO or president of an organization, along with its senior leadership, define, shape, and evolve the leadership culture of that organization. For the purposes of our journey toward more collaborative leadership and building on the work of Schein, Kouzes and Posner, McGregor, Argyris, and Parsons, we will define a *leadership culture* this way:

> *A leadership culture drives the behavior of an organization in its people relationships, work processes, organization design, and its outcomes. It reflects the assumptions and beliefs senior leadership have about the workforce, their principles and values as manifested in their behaviors, and their ethical conduct toward others.*

A leadership culture may reflect any of the three leadership paradigms we have discussed so far—Power, People, or Principle—as well as the Collaboration Paradigm of leadership to be discussed later in this chapter. The normative orientation of the leadership culture, however, will determine the types of outcomes that the organization delivers. It reflects the following:

- **Assumptions and Beliefs:** What senior leaders believe about the workforce, whether they are lazy and irresponsible or are social creatures, responsible, hardworking, and wanting to be respected. These basic underlying assumptions about people, what it takes to motivate them, and how to get work done are critical to how leadership defines, shapes, and evolves the culture.
- **Principles and Values:** There are choices to be made about principles and values in the organization: trust or fear, transparency or opaqueness, integrity or unethical conduct, respect or discrimination, "I" or "We," individualistic or collectivist values, limited engagement or high engagement and ownership.
- **Behaviors:** How senior leadership behave toward each other and the workforce: authoritarian and control oriented or authentic, humble, and collaborative; will they walk the talk, will they seek to align the workforce with the vision and mission, and will they engage the workforce or maintain full control?
- **Ethical Conduct:** High standards of ethical conduct usually guide senior leadership's behavior, but sometimes there are leaders who choose to breach those principles and values. Sometimes there is conduct toward individual workers, such as sexual harassment, that fundamentally breaches the ethics of the organization. How these ethical breaches are handled reflects whether the leadership culture is truly ethical and accountable.

The sum total of the choices senior leadership makes ends up defining, shaping, and evolving what we have called the *predominant leadership culture*. But what are the outcomes this culture produces?

Leadership Culture Outcomes

Let's refer back to the systems model from Chapter 1, to which we will now add four types of outcomes that flow from the predominant leadership culture. Figure 2.3

represents the addition of these four outcomes to the model: relationship, results, reputation, and alignment.

- **Relationships:** The result of how the organization's culture shapes people processes like interpersonal relations, team dynamics, and professional development is the quality and character of relationships people have with each other. Those relationships may be fear- or trust-based; negative or positive; "I" or "We" oriented; competitive, cooperative, or collaborative; and conflict-resolving or conflict-avoiding.
- **Results:** Business results are the result of the intersection of how people work together to implement business processes to get the work of the organization done. Business results are typically revenues, profitability, sales volume, stock price, quality, or customer satisfaction.
- **Reputation:** The result of a company's culture and what the organization does is its reputation; that is, what others say in the marketplace about the organization, its ethical conduct, its character, its standing, or its renown. The degree to which it reflects its cultural norms will determine whether its reputation is positive or negative.
- **Ownership and Alignment:** Ownership is a core principle of a collaboration; the workforce owns the organization's leadership culture, vision, mission, and strategy; people own their jobs and take full responsibility for the success of their team, mission, and the organization; it is the key to high trust and productive energy of the workforce. Alignment is the degree to which the entire organization's workforce, from the C-suite to the front lines, is aligned with the leadership culture, vision, mission, and strategic direction of the organization.

At the center of the systems model is leadership. Its responsibility and obligation is to be aware of and orchestrate these relationships and their evolution. Organizations are dynamic, organic, living entities that require focused leadership. Leadership must comprehend and honor the ethos of the system—its history, legacy, rituals, customs, language, and traditions.

How Leaders Drive Culture

We have established that there is a one-to-one correlation between the assumptions and beliefs, principles and values, behavior, and ethical conduct of senior leadership and the leadership culture. We are clear about the origins of leadership culture. But leaders also continue to shape, reshape, or evolve that leadership culture over time. They do so in a very complex organizational system. Given this complexity, senior leadership do have a number of levers that they can pull to influence the direction of the organization's predominant leadership culture. Schein has suggested two sets of levelers, or what he calls "primary embedding mechanisms" that enable leaders to embed their assumptions, beliefs, and values in the culture:[27]

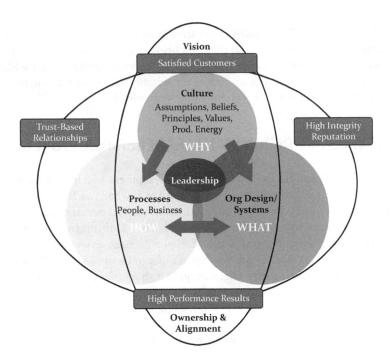

FIGURE 2.3 Systems Model With Outcomes.[26]

- **Primary Embedding Mechanisms: How Leaders Communicate Their Assumptions to the Workforce:** These include what leaders pay attention to, measure, and control; how they react to critical incidents and organizational crises; how they role model, teach, and coach; how they allocate resources, rewards, status or accountabilities; and how they recruit, select, promote, and communicate.

I would add to this important list *how leaders engage the workforce and the degree to which they give them ownership over the vision, mission, culture, work processes, change initiatives, and their own jobs.* Schein continues with:

- **Secondary Reinforcing and Stabilizing Mechanisms:** The organization's design and structure, systems and procedures, rites and rituals, physical space, stories about important events and people, and formal statements of organizational philosophy, creeds, and charters.

In my experience, most new senior leaders who have been hired into an existing organization do not understand the power of the leadership culture, how it has been created, or even their role in it. In their first 100 days, they typically go on a "listening tour," meet with first- and second-tier leadership, and then start making changes to the structure of the organization so they can bring in their own team, redo the strategy, craft a new vision, or introduce a new product/service. Rarely do they address the leadership culture. This short-term strategy inevitably backfires, leading to yet more structural change—such as a search for a new senior leader.

THREE TYPES OF PREDOMINANT LEADERSHIP CULTURES

Kristen, the Vice President for Learning and Development of a 15,000-person global human resources firm, had only been in her role a year when her Executive Vice President called her into his office and complained about the performance of her staff. They were not executing their commitments on time. Her internal customers were complaining to him about her staff's lack of responsiveness, as well as the high cost of their services. He warned her to get her ship in order or he would consider outsourcing her entire group. Needless to say, this was quite a shock; she had what is known as a "burning platform" and decided it was time for radical change. Like most new executives, she had already reorganized the department, with new people in leadership roles and a new organization chart. But as we have learned, structural change alone will not "fix" ingrained behaviors. She knew from her previous job that she now needed to transform her department's culture.

The first step was to find out what the current state was for the culture she inherited and to determine the desired state of the culture. She decided to do a culture audit using two tools that had been developed by Human Synergistics International (HSI). The first tool was the Organizational Culture Inventory® (OCI®), which would measure the current state of her culture on 12 behavioral dimensions and the levers for change. The second, the Organizational Culture Inventory-Ideal® (OCI-Ideal®) would measure the culture her workforce desired.[28] Kristen assembled her leadership team to be briefed on this entire process.

Overview of the OCI® Cultural Assessment[29]
Because *culture* has appeared to many business leaders to be "soft" and is hard to understand, we have needed a way to measure it to make more concrete. There are many instruments in the market that purport to measure an organization's climate and culture, but given McGregor's work on the social and relationship orientation of people in the workplace and Schein's work in defining *cultural DNA*, what has been needed is an instrument that could assess the behavioral expectations people have about their workplace, feelings, perceptions, and experience of what it will take for them to succeed.

Enter the OCI® that Kristen found and decided to use, an instrument developed by Dr. Robert Cooke and J. Clayton Lafferty of HSI. Dr. Cooke, CEO of HSI and associate professor emeritus of management at the University of Illinois, Chicago, led the development and validation of the OCI®. There are 12 behavioral norms he identi-fied, four of which are constructive and facilitate problem solving, decision-making, teamwork, productivity, and long-term effectiveness. Eight of the behavioral norms are passive/defensive or aggressive/defensive and detract from effective performance.

What are *behavioral norms?* HSI defines them this way:[30]

> *As a component of culture, behavioral norms are shaped by the commonly shared assump-tions, beliefs, and values of organizational members ... and lead to the general patterns of work-related behaviors and attitudes that may be observed. ... These behavioral norms guide the way in which members approach their work and interact with one another.*

What the OCI® is measuring relates directly to our earlier definition of a *leadership culture* and builds on the work of Schein, McGregor, Argyris, Bennis, and many others. The OCI® is administered to individuals or groups. Results reveal their beliefs about the behavioral expectations that operate within the organization, or the "current state" of the operating culture. The OCI-Ideal® asks a set of questions that measure the indi-vidual's or group's "desired state" for the culture.

Since 1976 Cooke and HSI have administered both the OCI® and related instru-ments to over 4 million respondents in more than 70 countries at companies like IBM, Ford, General Electric, and Motorola. As an indicator of its cross-cultural import, the OCI® has been translated into 35 different languages. His work has been supported by the National Science Foundation, the National Institute of Education, and the National Commission for the Protection of Human Subjects and, among other awards, has won the Douglas McGregor Memorial Award for Excellence in the Applied Social Sciences.

These instruments increase our understanding of three types of predominant leader-ship cultures by focusing on behavioral norms that members of a workforce are expected to honor if they are to succeed in that organization. These three leadership cultures are (1) Passive/Defensive, (2) Aggressive/Defensive, and (3) Constructive. Cooke and Szumal, in research reported in 1994, validated the behavioral measures of these leadership cul-tures in terms of their impact on problem-solving effectiveness in 61 groups. They found that constructive styles were positively correlated with problem-solving effectiveness, passive styles were negatively correlated, and aggressive styles had mixed results.[31]

In 2000 Cooke and Szumal published the results of their analysis of over 2 million respondents in thousands of organizations throughout the world. In measuring the "cur-rent state" of their leadership cultures versus the "desired state," they found similar results:[32]

- There was a preference for constructive behaviors, moderate to weak prefer-ences for aggressive/defensive behaviors, and weak preferences for passive/defensive behaviors.
- Across industries people wanted to work in constructive cultures.
- Emphasis on defensive norms were found in organizations in countries with stronger collectivist, power distance, and conflict avoidance values.

- Constructive norms are those most likely to promote performance regardless of the types of organization type.

A Typology of Leadership Cultures

There are three types of leadership cultures, and each has four behavioral norms.[33] Each culture will be described in general terms first—its philosophies, beliefs, and values—followed by the four behavioral norms used to evaluate the respondents' current and desired workplace culture, and finally the types of outcomes from that culture.

1. **Passive/Defensive Leadership Cultures**[34]

    - **Overall Description:** Reflecting the Power Paradigm and Scientific Management, passive/defensive leadership cultures are about control and security, pleasing one's superiors, avoiding conflict, playing by the rules, and following orders, expectations that are reinforced through punishments, structures, systems, and technologies. Fear drives this culture, especially if you disobey orders. The focus is on output, so individuals subordinate their preferences to those of the power structure. This culture results in unresolved conflicts, high turnover, low motivation, little innovation, and low productive energy.
    - **Philosophies, Values, and Beliefs:** A passive/defensive culture's dominant belief is the need for a high degree of structure and control, strict rules, narrow job descriptions, close supervision, and standardization.
    - **Four Cultural Norms:**

        ○ **Approval:** Conflicts are avoided; relationships are superficial; there is a focus on getting approval, agreeing with others, being liked, having a low level of ownership of decisions reached, and backing up those with the most authority.
        ○ **Conventional:** Conformity, following rules, making a good impression, accepting the status quo, not rocking the boat, and avoiding confrontations are important; it's about rules, procedures, and traditions.
        ○ **Dependent:** Organizations are nonparticipative, hierarchical, and create dependence among the workers; the workforce is expected to do what it's told, even if it's wrong; individual initiative is discouraged; and performance tends to suffer.
        ○ **Avoidance:** Working here is like walking through a minefield; mistakes are punished, so workers will shift blame to others; workers are noncommittal, put things off, and wait for others to act first.

    - **Outcomes:** This is not a pleasant or empowering place to work; workers are demotivated and unhappy, and productive energy is low; people avoid taking responsibility and may avoid work; there is lots of conflict, but because of conflict avoidance, people leave or shut down emotionally.

2. **Aggressive/Defensive Leadership Cultures**[35]

- **Overall Description:** This leadership culture also reflects the Power Paradigm approach to leadership, but with a twist. In this culture, workers are expected to be aggressive and forceful to protect their own individual security and status. You are expected to appear to be competent even if you don't feel that way; you never admit weakness, mistakes, or shortcomings. It's about looking like you're perfect and not about your well-being. Fear drives this culture, where there are punishments and terminations to enforce production, reflecting a lack of respect for the humanity of the workforce. You can imagine that their productive energy is low while their output is relatively high to avoid the consequences.

- **Philosophies, Values, and Beliefs:** Success is the result of avoiding mistakes and failure; people are merely a means to the end; workers are highly individualistic; the belief is that by making them compete against each other, and to keep their jobs, they will be productive; financial assets are valued over people; the short term is valued over the long term; survival of the fittest with a premium on bluster and arrogance.

- **Four Cultural Norms:**

  o **Oppositional:** This culture is about confrontation and criticism, where workers gain status and influence by opposing the ideas of others and pointing their flaws, act hard to impress, refuse to accept criticism, and question the decisions others make.

  o **Power:** Control and authority are important; workers are rewarded for "taking charge"; forget participation in decision-making; never relinquish control; build your empire; demand loyalty; play politics to gain influence.

  o **Competitive:** Winning is valued; others are expected to lose; people have to be right rather than in relationship, compete rather than cooperate, and maintain an image of superiority.

  o **Perfectionist:** The shy need not apply; people are expected to be perfect, detail-oriented, work hard, never make a mistake, have high goals, stay on top of everything, and forget work-life balance.

- **Outcomes:** This is a dog-eat-dog existence. Think about the New York Stock Exchange or a highly aggressive sales organization. Externally, the outcomes are predictable—aggressive and argumentative behavior toward customers, and poor service quality. Internally, there is a high degree of competition, conflict, shaming and blaming others, win-lose battles, and a lack of cooperation either within the business unit.

3. **Constructive/Collaborative Leadership Cultures**[36]

- **Overall Description:** Roethlisberger, Maslow, McGregor, Argyris, and Bennis would be proud. The assumptions, beliefs, and values of the People and Principle Paradigms are very much evident in this culture. Workers are encouraged to work with each other, support each other on tasks, reach their full potential, and build strong, trust-based relationships. There is respect for people's needs, a high degree of engagement, two-way communications, and empowerment. As a result, there is low turnover, high motivation, innovation, productivity, and very high levels of productive energy.

- **Philosophies, Values, and Beliefs:** There is a fundamental belief in the goodness of the workforce that they want to work hard and contribute. Because of this trust, workers are encouraged to experiment, take risks and learn, and set challenging goals. If you invest in the workforce, they will learn, grow, and give dividends to the organization. Leaders believe they need to model the behavior they wish to see.

- **Four Cultural Norms:**

  - **Achievement:** People are valued who set and achieve their own realistic goals, problems are effectively solved, risks are taken, and a standard of excellence is pursued.

  - **Self-Actualizing:** This culture values creativity, quality over quantity, individual growth and task achievement; people enjoy their work, innovate, take on new activities, develop themselves, and maintain their personal integrity.

  - **Humanistic/Encouraging:** Workers are expected to show concern for and help each other and be willing to be helped, there is a high degree of participation, conflicts are resolved constructively, and there is team-based problem-solving.

  - **Affiliative:** Workers are expected to be open, friendly, cooperative, and tuned in to the needs of their teams or work groups; the focus is on the success and satisfaction of the group, teamwork, self-management, and interdependence.

- **Outcomes:** This is a great place to work. It is highly engaged, open, team-based, and collaborative. Customers are treated with integrity; there is a high level of responsibility for quality service/products, low turnover, high motivation and job satisfaction, cross-functional collaboration, and mutual support.

The Circumplex[37]

The OCI® uses a tool called the *Circumplex* to summarize the scores from respondents according to their answers to specific questions for each behavioral norm. What emerges is a picture of the organization's predominant leadership culture that is grounded in the perceptions and points of view of its workforce. Figure 2.4 represents the Circumplex without any data clusters for behavioral norms. Each of the 12 behavioral norms is arranged in the Circumplex based on the leadership culture cluster it is in. Behavioral norms at the top of the Circumplex promote the satisfac-

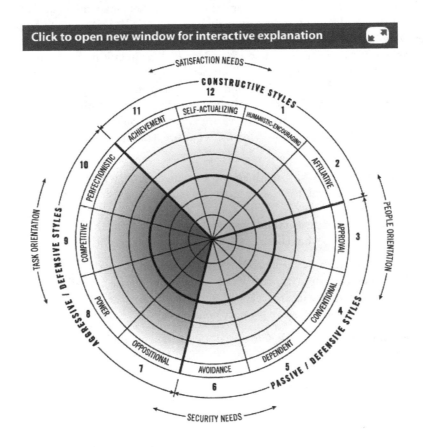

FIGURE 2.4 The OCI Circumplex.

tion needs of members and behaviors that enable them to fulfill those needs such as achievement and affiliation. Behavioral norms toward the bottom promote security needs and require self-protective behaviors such as acceptance or avoiding failure.

Behavioral norms on the right side promote people-oriented behaviors; on the left side are task-oriented behaviors.

When respondents complete the OCI® and the OCI-Ideal®, their answers are recorded on the pertinent norm, and the strength of those answers is represented by the concentric circles. The more those circles are filled, the stronger the culture is on that behavioral norm.

Current State vs. Desired State Leadership Cultures

Returning to our story about Kristen and the culture of her department, her leadership team felt they had enough information about how the OCI® was going to help them. They were impressed with its clarity and validity. Once and for all they were going to be able to get their arms around what their leadership culture was, what they all wanted, and how they could begin to improve things to avoid being outsourced. The OCI® and OCI-Ideal® were administered to a high percentage of her 250 people. Their results are found below. Figure 2.5 is their "current state" leadership culture. Kristen's leadership culture was primarily Passive/Defensive, although there was also a strong representation of the Aggressive/Defensive culture as well. The two primary behavioral norm findings were:

- **Primary Style is Approval:** People are expected to switch priorities to please others, do things for the approval of others, and back up those with the most authority.
- **Secondary Style is Dependent**: People are expected to please those in positions of authority, do what is expected, and check decisions with superiors.

The team was not terribly surprised by these findings and quickly pivoted to the type of leadership culture they wanted, which is shown in Figure 2.6. Like HSI's other 4 million respondents, the desired leadership culture for Kristen's department was constructive/collaborative. The two primary behavioral norm findings were as follows:

- **Primary Style is Achievement: 98%:** Ideally, people should be expected to know the business, pursue a standard of excellence, and think ahead and plan.
- **Secondary Style is Humanistic-Encouraging: 98%:** Ideally, people should be expected to resolve conflicts constructively, encourage others, and be a good listener.

This time, the leadership team was both surprised and pleased with how much they agreed about the type of culture they wanted. Now the hard work would begin, focusing on how they would move from their current culture to the desired one. A list of strategic priorities was developed, a set of action steps was quickly identified, and members of the team stepped up to take responsibility for leading each of them.

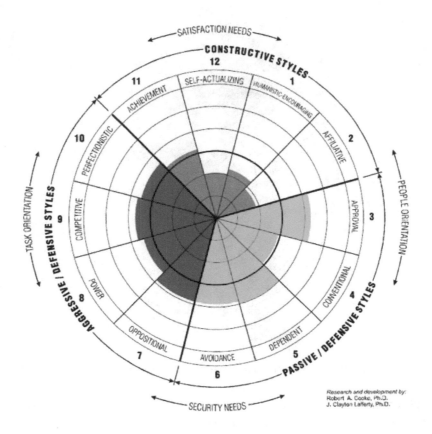

FIGURE 2.5 Current State Leadership Culture of Kristen's Department.[38]

A year later, I went back to see how far the client had come in achieving their strategic goals. They had not made much progress. They had chosen not to begin a structured culture change initiative, which would have given them specific tools and processes to become a constructive/collaborative culture. It reminded me of something Dr. Cooke had told me: "Left to our own devices, we will default back to either a passive/defensive or aggressive/defensive posture. Becoming a constructive/collaborative culture must be consciously considered and invested in."[39] Put another way, and paraphrasing a country-and-western song by the Dixie Chicks, it's about people reverting to old behavior, or coming back to "the freedom of my chains,"[40] even if they are disempowered by the "chains" of control and hierarchy. Kristen's group reverted to what they were comfortable with, even if it meant they would likely be outsourced.

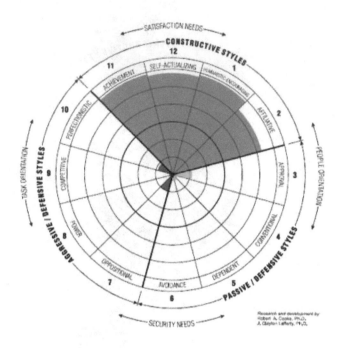

FIGURE 2.6   Desired State Leadership Culture for Kristen's Department.

People resist change almost as a reflex, especially if they have to change their behaviors, which is why culture change is so slow.

THE PRINCIPLE PARADIGM OF LEADERSHIP: TOWARD A COLLABORATIVE LEADERSHIP CULTURE

The learning team was excited. Learning about the Power and People Paradigms, along with understanding the power of leadership cultures, had been very helpful in providing them a perspective on how we have gotten to this point in the development of leadership theory and practice. Now they wanted to focus on what was most important to them and their future—the foundations of the Principle Paradigm of leadership, and how it laid the foundation for the Collaboration Paradigm. They had a lot of questions: What is the Principle Paradigm of leadership? What are its assumptions and beliefs, its principles and values? They were looking for answers.

In 1990, toward the end of the Transitional Period of leadership, Stephen R. Covey published a major book called *Principle-Centered Leadership*, which followed his book

The 7 Habits of Highly Effective People.[41] Covey was a businessman, author, and well-known speaker whose *7 Habits* is considered one of the most influential leadership books of all time. His book on leadership was a logical next step in our journey and represented a sea change in how we began to think about leadership at the time. His books came at the same time that the World Wide Web was launched and we entered the Digital Age. It was a time when we needed new thinking about how to lead organizations.

At a Fortune 100 company in the 1990s, where I worked for about four years as a leadership and collaborative change consultant, there was a significant amount of frustration among leaders about the persistence of the Power Paradigm. There were leaders trying other approaches, ranging from self-managed teams and participatory management to reengineered management and the early days of collaboration, which gave the company its "program-of-the-month" reputation. My leader I worked with worked hard to bring this principle-based approach to his IT organization. There was a leadership "culture war" going on inside the company, and Covey's work was a breath of fresh air. Everyone was talking about *The 7 Habits*, and they paid for many senior leaders to attend a weeklong training session.

Covey's Principle-Centered Leadership[42]

Covey called for a *paradigm shift* and claimed that principle-centered leadership was that shift:

> *Principle-centered leadership introduces a new paradigm—that we center our lives and our leadership of organizations and people on certain "true north" principles ... certain inviolate principles—natural laws in the human dimension that are just as real, just as unchanging, as laws such as gravity are in the physical dimension. Principles are not invented by us or by society; they are the laws of the universe that pertain to human relations and human organizations ... such ... as fairness, equity, justice, integrity, honesty, and trust.*[43]

By recognizing the need for a shift in how we think about leadership, Covey helped us move toward the 21st Century and the central focus of this book—collaborative leadership. Finally, here was a champion for the next step on our collective leadership journey. Here are four key parts of principle-centered leadership:

- **Four Levels of Leadership:** Each level has a core principle: personal (trustworthiness), interpersonal (trust), managerial (empowerment), and organizational (alignment). Trust is at the core of these four levels. He saw *trustworthiness* being based on one's character and competence, and *trust* as the emotional bank account between people that enables us to have win-win relationships that have empathy, synergy, and interdependency.[44] In my work, trust is essential for relationships and teamwork and is central to leaders' credibility so they can do their job. It is the glue that holds organizations together.

- **Three Types of Power:** Covey references three types of power, the first two of which we discussed are Theory X and the transitional period for leadership:

  o **Coercive power:** Fear-based; is about control; represents the motivational driver in the Power Paradigm
  o **Utility power:** Focuses on benefits that come to workers if they follow the leader
  o **Principle-centered power:** When leaders trust their people, believe in them and what they are trying to accomplish[45]

Principle-centered leadership shifts the conversation about leaders and the people who work with them to trust as the organizing principle. Covey helps us move past the power vs. people distinction toward a people-principle distinction—that leadership is about gaining the trust of the people you work with. First, however, you must trust yourself, which is the starting point for the collaborative leadership journey.

- **The Principle-Centered Leadership Paradigm:**[46] In articulating his paradigm, Covey first distinguishes it from what we have called the power and People Paradigms and sets forth what in effect are his assumptions and beliefs that are the cornerstones of this approach to leadership. People are not just resources or assets or just social or psychological beings; they are also spiritual beings and want to be treated as whole people. People want meaning or purpose in their lives and want to be believed in. People want to contribute to the accomplishment of worthwhile objectives.

Based on these assumptions, the core principles of this paradigm are fairness, kindness, efficiency, and effectiveness. Covey then brings it all together in what is, in effect, his systems model of leadership, shown in Figure 2.8. If you map this against our systems model (Figure 2.7), you will see that most of the elements are aligned. Of

---

PRINCIPLE PARADIGM OF LEADERSHIP

CULTURE: Principles are immutable truths; trust is central to all relationships; emotional bank accounts; integrity essential for any effective leader; interdependence

LEADERSHIP: Principle-driven; focus on trustworthiness and integrity; inside-out; people-centric in a hierarchical system; situational

PROCESSES: Teams are how work gets done; two-way communications; high engagement; effectiveness and efficiency

ORGANIZATION STRUCTURE/DESIGN: Still hierarchical; hub-and-spoke transactional; interdependence of systems

FIGURE 2.7   The Principle Paradigm of Leadership.

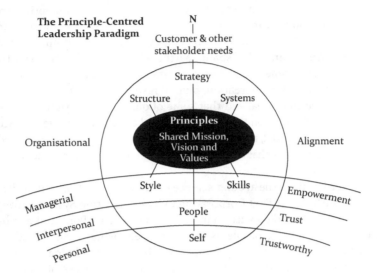

The Principle-Centred Leadership Paradigm

FIGURE 2.8 Covey's Principle-Centered Leadership System.

particular note is that while *collaboration* is not a central focus in Covey's work, the principle-focused approach opens the door for us to explore the assumptions and beliefs, and principles and values of collaborative leadership.

THE COLLABORATION PARADIGM OF LEADERSHIP

Morare was so excited to share with the learning team something about collaboration from Zulu culture in South Africa. "There is," he said, "a saying in our language called 'Ubuntu: Motho ke motho ka batho,' which means "You are what you are because of others," or put another way, "I am because we are." The team was impressed with his passion about his cultural heritage and wanted to learn more. It pointed the way to some important questions: What were the origins of the Collaboration Paradigm? What type of culture was it? What were the assumptions, beliefs, and principles that reflected the foundation of a collaborative leadership culture?

Origins of the Collaboration Paradigm
It was 1979, and I was beginning my management consulting career in Washington, DC. I had just finished an assignment at a nonprofit focused on community economic development, and created my first company, called the Community Development Collaborative. I had no idea what that meant at the time, but I knew that the only way for

low-income and minority communities to develop was through public-private partner-ships—that is, collaboration among a range of stakeholders who would work together to invest in small business, create jobs, and empower them. My company changed its name as African-American and Hispanic partners joined, and for the next ten years we worked with low-income and minority communities in cities across the country, building a methodology for co-creation, mutual respect, trust, and empowerment. It was during this time that I realized that some of our change initiatives were failing because we had not focused on the culture. I added the culture circle to Talcott Par-sons's content/process model, resulting in the Systems Model in Figure 2.3, and began to build tools and processes that linked culture to behavior—how people worked with each other collaboratively.

In 1989, after learning the art and science of group facilitation, I had the opportunity to work with the DuPont Corporation in its Information Systems group. Over the next four years, I worked with many teams, both at DuPont and a subsidiary, Conoco, to help them solve problems collaboratively using "team-based manage-ment." Self-managed teams were popular, but DuPont quickly learned they were unwilling to be held accountable. If we could develop a process of empowerment that would also ensure accountability, this could be really helpful to DuPont and companies everywhere. This was the origin of *collaborative teams* that were both empowered and accountable. My client asked me a central question in my work: "All this talk about 'collaboration' is well and good, but *how* will it actually work?" There had to be a practical application that could truly be helpful, which became the central focus of my work.

What emerged was a trifecta: (1) The critical role of culture in transforming work relationships and workplaces, (2) The need to answer the "how" question by having a realistic and practical methodology for true collaboration, and (3) The need for a wholesale replacement for the Power Paradigm because the world had dramatically changed. What an extraordinary opportunity to make a difference in the lives of people in every workplace. What resulted was the Collaborative Method.

At DuPont, I was tasked by headquarters to go to the Gulf Coast of Texas to work with three competing IT groups who were each serving different customers but needed to work more effectively together in order to beat their main competitor, Dow Chemi-cal. In working with the leadership team, I asked them, "What do you need in order to be able to work together effectively?" This question started an extraordinary journey that eventually led to an integrated, collaborative, team-based Information Systems Gulf Coast and to the creation of what became known as the Collaborative Team Governance Process. They needed to know how to make decisions, how to disagree with each other constructively, how to communicate across time and distance, and how to hold each other accountable. These became their operating agreements, which they agreed to by 100% consensus, but more importantly, they revealed some critical principles and values that became known as the collaborative work ethic. The most important principle for this team seemed to be *ownership*. Because of their 100% consensus decisions on their Operating Agreements, they truly "owned" them, took care of them, and then took this principle forward into all of their work.

This team had amazing success. Over the next 18 months, they totally transformed their now unified organization, became team based, went from five levels of management to three, from a 1-to-5 span of control to a 1-to-50 span, adopted a team-based performance management system, increased their internal customer satisfaction by 60% in the first year, became the low-cost supplier of information systems in their business, and became self-sufficient in sustaining their collaborative leadership culture over the next several decades. What was particularly rewarding was when they received the first-ever *Excellence in Organization Development Award* from the Association for Talent Development, the country's leading organization development professional association.

This experience at DuPont gave birth to the creation of the *Collaboration Paradigm* of leadership, its assumptions and beliefs, principles and values, demonstrated behaviors, and ethical conduct and how it is expressed at the levels of individual leaders, teams, and organizations as they change and evolve, and potentially at the global level.

This notion of a shared identity, responsibility, and accountability reflects a deep respect for all and a culture that connects my personal identity to that of the group. It reflects a profound belief in the goodness of people, that they have meaning and value to others, and that we are charged with ensuring their safety, empowerment, and ability to fulfill their dreams. In effect, *ubuntu* is collaboration.

The Collaboration Paradigm of leadership comes from the very deep heritage of the People Paradigm and particularly the work of Douglas McGregor, who helped us understand that people have feelings, emotions, and value; are social; and want to work with others in teams. He helped us understand that workers are responsible, like to work, want to contribute, and prefer rewards and development rather than fear and punishment. McGregor even pointed out that people prefer to collaborate rather than compete, though he could only hope that would happen in the future. Dr. McGregor, the future is here!

The Collaboration Paradigm of leadership also found important cornerstones of its foundation in the work of Covey's principle-centered leadership. The next level of humanistic leadership assumes not only that people want to work hard and are responsible, but that they want meaning and purpose in their lives, want to be believed in and trusted, and want to be engaged in the business of the business. While Covey helped build the principle platform, he did not build on McGregor's hope for collaboration in the future. From Cooke's work we discovered that the constructive/collaborative leadership culture was the preferred way of working for millions of people in 70 countries around the world.

Thus, clearly articulating the culture of the Collaboration Paradigm is the logical next step in the evolution of leadership.

Leadership's 4ᵗʰ Evolution: The Collaboration Paradigm

A careful reading of the history and evolution of the relationship between leaders and the workforce since the early 1900s, along with insights about the essence of human nature, the human psyche, group dynamics, organizational theory, behavior, and development, all point us toward this moment in time. It is time for our leadership paradigm to evolve again—this time to collaboration. This pivoting away from hierarchy, transactional, and transitional leadership is essential for the fulfillment of the most fundamental needs of human beings who work. It is essential to chart a new course in our continuing journey for a more perfect way to work with each other. Even more important, it is essential to our survival if we hope to save our planet.

In terms of collaboration in the workplace, the essence of this leadership philosophy is this: *People want to be trusted, respected, and honored for who they are as responsible and accountable human beings; they want to be safe and to own their jobs and the workplace so that they can be their best selves and do their best work.*

Assumptions and Beliefs of the Collaboration Paradigm

Here are the key assumptions and beliefs about people in the workplace that are the underpinnings of a collaborative leadership culture:

- **Inherent Goodness:** People are inherently good and have intrinsic value. They are responsible, are eager to work hard, can be trusted to do their best, and are accountable. They do not need to be motivated by fear or control. They need to be engaged.
- **Significance—People Want to Matter:** People want to matter in life, in their relationships, and at work. They have intrinsic value. They want to be treated like adults, to work interdependently, and to make a difference in their work, their lives, and the lives of others. They are not interchangeable parts in a machine that can be disposed of when they are considered to be no longer "useful" by the powers that be.
- **Meaning and Contribution:** People need to have meaning or a sense of purpose in their lives and work. They need an answer to the questions of why they are here on this planet and what value they can add by being here. Meaning is not found in "just having a job." It is found in the vision, mission, and goals of the organization they work for, in how they are treated by leadership, and in how their job connects to the larger purpose of the organization. Meaning is found in the contributions they make to tasks, goals, and overall achievements of the organization.

- **Dignity, Honor, and Respect:** People want their dignity to be honored and respected by others in their teams and organizations. This means they are respected for who they are as individuals, regardless of their gender, race, religion, cultural heritage, sexual orientation, or age. It means they are honored and respected for the gifts they bring to the organization. Their dignity is not up for debate, debasement, or dishonor.
- **Trust:** The cornerstone for any human relationship is trust. We cannot function effectively without it. Everyone wants to be trusted in the workplace to do their best work.
- **Ownership:** People take care of what they own—they don't wash rented cars. They need to have psychological ownership over the organization's vision, mission, goals, their own jobs, and any change initiatives that will affect their work lives.
- **Psychological Safety:** To do their best work and to be their best selves, people need to feel psychologically, physically, and emotionally safe in their workplaces. This means no fear-based or compliance-oriented leadership, retribution, intimidation, actual or perceived, harassment, or assault.
- **Learning and Development:** People want to learn and grow, to know that they have a future where they are working, that there is opportunity to develop, and that leadership is taking a direct interest in their development.
- **Appreciation and Acknowledgement:** People are starved for authentic acknowledgement and appreciation from others, which adds significantly to what Covey has called the emotional bank account.[47] Appreciation and acknowledgement create connection, amplify one's feeling of self-worth and self-esteem, and open up the opportunity for a deeper relationship.

Work gets done through people. If the workforce knows their leadership is operating on the basis of these assumptions and beliefs, not only will the productive energy of the workforce be exceptionally high, but the business will have a significant competitive edge in the marketplace.

The Seven Principles of the Collaborative Work Ethic[48]

Building on these assumptions and beliefs we have just discussed, there are seven principles in the collaborative work ethic, which provide the foundation for collaborative leadership. They are trust, ownership, integrity and ethics, honor, mutual respect, full responsibility, and accountability.

Principle 1: Trust:[49] Trust is the fundamental building block in human relationships. It is at the root of how we treat each other. It is a principle that governs how we perceive ourselves and how others see us. *Merriam-Webster* defines *trust* as assured reliance on the character, ability, strength, or truth of someone or something; one in whom confidence is placed; a charge or duty imposed in faith or confidence, or as a condition of some relationship.[50]

In the collaborative leadership context, trust can be thought of in at least three ways. First, it is a principle, a cornerstone of how we choose to live our lives, and a standard we use to evaluate our own actions as well as those of others. It is an expression of what we value most in ourselves and others. It is a frame of reference or way of looking at things. It is the glue that holds our relationships together over time and distance.

Second, trust is a measure of our self-esteem; that is, how we feel about ourselves. Without it, we may give up hope. With too little of it, we may be more suspicious of others than is needed. When we have high self-esteem, we usually flourish and are more able to trust others. There is no pride with trust—only humility and grace. There is no arrogance—only the recognition that we all make mistakes.

Third, trust comes from the inside out. We must first be trustworthy, which means clarifying our values, learning new skills to support those values, and then behaving accordingly, or *trust competence*. The development of trust competence is perhaps the most critical challenge we face as individuals, teams, and organizations. Words are cheap. It is actions that determine if we can be trusted. One's trust competence is fairly easy to measure because it will be reflected in what others say about us. It will show up in the quality, character, and effectiveness of our relationships with them.

To trust another reflects our confidence in their character, our faith in their capacities, that we can count on them, and our reliance or even dependence on their taking care of something that is important to us. Trust is usually conditional and not given lightly. To trust another is a reflection of how we perceive their integrity and our confidence in them, that they are responsible and will do what they say they are going to do.

Without trust, our relationships become merely transactions. With trust, there is the true potential for deep collaboration. Most of us enter our relationships with others somewhere along a continuum that reflects the degrees of trust we have in each other. Some people begin their relationships from a position of trust, with a belief that there is credibility and integrity, that trust is given without it having to be earned. For others, trust must be earned over time, proved by one's deeds matching their words.

Principle 2: Ownership: People take care of what they own—they don't wash rented cars. If individuals own their homes or cars, they tend to take care of them. If individuals are given ownership of their jobs, rather than just being given a set of roles and responsibilities, they will perform them excellently. If teams own their work, they will be more willing to be held accountable for the results. Consensus decision-making is how team members create ownership of their work. If organizations give ownership of change processes to the people affected by them, the resistance to the change will drop dramatically.[51] If nations around the globe own the solution to a problem like climate change, they will be more likely to implement it. Of all the principles in the collaborative work ethic, the ownership principle is the one that most clearly distinguishes collaboration from any other approach to leadership. There is no workforce ownership in the Power Paradigm. There is slightly more ownership in the People Paradigm in the form of participatory management. In the Principle Paradigm there is a focus on building commitment, which is a form of ownership. But in a collaborative leadership culture, ownership is foundational and core; it transforms how people think about themselves, their work, their teams, and their organizations. With ownership comes high levels of productive energy.

Principle 3: Integrity and Ethics: *Merriam-Webster* defines *integrity* as the "firm adherence to a code of moral values."[52] Put another way, leaders are seen as having high integrity when their actions match their words as well as their intent, or what is commonly referred to as walking the talk. If leaders are viewed as being ethical, respectful, responsible, and accountable, they are viewed as having high integrity. If a leader lies, cheats, steals, manipulates, intimidates, or harasses, this is considered a breach of integrity and a violation of ethical conduct. Collaborative leaders are ethical above reproach.

Merriam-Webster defines *ethics* as a "set of moral principles, a theory or system of moral values", and "the principles of conduct governing an individual or a group".[53] People's integrity is at the core of their ethical code and conduct. Ethical conduct is an essential condition for a collaborative leadership culture that is built on trust, honor, dignity, respect, and accountability. Ethical leaders can be counted on to do the right thing when faced with difficult choices. Ethical leaders will put acting with integrity above their self-interest. They will always do what is best for the organization rather than for any special interest.

Principle 4: Honor: *Semper Fidelis*, which means "always faithful," is the US Marine Corps motto, which reflects a code of honor among soldiers. It is their bond, their word, their commitment to one another. Honor is a mark of distinction, one's reputation, and the regard that others have for us. To be honorable means the leader has high integrity and can be counted on. In a collaborative workplace, honoring one's commitments and agreements is an essential building block for the success of the team and the organization. Because we are more interdependent and must count on each other, we need to know we are working with honorable people.

Principle 5: Mutual Respect: There are three levels of mutual respect to consider: self-respect, respecting others, and a leadership culture of respect. *Self-respect* is about one's self-esteem. It is the regard that I have for myself, my self-confidence, competence, self-trust, and sense of purpose. Self-respect is not something I do. It is not something I can get by going to a workshop. It is something I have, and we all have it to some degree or another. Developing and nurturing my self-respect is part of my leadership journey, the inside-out exploration of who I am, what I stand for, and how I will act toward others. My level of self-respect will determine how I respect and treat others, as well as whether others will respect me. If I have high self-respect, I will not need to belittle, discriminate against, deride, criticize or manipulate others. High levels of self-respect usually exist when we have been respected by others from our earliest years. We were listened to, honored, and celebrated. A collaborative leadership culture is a safe place where all are respected. *Respecting others* means we have the highest regard for others, without any consideration of their gender, race, color, religion, culture, country of origin, sexual orientation, or age. This is a very high standard, which contributes to the building of high levels of trust, particularly on cross-national teams. In a collaborative workplace, respecting others means that respect is reciprocal, that it is received and given with grace. *A leadership culture of respect* honors the dignity, competencies, and gifts each person brings to the workplace. It values all people for who they are and where they are in their growth and development, invests in their continued development, appreciates and acknowledges their contributions, and empowers them to be their best selves and to do their best work.

Principle 6: Full Responsibility: There are two types of full responsibility—being responsible for yourself and being responsible to others. *Being fully responsible for myself* is an individual act of commitment. It means that I own, and am responsible and accountable for, the assumptions I make, the beliefs I hold, my attitudes toward others, my behaviors, and the actions I take. It means I am willing to be held accountable for my behaviors and actions. I am open to receiving feedback and to modifying my behaviors if they are found to be disrespectful, out of integrity, or unethical. It means I do not blame and shame others for behaviors or actions that I own. It means that, at the end of the day, others can trust and count on me. In a collaborative leadership culture, being fully responsible for myself means I am trustworthy and a person of integrity. *Being fully responsible to others* means I care about my colleagues, team members, and the organization, that I will be aware of and acknowledge issues or problems that may be obstacles to our effectiveness, that I will show up, speak up, and step up to address them. In a collaborative leadership culture, if someone is behaving unethically, I will have a direct conversation with them in an effort to resolve the issue. If that fails, I will escalate the issue until there is someone in the organization who addresses it to ensure team and organizational integrity.

Principle 7: Accountability: In a collaborative leadership culture there are two types of accountability: self-accountability and holding others accountable. *Self-accountability* is about "owning up" to your mistakes. It is the "Blue Angels Principle."[54] This US Navy precision flying team flies six F/A-18 Hornet jets at 700 mph, often at 18-inch wing separation through hundreds of acrobatic maneuvers in a 45-minute air show. Mistakes can be fatal, so if you make a mistake, everyone knows it, and you are expected to own up to it at the debriefing, explain what you learned, and commit to it never happening again. In a collaborative leadership culture, self-accountability is very powerful; it strengthens my trust in you because I know that if you make a mistake, you will own up to it. It's about getting better. It means I am willing to accept the consequences for my behaviors or actions. *Holding others accountable* is where the "rubber hits the road" in collaboration. You can run but you cannot hide. We are all accountable to each other. This means we hold each other to the highest standards of collaborative and ethical conduct, not from a place of authority or control, but from a place of compassion, growth, and development. If someone on our team is consistently not doing their fair share, if they are behaving unethically, we first will seek to understand why they are behaving this way. Empathy and active listening are used, through direct or difficult conversations, to get to the root cause. Perhaps there are concerns outside of work that are driving this behavior. Perhaps it's just the wrong fit for the person. In a collaborative workplace, this approach to accountability requires the highest degree of integrity combined with emotional intelligence, but if the situation cannot be resolved, it can lead to the person being asked to leave the team or company.

SUMMARY AND CONCLUSION: THE 21ST CENTURY REQUIRES THE COLLABORATION PARADIGM

What got you here won't get you there.
—Marshall Goldsmith[55]

In terms of leadership paradigms, we have been wandering in the wilderness since 1960. Many leaders still use the principles and practices of the 20th Century Power Paradigm to run their 21st Century Digital Age companies. Some are more benevolent and realize that people do the work of their organizations, and have adopted some of McGregor's ideas from the People Paradigm. Yet others have become more participatory, have adopted vision statements and codes of ethics, but are still transactional, or cooperative, in their style. Still others are team based, have positive learning and development programs, and have all the appearances of being more people-centric but remain firmly entrenched in the hierarchical construct. A few companies reflect the values and practices of the Principle Paradigm, while still fewer have adopted a collaborative leadership culture. We are still in the transitional period with no end in sight, even though we have learned that the preferences of workers around the world are for collaboration. It is time for the Leadership's 4th Evolution—Collaboration.

We know that in the 21st Century, technology will accelerate at close to a billion times in the next 30 years, which will force organizations to adjust, adapt, or die. We saw in Kristen's organization that, even when faced with their own hard data and the possibility of losing their jobs, they still resisted change. As a consequence of this phenomenon, organizations are not changing at a rate anywhere close to the rate of technological change. Globalization is causing businesses to become more networked and virtual. The volatility, uncertainty, complexity, ambiguity, and interdependence of global markets means business leadership cultures must adapt or face being disrupted out of business. We know that as of 2025 the Millennial generation is 75% of the global workforce and that they prefer to work collaboratively. We also know that the world faces existential threats like climate change, nuclear proliferation, disease pandemics, and famine.

We are simply not prepared for the 21ˢᵗ Century, as individuals, teams, organizations, nations, or as a planet. What got us here is the Power and People Paradigms, plus a half century of wandering in the cultural wilderness where we have tried everything to see what would work best. Even the Principle Paradigm, while helping shift the focus from Power to Principle, still resides within the hierarchical construct.

It took 60 years to fully realize the anomalies of the Power Paradigm, and McGregor gave us the foundations for the People Paradigm. It then took another 30 years to get us to the understanding that leadership should be principle-based, and Covey gave us the Principle Paradigm. It took us another 10 to 15 years to realize we needed to evolve to the next paradigm—and the Collaboration Paradigm of leadership came into existence. The essence of Collaborative Leadership is this: *People want to be trusted, respected, and honored for who they are as responsible and accountable human beings, and they want to be safe and to own their jobs and the workplace so that they can be their best selves and do their best work.*

What are we waiting for? Leaders have a choice—they can rearrange the chairs on the deck of the *Titanic*, or they can embrace a cultural platform that gives us the best chance of meeting these challenges, and potentially save the planet.

You are now ready to take the next step of our leadership journey where you will learn about the rest of the Collaboration Paradigm.

CHAPTER REVIEW AND REFLECTIONS

Learning Objectives:
Let's reflect on the learning objectives for this chapter:

- Understand what the *culture* of an organization is and how it shapes the ways people work together
- Understand what a *leadership culture* is and how it shapes the organizational system; how leadership's assumptions beliefs, and values affect how the organization actually works
- Be introduced to a typology of three types of leadership cultures present in most organizations: passive/defensive, aggressive/defensive, and constructive/collaborative
- Learn about Stephen Covey's *principle-centered leadership* and the Principle Paradigm of leadership

- Learn about the cultural dimension of the Collaboration Paradigm of leadership—its assumptions, beliefs, and principles

Initial Questions Revisited, and For Reflection:

At the beginning of this chapter, you were asked to consider the questions below as you did your reading. What did you discover? What were your key learnings?

- *How do you define* organizational culture, *and why do you think it is important?*
- *When you hear the term* leadership culture, *what does that mean to you?*
- *What type of leadership culture would you prefer to work in, and why?*
- *What is your definition of a* collaborative leadership culture?
- *How important is trust to you in any relationship, as well as at work, and why?*

ADDITIONAL READINGS

- Covey, Stephen R. *The 7 Habits of Highly Effective People.* New York: Free Press, 1989.
- Covey, Stephen R. *Principle-Centered Leadership.* New York: Free Press, 1990.
- Marshall, Edward M. *Building Trust at the Speed of Change: The Power of the Relationship-Based Corporation.* New York: AMACOM Books, 2000.
- Marshall, Edward M. *Transforming the Way We Work: The Power of the Collaborative Workplace.* New York: AMACOM Books, 1995.
- Schein, Edgar H. *Organizational Culture and Leadership.* 5th ed. Hoboken, NJ: Wiley, 2017.
- Szumal, Janet L., and Robert A. Cooke. *Creating Constructive Cultures.* Plymouth, MI: Human Synergistics International, 2019.

ENDNOTES

1 Louis Gerstner, *Who Says Elephants Can't Dance* (New York: HarperBusiness, 2002); emphasis added.
2 Martha Lagace, "Gerstner: Changing Culture at IBM," Harvard Business School, December 9, 2002, https://hbswk.hbs.edu/archive/gerstner-changing-culture-at-ibm-lou-gerstner-discusses-changing-the-culture-at-ibm
3 Anthony Taylor, "What Does "Culture Eats Strategy" Mean for You and Your Organization? https://www.smestrategy.net/blog/what-does-culture-eats-strategy-mean-for-you-and-your-organization
4 *Financial Times,* August 20, 2012, quoted in Andrew Leigh, *Ethical Leadership: Creating and Sustaining an Ethical Business Culture* (London: Kogan Page, 2013), p. 14.

5 John Kotter, cited in Andrew Leigh, *Ethical Leadership: Creating and Sustaining an Ethical Business Culture* (London: Kogan Page, 2013), p. 12.

6 Edgar Schein, *Organizational Culture and Leadership*, 5th ed. (Hoboken, NJ: John Wiley & Sons, 2017), p. 6.

7 Ibid.

8 Schein, op. cit., pp. 17–25.

9 Schein, op. cit., pp. 17–25.

10 Schein, "Cultural DNA Workshop," op. cit.

11 Douglas McGregor, *The Human Side of Enterprise* (New York: McGraw-Hill, 2006), p. 179–180.

12 Ibid., 181, 183.

13 Andrew Leigh, *Ethical Leadership: Creating and Sustaining an Ethical Business Culture* (London: Kogan Page, 2013), p. 15.

14 Andrew Leigh, Ibid.

15 Boris Groysberg, Jeremiah Lee, Jesse Price, and J. Yo-Jud Cheng, "The Leaders Guide to Corporate Culture: How to Manage the Eight Critical Elements of Organizational Life," *Harvard Business Review,* January–February 2018, pp. 4.

16 Ibid.

17 Geert Hofstede and Gert Jan Hofstede, *Cultures and Organizations: Software of the Mind* (New York: McGraw-Hill, 2005), pp. 2–3.

18 Ibid., pp. 281–284.

19 This definition was developed by the author over a period of 35 years and is a cultural assessment measure in the Collaborative Interdependence Index©, which has been used by teams and organizations to determine how collaborative and interdependent they are; also, over 500,000 people have been asked the question "What percentage of you is your employer getting?" with responses typically in the 30–40% range for hierarchical/Power Paradigm organizations and 70–80% for collaborative/Principle Paradigm organizations.

20 Schein, op. cit., p. 45.

21 Schein is quoted in Penny Pennington, Christine Townsend, and Richard Cummins, "The Relationship of Leadership Practices to Culture," *Journal of Leadership Education* (Summer, 2003): V 2, Issue 1, p. 28.

22 Jim Whitehurst, "Leadership Can Shape Company Culture through Their Behaviors," *Harvard Business Review,* October 13, 2016, p. 3

23 Tomas Giberson, Christian Resick, Marcus W. Dickson, Jacqueline K. Deuling, Kenneth R. Randall, Malissa A. Clark, "Leadership and Organizational Culture: Linking CEO Characteristics to Cultural Values," Springer Science+Business Media, LLC, (April 26, 2009), https://www.researchgate.net/publication/225810720_Leadership_and_Organizational_Culture_Linking_CEO_Characteristics_to_Cultural_Values

24 Pennington et al., op. cit., 27–28.

25 James Kouzes and Barry Posner, *The Leadership Challenge*, 6th ed. (Hoboken, NJ: Wiley, 2017).

26 This systems model of an organization was developed by Dr. Edward M. Marshall over a 35-year career as a leadership and organizational change consultant with companies of all sizes on five continents. It has been validated by hundreds of senior leaders who helped Dr. Marshall understand the interactions of the elements of this model. As noted in Chapter 1, this model builds on the work of Talcott Parsons, *The Social System* (London: Routledge & Kegan Paul 1951).

27 Schein, *Organizational Culture and Leadership*, Chapter 10, "How Leaders Embed and Transmit Culture," pp. 181–206.

28 Organizational Culture Inventory® (OCI®), "Identify your organization's culture and learn how to turn it into a competitive advantage," Human Synergistics, International, Plymouth, MI, 2000.

29 This section is based on an interview and data from Dr. Robert Cooke, March 25, 2019, and May 27, 2019; also the HSI website that summarizes Dr. Cooke's background: https://www.humansynergistics.com/about-us/our-people/robert-a-cooke

30 Human Synergistics and Center for Applied Research, *Organizational Culture Inventory, OCI®: Interpretation and Development Guide* (Plymouth, MI: Human Synergistics/Center for Applied Research, 2009).

31 Robert A. Cooke and Janet L. Szumal, "The Impact of Group Interaction Styles on Problem-Solving Effectiveness," *Journal of Applied Behavioral Science* (December 1994): 15, pp. 415–437.

32 Robert A. Cooke and Janet L. Szumal, "Using the Organizational Culture Inventory® to Understand the Operating Cultures of Organizations," in *Handbook of Organizational Culture & Climate*, ed. Neal M. Ashkanasy, Celeste P. M. Wilderom, and Mark F. Peterson (Thousand Oaks, CA: Sage Publications, 2011), 149–151; see also Janet L. Szumal and Robert A. Cooke, *Creating Constructive Cultures* (Plymouth, MI: Human Synergistics International, 2019).

33 While Cooke and Szumal do not specifically use the word *collaborative* to describe the third leadership culture, the norms used to measure it are decidedly collaborative, which will be discussed specifically in the next section of this chapter.

34 This section is based on Human Synergistics and Center for Applied Research, *Organizational Culture Inventory*, pp. 32–47.

35 This section is based on ibid., pp. 50–67.

36 This section is based on ibid., pp. 12–31. Please note that the word *collaborative* was added to *constructive* by this author, based on his experience at a 2016 HSI workshop on the OCI®, and an interpretation of the norms, which are collaborative in both intent and actuality.

37 This section is based on ibid., p. 6.

38 This research was conducted by Dr. Edward Marshall, who is certified in the OCI®, under a consulting contract with this organization. HSI calculated the results of the surveys, and Dr. Marshall provided the client feedback.

39 Robert A. Cooke, interview by the author, March 25, 2019.

40 Dixie Chicks, *Loving Arms*, first published by Tom Janis in 1973; YouTube, https://www.youtube.com/watch?v=lcostCWCk9g

41 Stephen R. Covey, *Principle-Centered Leadership* (New York: Free Press, 1990); Stephen R. Covey, *The 7 Habits of Highly Effective People* (New York: Free Press, 1989).

42 This section is based on Covey, *Principle-Centered Leadership*, ibid.

43 Covey, ibid., p. 18.

44 Ibid., p. 31.

45 Ibid., pp. 101–105.

46 Ibid., pp. 176–186.

47 Stephen R. Covey, op. cit.

48 This section on principles is based on, and in some cases taken from, Edward Marshall's books: *Transforming the Way We Work*, op. cit., and *Building Trust at the Speed of Change: The Power of the Relationship-Based Corporation* (New York: AMACOM Books, 2000).

49 To read more about the meaning and practice of trust, see Dennis Reina and Michelle Reina, *Trust and Betrayal in the Workplace* (Oakland, CA: Barrett-Kohler, 2015); Stephen M. R. Covey, *The Speed of Trust* (New York: Free Press, 2006).

50 https://www.merriam-webster.com/dictionary/trust?src=search-dict-box

51 In close to 100 change processes facilitated over 35 years, when leadership gave ownership of the change to the workforce, the change success rate was about 80%.

52 https://www.merriam-webster.com/dictionary/integrity

53 https://www.merriam-webster.com/dictionary/ethics

54 https://www.blueangels.navy.mil/; I learned the principle of self-accountability in the Blue Angels from my colleague and friend Captain Kent Ewing, former Captain of the USS America aircraft carrier, and a former Navy fighter pilot.

55 Marshall Goldsmith, *What Got You Here Won't Get You There* (White Plains, NY: Disney Hyperion, 2007).

Figure Credits

CHAPTER THREE

The 4th Evolution of Leadership Culture: Collaboration

Collaboration will be the critical business competency of the Internet age.
—James M. Kouzes, *The Leadership Challenge*

"*F*INALLY," ANA said, "we get to focus on collaboration and the Collaboration Paradigm of leadership." *The learning team had gathered for their weekly meeting over lunch to review their next assignment. They were energized by what they had learned about the critical role of leadership culture in an organization, the three types of leadership cultures, and the core principles of the collaborative work ethic. It all made sense. They saw the natural evolution of leadership paradigms, from Power to People to Principle, and how Collaboration was the next step on the journey. As millennials and Gen Xers, they fully understood why this shift was so critical to their own preferred way of working, and for the organizations they worked in to be able to adapt to the rapid rate of change.*

They were grounded in the historical precedents of organizational behavior and leadership, as well as the cultural cornerstones of collaboration, but now wanted more specificity about what "collaboration" is and what this 4th Evolution of Leadership was. Hanyue shared his confusion about the meaning of "collaboration," because he thought he collaborated all the time on social media and through online teamwork. Linda thought that it was about cooperation, while Morare suggested it was a way of life. Ana felt "collaboration" was more situational than an overarching approach to leadership. Clearly, there was work to do.

Their next assignment was designed to help the team understand collaboration, starting with four questions in their assignment:

- *Of the six key thought leaders to be discussed, how do they contribute to our understanding of collaboration?*
- *As you review the Collaboration Paradigm of leadership, in what ways is it different from the Power, People, and Principle Paradigms?*

- *How do the principles of the Collaborative Work Ethic fit with your view of leadership?*
- *As you think about the definition of collaboration and how it has evolved over time, how is it distinct from cooperation and digital collaboration?*

LEARNING OBJECTIVES

By the end of this chapter, you will:
- Understand the contributions of *six key thought leaders* to the development of *collaboration*
- Build on our understanding of collaborative culture as we define the *Collaboration Paradigm of leadership*
- Understand a 21st-Century definition of *collaboration* as a way of life, a way of working, and how it is distinct from other definitions of collaboration
- Make the case that it is time to adopt the 4th Evolution of Leadership for the 21st Century—Collaboration

THE MAIN POINT OF THIS CHAPTER

In the 21st Century, the stakes are high, the pace is fast, change is constant, disruption is inevitable, technological changes are accelerating faster than human organizations are adapting, and where culturally diverse teams are working virtually in globally networked organizations, it is even more critical than ever to create collaborative leadership cultures. But what is *collaboration*? Is it a buzzword, a fad, a tool, a process, or a completely different way to lead? What is the 4th Evolution of leadership, collaboration, and how is it different from the power, people, or Principle Paradigms?

There is confusion about what *collaboration* is. Like our learning team, some believe it is the same thing as *cooperation*. Some believe it is *digital* communication. Still others believe that collaboration is just another fad that will pass with time. Still others believe the *consensus* is the enemy of collaboration in decision-making. In fact, *collaboration* is about people, relationships, and culture. It is a way of working and a way of life that enables us to be principled, be adaptive, and work interdependently with others to solve problems and create workplaces where people can be their best selves and do their best work. If collaboration is adopted broadly and becomes the predominant way in which organizations are led, it can ensure that we can not only transform and humanize the workplace but can also save the planet.

SIX KEY THOUGHT LEADERS AND THE COLLABORATION PARADIGM

Fads will come and go. The fundamental fact of man's capacity to collaborate with his fellows in the face-to-face group will survive the fads and one day be recognized. Then, and only then, will management discover how seriously it has underestimated the true potential of human resources.
—Douglas McGregor, *The Human Side of Enterprise*

Dr. McGregor, that time is right now. We have discussed the evolution of three leadership paradigms: Power, People, and Principle. To quickly review, in the early 1900s with the Industrial Revolution, Taylor's Scientific Management approach to leadership was based on power and control, the subordination of the workforce, and a focus on efficiency and "the one best way" of production. The Power Paradigm of leadership brought us hierarchy and a culture of fear and dependence, which remains the predominant way of leading well over 100 years later in the Digital Age.

In the 1930s Roethlisberger and his colleagues conducted the Hawthorne experiments, which found that the people who do the work in organizations want to matter. In 1957 Argyris argued that there was a significant number of anomalies in the Power Paradigm, leading to McGregor's groundbreaking book, *The Human Side of Enterprise,* which articulated what we have called the People Paradigm of leadership.[1] Over the next 30 years, leaders tried a range of approaches during what we have called the Transitional Period of leadership, because there was no universally accepted leadership methodology. The Power Paradigm, however, was the default approach to leadership.

In 1990, with the dawn of the internet, the digital age, and globalization of business, the Power Paradigm, even when modified by the People Paradigm, was unable to meet the needs of those realities. We needed another paradigm shift. Covey introduced us to principle-centered leadership in a book by the same name.[2] We began to see that true leaders, who had a high regard for people, had to take an inside-out journey to discover their core principles so that they could lead with integrity. The Principle Paradigm of leadership emerged and paved the way for a deeper understanding of how people could work in an interconnected and rapidly changing world. Schein's work on the role of culture and leadership, which was first written in 1985,[3] helped us understand the critical role that leadership cultures play in shaping how organizations work or don't work. Cooke's work in 1994 statistically proved that there are three types of leadership cultures and provided evidence that people prefer to work in constructive/collaborative work environments. All of this led to Marshall's early work in the 1990s on collaborative leadership, teams, and organizational change,[4] which was developed, tested, and strengthened in over 100 organizational change processes over 40 years. This led to the emergence of the 4th Evolution of Leadership in the first quarter of the 21st Century, Collaboration.

There are six key thinkers who have provided critical cornerstones to our understanding of collaboration: Kouzes and Posner's *five practices of leadership,*[5] Goleman's

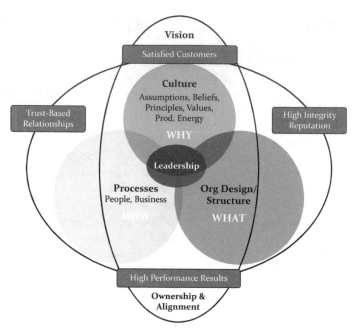

FIGURE 3.1 Collaboration Paradigm Systems Model.

emotional intelligence,[6] George's *authentic leadership*,[7] Senge's *learning organization*,[8] Greenleaf's *servant leadership*,[9] and Collins's *level 5 leadership*.[10] These thinkers will help us fill out the Collaboration Paradigm systems model (Figure 3.1).

Kouzes and Posner: The 5 Practices and 10 Commitments of Leadership[11]

In 1983, Kouzes and Posner's team began conducting research on the best leadership experiences about what motivated people to do their very best. Based on thousands of interviews, they found that these leaders had similar journeys, that leadership was about behavior, not personality, and that there are 5 key leadership practices and 10 commitments that withstood the test of time (Figure 3.2). They built on both the people and Principle Paradigms by advancing our understanding of true collaborative leadership, leadership that is based on the individual's credibility and integrity, provides clear direction, empowers the workforce, and provides inspiration and appreciation for those they work with. They see leadership not as a gene or an inheritance but as a relationship, and that it can be found anywhere in the organization. Leadership is not the exclusive domain of people at the top. They reject the Power Paradigm's premise that leaders have to use fear to motivate people. On the contrary, they argue that a relationship "characterized by mutual respect and confidence will

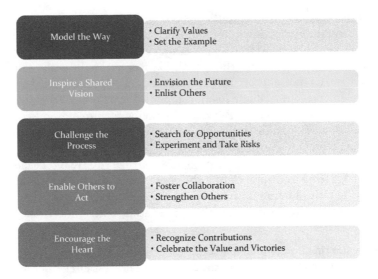

FIGURE 3.2   The 5 Practices and 10 Commitments of Leadership.

overcome the greatest of adversities and leave a legacy of significance."12 Here is a summary of their practices and commitments:

- **Practice 1 and Commitments 1–2—Model the Way:** Leaders clarify their values and set the example. Values clarification is the first step of the inside-out journey to becoming a collaborative leader. Setting the example is about the leader's integrity, consistent behavior, earning the respect of others, and doing what they say they are going to do. Both commitments belong in the Culture circle of the Collaboration Paradigm Systems Model.
- **Practice 2 and Commitments 3–4—Inspire a Shared Vision:** Leaders envision the future and engage others so that they are aligned and share these aspirations. They provide clear and inspiring vision for the project, team, or organization to help people find meaning in their work, feel like they belong, realize their dreams, and can be proud to work there. In the Collaboration Paradigm Systems Model, this commitment sits at the top of the model under vision. Getting others to align with that vision, leaders engage the workforce so they can unify around a common purpose. That commitment belongs in the ownership and alignment ellipse of the model.
- **Practice 3 and Commitments 5–6—Challenge the Process:** Leaders take the initiative, innovate, experiment, and take risks. It is okay to make mistakes and fail, as long as you learn from it. These commitments belong in the Process circle of the model.

- **Practice 4 and Commitments 7–8—Enable Others to Act:** Leaders foster collaboration by building trust and facilitating relationships, giving people a sense of ownership, as well as increasing self-determination and developing others' competence. While this sounds like it could be the entire Collaboration Paradigm, it represents one core culture element—to build trust—and two process elements—to facilitate relationships and build others' competence. They explicitly reject the Power Paradigm by saying "command-and-control techniques of traditional management no longer apply."[3] It is important to move from a culture of "I" to a culture of "We."
- **Practice 5 and Commitments 9–10—Encourage the Heart:** Leaders commit to recognizing and appreciating the contributions of individuals and to creating a spirit of community. Creating a spirit of community belongs in the Culture circle in the model, while appreciating contributions belongs in the Process circle.

As we leave the critical work of Kouzes and Posner, it is worth noting that all 5 practices and 10 commitments fit primarily in the culture and process circles of the Collaboration Systems Model, with a void in the organization design circle. Their work speaks to the critical importance of leadership focusing on culture and people to ensure the effectiveness of their organizations.

Daniel Goleman: Emotional Intelligence

In the new age of collaboration, leaders must become aware of their own emotions, be able to regulate them, and be aware of the emotions of others so that they can build trust, credibility, and respect. This is called emotional intelligence (EI). It is an absolutely essential competence at the center of collaborative leadership. It is not a skill. It is a way of being in relationship with yourself and others that lets them know you are self-aware, that you understand their joys, pains, frustrations, and desire to contribute and grow. It is glue. It binds us to each other, because everyone matters. As a result, EI enables leaders to build a culture of "We," in which people can be themselves, feel psychologically safe, take risks, and learn, and where they feel appreciated. EI is an essential component of the culture and leadership circles of the Collaboration Systems Model.

Without EI, leaders can be viewed as heartless, bureaucratic, or transactional technocrats who simply do not care about others. This feeds the Power Paradigm and undermines a leader's credibility because people intuitively know whether leaders really care about them. Emotional intelligence is especially important for 21st-Century leaders so they can motivate millennials and Gen Xers. If you are perceived as heartless or uncaring, these workers have choices and will vote with their feet.

During the Transitional Period of leadership, in 1990 John Mayer at the University of New Hampshire and Peter Salovey, provost of Yale University, were the first to coin the term *emotional intelligence* as a critical element of leading and managing. They defined it this way:

A set of skills [that] contribute to the accurate appraisal and expression of emotion in oneself and in others, the effective regulation of emotion in self and others, and the use of feelings to motivate, plan, and achieve in one's life.[14]

Their initial model of EI talked about the ability of leaders to be aware of their own emotions, understand the emotions of others—empathy—the ability to regulate or control one's own emotions, and the ability to use emotions in one's life.[15] By 2008 Mayer, Salovey, and Caruso had evolved the concept into a 16-step developmental model covering one's entire life.[16]

It was Daniel Goleman, however, who popularized the concept of EI as an essential leadership competence in his essential 2004 article in the *Harvard Business Review*, "What Makes a Leader."[17] In this article, his research showed that EI is an essential competency for being an effective leader, that it is twice as important as technical or analytical skills, or intellect. His construct of EI has five elements, which may be found in Table 3.1. He calls out empathy as being perhaps the most critical element of

TABLE 3.1 *Goleman's Concept of Emotional Intelligence*[19]

EI ELEMENT	DEFINITION	HALLMARKS
SELF-AWARENESS	The ability to recognize and understand your moods, emotions, and drives, and their effect on others	Self-confidence Realistic self-assessment Self-deprecating sense of humor
SELF-REGULATION	The ability to control or redirect disruptive impulses and moods The propensity to suspend judgment—to think before acting	Trustworthiness and integrity Comfort with ambiguity Openness to change
MOTIVATION	A passion to work for reasons beyond money or status A propensity to pursue goals with energy and persistence	Strong drive to achieve Optimism, even in the face of failure Organizational commitment
EMPATHY	The ability to understand the emotional makeup of other people Skill in treating people according to their emotional reactions	Expertise in building and retaining talent Cross-cultural sensitivity Service to clients and customers
SOCIAL SKILL	Proficiency in managing relationship and building networks An ability to find common ground and build rapport	Effectiveness in leading change Persuasiveness Expertise in building and leading teams

EI, because in a work world dominated by culturally diverse teams, *empathy* is what enables us to appreciate and understand the cultures and behaviors of others. There are three components to empathy:[18]

- **Cognitive:** The ability to understand another person's perspective, which enables leaders to explain themselves in meaningful ways and be inquisitive
- **Emotional:** The ability to feel what someone else feels, which is critical for working with anyone
- **Empathic Concern:** The ability to sense what another person needs from you

Leaders with high emotional intelligence are self-aware, are fully engaged with their teams and workforce, are grounded in principle, and have high value for the well-being and development of each of their workers. As a result, they will create leadership cultures in which people know they matter, where it is psychologically safe, and where people can do their best work.

These leaders will create cultures based on "We," not "I," in which the productive energy of the workforce is exceptionally high. For all these reasons, *emotional intelligence* is an essential attribute of collaborative leadership cultures.

Bill George: Authentic Leadership

In Shakespeare's *Hamlet,* act 1, Polonius says to Laertes: "This above all—to thine own self be true."[20] In a collaborative leadership culture, there is the freedom to be one's true self, to not have to position oneself to obtain favor, self-promote, or play politics to get ahead. Instead, there is a premium on leaders being their true, authentic selves. They have done their inner work, have become self-reflective, and are clear about who they are and what they stand for. They know their strengths, hot buttons, and weaknesses. They are learning beings who, because of their empathy, know that others are also learning.

We are transparent. Everyone knows, when we walk into a room, whether we are happy or sad, upset or feeling confident. So there is no reason to hide it. I once worked with a C-level executive who did not know he was transparent. Every morning when he walked into the office, his entire staff looked at his face, his gait, and how he held himself, to see what kind of day it was going to be. News traveled fast. By the time he got to his office on the sixth floor, the first-floor receptionist had used her network to alert people. Everyone was on pins and needles all the time because they did not know what to expect. Needless to say, this was not a leader who made people feel safe by being vulnerable and transparent. He had not done his work to discover his authentic self.

Bill George was Chair and CEO of Medtronic before becoming a professor at the Harvard Business School. Through critical life experiences of his own, and by taking his own life journey, George came to better understanding of who he truly was, and that he could not be effective as a leader if others saw him as being a phony. In research that George and his colleagues conducted, they discovered that leaders found their purpose and true, authentic selves through their life stories. There are six attributes of this authenticity journey: self-awareness, practicing your values and principles, balancing your extrinsic and intrinsic motivations, building your support team, staying grounded, and empowering people to lead.[21]

Here we see an integration of Covey's work on principle-centered leadership and the journey to self-awareness,[22] as well as Kouzes and Posner's five practices.[23] We are beginning to see the convergence of a number of elements of collaborative leadership: becoming one's true self, having high emotional intelligence, applying the five practices of leadership, and understanding the power of leadership culture—all contributing to the ability of leaders to create workplaces that empower the human spirit so that people can be their best selves, do their best work, and produce superior and sustainable results. In our model, *authentic leadership* belongs in the Leadership circle.

Peter Senge: The Learning Organization

A learning organization is "*a place where people are continually discovering how they create their reality.*"[24] With this 1990 definition came a new way of looking at organizations, one that has become a cornerstone of collaborative leadership culture. Senge, a professor at MIT's Sloan School of Management, saw that with the world becoming more interconnected, no longer could there be just one person doing all the learning for an organization. He rejected the Power Paradigm's construct that learning had to come from the top of the hierarchy. Instead, in *The Fifth Discipline,* he argues that all of us are natural learners, that it is part of who we are as human beings. He saw that global organizations, in competition with each other, with new technologies threatening to disrupt business models, needed to learn together on a global scale. He found that organizations had been hurting themselves by not investing in the talents and capabilities of their people so that learning was organization-wide. Finally, he suggested that "*the most salient reason for building learning organizations is that we are only now starting to understand the capabilities such organizations must possess.*"[25]

Again, as with the other key thought leaders of the time, Senge was part of the leadership renaissance that began in 1990, leading us toward the 4ᵗʰ Evolution of Leadership. In 1990 major advancements in business and technology were transforming our thinking about how to be competitive, how to be effective with our people, and how to adapt leadership approaches accordingly. There was a lot of experimentation with any number of leadership techniques and fads to achieve a balance between business results and effective human relationships. There was no "one right way". In that context Senge's work was a fundamental cornerstone of leadership's responsibility in creating a culture of learning.

To create a culture of learning, the leader must first be a lifelong learner who is willing to take risks, make mistakes, and learn as a result. The leader must have a sufficiently high level of self-confidence, be grounded in principle, have the emotional intelligence to engage the workforce in the same journey, and be authentic and humble.

It takes the leader's willingness to be vulnerable, open, and self-accountable to create a psychologically safe place for people to be able to learn.

It takes *discipline*. Senge, in his use of the term *discipline,* defined it as *"not an enforced order or means of punishment, but a body of theory and technique that must be studied and mastered to be put into practice; a developmental path for acquiring certain skills or competencies; practicing it makes you a life-long learner."*[26]

This applies to organizations and teams as well as individuals. It means making lifelong learning a habit that is practiced regularly. Table 3.2 presents the five disciplines for a learning organization, all of which are critical to a collaborative leadership culture, as represented in the Collaboration Systems Model.

Robert Greenleaf: Servant Leadership

The Transitional Period of leadership was a time of "revolutionary politics" in the United States. There was racial upheaval after the assassinations of the Rev. Dr. Martin Luther King and Robert F. Kennedy in 1968, riots in US cities each summer for years, corruption in Nixon's White House followed by a resignation, and an immoral war in Vietnam. Movements for racial justice, peace, freedom, women's rights, and workforce empowerment were just getting underway. This revolutionary fervor found its way into organizational behavior and how we thought about leadership, power, and control. The paradigm shift from power to people to principle was in full swing. For some, the change could not happen fast enough. Some talked about inverting the hierarchy pyramid and putting the leader on the bottom to serve the workforce, even though they were still tied to Power Paradigm thinking. Nonetheless, it was a radical thought at the time, and Robert Greenleaf gave it substance with his concept of *servant leadership,* which he defined this way: "A new moral principle may be emerging which holds that the only authority deserving of one's allegiance is that which is freely and knowingly granted by the led to the leader in response to, and in proportion to, the clearly evident servant stature of the leader."[28] By asserting that serving others was a moral principle, Greenleaf was a precursor to Covey's work two decades later. More importantly, he shifted our thinking about what gives a leader his or her credibility, respect, and trust—it comes from the workforce, based on the behaviors and beliefs of leadership, central to the work of Kouzes and Posner. Regarding serving others, Greenleaf noted the following:[29]

- It begins with caring for people and helping them grow; it focuses on teams and the organization.
- It is a conscious choice.
- Is how trust is built.
- It requires that leaders confront the reality of problems as a personal responsibility and as a way to realize their own integrity.
- It involves coaching and mentoring others.

TABLE 3.2 *The Five Disciplines of a Learning Organization*[19]

- **Systems Thinking (Model):**

  - A conceptual framework and body of knowledge and tools
  - The discipline that integrates the other disciplines, fusing them into a coherent body of theory and practice
  - Makes understandable the subtlest aspect of the learning organization

- **Personal Mastery (Leadership):**

  - The discipline of continually clarifying and deepening our personal vision, focusing our energies, developing patience, and seeing reality objectively
  - Starts with clarifying the things that really matter to us; living our lives in the service of our highest aspirations

- **Mental Models (Leadership):**

  - Deeply ingrained assumptions, generalizations, or even pictures or images that influence how we understand the world and take action
  - Starts with turning the mirror inward; learning to unearth our internal pictures of the world, bring them to the surface, and hold them rigorously to scrutiny
  - The ability to carry on learning conversations that balance inquiry and advocacy

- **Building Shared Vision (Vision):**

  - A genuine vision where people excel and learn because they want to
  - Involves the skills of unearthing shared pictures of the future that foster genuine commitment and enrollment rather than compliance

- **Team Learning (Process):**

  - Views the team as the fundamental unit of learning in an organization
  - Starts with dialogue, suspending assumptions and cocreating
  - Involves learning how to recognize the patterns of interaction in teams that undermine learning

---

- It is an exacting process and is hard to attain.
- The best test is whether those being served grow as people and are healthier, wiser, and more independent.

Greenleaf's contribution to our Collaboration Systems Model is the creation of a culture of service, not only by leadership toward the workforce, but by the workforce toward each other, as well as by serving the customer. If we truly commit to serving each other and the customer, we eliminate the political game playing that is such a toxic element of the power-based organization. It's no longer about getting ahead or positioning ourselves as the "smartest person in the room," it's about empowering and supporting each other, encouraging and acknowledging everyone's contributions and achievements, while getting the job done. In our model, creating a culture of service is in the culture circle.

Jim Collins: Level 5 Leadership

It was the end of the Transitional Period of leadership when, in his 2001 book, *Good to Great: Why Some Companies Make the Leap … and Others Don't,*[30] Collins provided a road map for leaders interested in making the transformational shift from simply good companies to great ones. Based on his research on 1,400 companies, he explicitly rejected the idea that it had anything to do with the CEO.

Collins was looking for something far deeper, the enduring principles for organizations that could sustain a company's greatness over time. He used this analogy: while engineering practices continue to evolve, the laws of physics remain largely the same. He saw this journey of discovery as being able to understand the underlying physics, the principles and laws, that remain true over time.[31]

One of those laws was Level 5 Leadership, the focus on humility and professional will. Achieving level 5 does not happen for many leaders. As Figure 3.3 shows, we start out our professional careers as individual contributors (level 1). After a few years, if we are diligent and hardworking, we are recognized as a contributing team member (level 2). If we are successful in helping our teams achieve their goals, senior leadership will ask us to become managers (level 3), and if we execute our responsibilities effectively and demonstrate an ability to engage, motivate, and facilitate the work of others, we are recognized and promoted to the role of leader (level 4).[32] From my own professional experience with several thousand managers and leaders over 40 years, I can tell you that this is the final resting place for well over 99% of them.

It is understanding the essence of level 5 leadership to which we now turn, to serve as a goal to which leaders can aspire and a way of thinking about the journey along the way. In effect, to move from level 4 to level 5 leadership, leaders must become a servant of others, give up their ego and need for control, make themselves vulnerable and open, be high in empathy toward others, and certainly ground their personal and professional lives in principle. Level 5 leaders are few and far between because the way in which they got to level 4 was most often based on the strength of their egos, their business acumen, and professional competence. In fact, when I have asked my graduate students at Duke University who they considered to be level 5 leaders, they always cite the names of political leaders who sacrificed their lives for the causes they believed in: Mahatma Gandhi, Martin Luther King, and Nelson Mandela. Egomaniacs need not apply.

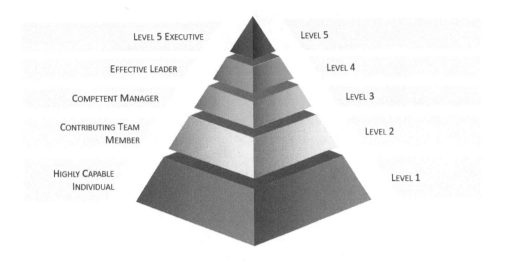

FIGURE 3.3 Level 5 Leadership.

Research by the Collins team discovered two key characteristics of a level 5 leader: professional will and personal humility, summarized in Table 3.3. Level 5 leaders are also self-aware and reflective. When there are successes, they give credit to others. When there are breakdowns or failures, they are self-accountable, are resilient, learn from the failure, and make the necessary corrections to ensure success.

A great example of level 5 leadership is the former President of India (2002–2007), A. P. J. Abdul Kalam. He was also a renowned space scientist who, at the Indian Space Research Organization, helped develop India's successful rocket and nuclear weapons programs. In a famous video, Dr. Kalam tells the story of how, as project director of one of the first missile launches, he overrode the decision of his scientists not to launch. The rocket fell into the Bay of Bengal. He blamed himself, in true level 5 style, and redoubled his efforts, engaged his team, and successfully made the next launch. Then he gave his entire team the credit for the success. No ego. Just personal humility and professional will.[33]

While Collins still presents his construct of leadership as a hierarchical pyramid, think of it more like Maslow's hierarchy of needs,[34] in which there are levels of personal development. Level 5 leaders represent the self-actualization of individuals who are truly empathic, authentic, transparent, collaborative leaders who care about the success of their people and organizations, and this attribute belongs in the leadership circle of the collaboration systems model.

TABLE 3.3 *Two Attributes of Level 5 Leadership*[35]

SUMMARY: THE TWO SIDES OF LEVEL 5 LEADERSHIP	
PROFESSIONAL WILL	**PERSONAL HUMILITY**
Creates superb results, a clear catalyst in the transition from good to great.	Demonstrates a compelling modesty, shunning public adulation; never boastful.
Demonstrates an unwavering resolve to do whatever must be done to produce the best long-term result, no matter how difficult.	Acts with quiet, calm determination; relies principally on inspired standards, not inspiring charisma, to motivate.
Sets the standard of building an enduring great company; will settle for nothing less.	Channels ambition into the company, not the self; sets up successors for even greater success in the next generation.
Looks in the mirror, not out the window, to apportion responsibility for poor results, never blaming other people, external factors, or bad luck.	Looks out the window, not in the mirror, to apportion credit for the success of the company—to other people, external factors, and good luck.

From the Transitional Period to the 4th Evolution

These six thought leaders have helped our thinking about leadership mature. Their research, consultation, and experimentation in response to transformational changes in markets, technology, global trade, and politics during the transitional period deepened our understanding of the role of culture and people processes in driving the ability of leaders to motivate, engage, and support their workers.

It is worth pointing out that these thought leaders did not focus on the structure or design of organizations, which reflects the evolution of our thinking about what leadership truly is. It's not about hierarchy, span of control, "leaders and followers," organization charts, or procedures anymore. There has to be some kind of design, but by 2000, how organizations were structured was in flux. For example, one of the key pioneers in new organizational structures was a former DuPont executive, W.L. Gore, who founded W.L. Gore in 1958. He created a "non-organization" structure called the "lattice," or networked, organization.[36] He kept the size of his operations to 200 people so that people knew each other. He was easily 40 years ahead of his time.

We owe a debt of gratitude to Kouzes and Posner for their 5 Practices and 10 Commitments of leadership; to Daniel Goleman's popularization of emotional intelligence as a critical success factor for leaders; to Bill George for helping us understand the importance of leaders going on their personal journey to find their true, authentic selves; to Robert Greenleaf for turning the power pyramid upside down and helping us see the importance of creating a culture of service; to Peter Senge for helping us understand the importance of creating a culture of learning in our organizations and committing as leaders to being lifelong learners; and to Jim Collins for providing us with the twin goals of professional will and humility in Level 5 Leadership.

THE 4TH EVOLUTION OF LEADERSHIP: THE COLLABORATION PARADIGM

The 4th Evolution of Leadership emerged in 2018–20, as the result of a confluence of forces impacting businesses. The rate of volatility, uncertainty, complexity, and ambiguity was accelerating; Millennials becoming 75% of the global workforce by 2030, requiring a new approach to business leadership; and governments were given their final warning about climate change in 2018 by the United Nations—we have until 2030 to prevent the irreversible collapse of our global ecosystem.[37] The urgency to articulate what collaboration and collaborative leadership truly are for the 21st Century could not be greater. This urgency, in fact, gave birth to this book.

Our purpose here is to define the complete paradigm for the 4th Evolution of Leadership—a theory of collaboration. While the primary formulation of this paradigm is about the work we need to do inside organizations, in Chapter 10 we will apply it specifically to how global leaders can address global warming, an imminent existential threat.

For the workforce and leadership, the bottom line of this evolution for 21st Century leadership is this:

> *People want to be trusted, respected, and honored for who they are as responsible and accountable human beings; to be safe; and to own their jobs and the workplace so that they can be their best selves and do their best work.*

The culture, leadership, processes, and organization design are shaped by this fundamental assumption.

Culture: What Shapes Behavior in Organizations

In Chapter 2 we did a deep dive into what a collaborative culture is. We will summarize the key points since it is the essential starting point for how organizations, and the people in them, behave and work together. Culture shapes behavior in organizations. Here is a quick review of their essence:

- **Assumptions and Beliefs About People:**
  - **Inherent Goodness:** People are inherently good and have intrinsic value. They are responsible, are eager to work hard, and can be trusted to do their best.
  - **Significance—People Want to Matter:** People want to matter in life, in their relationships, and at work. They have intrinsic value.

- ○ **Meaning and Contribution:** People need to have meaning, a sense of purpose in their lives and work.
- ○ **Dignity, Honor, and Respect:** People want their dignity to be honored and respected by others in their teams and organizations. They are honored and respected for the gifts they bring to the organization.
- ○ **Trust:** The cornerstone for any human relationship is trust. We cannot function effectively without it.
- ○ **Ownership:** People need to have psychological ownership of their work.
- ○ **Psychological Safety:** People need to feel psychologically, physically, and emotionally safe in their workplaces.
- ○ **Learning and Development:** People want to learn and grow and have leadership take an interest in their development.
- ○ **Appreciation and Acknowledgement:** Appreciation and acknowledgement create connection, amplify one's feeling of self-worth and self-esteem, and open up the opportunity for a deeper relationship.

- **The 7 Principles of the Collaborative Work Ethic:**

  - ○ **Principle 1:** **Trust:** Trust is the fundamental building block in human relationships. It is a principle that governs how we perceive ourselves, governs how others see us, and guides how we choose to lead our lives and work with others.
  - ○ **Principle 2: Ownership:** People take care of what they own—they don't wash rented cars. They have a right to own their job, the work culture, and the vision, mission, and strategy of the organization. The ownership principle is what makes collaborative leadership distinct. It produces high levels of trust, responsibility, accountability, and productive energy.
  - ○ **Principle 3: Integrity and Ethics:** Collaborative leaders are ethical above reproach. They will always do what is best for the organization rather than any special interest.
  - ○ **Principle 4: Honor:** To be honorable means the leader has the highest integrity and can be counted on.
  - ○ **Principle 5: Mutual Respect:** Self-respect is about self-esteem; it is not something I do. It is something I have. Respecting others means we have the highest regard for others, without any consideration for any characteristics. A leadership culture of respect honors the dignity, competencies, and gifts that each person brings to the workplace, values them, and invests in their continued development.
  - ○ **Principle 6: Full Responsibility:** Being fully responsible for myself means I am responsible and accountable for who I am, what I say, and what I do.

Being fully responsible for others means I will show up, speak up, and step up to address any challenges facing my colleagues.

- ○ **Principle 7: Accountability:** Self-accountability is about "owning up" to your mistakes. Holding others accountable means we hold each other to the highest standards of collaborative and ethical conduct from a place of compassion, growth, and development.

- **Artifacts:** Every organization has an identity that is defined by a range of artifacts including its history and how the company came into being, how it grew, and what its achievements have been. Often this is found in the "About Us" section of a company's website and includes a timeline. Sometimes there are corporate legends about how the company got started. I remember one client whose first contract was signed on the hood of an old Studebaker car, which to this day remains in the lobby of the client's main office. Whenever the client got a new contract, everyone gathered around the Studebaker to hear about it.

  Every organization has customs that are unique to how it works. There is a unique language that includes terms of art specific to their culture. There are often "language taboos," words you're not supposed to use because they remind people of a particularly negative experience. When I worked in one Fortune 100 company, I was told by a senior executive *not* to use the word "collaboration." When I asked him why, he told me that in World War II, he was part of the D-day invasion into France, where the *collaborateurs* of Vichy France were working with the Nazis.

- **Productive Energy of the Workforce:** We know that work only gets done through people. From a competitive standpoint, the most significant differentiator between companies will be the degree to which the *productive energy* of the workforce has been fully engaged at the individual, team, and organizational levels. *Productive energy* is defined as:

  What workers are willing to give of themselves to the enterprise, it reflects their pride in the organization, their self-esteem, how they are treated by leadership, their level of engagement, the degree of trust and ownership in the culture, their willingness to take risks and go the extra mile, and the degree to which they feel respected, honored and appreciated.[38]

Leadership: Manifests the Culture in Their Behavior

At the center of our systems model is the leadership circle. Leadership's responsibility, indeed its obligation, is to understand systems thinking and to be aware of the complexity of these relationships and their interactions, dynamics, and ever-evolving nature so they can more effectively facilitate the development of the organization. Organizations, as systems, are dynamic, organic, living entities that must be attended to on a daily basis. Leadership must comprehend and honor the ethos of the system—its history, legacy, rituals, customs, language, and traditions. Most importantly, leadership needs to appreciate the primacy of the predominant leadership culture as the primary driver for all that happens in the organization. There are four dimensions to our understanding of collaborative leadership: (1) Definition, (2) Key attributes, (3) Key behaviors, and (4) Essential roles.

- **The Definition of Collaborative Leadership:**

Collaborative leadership provides a clear vision, mission, and strategy for the organization, department, or team. It creates and sustains a "We" culture, grounded in the assumptions and beliefs about people and the principles of the collaborative work ethic. It empowers people to be their best selves and to do their best work so they can produce superior, sustainable results. Collaborative leadership can involve anyone, at any level of the organization, at any time in service of the values, vision, mission, and strategy of the organization. It is a philosophy of service, lifelong learning, and integrity that builds psychological safety, ownership, and trust.

- **10 Key Collaborative Leadership Attributes:**
  - **Ethical Above Reproach:** Collaborative leaders have the highest integrity and ethically are above reproach; without ethics, leaders cannot build trust or be credible.
  - **Principle Based:** Collaborative leaders practice the seven principles of the collaborative work ethic.
  - **A Clear Purpose:** Collaborative leaders know why they are on this planet, understand their mission, and find meaning in their work and relationships.
  - **Credible and Trustworthy:** Collaborative leaders are both credible and trustworthy. They have the competence, demeanor, and executive presence to be credible, have done their inner-journey work to build self-trust, and can be trusted by others.
  - **Collaborative Mind-Set:** Collaborative leaders focus on building high-trust relationships first, the leadership culture, create psychological safety and ownership, through engagement of the workforce, and ensure the organization can adapt to a changing market. They know that work gets done through people and are people-centric.
  - **Emotionally Intelligent:** Collaborative leaders have high EI, are self-aware, are self-reflective, and do their inner work on a regular basis.
  - **Facilitative:** Collaborative leaders are facilitators of relationships and processes and ensure that there is ownership and buy-in.
  - **Optimistic and Inspiring:** Collaborative leaders maintain a high level of optimism toward the organization, the workforce, and their work, and when

there are challenges or breakdowns, these leaders are optimistic, encouraging, and supportive.

- ○ **Leadership Will:** Collaborative leaders have a deep reservoir of willpower and persistence in the face of extraordinary challenges. They never ever give up. They come from their commitment, purpose, values, and principles and consciously choose to stay the course.
- ○ **Leadership Discipline:** Collaborative leaders are disciplined; they work hard to stay on track; honor their principles and standards; grow trust, respect, and ownership; and produce results.

- **Collaborative Leadership Behaviors:** If an organization is to have a collaborative leadership culture, it is incumbent upon those who provide leadership for that organization to behave collaboratively at the levels of self, others, and organization (see Table 3.4).

TABLE 3.4   *Summary of Collaborative Behaviors*

COLLABORATIVE BEHAVIORS AT THE LEVEL OF SELF	COLLABORATIVE BEHAVIORS WORKING WITH OTHERS	COLLABORATIVE BEHAVIORS AT THE ORGANIZATION LEVEL
SELF-AWARENESS AND REFLECTION	Connecting	Building trust and credibility
FEEDBACK AND LEARNING	Engaging	Inspiring and aligning
SELF-ACCOUNTABILITY	Facilitating	Systems thinking
	Nurturing	Adapting

- **Essential Collaborative Leadership Roles:**
  - ○ **Chief Cultural Officer:** The Chief Cultural Officer for whatever group or team of people they are working with involves nurturing and growing the collaborative leadership culture of the organization. To do so, leaders must build and strengthen the collaborative leadership culture; create and ensure it is ethical; ensure the safety of the workforce—psychological, physical, and emotional; build ownership and trust; and appreciate the workforce.
  - ○ **Steward:** Stewards take care of the organization's code of ethics, vision, and mission; ensure their organization is responsible and taking care of the planet; and hold the aspirations, expectations, and professional futures of the workforce in their hands.
  - ○ **Visionary:** Alignment involves the organization's values, ethics, vision, mission, strategy, people and work processes, and design. Collaborative leaders

imagine the future, find a common purpose that is meaningful to the workforce, and then engage them to build ownership.

○ **Sponsor:** Sponsors ensure there is alignment between the work of subteams and the overall strategy of the organization, ensure there is a free flow of information and communication between them, and provide resources and "air cover" from organizational politics.

○ **Facilitator:** Facilitators are the essential link for a collaborative organization getting its work done. They build high levels of psychological safety, ownership, and trust in the teams they work with; ensure inclusion of all members in team meetings, processes, projects, or initiatives; empower them to be their best selves and do their best work; build synergy among team members; make the necessary interventions in interpersonal dynamics; and maintain the psychological health and well-being of the team. They are self-aware, have high emotional intelligence, are ethical above reproach, honor team confidentiality, and are respected, objective, and self-accountable.

○ **Communicator:** Collaborative leaders engender a high degree of credibility when they communicate with their teams, units, departments, or overall workforce with openness and clarity and when their intention is to have a dialogue, feedback, and a conversation. There are four key rules: tell the truth, develop four-way communications, promote dialogue, and actively listen.

○ **People Developers:** Collaborative leaders honor, respect, develop, and grow the people they are working with. They are coaches, help develop people, are mentors, and heal broken relationships.

○ **Change Agents:** Collaborative leaders recognize that when changes occur, it is the workforce who will have to absorb the impacts, make the changes, and make whatever adjustments are required. As a result, they use a "culture-first" approach to change to build ownership, alignment, and trust around the change. People take care of what they own. With a culture-first ownership strategy, resistance and costs are significantly reduced, speed is increased, and the effective adjustment to the change is made.

Process: How Work Gets Done

There are two types of processes that enable work to get done: people and business.

• **People Processes:**

○ **Teams Are How Work Gets Done:** Work gets done through teams of all kinds. In collaborative teams, there are no formally designated team leaders, but rather highly trained internal facilitators who are rotated over time. Teams are created using the Collaborative Team Governance Process

(Chapter 7), where members agree on a set of Operating Agreements for how they work with each other and a Charter for what they will do. Teams are created by senior leadership to ensure their alignment with the organization's strategy and are empowered and accountable.

- ○ **Facilitators Are an Essential Resource:** Teams have skilled facilitators who ensure engagement and ownership. The facilitator's role is to be objective, focus on protecting the team's process and its members, address any team dynamics issues, and ensure the team's development. Facilitators perform an essential staff function in a collaborative organization and may be called on to design and implement meetings, processes, or change initiatives.
- ○ **Transparent Communications:** Communications are at least two-way, open, transparent, and constant. There is a free flow of information and no "mystery house" where people don't know what is going on.
- ○ **Differences and Conflicts:** A divergence of views is encouraged, as people cocreate solutions to critical issues and problems. There is no "group-think" in a collaborative workplace; rather, people commit to working through their differences and conflicts for resolution. Conflicts are not swept under the rug.
- ○ **Accountability:** People hold themselves and each other accountable for their work and for mistakes they make.
- ○ **Human Resources/People Functions:** Leaders are responsible for people functions in a collaborative organization, which includes team-based rewards and recognition and hiring, firing, and promotion decisions, and training and development are tailored to the needs of the organization. Retention of the workforce increases when the right people are placed in the right jobs at the right time and then given ownership of and responsibility for their work. Individual professional development is an ongoing responsibility of leadership and the individuals themselves.

- • **Business Processes:**
  - ○ **Internal Functions:** The organization's customers or clients get their needs met through the implementation of collaborative business processes, including marketing, sales, information technology, research and development, supply chain, and production.
  - ○ **Process Improvements:** There may be any number of internal initiatives underway to improve the organization's business process performance through robotics, artificial intelligence, block chain, continuous improvement, lean manufacturing, or process redesign.

- ○ **Collaborative Processes:** The level of efficiency, effectiveness, and innovation will increase with the application of collaborative principles and behaviors.

Organization Design: How the Organization is Structured

Collaborative organizations are flat, networked, and team based, often with only two or three levels of management, whose roles are facilitative rather than control. There are no organizational silos, since those impede communications and true collaboration across the organization. Silos become power centers or fiefdoms that get in the way of solving problems and meeting customer/client needs. People typically have a "home team"/function, which is their primary role in the organization; they may be detailed to other teams or functions to address a particular need, but they do not have two bosses. The relationship between leaders and managers is facilitative rather than being based on control, and teams are governed by charters and internal performance criteria. There is, however, coaching and mentoring to support workforce development. Technology, information systems, data analytics, data management, and cybersecurity are the lifeblood of the organization and are heavily invested in to ensure the sustainable success of the organization. What the organization does, what it produces or provides to others as services, is the reason why people join the enterprise.

Collaboration Paradigm Outcomes

There are four organizational outcomes in our Systems Model:

- **Relationships:** The primary outcome of collaborative relationships and how they are built, developed, and sustained is *high trust.* Because these relationships are governed by principle, operating agreements, a charter, and consensus agreement among team members, trust is increased between individuals, within teams, across teams, and between the workforce and leadership. It creates a "We" culture and high trust, resulting in higher levels of *productive energy.*
- **Results:** With higher productive energy, innovation, commitment to quality, and effective and efficient processes, the *bottom line* of the organization will increase—sales volume, profitability, quality, and customer satisfaction. Results are more likely to be *sustainable* because of lower turnover and higher-quality members of the workforce.
- **Reputation:** An organization's reputation can be seen as what others say about it when they are not present. If there is alignment between the culture of the organization and what the organization does, it will have a *reputation for integrity.* A reputation of high character, ethical conduct, and a constructively collaborative culture enable the organization to focus on *excellence and sustainable* contributions to the market and society at large.

- **Ownership and Alignment:** When there is a high degree of ownership and alignment across the entire organization of its culture, vision, mission, and strategy, the organization will have higher level of *productive energy* in the workforce and *agility and momentum* in how it competes in the market.

DEFINING COLLABORATION IN LEADERSHIP'S 4TH EVOLUTION

When I first began consulting, my company was called the Community Development Collaborative. I had learned from my work in community economic development, and specifically public-private partnerships, that we had to find new ways to work together. In these partnerships, we created a process whereby low-income groups, the city, a major local bank, and the Federal government worked together to create small businesses, create jobs, and develop communities. But at that time there was no leadership philosophy, belief system, or paradigm that was called *collaboration*. By the early 1990s, there was initial discussion about collaboration by individual business leaders, but there was skepticism and even a rejection of the term by most. By the spring of 1995, however, *collaboration* took its next step in the evolution of leadership constructs when it officially became a business "buzzword" that everyone was using. In fact, when I published *Transforming the Way We Work: The Power of the Collaborative Workplace* in March of that year,[39] I was specifically asked during interviews by the news media whether it was just a buzzword and a passing fad. Based on the work I had been doing at DuPont, Conoco, and Marriott at that time, I responded with an emphatic "no." Rather, it was clear we were *just* beginning to understand what it meant and had a long way to go. At that time, people were still talking about self-directed work teams, team-based management, and business process reengineering.[40]

From 1989 through 2019, I worked with hundreds of leaders and managers on more than 100 projects of all kinds to better define what *collaboration* meant in the context of real work in real time. The full articulation of the Collaboration Paradigm of leadership (Figure 3.1) represents the result of this hands-on, roll-up-your-sleeves approach that helped me document what it takes for a leader, team, or organization to be collaborative. This work was cocreated with my clients, to whom I am deeply grateful for the privilege of being on their journey with them. I am very clear that I am merely a member of that cocreation team and that they did all the hard work.

My understanding and definition of *collaboration* is not theoretical. It is grounded in the practical reality of working with these leaders and teams who were solving thorny business issues, and in the facilitation of collaborative processes of all kinds in different work cultures on five continents. It is grounded in work in large companies and small on those continents. When clients asked how to measure the success of their collaborative efforts, valid and reliable measurement tools were created. When they asked to build their internal facilitative capabilities so they could be self-sufficient

SIDE BOX 3.1: COOPERATION VS. COLLABORATION

As Kouzes and Posner have suggested, there is indeed a similarity between cooperation and collaboration—they both require people to help each other. However, there is a very critical distinction to be made. *Cooperation* is an exchange between two people—for example, I ask you for information so I can get a report done; if I have been nice to you, and you want to help me because it is in your own interest, you will give me the information. Otherwise you are not required to do so. You can say "no," drag your feet, or give only partial information. *Collaboration*, on the other hand, is when you both own the project, have agreed to the rules for how team members are going to work, and have mutual respect, responsibility, and accountability for the outcome. *Collaboration requires a deeper level of engagement, while cooperation is merely an exchange.*

and not be dependent on outside consultants, a suite of training programs was developed around collaborative meetings, teams, and organizational change.

My understanding of *collaboration* is evergreen, adapting to changes in markets, demographics, technology, as well as business and global trends. Since 2010 it was clear that collaboration is here to stay as a way of leading and managing, in large part due to the globalization of business, the digital revolution, the need for flatter, networked organizations, and the demographics of the new generations of leaders who expect collaborative workplaces. It was also clear that in spite of all the work that had been done up to that point, we were only in the early stages of the full articulation of collaborative leadership cultures. Now I am convinced collaborative leadership is the only way we will survive in the 21st Century.

A Range of Definitions

The predominant leadership culture in most organizations today remains the Power Paradigm, with top-down power and control, hierarchical structures, fear-based motivational systems, and varying degrees of enlightenment being implemented by some leaders. Because leaders are still emerging from the transitional period of leadership, there is no consensus on a shared definition of *collaboration*. Let's explore some of the key thinkers to get some perspective on different ways the term has been defined.

- **Robert Cooke and Three Types of Leadership Cultures:** Cooke's work on the constructive/collaborative leadership culture, discussed at length in Chapter 2, significantly advanced our understanding of leadership cultures and the four types of behavior for a collaborative culture.[41]

- **Kouzes and Posner and the Collaboration Commitment:** Fostering collaboration is one of their ten leadership commitments. They cite *Merriam-Webster*'s definition of *collaboration* as "to work jointly with others together, especially in an intellectual endeavor," but also conflate it with the idea of *cooperation*, which is defined in a similar manner. They see collaboration as a "social imperative" that requires fostering a climate of trust and facilitating relationships.[42]

- **Tamm and Luyet and Radical Collaboration:** These authors have also conflated collaboration with cooperation by defining it as "an attitude of cooperation and mutual success, and supporting each other's interests and goals." They believe that true collaboration is an inside-out process for the individual, not the organization. Indeed, it does start inside of the individual, as well as for teams and organizations as they learn how to become a "We" culture. They have put forth the idea of a "Green Zone" (collaborative), vs. a "Red Zone" (passive/defensive or aggressive/defensive) culture, where the green culture is an environment where individuals collaborate to build mutual success, listen actively, and welcome feedback.[43]

- **Senge and How Work Gets Done:** Senge's mention of collaboration comes from his interview of Anne Murray Allen, former head of information technology and strategy for Hewlett-Packard's Ink Division, in which she talks about their business of knowledge and the role of collaboration:

  Knowledge is what we know how to do, and we do things with one another. ... Collaboration is the flip side of knowledge management. You can't talk about one without the other. So to manage knowledge you need to address collaboration and tools that help people collaborate.[44]

- **Hanson and Cross-Unit Collaboration:**[45] In 2009 Morten Hansen published a book called *Collaboration,* in which he defines the term as being cross-unit collaboration based on a particular situation where people need to work together on a project or task. He suggests a three-step approach

SIDE BOX 3.2: DIGITAL COLLABORATION AND PEOPLE COLLABORATION

Today's business requires both digital collaboration—the use of technical means to convey information and data and to communicate—and people collaboration, which is how people work together, make decisions, solve problems, and deliver results, which may or may not require digital means of communication. In the Digital Age, however, there is a view that if we have a webinar, attend a teleconference, or interact on social media, this is collaboration. It usually is not. *Digital collaboration is technology-based and -driven. People collaboration is people- and relationship-based and is grounded in the governance principles of a collaborative leadership culture.*

SIDE BOX 3.3: SITUATIONAL COLLABORATION VS. COLLABORATION AS A LEADERSHIP CULTURE

Hansen is essentially limiting the scope of collaboration to specific situations, or what can be called *situational collaboration* for cross-unit work. In effect, this makes collaboration a tool or a process, like having a hammer or saw in your tool box that you use once you have determined whether it will do the job. Otherwise, it's not necessary. I disagree with this limited view. As we have seen in Cooke's work and in the development of the Collaboration Paradigm, *collaboration is a leadership culture* that shapes the behaviors, processes, leadership, and structure of the organization. *Collaboration is not just a situational tool. It is a philosophy grounded in core beliefs and assumptions about human nature, a set of principles, concepts, and behaviors that shape the leadership culture of an organization.*

to what he called "Disciplined Collaboration": (1) Evaluate opportunities for collaboration, (2) Spot barriers to collaboration, and (3) Tailor solutions to tear down the barriers. He sees "Disciplined Collaboration" as letting *"units work independently when that approach produces the best results. ... To be disciplined about collaboration is to know when not to collaborate."*

- **Ricci and Wiese and the Collaborative Imperative:** John Chambers, former CEO of Cisco Systems, is well known for his advocacy for more collaboration in the workplace.[46] Two of his lieutenants, Ron Ricci and Carl Wiese, were involved in the implementation of his vision, and they articulated it in terms of Cisco's culture, leadership, process, and technology. They defined "true collaboration" as enabling *"small groups of specialized players, that might include people from different departments, customers, partners ... to work better together."*[47] In terms of the organization design, in 2009 Chambers created his idea of a collaborative decision-making structure, where executives from across the business sat on councils and committees. It is not clear what their governance process was or whether they had an effective way to make decisions or resolve differences. But when revenues fell, two years later in 2011, Chambers restructured the company yet again, getting rid of the councils and committees. It was followed in short order by layoffs and the elimination of some product lines.[48] Perhaps part of the problem was in their understanding of how to make collaborative decisions. On this point, Ricci and Wiese made this claim: "Let's be clear—collaboration is not about achieving consensus. In fact, consensus is the enemy of collaboration."[49]

- **Marshall's 1995 Definition of Collaboration:** We learned earlier that *collaboration* was defined by *Merriam-Webster* as working together.[50] *Merriam-Webster* also defines *collaboration* as working with the enemy, as in *collaborateurs*. In my first book on collaboration, *Transforming the Way We Work: The Power of the Collaborative Workplace*, collaboration was viewed as the replacement for hierarchy.[51] Based on my work with companies and leaders up to that time, *collaboration* was defined as:

> *A principle-based process of working together which produces trust, integrity, and break-through results by building true consensus, ownership, and alignment in all aspects of the organization. Collaboration is a way of life, a values-based framework which enables us to meet our fundamental needs for self-esteem, respect, trust, and integrity in the workplace. Put another way, collaboration is the way people naturally want to work.*[52]

Collaboration was seen as:

- **A Decision-Making Framework:** Making decisions based on principle rather than power or personality. Collaboration helps us decide when and how to use any particular approach to improve performance and how to engage the workforce in its implementation. It is just as concerned with relationships as it is with bottom-line results.
- **A Common Denominator for Relationships:** For engaging all members of the workforce, since its core values and beliefs are the basis for building trust-based relationships.
- **A Set of Methods and Tools:** Help the workforce become aligned, take ownership of and responsibility for the success of the enterprise, and build an organizational system that produces sustained high performance.
- **A Total Shift:** Collaboration is not a program, a technique, or a partial solution. It is a total shift in the way we work together and think about our customers.

SIDE BOX 3.4: CONSENSUS AND COLLABORATION

Perhaps Cisco did not know *how* to make consensus decisions where people are encouraged to disagree and work *through their differences*. Not having a methodology for consensus decision-making leaves any team, council, or committee with few alternatives but to revert to compromise and majority rule decisions. This means there is always a disgruntled minority who do not fully own the decisions. Contrary to Ricci and Wiese's view, *achieving consensus is at the core of how collaborative teams work and how a collaborative leadership culture of ownership, trust, alignment, responsibility, and accountability are achieved.* Without consensus-based governance, there is a strong likelihood the culture will revert to a benevolent form of hierarchy.

○ **A New Work Ethic:** Collaboration provides long-term stability for the workplace because it is a work ethic that recognizes that work gets done through people, people want and need to be valued, and any change must be owned by those implementing it if it is to be successful.[53]

The 4th Evolution's Definition of *Collaboration*

The world has changed dramatically since 1995, but the core of the 1995 definition of *collaboration* lives on, and with over two decades of application in a wide range of business situations, it is even more clear now than before that *collaboration and the Collaboration Paradigm of leadership is the replacement for hierarchy and the Power Paradigm*. We now have a deeper, systems-based understanding of the central tenets of collaboration as a leadership culture, a philosophy, and a way of life. While we are still in the "early years" of implementing this culture in organizations, in the 21st Century collaboration is the only way we can effectively and humanely address our organizational, societal, and global challenges. Our 21st-Century definition is:

> *Collaboration is a leadership culture paradigm, a comprehensive systems perspective on the culture, leadership, processes, and organization design of any organization. It is grounded in an explicit set of core beliefs and assumptions about people in organizations, and in the seven principles of collaboration that shape the culture. This paradigm informs every aspect of how an organization works.*

Let's consider a number of dimensions of this definition:

- **Fundamental Assumption:** People want to be honored for who they are as human beings, as well as professionals, and want to be empowered by the leadership culture to be their best selves so they can do their best work.
- **A Way of Life:** Collaboration is a way of living, a belief system that results in specific conscious choices leaders make to treat others with honor and respect, cocreate solutions, listen and engage, work through differences, and do what is best for the good of all.
- **A "We" Culture:** A fundamental shift in collaborative leadership cultures is from the "I" culture, individually based, to the "We" culture, where we subordinate our individual preferences to what is best for all. This means a commitment to do what is best for the team, the organization, the customer, or in global organizations, what is best for the planet. It means individuals state their views, create mutual understanding, and work through differences to achieve the best outcome for all.
- **Empowered to Be Their Best Selves and to Do Their Best Work:** The ultimate goal of collaboration is to create workplaces that empower people to be their best selves, do their best work, and produce superior and sustained results.

- **Ownership and Trust:** These two principles are the bedrock of true collaboration and distinguish it from any other kind of leadership culture. Without ownership there is no trust; without trust there is no credibility or effective teams and organizations.
- **A Safe Workplace:** To do their best work and be their best selves, the workforce must feel psychologically, physically, and emotionally safe and must feel free from fear, retribution, bullying, harassment, or discrimination. Collaboration is grounded in trust not fear, principles not power, accountability not blaming and shaming, and the practice of ethical behavior and conduct—which make it safe.
- **An Ethical Workplace:** Collaborative leaders are ethical above reproach. They practice the seven principles of the collaborative work ethic with a focus on integrity and honor.
- **Comprehensive:** Collaboration can happen at the individual, team, organization, or global levels. It is a framework for how we can live and work, no matter where we are.

SUMMARY AND CONCLUSION: COLLABORATIVE LEADERSHIP'S TIME HAS ARRIVED

We live in an era of constant change, disruption, accelerated technology, new generations of workers who are more diverse and global, and with a planet facing existential threats. Yet the predominant leadership paradigm in organizations remains 20th Century power and fear. McGregor and Argyris helped us see the anomalies in that Power Paradigm, which opened the door to new thinking about the importance of people, their motivations, needs, feelings, dreams, and expectations, and how the leadership paradigm needed to mature and change. Our thinking certainly changed, but from 1960 until the present day, power, control, and fear remain

SIDE BOX 3.5: CASE STUDY: FOUNDATIONS, INTERNATIONAL

In 2000, the founder of a midwestern manufacturing company, which we will call Foundations International, realized that if it was going to grow, he would need to adopt a different approach to leadership. Together, over the next five years, we transformed their leadership culture from a top-down hierarchy to a flatter, collaborative team-based organization. Then, after the September 11, 2001, attacks on the World Trade Center in New York, the stock market took a deep dive, and six months later the ripple effects hit his company's bottom line.

In a special Senior Leadership Team meeting, the issue was how they would survive. They had tapped out their credit line, and projected sales were down. The conversation quickly turned to "right-sizing," or terminating 15% of the workforce. The general manager of the manufacturing operation, which had one-third of the workforce and would be most directly impacted, took this pending decision back to his team at the plant. They had been formed as a collaborative team and felt responsible for the well-being of their entire workforce.

SIDE BOX 3.5: (CONTINUED)

Terminating 15% of their skilled workers, they knew, was just the beginning. When business came back, they could not guarantee these same workers would want to come back. Rather than terminating them, the entire workforce agreed to work four days a week rather than five and take a cut in pay so that all workers could stay on the job. It was a collective, collaborative decision that honored the entire workforce. Individual needs were subordinated to the good of all. It was a smart business decision as well. When business came roaring back the next year, they were able to meet the demands and had maintained the loyalty of their workers as well.

the predicate for organizational leadership. Even the emergence of Covey's Principle Paradigm did not result in much movement, though it solidified the collaborative foundation.

The dawn of the 21st Century brought with it the Digital Age, globalization, and younger generations of workers, along with the existential threat of global warming. There was new impetus for a transformation of how people worked with each other. From its early beginnings in the late 20th Century, *collaboration* has emerged as the 4th Evolution of Leadership paradigm, after Power, People and Principle. First considered a buzzword and fad, it was then found to be a tool or a process. We did not fully understand, at that time, the incredible power that collaboration holds for our ability to transform ourselves, our relationships, the workplace, and the planet.

In this chapter we reviewed the work of six major contributors to the development of the Collaboration Paradigm of leadership, including Kouzes and Posner's five practices, Goleman's emotional intelligence, Senge's learning organization, Greenleaf's servant leadership, and Collins's Level 5 Leadership. Each of their contributions was focused on culture and process, with no focus on organization structure. Then we defined the core elements of the Collaboration Paradigm using the systems model, which is the foundation for the rest of the book. Find a quick overview of that paradigm in Figure 3.4.

Finally, we cleared up the confusion around what *collaboration* is and what it isn't, arriving at a 4th Evolution definition of collaboration. After all that has been said, collaboration is about people, optimism for the human race, and how to realize our full human potential as human beings, teams, and organizations. It is a principle-based foundation, the rudder of a huge vessel, that will guide us through the stormy waters of our volatile world. Collaboration holds out our best hope as a human race to survive this next century and beyond.

Collaboration Paradigm of Leadership

Culture: People are inherently good and have intrinsic value, want to matter and contribute; psychological safety, ownership and trust are critical for successful collaboration; 7 Principles of the Collaborative Work Ethic; productive energy of the workforce increases with collaboration

Leadership: Ethical above reproach; principle-based; credible and trustworthy; optimistic, facilitative; self-aware; high EI; self-accountable; chief cultural officer, steward, communicator, and people developer

Processes: People: teams are how work gets done; facilitators are an essential resource; transparent communications; conflict resolution and accountability; Business: cross functional collaboration; process improvements to improve performance

Organization Design/Structure: Flat, networked and team-based; few levels of manageme gone

Outcomes: Trust-based relationships; superior results; ethical reputation; high ownership and alignment

FIGURE 3.4   The Collaboration Paradigm of Leadership.

CHAPTER REVIEW AND REFLECTIONS

Learning Objectives:

Let's reflect on the learning objectives for the chapter and summarize what you have learned:

- Understand the contributions of *six key thought leaders* to the development of collaboration.
- Build on our understanding of collaborative culture as we define the *Collaboration Paradigm of leadership.*
- Understand a 21st-Century definition of *collaboration* as a way of life, a way of working, and how it is distinct from other definitions of collaboration.
- Make the case that it is time to adopt the 4th Evolution of Leadership for the 21st Century—Collaboration.

Initial Questions Revisited, and For Reflection:

At the beginning of this chapter, you were asked to consider the questions below as you did your reading. What did you discover? What were your key learnings?

- *Of the six key thought leaders to be discussed for their major contributions to our understanding of collaboration, which one has the greatest impact on how you want to lead or manage, and why? How does that thought leader's contribution strengthen our understanding of collaboration?*

- *As you review the Collaboration Paradigm of leadership, in what ways is it different from the Power, People, and Principle Paradigms?*
- *Given the principles of the Collaborative Work Ethic, how have they influenced your view of leadership?*
- *As you think about the definition of collaboration and how it has evolved over time, how is the 4th-Evolution definition of it distinct from cooperation, digital collaboration, and situational collaboration?*

ADDITIONAL REFERENCES

- Collins, Jim. *Good to Great.* New York: HarperCollins, 2001.
- Goleman, Daniel. *Emotional Intelligence.* New York: Bantam Books, 1995.
- Kouzes, James, and Barry Posner. *The Leadership Challenge.* 6th ed. Hoboken, NJ: Wiley, 2017.
- Marshall, Edward M. *Transforming the Way We Work: The Power of the Collaborative Workplace.* New York: AMACOM Books, 1995.
- Senge, Peter M. *The Fifth Discipline.* New York: Crown, 2006.

ENDNOTES

1   Chris Argyris, "The Individual and the Organization," *Administrative Science Quarterly* 2, no. 1 (June 1957): 1–24; Douglas McGregor, *The Human Side of Enterprise* (2006; reprinted., New York: McGraw-Hill, 1960).

2   Stephen R. Covey, *Principle-Centered Leadership* (New York: Free Press, 1990).

3   Edgar H. Schein, *Organizational Culture and Leadership,* 5th ed. (Hoboken, NJ: Wiley, 2017).

4   Edward M. Marshall, *Transforming the Way We Work: The Power of the Collaborative Workplace* (New York: AMACOM Books, 1995).

5   James Kouzes and Barry Posner, *The Leadership Challenge,* 6th ed. (Hoboken, NJ: Wiley, 2017).

6   Daniel Goleman, *Emotional Intelligence* (New York: Bantam Books, 1995).

7   Bill George, Peter Sims, Andrew N. McLean, and Diana Mayer, "Discovering Your Authentic Leadership," *Harvard Business Review,* February 2007.

8   Peter M. Senge, *The Fifth Discipline* (New York: Crown Publishing Group, 2006).

9   Robert Greenleaf, *Part I: The Servant Leader Within* (Atlanta, GA: Greenleaf Center for Servant-Leadership, 1970), pp. 31–44.

10 Jim Collins, *Good to Great* (New York: HarperCollins, 2001).

11 This section is based on James M. Kouzes and Barry Z. Posner, op. cit., pp. 3–26, and Chapters 3–12.

12 Ibid., p. 2.

13 James Kouzes and Barry Posner, *The Leadership Challenge*, 4th ed. (New York: Wiley, 2007), p. 21.

14 Peter Salovey and John D. Mayer, "Emotional Intelligence," *Imagination, Cognition, and Personality* 9 (1990): pp. 185–211.

15 Peter Salovey and John D. Mayer, *Emotional Intelligence* (Amityville, NY: Baywood, 1990).

16 John D. Mayer, Peter Salovey, and David R. Caruso, "Emotional Intelligence: New Ability or Eclectic Traits?," *American Psychologist* 63, no. 6 (September 2008): pp. 503–517.

17 Daniel Goleman, "What Makes a Leader?" *Harvard Business Review, Best of 1998*, January 2004, pp. 1–10.

18 Daniel Goleman, "What Is Empathy?" *Harvard Business Review*, December 2013, p. 160.

19 Goleman, Ibid.

20 William Shakespeare, *Hamlet, Prince of Denmark*, Act 1, Scene 3.

21 Bill George, Peter Sims, Andrew N. McLean, and Diana Mayer, "Discovering Your Authentic Leadership," *Harvard Business Review*, February 2007, pp. 1–8.

22 Stephen R. Covey, *Principle-Centered Leadership* (New York: Free Press, 1990).

23 James Kouzes and Barry Posner, *The Leadership Challenge*, 6th ed. (Hoboken, NJ: Wiley, 2017).

24 Peter M. Senge, *The Fifth Discipline*, in *Classics of Organizational Behavior*, 4th ed., ed. Walter Natemeyer and Paul Hersey (Long Grove, IL: Waveland Press, 2011), pp. 591.

25 Peter M. Senge, *The Fifth Discipline* (New York: Crown, 2006), p. 4–5.

26 Senge, *The Fifth Discipline*, p. 590.

27 Senge, *The Fifth Discipline*, pp. 6–11.

28 Greenleaf, *Part I: The Servant Leader Within*, 33.

29 Ibid., 36–40.

30 Jim Collins, *Good to Great: Why Some Companies Make the Leap ... and Others Don't* (New York: HarperCollins, 2001).

31 Ibid., 15.

32 Ibid., 20.

33 A. P. J. Abdul Kalam, *Panel Discussion at the Aspen Institute of India*, YouTube, May 8, 2009, https://www.youtube.com/watch?v=q57FCLQUR94

34 Abraham H. Maslow, "A Theory of Human Motivation," *Psychological Review* 50, no. 4 (1943): pp. 370–396.

35 Jim Collins, *Good to Great: Why Some Companies Make the Leap ... and Others Don't* (New York: HarperCollins, 2001). p. 36.

36 Gary Hamel, "W.L. Gore: An Innovation Democracy," in *The Future of Management* (Boston, MA: Harvard Business School Press, 2007).

37 United Nations, "Only 11 Years Left to Prevent Irreversible Damage from Climate Change, Speakers Warn during General Assembly High-Level Meeting," March 28, 2019, https://www.un.org/press/en/2019/ga12131.doc.htm

38 This definition was developed by the author over a period of 40 years and is a cultural assessment measure in the Collaborative Interdependence Index®, which has been used by teams and organizations to determine how collaborative and interdependent they are; also, over 500,000 people have been asked the question "What percentage of you is your employer getting?," with responses typically in the 30–40 percent range for hierarchical/power paradigm organizations and 70–80 percent for collaborative/principle paradigm organizations.

39 Edward M. Marshall, *Transforming the Way We Work: The Power of the Collaborative Workplace* (New York: AMACOM Books, 1995).

40 Michael Hammer and James Champy, *Reengineering the Corporation* (New York: Harper Collins, 2001).

41 Robert A. Cooke and Janet L. Szumal, "The Impact of Group Interaction Styles on Problem-Solving Effectiveness," *Journal of Applied Behavioral Science,* 30:4 (December 1994), pp. 415–437.

42 James M. Kouzes and Barry Z. Posner, *The Leadership Challenge* (New York: Wiley, 2007), pp. 223–224, 362.

43 James W. Tamm and Ronald J. Luyet, *Radical Collaboration* (New York: HarperCollins, 2004), pp. 8, 17–18, 267.

44 Peter Senge, *The Fifth Discipline* (New York: Crown, 2006), pp. 269–270.

45 Morten T. Hansen, *Collaboration: How Leaders Avoid the Traps, Create Unity, and Reap Big Results* (Boston, MA: Harvard Business Press, 2009), pp. 14–19, 44.

46 Morten T. Hansen, "How John Chambers Learned to Collaborate at Cisco," *Harvard Business Review,* March 4, 2010. https://hbsp.harvard.edu/product/H004FN-PDF ENG?Ntt=morton+hanson+%2B+john+chambers&itemFindingMethod=Search

47 Ron Ricci and Carol Wiese, *The Collaborative Imperative: Executive Strategies for Unlocking Your Organization's True Potential* (Cary, NC: Cisco Systems, 2012), p. 2.

48 Brad Reese, "Management Vision of Cisco CEO John Chambers under Fire," Network World, August 7, 2009, Brad Reese, "Management Vision of Cisco CEO John Chambers under Fire," Network World, August 7, 2009; Jim Duffy, "Cisco Restructures, Streamlines Operations," Network World, May 5, 2011, Jim Duffy, "Cisco Restructures, Streamlines Operations," Network World, May 5, 2011.

49 Ron Ricci, "Why Consensus is the Enemy of Collaboration," Cisco, August 6, 2012, https://community.cisco.com/t5/collaboration-voice-and-video/why-consensus-is-the-enemy-of-collaboration/ba-p/3664849

50 https://www.merriam-webster.com/dictionary/collaborate

51 Edward M. Marshall, *Transforming the Way We Work: The Power of the Collaborative Workplace* (New York: AMACOM Books, 1995).

52 Ibid., pp. 4–5.

53 Ibid. p. 5–6.

Figure Credits

Fig. 3.2: Source: https://traitsandbehaviors.wordpress.com/.
Fig. 3.3: Marua da Silva, "Level 5 Leadership, from "Humility + Will = Level 5"," https://www.learningapprentice.com/good-to-great-level-5-leadership/. Copyright © 2019 by The Learning Apprentice.

Collaborative Leadership

CHAPTER FOUR

The Collaborative Leader

*A leader is best when people barely know they exist, when their work
is done, their aim fulfilled, they will say: we did it ourselves.*
—Lao Tzu, 6th Century BCE[1]

"*IT'S REALLY beginning to make more sense to me,*" *remarked Priyanka as the
team gathered in a library conference room for their weekly meeting. "I now
see that what we thought was collaboration, social media, is really digital communication, and that collaboration is really a way of working with others and a
way of life." The rest of the team members were nodding their heads in agreement.
Ana said she appreciated knowing more about the thought leaders who had contributed to this 4th Evolution.*

*Morare said he had grown up in a culture that was collaborative, especially
in how people cared for each other, but now he saw the breadth and depth of the
Collaboration Paradigm and a dramatic shift in how we think about leadership
over the last 100 years. "Yes," Linda responded, "but it's really clear that while
collaboration is the culture we all want, it is not the culture most organizations
have. We're still stuck with the Power Paradigm—it needs to go."*

*Hanyue sat observing his teammates thoughtfully and said, "I want to be a
collaborative leader, but what does that mean? Is it just facilitating a meeting?
Is it about how to help others?" He also wanted to know more about how the
Collaboration Paradigm of leadership would help him understand the attributes
of a collaborative leader, how they are expected to behave, and what roles they
play in an organization. The team turned to their next assignment and saw they
had five questions to reflect on as they reviewed this chapter:*

- *Given the definition of "collaborative leadership," in what ways does this fit
with your own approach to working with others?*
- *Of all the attributes of a collaborative leader, which are the three that best
define who you are now as a leader? What are the ones you would like to
be better at and are willing to work on?*

- *In reviewing the behaviors of collaborative leaders, how would you rate yourself?*
- *Given the roles of collaborative leaders, where are you the strongest and what will you work on?*
- *Given what you have learned about collaborative leadership, are you ready to consciously choose to take the journey?*

LEARNING OBJECTIVES

By the end of this chapter, you will:

- Define what a *collaborative leader* is
- Understand what the *key attributes* of collaborative leadership are and how they are distinct from those of the hierarchical, power-based leader
- Learn about how collaborative leaders *behave* at three levels: themselves, those they work with, and at the organizational level
- Understand the *essential roles and responsibilities* of collaborative leaders
- Decide whether you wish to make the conscious choice to become a collaborative leader

THE MAIN POINT OF THIS CHAPTER

It was time for the consulting assignment with the information systems leadership team to end. We had done what we had set out to do: the organization's culture, work processes, and structure had been transformed into a collaborative, team-based business focused on the customer. Walter was the leader who reported to the plant manager in a fairly steep hierarchy. Walter and his colleagues knew that if they were going to beat the competition in this IT services business, they would need to find a different way to work. After 18 months, the leadership team had significantly changed every aspect of the organization of a couple hundred engineers. It was time to turn over the reins. They were ready to assume their collaborative leadership responsibilities.

In our close-out meeting, I asked the team: Who is the leader? Who will ensure there is a high level of ownership as the change process continues? Who will identify when interventions are needed to keep the team and organization on track? I did not at all expect their answer: "We are the leader!" they answered in unison. It was almost as if they knew the question was coming. They went on to say:

> We're going to rotate the responsibilities for designing, facilitating, and following up our meetings in teams of two, for four-month terms. We will continue to use our collaborative team governance process to shape how we work with each other here

> *and across the organization. When we need inspiration, Sam will provide it. When we make decisions that may not be 100% consensus, Jeff will challenge us. When a difficult conversation is needed, Victoria will help us through it. When we need to engage our workforce, their teams, and make sure everyone is aligned and owns our future direction, we will all step up to take that on.*

Thirty years later, this organization is still a collaborative leadership culture and organization.

We are living in the new age of collaboration. The world we live in is highly volatile, disruptive, high speed, networked, and global. We cannot lead effectively in the 21st Century using the 20th Century's power-based approach. It is out of step with our current reality. It's no longer about authority and control. It's about influence, insight, and engagement. It's about creating the environment within which people can find meaning and purpose in their work lives and relationships. It's about ensuring psychological safety, ownership, and trust. At the end of the day, it's about empowering people to be their best selves so they can do their best work and produce superior results.

In the 21st-Century collaborative workplace, leadership is a function, not a title or position. Leadership in a meeting, team, business unit, or organization is based on the situation or circumstances and the gifts, talents, skills, and insights of any given individual. Anyone can lead their team or the organization based on their unique gifts, talents, knowledge, and skills. Everyone can be a servant leader. Everyone can foster trust and ownership and can nurture and support each other.

Becoming a collaborative leader is a journey that takes commitment, time, and reflection. It involves a number of steps, not the least of which is whether you want to take the journey. Not everyone is cut out to be a collaborative leader from a values, talent, or skills perspective. Some may not want or be able to subordinate their ego and ambitions to the good of the whole, where to them "I" is more important than "We." Others may want to become a collaborative leader but don't know how to get from where they are now to where they are considered by others to be collaborative.

To help you make a conscious choice about whether you want to go on this journey, let's focus on defining *collaborative leadership* for the 21st Century, explore who these leaders are in terms of their qualities and *attributes*, the *behaviors* they demonstrate toward the people they work with, and their *roles* and responsibilities with the workforce.

DEFINING COLLABORATIVE LEADERSHIP

We are all familiar with the iconic alien coming to Earth and asking to be taken "to your leader" (Figure 4.1). Implicit in this instruction is that there is one leader who is in charge, though as we have learned, in a collaborative leadership culture, anyone

FIGURE 4.1   "Take me to your leader."

can be a leader. The idea that anyone can be a leader is particularly challenging for the leadership development industry, which has been built on the presumption that there is indeed one leader at the top of every organization, and that young professionals and corporations must invest hundreds of millions of dollars to obtain the training, degrees, and certificates that will ensure their ability to climb the ladder. How disconcerting to discover that people may not want to climb the ladder but just provide superb service to others and have a good life.

In the 21st Century Digital Age, gone are the days when business leadership is the exclusive domain of a few people at the top of the organization. Because our world has changed so dramatically, the old assumptions and constructs about leadership are either disappearing or no longer apply. The heroic or charismatic leader of the 20th Century creates dependence that thwarts the ability of those working to collaborate, create, innovate, and execute. The 20th Century cult of personality that characterized so many companies now undermines the culture of empowerment demanded by 21st Century Millennials. The ego-driven, power-based, politicking leaders who created aggressive/defensive or passive/defensive leadership cultures in the 20th Century will find it next to impossible to be effective in the relationship-based, flat, team-driven, and nurturing constructive/collaborative leadership culture of the 21st Century. The requirements of 20th Century hierarchy to go up the chain of command to get a decision only compromises the capacity of the 21st Century globally networked organization to make decisions on the spot, at the lowest level possible. The Power Paradigm is simply out of step with the realities of the 21st Century.

The new age of collaboration requires a different kind of leadership, leadership that is ethical, principle-based, and believes in the inherent goodness of the workforce. The new leadership understands that the 21st Century workforce wants to find meaning in their work, they want to work hard, make a difference, and succeed. They want to connect with others, build strong trust-based relationships, innovate, and take on projects that challenge their intellect. It's no longer just about money, title, or climbing a ladder to nowhere. It's about a quality of life, connection, service, and making a difference. Of course they want a good salary and benefits, but these are extrinsic motivators. The 21st Century workforce needs to be intrinsically motivated.

Collaboration, as leadership's 4th Evolution, upends the Power Paradigm and transcends it by creating an entirely new leadership theory. Collaborative leadership is not about power, authority, fear, or control. It is about people, principle, relationship, psychological safety, ownership, trust, and empowerment. Collaborative leadership, as shown in Table 4.1, is about honoring nine collaborative beliefs about the workforce, and the 7 Principles of the Collaborative Work Ethic. In honoring these beliefs and principles, collaborative leadership brings to the 21st Century workplace the potential for transforming entire organizational systems, work relationships, business processes, and customer relationships.

How, then, do we define collaborative leadership? Let's start with our definition of *collaboration*:

> *Collaboration is a leadership culture paradigm, a comprehensive systems perspective on organizations that is grounded in an explicit set of core beliefs and assumptions about people in organizations and in the 7 Principles of the Collaborative Work Ethic that shape the culture. This paradigm informs every aspect of how an organization works.*

In this context, we define *collaborative leadership* as:

> *Collaborative leadership is an ethical, principle-based philosophy of service that builds a leadership culture of psychological safety, ownership, and trust that*

TABLE 4.1 *Collaborative Leadership Beliefs and Principles*

9 COLLABORATIVE BELIEFS ABOUT PEOPLE	7 PRINCIPLES OF THE COLLABORATIVE WORK ETHIC
People are inherently good and want to work hard.	Trust
People want to matter.	Ownership
People need meaning and a sense of purpose in their work and want to contribute.	Integrity and Ethics
People need dignity, honor, and respect.	Honor
People want to be trusted and to be able to trust others.	Mutual Respect
People take care of what they own at work.	Full Responsibility
People need psychological, physical, and emotional safety to be their best selves and do their best work.	Accountability
People want to learn, grow, and develop.	Full Responsibility
People want to be appreciated and acknowledged for their contributions.	Honor

empowers the workforce to be their best selves so they can do their best work and produce superior results.

This definition dispels five myths about leadership that have been carried forward from the 20th Century Power Paradigm:

- **Myth 1—There Will Always be Hierarchy:** False. With the internet, open systems, and distributed leadership, as well as flat, team-based, networked, global organizations, hierarchical leadership is inefficient and ineffective. Psychological safety and trust replace fear and control as leaders at all levels emerge to take full responsibility for the effective and efficient management of the organization.
- **Myth 2—There is Only One Leader at the Top:** False. There is no presumption that only one person is the leader, though there are levels of leadership based on the needs of the business. In a flat, networked collaborative organization, there may be up to three levels, though their primary roles are strategic guidance and facilitation of process and outcomes.
- **Myth 3—Leaders are Only Born:** False. There is also no presumption that "leaders are born, not made." Anyone can be a collaborative leader at any given time, depending on the situation and the abilities of the individual. Anyone can become a collaborative leader if they go on their journey.
- **Myth 4—There are Always Followers:** False. In collaborative leadership, there is no presumption of "leaders and followers," which also dominates the current way in which leadership is discussed in higher education, the literature, and common parlance. In collaborative leadership, the conversation is about how best to get the work done and who needs to be involved, not who follows whom. Anyone can be a leader or follower at any time, depending on the situation. Collaborative leaders are not concerned about how many "followers" they have because it's about making a difference, not about being important.
- **Myth 5—Collaborative Leadership is Just a Style:** False. Collaborative leadership is not a "style" at all, as suggested by Hansen.[2] It is a philosophy, a way of being and working with others. It is true some leaders are more collaborative than others, but anyone can be on their journey to becoming more collaborative in their beliefs, principles, behaviors, and work practices. It is a learning process and is not static. You never "arrive" because we are all works in progress.

Collaborative leadership has the potential to be truly transformational at all levels of an organization. For individuals, it can help them become more facilitative, empathic toward others, and focused on the good of the organization. For teams, it can transform members' work relationships, helping them rise above politics and shift the focus to synergy, service, and superior results. For business units or departments, it can transform their cross-functional relationships by taking down the silo walls that keep them from working collaboratively, engage and align their workforces, and accelerate the ability of the organization to adapt to the quickly changing terrain. For organizations, collaborative leadership can transform their visions and missions and help them achieve extraordinary goals. For leaders on the world stage, collaborative leadership can transform how difficult global problems can be resolved. They can move beyond that 19th Century concept of national self-interest and focus on meeting the needs of all the people on our planet, particularly those in greatest need.

KEY ATTRIBUTES OF COLLABORATIVE LEADERS

In their research on the characteristics of the most admired leaders, Kouzes and Posner developed a list of 20 characteristics, surveyed over 75,000 people around the globe, and asked them for their top seven. For 30 years they have reported the results for the top four characteristics, and the top four have not changed during that time. In 2016, they were as follows:[3]

- **Honest** (89%): worthy of trust; integrity and character; tells the truth; tied to values and ethics
- **Forward-looking** (71%): vision; concern for the future of the organization
- **Competent** (69%): ability to get things done; inspires confidence
- **Inspiring** (69%): enthusiastic, energetic, and positive about the future; uplifts spirits; able to communication the vision in a way that motivates; speaks to people's need for meaning in their lives

Leaders of organizations were not admired for their controlling behavior, aggressive drive, fostering competition, or motivating people through fear. What is particularly striking in the Kouzes and Posner data is that nothing has changed in 30 years in terms of what people want to see in their leadership. All of these attributes align with collaborative leadership and where we are headed for the rest of this century.

In my work with hundreds of business leaders and managers who aspired to be collaborative leaders, 10 key attributes kept showing up:

- **Ethical Above Reproach:** Collaborative leaders have the highest integrity and ethically are above reproach. Leigh helps us understand what it means to be an ethical leader:[4]
  - They have a moral compass with integrity at its center.
  - They demonstrate that ethical behavior is a priority, with no apologies.

- ○ They communicate clear expectations and set the tone for others that they behave ethically.
- ○ They walk the talk and practice ethical decision-making.

- **Principle-Based:** Collaborative leaders work with others from a clear set of principles rather than power, politics, or personality. They practice the 7 Principles of the Collaborative Work Ethic: trust, ownership, integrity and ethics, honor, mutual respect, responsibility, and accountability. They behave toward others, make decisions, and solve problems in ways that are grounded in these principles.

- **A Clear Purpose:** Collaborative leaders have done their journey work, know why they are on this planet, know what their mission is, and have found meaning in their work and relationships. They have high self-esteem, and as a result they are service-oriented and stewards of the well-being of others and the planet.

- **Credible and Trustworthy:** Collaborative leaders are both credible and trustworthy. Kouzes and Posner have made credibility the "foundation of leadership."[5] The workforce must believe in their leaders, that their word can be trusted, and that they have the competence to lead. They have done their inside-out work and built self-trust, which involves clarifying their own personal values, their self-respect, and their honor and dignity.[6]

- **Collaborative Mindset:** Collaborative leaders are focused on relationships first, the leadership culture, building psychological safety, ownership, and trust through engagement of the workforce, and ensuring the organization can adapt to meet the demands of the market.[7] These leaders are humanists at heart. They know that work gets done through people, are inclusive of all types of people, and move beyond their own egos. They have what Tamm and Luyet call *collaborative intention,* when leaders are authentic, non-defensive, and make a commitment to the mutual success of their relationships.[8] They are service-oriented leaders and demonstrate Level 5 humility toward those with whom they work.[9]

- **Emotionally Intelligent (EI):** Collaborative leaders have high EI. They are self-aware and not in denial about their own behavior and its impacts on others. They are self-reflective and do their inner work on a regular basis. As Salovey, Mayer, and Goleman helped us understand, having high EI means a high degree of empathy toward others and self-regulation of their own emotions.[10] They practice the habit of mindfulness which Rick Hanson sees defines as *"staying present in the moment ... rather than being distracted."*[11] They make themselves vulnerable to others, are open and transparent, and commit to being lifelong learners.[12]

- **Facilitative:** Collaborative leaders have no need to control others. Instead, they are facilitators of relationships and processes, and they ensure that there is ownership and buy-in along the way. Their facilitative style is open, engaging, actively listening, encouraging, supportive, and focused on ensuring that members of the workforce have full ownership of whatever they are working on. In this way they empower others and create a work culture in which people can be their best selves and do their best work.

- **Optimistic and Inspiring:** Collaborative leaders maintain a high level of optimism toward the organization, the workforce, and their work. When there are challenges or breakdowns, these leaders are encouraging and supportive. They bounce back, learn from the challenges, and reassure those they are working with that anything is possible if they apply themselves. They inspire others to excel, to go beyond, to think out of the box, and to innovate.

- **Leadership Will:** Collaborative leaders have a deep reservoir of willpower and persistence in the face of extraordinary challenges. They never ever give up. They come from their commitment, mission, values, and principles, and they consciously choose to stay the course when that course is the right thing to do.[13] Collaborative leaders are resilient and have grit. Hanson defines grit as "dogged, tough resourcefulness. It's what remains after all else has been ground down."[14] Having a strong will also means you are adaptive, adjusting to the ever-changing realities around you. Finally, it is about being courageous, speaking truth to power in a way they can hear, taking a stand for what is right, ethical, and just. It is standing up for others to ensure their physical, psychological, and emotional safety.

- **Leadership Discipline:** Collaborative leaders are disciplined. They work hard to stay on track; honor their principles and standards; grow trust, respect, and ownership; and produce results. Collaborative leaders' discipline reflects their personal integrity and the conscious choices they make. Discipline means there is consistency in the application of collaborative principles, and there is patience in the face of resistance or skepticism. Finally, there is a high level of self-accountability where collaborative leaders accept responsibility for mistakes they have made and then learn from them and grow.[15]

These attributes are intended to provide a framework that helps us understand who is a collaborative leader. These attributes can be used as criteria to assess where one is stronger or wants to grow. They provide a goal to which leaders can aspire. It can be used as a recruitment and hiring screen, as well as a professional development tool, so that organizations hire and develop collaborative leaders.

We might ask ourselves, "If I am strong on only five of the ten criteria—does that mean I am not a collaborative leader?" Not at all. It means that you are strong on the five criteria, are on your journey, and can now focus on developing yourself in the other five. In my professional career, there have been only a few leaders who met all ten of these criteria. So this profile is not intended to exclude people. Instead it is intended to be a set of aspirational criteria toward which leaders work as part of their journey.

KEY COLLABORATIVE LEADERSHIP BEHAVIORS

Our reputations in organizations are usually based on how we treat others, rather than what we know. This is especially true in a collaborative leadership culture where the quality of relationships and the level of trust and respect are determinants of how well the organization is going to function as well as the productive energy of the workforce. Collaborative leadership behaviors happen at three levels: (1) Self, (2) Work with others, and (3) Organizational. These behaviors derive directly from the attributes of collaborative leaders and the Collaboration Paradigm.

Collaborative Behaviors at the Level of Self

There are three sets of collaborative behaviors that reflect a high level of emotional intelligence and enable the leader to self-regulate and make course corrections.

- **Self-Awareness and Reflection:** It is incumbent on the collaborative leader to maintain a high level of self-awareness, to be vigilant at all times about how they feel about themselves and others, how they are interacting with others, and the impact of their behavior on others. To do so requires them to have a habit of reflection and mindfulness whereby they are actively meditating, asking themselves good questions, and journaling to remain connected to the world around them. This is a daily habit that ensures the leader is grounded in reality.

- **Feedback and Learning:** I once had a coach who asked me three questions: (1) What messages are you getting from the universe? (2) Are you listening? and (3) If so, what are you going to do about it? We get "messages from the universe" every day in many different ways. It may be direct feedback we get from others, something that happens to us, an article we read, or a podcast we heard. These messages may show up when we take a shower, drive to work, or exercise. What is critically important is that we listen for this feedback so we remain conscious about the world around us. Each piece of feedback, each message, gives us an opportunity to learn about our behavior and how we impact others. It gives us a chance to self-correct.

- **Self-Accountability:** We discussed the principle of Self-Accountability in Chapter 3. Now you get to practice it. Based on the feedback received and your reflections, there may have been an adverse impact on an individual, group of individuals, team, or the organization. You get to be right or in relationship. If you wish to be in relationship with those you have hurt, the next step is to hold yourself accountable to them, share what you have learned, and commit to not repeating that behavior. There may be times when it even becomes necessary to ask for forgiveness, which can be very healing.

Collaborative Behaviors Working with Others

There are four collaborative leadership behaviors when working with others, whether it is a small group of people, a team, or a larger group of colleagues: (1) Connecting, (2) Engaging, (3) Facilitating, and (4) Nurturing. Within each of these four categories there are specific ways in which collaborative leaders can behave:

- **Connecting:** In a collaborative leadership culture, the most important thing leaders can do is connect with the people with whom they work. It is a quintessential aspect of our humanity to recognize the existence of another human being. In a collaborative culture this means first, you have to show up, both physically and emotionally. Second, you are fully present with others, which means not being distracted or multi-tasking, and being willing to engage. Third, you actively listen to others with your eyes, ears, and heart. So often leaders listen only with their ears, and listening becomes more of a transaction than part of the relationship. Or the leader listens from an assumption, expectation, or judgment about the person. People know when they are not truly being heard. Fourth, collaborative leaders empathize with others. They look for what is *behind* what is being said, putting themselves in the other's shoes, and understanding the other's context.

- **Engaging:** Once there is a credible connection, collaborative leaders engage others on the topic at hand. This involves collaborative leaders communicating with their colleagues in a dialogue, information exchange, or feedback. Second, collaborative leaders ask good questions that challenge their colleagues to think, at the same time they are actively listening for the responses. Third, these leaders build ownership among their colleagues of their work. With ownership come trust, responsibility, and accountability. Fourth, these leaders will build trust-based relationships. Finally, engagement results in leaders being able to empower individuals, teams, and the workforce because there is respect, trust, and ownership.

- **Facilitating:** Facilitating behavior is the essence of collaborative leadership, where the leader is service oriented, which means these leaders ask for the desired results of a meeting, team process, business process, or organizational strategy. Those outcomes then help determine how the group, team, or organization is facilitated so they are achieved. Second, they engage others by asking good questions, move the agenda along, summarize it, and bring discussions to a close. Third, facilitative, collaborative leaders protect the group and the integrity of its process. Finally, collaborative leaders ensure the participants of a team reach true consensus by working through their disagreements.

- **Nurturing:** Collaborative leaders come from a place of nurturing and support for the people they work with. Which is one of the five leadership practices cited by Kouzes and Posner—to "Encourage the Heart."[6] They give constructive feedback to their teammates, colleagues, and the workforce. They provide a range of support to others, including working through organizational issues, helping individuals learn and grow by coaching them, providing professional development assistance, or just being available as an active listener. Collaborative leaders may be asked to intervene in a given situation, where they may need to mediate the challenge or help the participants heal a broken relationship. Finally, collaborative leaders show appreciation for or acknowledgement of the contributions of the workforce.

These four collaborative leadership behaviors result in a high level of motivation for the workforce, promote synergy, and result in high levels of productive energy.

Collaborative Behaviors at the Organizational Level

At the level of the organization, collaborative leaders are focused on what is best for the organization overall. They work to create what Cooke called the constructive/collaborative leadership culture that reflects these four behaviors:[17]

- **Achievement:** People are valued who set and achieve their own realistic goals; problems are effectively solved; risks are taken; and a standard of excellence is pursued.
- **Self-Actualizing:** This culture values creativity, quality over quantity, individual growth, and task achievement. People get to enjoy their work, innovate, take on new activities, develop themselves, and maintain their personal integrity.
- **Humanistic/Encouraging:** Workers are expected to show concern for and help each other and be willing to be helped; there is a high degree of participation, conflicts are resolved constructively, and there is team-based problem solving.
- **Affiliative:** Workers are expected to be open, friendly, cooperative, and tuned in to the needs of their teams or work groups. It's about the success and satisfaction of the group in addition to an individual's self-actualization. It's about teamwork, self-management, and interdependence.

To help create this kind of leadership culture, collaborative leaders manifest four types of behavior:

- **Build Trust and Credibility:** They build trust and credibility with the workforce by walking the talk of the collaborative principles.
- **Inspire and Align:** They inspire the workforce with a clear vision that gives them a sense of purpose and meaning in their work, and then align them around that purpose.

- **Systems Thinking:** Collaborative leaders think from a systems perspective, recognizing the importance of the interactions of culture, process, and organization design with leadership and the outcomes of the organization. This also enables them to think strategically about where the organization is headed and how it is developing.
- **Adaptation:** They adapt to the wide array of changes that impact the organization, both internally and externally.

ESSENTIAL ROLES OF COLLABORATIVE LEADERS

The first responsibility of a leader is to define reality. The last is to say thank you. In between the two, the leader must become a servant and a debtor. ... To be a leader is ... to make a meaningful difference in the lives of those who permit leaders to lead.

—Max DePree, *Leadership Is an Art*[18]

The executive leadership team at a top-tier technology company was reflecting on their journey as a team to become collaborative leaders. It certainly had not been easy. But they had made great progress adopting new behaviors and walking the talk. "I wish we could have always been leading this way," said the CIO. "It was so hard to establish our credibility with our workforce before, and our business suffered as a result." The chief R&D officer responded, "Now I can look my workforce in the eye and tell them the truth about where we are and need to go, and I am able to hear them tell me *their* truths." It wasn't always that way. This was a tough, command-and-control, bottom-line results, shareholder-value-comes-first kind of an organization. Collaboration did not come easily to them. In fact, it was a struggle as they redefined their leadership culture, work processes, and organization design.

This team realized that as a result of the new realities of the market, their diverse Millennial workforce, their highly interdependent relationships across the business, and exacting competition that was trying to disrupt their historical success, they had to adopt the new roles of collaborative leaders.

Collaborative leaders represent a completely different approach to how they work with others. Their primary mission is to create leadership cultures that empower the workforce to be their best selves and do their best work so that they can produce superior results. This collaborative leadership culture, as we have already discussed, is based on the core beliefs and 7 Principles of the Collaborative Work Ethic, where building psychological safety, ownership, and trust are their central responsibilities.

Collaborative leaders are systems thinkers. In the Collaboration Paradigm (Figure 3.1 in Chapter 3), at the center of the model is leadership, whose responsibility—indeed, obligation—is to be aware of and orchestrate the complexity of the connections, relationships, dynamics, and ever-evolving nature of the organization's culture, people and work processes, and organization design.

Collaborative leaders are facilitative rather than authoritative. They ask rather than tell. They engage rather than dictate. They co-create rather than dominate. They motivate by building ownership and trust rather than through fear and control. They genuinely care about the people they work with. Their goal is to increase the level of self-trust, tap into their hidden productivity, release their full potential, and build a strong sense of ownership of the business. They engage the workforce in making critical business decisions and solving business problems. The collaborative leader understands that culture and people drive the business rather than technology, strategy, finance, or shareholders. These leaders hone their people and process skills in meeting management, team development, small group dynamics, conflict resolution, and change management. Collaborative leaders sponsor people's success. They are champions of learning and catalysts for change so that the organization and the workforce can adapt and evolve in a healthy way.

Remember Lao Tzu's prescient adage in the 6th Century BCE about collaborative leadership: *"A leader is best when people barely know they exist, when their work is done, their aim fulfilled, they will say: we did it ourselves."*[9] When collaborative leaders are successful, they will be hardly noticed, in the background, because they have been so successful at developing their people, teams, and organization to be self-sustaining as a collaborative leadership culture. The workforce will say, "This is a great place to work." It is a highly engaged, open, team-based, and ethical workplace. There is low turnover, high motivation, job satisfaction, and productive energy, and the workforce works seamlessly across functions, time zones, and cultures. Customers are treated with integrity, there is a high level of quality in the services/products, and innovation is encouraged.

There are eight essential roles for the collaborative leader, some of which are appropriate primarily for senior leaders responsible for an organization. A number of the roles, like facilitator, however, are for anyone who steps up to lead a meeting, team, initiative, or process. All of the roles can become part of any organization's professional development process.

1. **Chief Cultural Officer (CCO):** Collaborative leaders are the CCO for whatever group of people with which they work. Their overall responsibility is to nurture and grow the collaborative leadership culture of the organization. Here are some actions they can take:

   • **Build and Strengthen the Collaborative Leadership Culture:** Collaborative leaders own the core beliefs and the principles of the Collaboration Paradigm. They have a responsibility to discuss them publicly in meetings, teams, or organizational settings so they remain front and center. This means that decisions, large and small, are based on principle, rather than power, politics, or the personality. It means creating a "We" culture, a sense of community where the good of all is more important than "I," ensuring that the work environment is collaborative rather than competitive, and that rewards and recognition are for teams rather than individuals. It means a culture of service to each other, learning from each other, cocreating solutions to problems, and working seamlessly across boundaries of any kind.

- **Create and Ensure an Ethical Culture:** Collaborative leaders are ethical above reproach. They bring their integrity to bear in every aspect of their work. They set the highest standards of ethics for the people they work with. Ethics and ethical standards become part of the daily fabric of the workplace, are regularly discussed, and are applied to decisions that are being made. They also hold people accountable for unethical conduct and ensure that there is effective follow-through.

- **Ensure the Safety of the Workforce:** We live in challenging times when it comes to the respectful and ethical treatment of women, people of color, different religions, and people with different sexual identities or physical or mental disabilities. Collaborative leaders create and ensure that the workplace is a safe place to work, physically, psychologically, and emotionally. Harassment, intimidation, or discrimination of any kind is not tolerated and is considered a violation of the organization's ethical code. Fear should not exist in a collaborative leadership culture. If it does, it is the role of collaborative leaders to root it out.

- **Build Ownership and Trust:** An absolutely central role for collaborative leaders is to create a culture of ownership and trust across the organization.[20] People take care of what they own, so collaborative leaders ensure that members of the workforce own the values, vision, mission, and strategy of the organization; that they own their jobs and the projects they are working on, and that they own any change initiatives in the organization. Ownership is engendered through high-engagement strategies, four-way communications, the Collaborative Team Governance Process (see Chapter 7), and by having dialogues around a range of topics. Trust is the result of this investment in building ownership, and with that comes leadership credibility.

- **Appreciate the Workforce:** One of the greatest motivators for an individual, team or organization is appreciation and acknowledgement for their contributions and hard work. Collaborative leaders do as Kouzes and Posner have urged, to "Encourage the Heart,"[21] by recognizing people and teams for their work, celebrating successes, and encouraging them to learn and grow an environment of gratitude and appreciation.

2. **Stewards:** Max DePree tells us that leaders are the stewards of an organization's value system.[22] There is much to be taken care of in a collaborative organization, not the least of which is the code of ethics, vision, and mission. Collaborative

leaders also hold the organization "in trust for the greater good of society."[23] In light of our existential challenges, this stewardship role is especially important for every collaborative leader. Regardless of the type of organization or what it does, every organization and leader have a duty to ensure their organization is responsible and taking care of the planet. They also are holding the aspirations, dreams, hopes, expectations, and professional futures of the workforce in their hands. In everything they do, collaborative leaders must honor this sacred trust.

3. **Visionaries Who Align the Organization:** The spine of any organization is the degree of alignment that exists throughout the workforce on a wide range of issues. In the Collaboration Systems Model, there is an alignment ellipse that traverses the system from top to bottom, connecting all parts of the organization. At the center of that ellipse is leadership. It is collaborative leadership's responsibility to ensure that all parts of the organization are aligned and working in the same direction. Alignment involves the organization's values, ethics, vision, mission, strategy, people and work processes, and design.

Collaborative leaders, therefore, play a critical role in what Kouzes and Posner call "Envisioning the Future," where you imagine the possibilities and find a common purpose that is meaningful to people, and to which they can commit. Then you engage the workforce, appealing to a common set of ideals and bringing the vision to life.[24]

When Marriott's Residence Inn brand was first created, leadership took the entire staff away for a week to create the vision and mission for the organization. They wanted everyone to own it. The passion, excitement, and energy that this process created was palpable for years to come. Like Residence Inn, collaborative leaders engage the entire workforce to take ownership of the values, ethics, vision, mission, and strategy of the organization. This ensures alignment and builds trust and credibility.

There are several other types of alignment collaborative leaders need to pay attention to:

- **Market Alignment:** Ensures the company is strategically positioned relative to its competitors, that its unique and value-added role is clear, and that its strategic direction is focused
- **Customer Alignment:** Meets the needs and interests of its customers
- **Workforce Alignment:** Engages the full energies and productivity of the workforce, focused on the company's vision and strategy
- **Leadership Alignment:** Leaders and members agree on the strategic direction, people and business processes, and products and services being delivered

4. **Sponsors:** Collaborative leaders have a key role as sponsors. If they are on the senior leadership team, it may ask a functional or cross-functional team to complete a specific task within a specific time frame. The senior team then asks

one of its members to be the sponsor of that team, ensure there is alignment between its work and the overall strategy of the organization, and ensure there is a free flow of communication between them. Sometimes the team's task is of sufficient size that it needs to create working groups to get the work done. It will also have a sponsor for each of those working groups. In all cases, the work of the sponsor has been agreed to by their governing body, whether it is a senior leadership, departmental, networked, or other team.

The primary role of a Sponsor is to ensure the success of the team. This means that in addition to the roles of alignment and communication, sponsors provide strategic direction in the form of an initial charter that spells out the mission, tasks, timeline, and boundary conditions for the team's work. They provide the necessary resources and "air cover" should the team run into resistance within the organization. They coach and support the team as it works through its charter. Finally, they monitor the team's work and keeps senior leadership informed on its progress.

The Sponsor plays a pivotal role in a flat, team-based, networked organization, ensuring that there is effective internal alignment, communications, and implementation of team charters. This is how a collaborative organization gets its work done.[25]

5. **Facilitators:**

> *Group members genuinely appreciate a leader who facilitates their lives rather than promoting some personal agenda. Because the leader is open, any issue can be raised. Because the leader has no position to defend and shows no favoritism, no one feels slighted; no one wishes to quarrel.*
>
> —Lao Tzu, 6th Century BCE

The role of facilitator is a sacred responsibility in a collaborative leadership culture. Facilitators are the essential link for a collaborative organization getting its work done. Their primary roles are to build high levels of psychological safety, ownership, and trust in the workplace; engage people; and empower them to be their best selves so they can do their best work. They also build synergy among team members, make the necessary interventions, and maintain the psychological health and well-being of the group, team, or organization. It is a difficult job because of the complex human interactions they must address, some of which will be addressed in a later chapter.

- **A Key Distinction: Collaborative Leaders vs. Facilitators:** I need to make a very clear distinction about a role conflict: *business or organizational leaders with formal authority should not be facilitators*—it is a direct conflict of interest. The conflict is that they have the formal power to conduct the performance appraisals of team members and give out bonuses, raises or promotions. Facilitators, on the other hand, have no formal power. They are objective third parties for teams, processes, or initiatives, who only have the informal power of influence based on their credibility. In addition, their job is to protect the team, to be a neutral person whose only interest is the health, well-being, and success of the team. When the roles of leader and facilitator are conflated, it not only creates confusion in the minds of the team members, it also thwarts their willingness to speak up, thereby defeating the purposes of the team. Most people will not speak truth to power and are easily intimidated by, or are fearful of, formal leaders in an organization—in large part because we are still dealing with the legacy of the Power Paradigm. The job of these formal leaders is to identify the right type of facilitator, invest in the person's skills development, and ensure that the person has the independence of action to perform his or her primary roles.

"Why, then," you might ask, "are you including facilitator as a role for collaborative leaders?" It is because all collaborative leaders do not necessarily have formal power or authority. Remember, anyone can be a collaborative leader, depending on the situation, their skill set, and willingness to step forward. A facilitator is a collaborative leader, but not all collaborative leaders can be facilitators. This distinction also applies to the conflict noted above, between collaborative leaders with formal authority and their being a facilitator. Never the twain should meet.

- **7 Key Attributes of Facilitators:** What kind of person, then, is a facilitator? Our focus here is on the internal facilitator. Organizations can, of course, hire trusted external facilitators if they wish. The same attributes, skills, and roles will still apply. They have a number of key attributes and key roles and skills, without which they cannot be successful in their jobs.

  - **Ethical Above Reproach:** They have the highest standards of ethical conduct and act accordingly.
  - **Self-Aware:** Facilitators are highly self-aware individuals, are reflective, and are clear about their "hot buttons" that may cause them to overreact and undercut their effectiveness.
  - **High Emotional Intelligence:** They have a high degree of EI, particularly in the areas of empathy toward others and their ability to self-regulate.
  - **Credible and Trustworthy:** To be successful, they must be credible and trustworthy, as judged by the members of the team. Everyone knows who they can trust.
  - **Confidential:** They keep internal team processes confidential and adhere to the team's operating agreements.
  - **Respected:** Facilitators are widely respected within the organization and are often informal influencers.
  - **Objective:** They must be objective to call situations for what they are.
  - **Relationship-Centric:** They are focused on relationships first and empowering people to be their best selves.[26]

- o **Service-Oriented:** They serve the team and its members, ensure there is a free flow of information, and ensure alignment.
- o **Self-Accountable:** Facilitators hold themselves accountable with the people they work with.

- **10 Key Roles and Skills of Facilitators:**[27]

  - o **Small Group Psychology and Dynamics:** Facilitators must have a working knowledge of small group psychology and dynamics—individual use of power; behaviors like manipulation, controlling, dominating, resisting, disrupting, blaming, and shaming; and team dynamics, such as achieving consensus, working through disagreements, building trust and cohesion, handling breakdowns, or dealing with emotional outbursts.
  - o **Discovery:** Facilitators are often called on to do fact-finding about a team and its dynamics, an interpersonal problem that is disrupting the team, or larger organizational issues facing a team or leaders. They design and conduct objective interviews, do fact-finding, write objective reports, and make presentations about the results.
  - o **Group Facilitation:** Facilitators must know the basics of group facilitation, as well as advanced facilitation that can address team dynamics or dysfunctions. They create a psychologically safe space so team members will speak. They help members work with each other, solve problems, and make decisions.
  - o **Achieving Consensus:** The facilitator must know how to help a team reach true consensus on an agreement. This means respecting the diversity of opinions as the team works through differences to achieve full ownership of their decisions.
  - o **Collaborative Meetings:** Work gets done in meetings, whether in person or online, and the facilitator must know how to design and facilitate both types.
  - o **Collaborative Teams:** Teams are the primary unit of work and change in an organization, so facilitators must know how to implement the Collaborative Team Governance Process, help the team manage their internal processes so they fulfill their charter, and engage and work with other stakeholders as needed.
  - o **Preventions and Process Interventions:** Breakdowns always happen in meetings and teams. Collaborative facilitators know how to prevent them before they happen, as well as how to intervene when they do, so that the work of the team can proceed and team members own the outcomes.
  - o **Difficult Conversations:** There are always difficult conversations to be held. Facilitators know how to conduct them in a way that respects the dignity of the individuals involved. They help the participants work through

their issues. The goal is congruence, ensuring that the truth for all parties is told in a way that is respectful and supportive.

○ **Healing:** Often teams have broken relationships, or there is history that gets in the way of these members working well together. Facilitators step in to support the members in healing their relationship.

○ **Nurturing:** Facilitators nurture the spirit, motivation, and productive energy of the team by showing their appreciation and gratitude for the work they have done.

6. **Communicators:** Collaborative leaders will engender a high degree of credibility when they communicate with their teams, units, departments, or the overall workforce with openness and clarity. All too often, senior leadership communications are periodic, transactional in tone, nontransparent, and one way. In a collaborative leadership culture, there is no need for a "public relations" function, which puts a spin on what senior leaders say. Often leaders try to "keep the lid on" certain events, like a drop in revenues or a pending merger or layoffs. What they do not understand is that every organization has a very vital and active informal network, especially with social media, and everyone knows anyway. As one executive once said to me, "I am the last one to know." Organizations have no secrets. They are transparent. So leadership might as well go ahead and tell the truth, engage people in a conversation, and if necessary, cocreate solutions to challenges they are facing. Rather than be fearful of what the workforce will do with adverse information, collaborative leaders tell the truth and engage them is addressing the issues. Here are four key rules collaborative leaders have in the area of communications:

- **Tell the Truth:** There is no need for a cover up, sleight of hand, or a public relations campaign to spin or sugarcoat information. A collaborative workforce expects to be trusted by leadership. They appreciate candor and transparency. Telling the truth increases leadership's credibility and shifts the conversation to shared problem solving.

- **Four-Way Communications:** Collaborative leaders create a four-way communication system—vertical and horizontal. The intention of this system is to have a robust dialogue in the organization about the issues that matter. Everyone's opinion matters and has equal merit. "All-hands" teleconference calls that everyone attends can kick off the process of exchange and dialogue by having a range of mechanisms to discuss and provide feedback to leadership. Zoom offers the chance for breakout sessions online to enhance dialogue. Team members can be asked to present specific agenda items as well.

- **Promote Dialogue:** Collaborative leaders are committed to, and promote the art of, dialogue across the organization. These are open, honest, and candid conversations about things that matter to the organization and its departments, teams, or members. Politics, power, hidden agendas, and ego have no place in these dialogues. Chrislip has helped us understand the importance and the depth of dialogue by defining it as creating shared meaning and mutual learning, building group capacity to do adaptive work through active listening and constructive inquiry and advocacy, legitimizing and clarifying diverse perspectives, and having new possibilities and relationships emerge.[28]

- **Active Listening:** An absolutely essential skill for collaborative leaders is active listening; leaders listen with their emotional intelligence, from a place of respect and appreciation for what is actually being said. They listen with their ears, eyes, and heart. They reflect back what they have heard to the other's satisfaction. They demonstrate deep respect for others.

7. **People Developers:** Work gets done through people. It's all about relationships—that is how results get produced. If the leader is only focused on producing bottom-line results, people become a transaction, a means to an end. So a central role of collaborative leaders is to honor, respect, develop, and grow the people they are working with. There are at least four ways people can be developed:

   - **Coach:** Collaborative leaders can serve as coaches to their team members. As coaches, they use their emotional intelligence to listen, reflect, and provide constructive feedback to colleagues and people they work with, not from a position of power, but from a place of learning and growth. When people need help, they are there to support them. Finally, they motivate those they work with through encouragement, appreciation, and gratitude.
   - **Mentor:** Collaborative leaders can be mentors to a few of the people they work with. Different from coaching, mentors usually have seniority in the organization or are outside of the organization. The Association for Talent Development has identified four key things they do: They provide advice and guidance, share their experience and expertise, and serve as a sounding board; are a champion and cheerleader who offers encouragement and support, helps mentees move out of their comfort zone, and celebrates successes; are a resource and connecter to key people; and tell the mentee the truth in order to help them move forward.[29]
   - **Healer:** Collaborative leaders, like facilitators, help the people they work with heal relationships that have broken down. This does not mean rescuing them or enabling bad behavior by making excuses for them. It does mean to help them work through whatever pain they are feeling and empowering them to deal directly with the other person.

- **Capacity Builder:** Collaborative leaders look for opportunities for the people they work with to learn new skills, tools, and processes, but more importantly, opportunities where they can grow as professionals.

8. **Change Agents:** Organizations are facing a myriad of change challenges ranging from market competition, disruptive technologies, artificial intelligence and robotics, the threat of a merger or acquisition, financial swings, reorganizations, demographic changes, and disrupters of all kinds. Change pressure is unrelenting and persistent. Agility and adaptiveness are essential. Resistance can prove fatal for an organization. In Power Paradigm organizations, leadership typically imposes the change on the workforce without consultation or engagement, changes are structure or process based, and the result is workforce resistance; negative impacts on speed, cost, and quality; and often change failure.

   Collaborative leaders, on the other hand, recognize that when changes occur, it is the workforce who will have to absorb the impacts, make the changes, and make whatever adjustments are required so the work can still get done. As a result, they use a "culture-first" approach to build ownership, alignment, and trust around the change. They trust the workforce to be able to absorb the reality of the change and make the necessary adjustments. They realize that people take care of what they own, and if the workforce does not own the change, they will resist it. With a culture-first ownership strategy, resistance and costs are significantly reduced, speed is increased, and the effective adjustment to the change is made.

   To build ownership, collaborative leaders transparently communicate about the change well in advance, create project teams to address change issues, ask for feedback, and strengthen the change process. When the process is launched, the project teams are re-tasked to lead that process. They are intimately involved every step of the way. The results of high levels of ownership are adaptiveness, little or no resistance, and successful implementation.

CHAPTER CONCLUSION: COLLABORATIVE LEADERSHIP FOR THE 21ST CENTURY

We are in a new era, a new Century, in which the contours of markets, technology, interdependence, demographics, and global threats require a new approach to leadership. The Power Paradigm, while useful in the early 20th Century, is out of step with 21st Century digital and global realities. The anomalies of the power, authority, fear, and control approach of hierarchy will simply not work with Millennials and GenXers. Collaborative leadership, which has evolved since the 1990s, has emerged as the outright replacement for hierarchy, even though hierarchy is still the predominant way organizations are still led. It is taught in our graduate schools and in our executive education programs almost with an air of indifference toward the transformed realities within which they operate. With the emergence of a fully developed Collaboration Paradigm of leadership, the 4th Evolution, we now have a Digital Age alternative.

In this light, we have defined *collaborative leadership* as an ethical, principle-based, humanistic, relationship-oriented way in which leadership creates and sustains workplaces that empower people to be their best selves and do their best work so they can produce superior results. Our definition is not constrained by the narrow casting of spans of control or with ladders leaders must climb. Instead, our definition of collaborative leadership reflects the recognition that in our networked world, anyone can show how they are a collaborative leader, depending on the situation, circumstances, their skill levels, and willingness to step forward. Yes, there are likely several levels of greater responsibility within a flat, team-based collaborative organization, but the focus is not on accumulating power or being important, but on meeting customer needs, serving each other, and solving problems. We've also discovered that anyone can be a collaborative leader if they so choose, but that it is a lifelong journey of learning new ways to behave and work with others, as we discard the shackles of hierarchy.

If you are trying to determine if a leader is collaborative or want to evaluate your own degree of collaborativeness, this list of key attributes is instructive: ethical, principle based, clear purpose, credible and trustworthy, collaborative mind-set, emotionally intelligent, facilitative, optimistic and inspiring, and having leadership will and discipline. These attributes are not intended to exclude or discourage people from the journey but to provide a framework that is grounded in theory, principle, and practice that can be used as a goal to which leaders can aspire.

We also learned that collaborative leaders exhibit behaviors that are quite different from the power- or ego-driven leader. They start from the inside, with a focus on self-awareness, reflection, feedback, and self-accountability. In working with others, their behaviors involve building psychological safety, ownership, and trust through connecting, engaging, facilitating, and nurturing. At the organizational level, collaborative leaders are all about building ownership, trust and credibility, alignment and inspiration, systems thinking, and adaptation summarized in Table 4.2.

We've discussed the key roles collaborative leaders play in ensuring that a collaborative culture is developed and sustained, and that whether they have a title or not, the facilitator's role is central to the functioning of the collaborative organization, without which work does not get effectively done.

The predicate for this entire conversation is the recognition that work gets done through people, who work in teams and conduct their work in meetings. In this culture, the glue that holds all of these relationships together is trust, not fear. Ownership is created by leaders trained in the art of facilitation, protected by leaders

TABLE 4.2   *Summary of Collaborative Leadership Behaviors*

COLLABORATIVE BEHAVIORS AT THE LEVEL OF SELF	COLLABORATIVE BEHAVIORS WORKING WITH OTHERS	COLLABORATIVE BEHAVIORS AT THE ORGANIZATIONAL LEVEL
Self-awareness and reflection	Connecting	Building trust and credibility
Feedback and learning	Engaging	Inspiring and aligning
Self-accountability	Facilitating	Systems thinking
	Nurturing	Adapting

who are sponsors and CCOs, guided by leaders who are ethical above reproach, and supported by leaders who nurture, appreciate, and acknowledge the gifts, hard work, intellect, and enormous contributions that every member of the organization makes. Table 4.3 provides a comparative summary of the Power and Collaboration Paradigms, based on our Systems Model, to help you understand the choices you have.

The next question, then, is whether you want to become a collaborative leader. To be fair, collaborative leadership is not for everyone. As we will learn in the next chapter, some leaders are so tied to the past, their power, their ego, and the need for control that they are unable to make the shift. Some leaders have experienced what I call a significant personal emotional event like a heart attack, a failed business, a lost child, a divorce, or other traumatic event that causes them to evaluate what is important in their lives. Still other rising leaders, particularly Millennials, will

TABLE 4.3   *Power vs. Collaboration Paradigms of Leadership*

DIMENSION	FROM POWER PARADIGM— HIERARCHICAL LEADERSHIP	TO COLLABORATION PARADIGM— COLLABORATIVE LEADERSHIP
CULTURE		
Trust and Credibility	Must be earned; credibility depends on the leader	Builds trust through ownership; highly credible
Ethics	Dependent on the leader	Ethical above reproach
Primary Driver	Fear as the motivator	Trust as the motivator
Cultural Focus	"I" culture; ego; individualistic; shareholder value	"We" culture; team based and collective (what is best for all)
LEADERSHIP		
Systems	Usually not systems thinkers	Systems thinkers
Leadership Style	Authoritative; power; commanding; few owners	Facilitative; principled; asking; everyone an owner

(Continued)

TABLE 4.3 *Power vs. Collaboration Paradigms of Leadership (Continued)*

Self-Awareness	Not usually self-aware	High self-awareness; reflective; learning and growing
Leadership Focus; Mindset	Control; exclusive; efficiency; structure; authority; dominate	Empowering; inclusive; effectiveness; cocreating
Emotional Intelligence	Low EI; not important	High EI; critical; empathy very important
PROCESSES		
Focus	Efficiency; cost reduction	Effectiveness; innovation
Working With Others	Transactional; task-oriented; tells; delegates; low emotional intelligence	Collaborative; relationship oriented; facilitative; asks; partners; high emotional intelligence
How Work Gets Done	Delegating	Partnering
Communications	Closed: one way	Transparent; four way
Decision-Making	One or a few make the decisions	Consensus decision-making
People Development	Boss; performance appraisals; promotions/demotions	Coach; feedback; mentor; capacity builder
Feedback	Not open to it	Welcomes constant feedback
Conflict	Avoided	Addressed for resolution
Rewards	Individual performance	Team performance and individual contributions
Accountability	Blame, shame, and transference; gets caught; asks for forgiveness	Self-accountability; team debriefs, learns, and grows
ORGANIZATION DESIGN/STRUCTURE		
Structure	Hierarchy; many levels; span of control; titles; ladder to climb	Flat; team-based; networked; few titles; focus on personal and professional development
Organizational Change	Structural change first; CEO-driven; imposed; high resistance	Culture first; ownership-based; engaged; low resistance
Productive Energy of the Workforce	Typically <40%; o to 10% after structural change	Typically 65 to 85%

find what is being discussed here as obvious and natural, and they may be uncertain why a book had to be written about it. To those who are open to collaborative leadership, welcome. To those of you who are not interested or find this inconsistent with your values, I offer this journey as an opportunity to check your assumptions and to assess your own aspirations, dreams, and what it is going to take to help you realize them.

CHAPTER REVIEW AND REFLECTIONS

Learning Objectives:

Let's reflect on the learning objectives for the chapter and summarize what we have learned:

- Define what a *collaborative leader* is.
- Understand what the *key attributes* of collaborative leadership are and how they are distinct from the hierarchical, power-based leader.
- Learn about how collaborative leaders *behave* at three levels: themselves, those with whom they work, and the organizational level.
- Understand the *essential roles and responsibilities* of collaborative leaders.
- Help you decide whether you wish to make the conscious choice to become a collaborative leader.

Initial Questions Revisited, and For Reflection:

- *Given the definition of collaborative leadership, in what ways does this fit with your own approach to working with others?*
- *Of all the attributes of a collaborative leader, which are the three that best define who you are now as a leader? What are the ones you would like to be better at and are willing to work on?*
- *In reviewing the behaviors of collaborative leaders, how would you rate yourself?*
- *Given the roles of collaborative leaders, where are you the strongest, and what will you work on?*
- *Given what you have learned about collaborative leadership, are you ready to consciously choose to take the journey?*

ADDITIONAL REFERENCES

- Archer, David, and Alex Cameron. *Collaborative Leadership: How to Succeed in an Interconnected World.* Boston, MA: Elsevier, 2009.
- Chrislip, David D. *The Collaborative Leadership Fieldbook.* San Francisco: Jossey-Bass, 2002.
- Hargrove, Robert. *Mastering the Art of Creative Collaboration.* New York: McGraw-Hill, 1998.
- Kouzes, James M., and Barry Z. Posner. *The Leadership Challenge.* San Francisco: Wiley, 2017.
- Tamm, James W., and Ronald J. Luyet. *Radical Collaboration.* New York: HarperCollins, 2004.

ENDNOTES

1   The quote from Lao Tzu comes from the *Tao Te Ching*, sixth century BCE, and has been modified to reflect that leaders may be women as well as men.

2   Morten T. Hansen, *Collaboration: How Leaders Avoid the Traps, Create Unity, and Reap Big Results* (Boston, MA: Harvard Business Publishing, 2009), pp. 143–165.

3   Definitions and categories come from James Kouzes and Barry Posner, *The Leadership Challenge*, 6th ed. (Hoboken, NJ: Wiley 2017), pp. 33–39; 2016 percentages come from: James Kouzes, The Wiley Network, March 31, 2016 https://www.wiley.com/network/professionals/leadership-skills/the-top-4-characteristics-of-admired-leaders

4   Andrew Leigh, *Ethical Leadership* (London: Kogan Page, 2013), pp. 87–99.

5   Kouzes and Posner, op. cit., pp. 25–44.

6   Edward M. Marshall, *Building Trust at the Speed of Change* (New York: AMACOM Books, 2000), pp. 53–63.

7   Edward M. Marshall, *Transforming the Way We Work: The Power of the Collaborative Workplace* (New York: AMACOM Books, 1995), pp. 69–76.

8   James W. Tamm and Ronald J. Luyet, *Radical Collaboration* (New York: HarperCollins, 2004), p. 9.

9   Robert Greenleaf, *Part I: The Servant Leader Within* (Atlanta, GA: Greenleaf Center for Servant-Leadership, 1970), 31–44; Jim Collins, *Good to Great* (New York: HarperCollins, 2001), p. 36.

10 Peter Salovey and John D. Mayer. *Emotional Intelligence*. Amityville, NY: Baywood, 1990; Daniel Goleman, "What Makes a Leader?" *Harvard Business Review*, January 2004, 1–10.

11 Rick Hanson, *Resilient* (New York: Harmony Books, 2018), pp. 23–48.

12 Peter M. Senge, *The Fifth Discipline* (New York: Currency Books, 2006); David Archer and Alex Cameron, *Collaborative Leadership* (Boston, MA: Elsevier, 2009), p. 121.

13 Marshall, *Building Trust ...* , op. cit., pp. 146–147.

14 Hanson, op. cit., pp. 77, 78–93.

15 Marshall, *Building Trust. ...*, op. cit., pp. 147–148.

16 Kouzes and Posner, op. cit., pp. 245–294.

17 Human Synergistics and Center for Applied Research, *Organizational Culture Inventory, OCI®: Interpretation and Development Guide* (Plymouth, MI: Human Synergistics/Center for Applied Research, 2009).

18 Max DePree, *Leadership Is an Art* (New York: Dell, 1989), pp. 11, 22.

19 Lao Tzu wrote the *Tao Te Ching* in the sixth century BCE; also in John Heider, *The Tao of Leadership* (Atlanta, GA: Humanics New Age, 1985); text was modified for gender neutrality.

20 For a more in-depth look at building trust, see Edward M. Marshall, *Building Trust at the Speed of Change* (New York: AMACOM Books, 2000); see also James M. Kouzes and Barry Z. Posner, *The Leadership Challenge* (New York: Wiley, 2007), pp. 221–247.

21 Kouzes and Posner, Ibid., pp. 245–294.

22 Max DePree, op.cit., pp. 11–22.

23 Larry Spears, "The Understanding and Practices of Servant Leadership," presentation at Servant Leadership Research Roundtable, Greenleaf Center for Servant Leadership, Regent University School of Leadership Studies, Virginia Beach, VA, August, 2005.

24 Kouzes and Posner, op.cit., pp. 95–116.

25 David D. Chrislip has done excellent work on the role of leaders in the nonprofit sector, where they perform a role similar to that of sponsor. He has also identified the roles a facilitator plays in the nonprofit sector, which is worth reviewing. Please refer to David D. Chrislip, *The Collaborative Leadership Fieldbook* (San Francisco: Jossey-Bass, 2002), p. 54.

26 Kouzes and Posner discuss the importance of facilitating relationships here: op. cit., pp. 206–216.

27 This section is based on my own work with clients and teams over 40 years, as a certified master facilitator. Also consider two sources: Chrislip, *Fieldbook*, and Robert Hargrove, *Mastering the Art of Creative Collaboration* (New York: McGraw-Hill, 1998), pp. 204–217.

28 Chrislip, op. cit., p. 96.

29 Morag Barrett, "What Exactly Is the Mentor's Role? What Is the Mentee's?" Association for Talent Development, January 21, 2014, https://www.td.org/insights/what-exactly-is-the-mentors-role-what-is-the-mentees

Figure Credits

Fig. 4.1: Copyright © 2013 Depositphotos/Nevada31.

CHAPTER FIVE

Becoming a Collaborative Leader

The quest for leadership is first an inner question to discover who you are. But there are no freeways to the future. ... There's only wilderness. To step out into the unknown ... we ... discover that the most critical knowledge ... turns out to be self-knowledge.

—James M. Kouzes and Barry Z. Posner[1]

*T*HIS WEEK, *the learning team decided to meet outside in the Quad. It was a beautiful day and they decided to change the venue for this all important conversation about the collaborative leadership journey. "Our last assignment on collaborative leadership made a whole lot of sense to me," Hanyue said to start the conversation. "At first, I was a bit taken aback by what seemed like an impossible list of attributes, behaviors, and roles. But then I realized that this is a replacement for hierarchy, and this is the kind of leader I want to be." The other team members were nodding their heads in agreement. Linda then said, "Our generation requires this kind of leadership. I don't ever want to work for someone who is always telling me what to do. I need them to trust I know what I'm doing, want to do my best, and want the organization to succeed." Again, there was a lot of agreement.*

Morare then challenged the group to think creatively about how they were going to make the transition. They were so used to operating in a hierarchical organization. They had also started this work committed to "climbing the ladder" to higher positions of authority. Collaborative leadership means flatter, networked organizations, where there is essentially no ladder. They knew that there would still be salary increases, but the focus was on the work, not the climb. This was going to take some adjustment of expectations and a realignment of motivations from power to service. Priyanka was ready to go on her journey, even though she had some trepidation. She opened up the assignment for the next week and found these five questions to reflect on:

- *Do you see yourself as a collaborative leader? In what ways (attributes, behaviors, and roles)?*

135

- *Why do you want to go on this journey? What are your greatest concerns? What do you see as the greatest potential benefits?*
- *Given the challenges many people face, barriers they must navigate, and steps on the journey to becoming a collaborative leader, how will you address them?*
- *Are you ready to make a conscious choice to go on this journey?*
- *What steps in the journey do you see being the most challenging?*

LEARNING OBJECTIVES

By the end of this chapter, you will:

- Understand what the *collaborative leadership journey* is and its benefits if you embrace the process
- Consider *who* is likely not to take the journey
- Discuss the *challenges or barriers* to becoming a collaborative leader and how they might be addressed
- Consider what is involved in making a *conscious choice* to go on this journey
- Review the *steps* in the collaborative leadership journey once you have made that choice

THE MAIN POINT OF THIS CHAPTER

In 2015 Ralph Stayer stepped down as CEO of Wisconsin-based Johnsonville Sausage, a position he held for 47 years. He expanded the butcher shop his father gave him into a $1.5 billion global business and the largest sausage brand in the United States.[2] What is more interesting is how he transformed himself as the leader of this business that enabled it to grow—through a collaborative leadership journey. Stayer may be one of the first business leaders to openly explore what it would take for him to transform himself from a command-and-control leader to a truly collaborative one and then go ahead and do it. In 1990 he wrote what is now a *Harvard Business Review* classic, called "How I Learned to Let My Workers Lead."[3] The story is told that in the early days, the sausage line ran outside Stayer's office above the factory floor. Every day at noon he would come out to taste the sausage by sticking his finger in the sausage line. Everyone below would stop and look up to see if the sausage quality met with his approval. If he gave a thumbs-up, they went back to work. If he gave a thumbs-down, there was work to be done to find out where the quality problems were. Fast-forward 20 years, and there was no sausage line outside Stayer's office. The line operators each had the authority to "pull the chain," to stop the sausage line if they believed there was something wrong with the quality. In between those two iconic events, there was a fundamental transformation of Ralph Stayer, his leadership style, and his company. His journey from a hierarchical, power and control executive to a collaborative, team-based, and empowering collaborative leader is highly instructive for what we are discussing in this chapter.

In the early years of his journey, he observed that his workers did not seem to care about their jobs. They were bored and made many mistakes. Their productive energy was low. They just did what they were told and then went home. The first step on his journey was self-awareness. As he said, "If I was going to fix what I had made, I would have to start by fixing myself. ... I was the problem so I could be the solution."[4] This moment was highly significant, because he took full responsibility for the situation and then consciously decided to go on his inside-out journey. He gathered data, or feedback, about what was happening in his company. He found that he had centralized control, was behaving aggressively, and had an authoritarian style, all of which made him and his workers unhappy. He concluded he needed to increase worker involvement in the business and came to the principle we have called ownership. His next step was to create a vision for the kind of company he really wanted:

> What I saw ... was definitely not an organization where I made all the decisions and owned all the problems. What I saw was an organization where people took responsibility for their own work, for the product, for the company as a whole.[5]

Over the next few years, he created a collaborative leadership culture that was based on the following observations about human behavior, similar to our collaborative beliefs:[6]

- People want to be great; if they aren't, it's management's responsibility.
- Influence what people expect and you influence how they perform.
- Expectations are driven partly by goals, vision, symbols, and language, as well as decision-making processes, production practices, and compensation systems.
- Learning is a process, not a goal.
- Organization results reflect the leader.

Stayer created an organization that transformed its entire business. As a result, the productive energy of the workforce and profitability for the company increased, and the company grew and grew. But it all started with the self-awareness and the journey of an extraordinary leader. As he said, "CEOs need to focus first on changing themselves before they try to change the rest of the company."[7]

Not all leaders are this self-aware. In fact, according to Morten Hansen's research on a sample of 185 leaders, only 16% were considered to be collaborative.[8] So there is much work to be done, not only by current business leaders but also by graduate programs, executive education, and corporate universities to transform their leadership curriculum to make collaborative leadership core to their programs.

Like what Ralph Stayer experienced, the collaborative leadership journey is an *inside-out process*. It usually starts with an event that causes leaders to stop and reflect on what is truly important in their lives. This self-reflection leads to self-awareness then expands to a deeper understanding of who they are as a human being, what matters to them, and what difference they want to make in the world. This journey is not for the faint of heart. It is clearly not for everybody. If, however, you see the market, technological, and demographic realities of our digital age, this journey will prepare you for the 21st Century.

DEFINING THE COLLABORATIVE LEADERSHIP JOURNEY

For nearly four decades, as an executive coach, I worked with over 100 leaders who decided to take this journey. Just like any climb to the top of a mountain, there was more than one way to get there. Some journeys took longer, and some were more difficult than others. Everyone started from a different place, each had different challenges and barriers, and each chose a different level of commitment. In each case, the inner work they did was extraordinary.

FIGURE 5.1   The Journey Begins.

One of the key lessons I learned in working with these leaders is that the true test of leadership is the individual's willingness to look at themselves, to do their inner work, and to explore where they get stopped in life and in relationships. The ability to see one's own self-imposed limitations, make a conscious choice to have it be different, be more constructive, and have a breakthrough to a new sense of self takes great courage. Nearly everyone who has gone on this journey has found great value in discovering new insights about themselves, new facets of their character, and new perspectives on their behavior and how they want to work with others.

The collaborative leadership journey is a gift to yourself, a commitment you make to look at all aspects of your values, assumptions, expectations, and behaviors. It is not a one-time event. It is a journey for life, a journey of continuous learning, growth and development. But what is this journey?

Defining the Collaborative Leadership Journey

This coaching journey was inspired in the 1990s by my sponsor at DuPont, Steven T. Miller, who as an engineering leader went on this journey himself. Together we discovered the critical steps in the process. About the same time, Stephen Covey published *The 7 Habits of Highly Effective People,*[9] which introduced us to the idea of an "inside-out" journey to discover our character, values and principles that shape our lives. That is where the collaborative leadership journey begins. Miller helped me understand the critical importance of applying your values and principles to every aspect of your life, both at work and at home. From there, I integrated key elements of 360 degree feedback, the outplacement coaching process, and the fundamentals of interpersonal relations into the process. Based on this work, this journey is defined as follows:

> An inside-out journey of self-discovery, self-awareness, and reflection that helps you define who you are as a human being and a professional, what you believe in, what you value, why you are here on this planet, and where you choose to go with the rest of your life. It is about your self-esteem, sense of self-worth, and the ground you stand on. It is a journey with no destination, but is about lifelong learning, growth, and development.

There are 5 key dimensions of the journey essential for its success:

- **Inside-Out and Self-Discovery:** Who we are, our assumptions, beliefs, values, attitudes and behaviors toward others all come from inside of us. They are based on what our family valued, how we grew up, our education, and our life experiences. The inside-out dimension of this journey offers an opportunity to take control of our lives, to accept the fact that we are in charge of who we are, in spite of what has happened to us in our lives.
- **Self-Awareness:** What kinds of impacts are we having on people around us? How do we know? Knowing our impact on others is essential to our ability to

show empathy toward them and to demonstrate our emotional intelligence so central to collaborative leadership. As Jeff Bezos, CEO of Amazon, has said, "Your brand (reputation) is what others say about you when you're not in the room."[10] One way of discovering our impact on others is understanding our leadership style, which can be discovered using instruments like the Myers-Briggs Type Indicator (MBTI), which is based on the groundbreaking work of Carl Jung.[11] Another helpful way to learn what others think about us is 360 degree feedback. Beyond the data, there are a number of questions for you on this journey: What are you going to do with it? What changes can you make? What changes are you willing to make? How will you go about that? What actions will you take by when? What kind of support do you need?

- **Reflection:** Without reflection, we may be subject to being reactive, constantly dealing with what is happening to us. We are often not consciously acting based on what we want to have happen in our lives, but more based on survival, pleasing others, or getting that next promotion. Without reflection, we are more susceptible to organizational politics, rather than operating on principle. Reflection involves quiet time alone, giving ourselves the opportunity to feel, think, and understand what is happening in our lives and how we can proactively address it. Reflection gives us the space to consider, understand, and choose if and how we want to respond. Reflection shifts us from reaction to being "response-able" professionals.

- **Getting Grounded:** All of this work helps us get grounded, to know who we are, why we are here on this planet, and how we want to work with others. Getting grounded happens especially through the daily practice of reflection. It is not just in times of uncertainty. It is every single day. Leaders who have high self-esteem, self-confidence, excellent relationships with others, and are doing superb work are grounded. They have done their inner work and are continuing to do it as they evolve and grow.

- **Conscious Choices:** If I am doing my work from the inside-out and am reflective, I will make more conscious choices about my work and life, about how I work with others, and how I collaborate as a leader. *Conscious* means I am aware of and knowledgeable about my values, ethics, beliefs, and attitudes and will behave accordingly. *Choice* is a decision I make in how to respond or behave toward others.

Is the View Worth the Climb?

Once a client asked me, "Is the view worth the climb? It sounds like a lot of work. What am I going to have to give up? What's the payoff?" I hesitated to answer the question because he was already doing his work. He was seeing the need to invest time, that perhaps assumptions he'd been working under were going to get called into question, and that he might have to change some of his behaviors. What was also especially interesting was that these very questions suggested his mindset, that this was an event, something he could buy with an investment of time. "I guess I need to get fixed," the CEO of a biomedical company said to me recently. This journey is not about getting fixed or giving things up. It is about revealing who you are, your strengths, challenges, and the opportunities you have to make conscious choices you control. You actually discover your true, authentic self. You get to open up and go on what Senge calls a journey of lifelong learning.[12] That is a view worth the climb.

There are 5 other benefits from this work:

- **Self-Esteem and Self-Confidence:** The journey not only increases self-awareness but also provides the foundation for your self-esteem, your core sense of who you are as a person. This in turn builds your self-confidence, which leads to more positive and collaborative relationships both at work and at home.
- **Empathy and Self-Regulation:** Because of the inside-out work and increased self-awareness, empathy toward others and the ability to self-regulate will be substantially increased.
- **Clarity of Direction:** This journey clarifies one's personal vision and mission, why we are on this planet, and a strategy for realizing hopes and dreams.
- **Humility:** We have learned that Level 5 Leadership is a combination of personal humility and professional resolve.[13] This journey will provide a sense of calm and self-acceptance, which in turn provides inner peace, leading to a level of humility that empowers others. This journey also results in a fierce resolve to achieve one's vision and mission through others, as well as persistence in the face of adversity.
- **Personal Mastery:** Making this a lifelong journey of personal and professional growth and development is about achieving what Senge calls personal mastery.[14] In collaborative leadership, personal mastery is when you arrive at the highest level of competence in the attributes, behaviors, and roles of collaborative leaders. It means coaching and mentoring others and empowering them to be more collaborative. It is about service to others and helping to save the planet.

WHO BECOMES A COLLABORATIVE LEADER

Collaborative leadership is not for everyone. For some it makes perfect sense or is the result of an event in their lives that has caused them to reevaluate what is important. For others, especially those tied to the Power Paradigm, it is a far more difficult choice. Here are several types of leaders who do not see collaborative leadership as their future.

Leaders Who Do *Not* Want to Become Collaborative

There are a number of leaders for whom collaboration is not a preference or a choice.

- **The Controller:** "I have worked hard for 20 years to get where I am now, I played by the rules of hierarchy, so why should I change now?" I have frequently heard this refrain. It is true most leaders of organizations grew up in the embrace of the Power Paradigm. It was the system they learned, the system in which they were developed and promoted. They like being in control and having the power, and for most of them, it is highly likely that, unless their organizations make a cultural transformation, they will not choose to become collaborative.
- **The Narcissist:** There are leaders for whom leadership is "all about me." They are climbers and don't care who they hurt on the way up. They are controllers, accumulate formal power, and know how to play organizational politics to get ahead. To become a collaborative leader means they would have to focus on "We" rather than "I," which threatens their power.
- **The Star:** There are leaders who are brought into an organization because of their star power or recognition in their field. These leaders will continue the behavior that made them successful up to this point, at the expense of others. To become a collaborative leader means sharing the adulation.
- **The Heroic Leader:** There are leaders who have to "save the day" and be the hero. They want to look good. This is more "I" behavior, which by definition rules out collaboration. Sometimes these leaders will start organizational "fires," crises that create drama and trauma in the organization, fires that only the heroic leader can put out. Collaboration is a threat to their power, so they snuff out any attempts to move toward this way of working.
- **The Reluctant Leader:** Some leaders are extremely introverted and shy, and even though they are respected by others across the organization for their technical and people skills and are urged to take a leadership role, they demure. Collaboration is how they naturally work, but they do not want to be a leader and will resist efforts to be promoted.
- **The Dissenter:** There are leaders who may choose not to consider taking this journey because they disagree with the belief system, values, or goals. They believe that "I" is more important than "We", that competition yields the best results even if it pits people against each other, and that collaboration is really "group think," where you lose your identity. Collaborative leadership is out of the question.
- **The Threatened:** Others harbor the belief that collaboration is simply "touchy-feely" stuff, even though building trust is some of the hardest work we can do. They often refer to it as "Kumbaya" moments, where people hold hands and hug each other. This derisive view of people who collaborate is often held by people who may be uncomfortable with their own feelings, feel insecure, and fear that collaboration will require them to be vulnerable. Collaborative leadership is out

of the question because it would require them to reflect, become self-aware, and see the impact of their behavior on others.

- **The Unwilling:** There are leaders who do not want to go on this journey because they have had a bad experience with a "program-of-the-month" that was called "collaboration." This experience so soured them on any other approach to collaboration that they have chosen not to have anything to do with it.

Leaders Who *Want* to Become a Collaborative Leader

Most people who seriously consider a shift in how they lead rarely do so because they woke up one morning and said, "Today I think I will transform my leadership philosophy." Usually, there is some significant event or series of events in their personal life or that of their organization that punctuate the necessity for a dramatic change. Some people begin the journey out of a genuine desire to try a new approach to leading and managing. Still others see the trends and recognize the new realities and, either out of altruism, good sense, or survival, actively seek out collaborative leadership.

Let's remember our definition of collaborative leadership from Chapter 4:

> *Collaborative leadership is an ethical, principle-based philosophy of service that builds a leadership culture of psychological safety, ownership, and trust that empowers the workforce to be their best selves so they can do their best work and produce superior results.*

There are six types of leaders who do want to take this journey:

- **The Millennial:** Fully 75% of the global workforce will be Millennials by the year 2025.[15] Collaboration and teamwork are how they have gone through school and how they prefer to work. They want a constructive/collaborative leadership culture, and if they do not find one, they will likely move to a different culture or start up a new venture. For this generation, the journey is a natural process, and one where they appreciate the opportunity to reflect on themselves and the development of their own brand.
- **The Futurist:** There are leaders who see the future and want to be sure they are prepared to lead in it. They find collaborative leadership as a natural and preferred way to work and want to go on their inside-out journey to fully develop their values, vision, mission, and behaviors.
- **The Legacy Leader:** There are leaders who are five to ten years away from retirement and want to leave a legacy of positive human relationships. They were raised in the "old school" of power-based leadership and have made a number of adjustments in their own style. They are now at a level in the organization, and at a point in their careers, that they can influence significant change in the culture and how people work together. They see the collaborative leadership journey as a way to discover and clarify their true, authentic self and the way they have always preferred to lead.

- **The Transformer:** This type of leader has had what can be called a significant personal emotional event that causes the person to reevaluate what is important in his or her life. These leaders consciously decide to make a rather abrupt and immediate change in how they lead in the future. They are most receptive to beginning the collaborative leadership journey.
- **The Pragmatist:** The pragmatist has risen through the ranks of formal power, is very reluctant to give it up, but sees the future's handwriting on the wall. Pragmatists are frustrated with the slowness of hierarchy and decide to experiment with other approaches. When none of these really work, they do some reading and research and realize that collaboration is the way they need to lead, decide to get an executive coach, and take the journey.
- **The Traditionalist:** The traditionalist is the least willing to try leading collaboratively. These leaders like things the way they are. They are conservers and rule followers, or they simply resist what they consider to be the latest "fad." They find themselves, however, in a rapidly changing work environment and do not know what to do. They receive encouragement from others to take the journey. They resist. And then something big happens at work—a Millennial is made their supervisor, or they are merged into a company with a more collaborative culture. After months of consideration, they decide to try the process. Their prospects for success are not very high, given their reluctance and resistance, but at least they have tried and may find value in what they learn about themselves.

Significant Personal Emotional Events: A Catalyst for Change

We noted transformers above as individuals who, as a result of a significant personal emotional event, consciously decide to make the shift to collaborative leadership. It is an emotional decision based on something that has happened to them to cause them to reevaluate who they are and what matters to them in life.

I recall one of my early coachees was Arthur, the chief operations officer of a midwestern manufacturing company. He had been at the company for 25 years and was well known for his rather intimidating command-and-control way of leading. When his direct reports went into his office during budget season, the word was that they better be more prepared than Arthur, or he would chew them out and send them back to the drawing boards to redo their budgets. On the shop floor, when Arthur showed up, everyone stopped working to see what he was going to say or do, similar to the early Ralph Stayer. They watched his every move—was he scowling, smiling, or sullen—and prayed that there was nothing wrong. He was known to fire people on the spot if they couldn't answer his questions. Arthur was particularly feared because he had started his career on the shop floor and knew all the tricks of the trade.

It was June, and the company was in the height of its production cycle. Business was good, and efficient operations were essential if they were going to meet the demand. Arthur got a call on Tuesday afternoon of the first week only to be told by his wife that his only son had died in an automobile accident. Arthur was extremely close with his son and was hoping that upon graduation from college, his son would join the company. Arthur rushed out of the plant and went home, not to return for two weeks. His heart was broken and his spirit crushed. He felt like his life had ended. During that two weeks, he spent a lot of time at the lake where he and his son had fished and camped, remembering those times together, weeping, and in utter despair about how he was going to move forward.

Inexorably, as he camped and fished, he began to regain his footing, and his thoughts turned to his workforce. He knew from his direct reports that things were going well back at the plant. They were doing fine without him. And that caused him to start asking some very basic questions about how he had treated his workforce. He realized that he didn't need to control them; he needed to trust them. He realized that his micromanagement and disrespect toward them was now unacceptable, and that he was going to change that behavior immediately. He also realized that his workforce was deeply unhappy, and that their unhappiness was also unacceptable. Life could be snuffed out at any second, and people needed to be honored every minute they were alive. He called up an executive coach and decided to begin his journey to collaborative leadership in earnest.

There are all kinds of significant personal emotional events, ranging from what Arthur experienced to a major health crisis like a heart attack, a stroke, or curable cancer, to a divorce, to being fired from a top-level position, or to the failure of a business. Bill George has called these "crucible moments."[6] Each of these events invokes a serious exploration of what is most important in life. Death, loss, failure, and brokenness are powerful forces for change in our lives. If we heed their call, we can turn our lives around. If we don't, they may happen again.

In observing individuals who have come through their significant event to the other side, and have taken their journey, I have observed some similar behaviors. Because they had a death or near-death experience, they took a hard look at themselves, their values, and their behaviors. They became more self-aware and spiritual. They tended to be less self-centered, less ego driven, and less concerned about control. They were focused on doing what was best for the workforce and the organization. They became more facilitative, engaging, dedicated to increasing ownership, and focused on work-life balance. Because of their experience, they had more empathy toward others and cared about making sure that they had the highest quality of work life possible.

SIX CHALLENGES IN BECOMING A COLLABORATIVE LEADER

You can choose to go on the collaborative leadership journey whether or not you have had a significant personal emotional event. You can choose to take the journey because you want to discover your authentic self, get grounded, or strengthen your ability to work with others. It is important, though, to go into the process with your eyes open.

There are some of the challenges other leaders have had to work on as they took this journey. I share these not to dissuade you from your own work, but to be transparent about the realities some have encountered. We know that nothing worth having is easy. If you want to be an Olympic champion in skiing, running, skating, or other sport, you begin practicing when you are six or seven years old. You make extraordinary sacrifices, focusing only on school and practice. Ten to 15 years later, if you haven't washed out, you may get your first opportunity to compete on the world stage. This journey is about you becoming the champion of your own life so that you can engage others self-confidently at work, home, or in your community.

While this journey may not be like training for the Olympics, it does require a high level of commitment, ongoing reflection, an openness to feedback from others, and lifelong learning. It is a journey without a destination other than realizing your full, authentic potential as a human being and professional. This journey is your inside-out work, work that helps you clarify your assumptions, beliefs, values, vision, mission, and legacy that will make you the truest version of yourself so that you can do your best work.

Every journey we take in life, whether it is across the country or to another part of the world, will experience roadblocks, barriers, or unforeseen challenges. We go on these journeys because we believe that they are worth the investment, just as years of practice is worth the chance to become an Olympic champion. In the collaborative leadership journey, the question is whether the results are worth the time and effort you invest. Is it worth making detours around the roadblocks, surmounting the barriers, and meeting the challenges head-on? Ultimately it is up to you to consciously decide to take it. In my experience nearly everyone who has taken this journey has typically said, "Why did I wait so long?"

Here are six critical challenges you may encounter on your journey. Each of them is described, as well as how it is addressed on your journey and what the potential outcomes are as a result of your work.

1. Personal History—From Reaction to Pro-Action

The Challenge: Each one of us has a set of assumptions and beliefs that are the beginning point for how we think about our role as a leader, how we behave, and how we treat others. These assumptions and beliefs are deeply rooted in how we were brought up, our education, and our life experiences. We have each been exposed to different behaviors and treatment and one degree or another of dysfunction, which helped shape our level of self-esteem or self-doubt. Whether we like it or not, we bring the consequences of that upbringing into how we view and work with others. We have different ideas about what is important at work, the value of people, the value of product, and the significance of process. Each of us has been educated differently, and bring different perspectives, philosophies, and paradigms about business to the table. We have also had different work life experiences, which affect how we behave toward others.

The reason our personal history is the first challenge on this journey is that to become a more collaborative leader we first need to be aware of and understand where we came from and the forces that shaped who we are, not as a story that is descriptive, as interesting as that may be, but as a way to explain who we are now and how we got to the assumptions, beliefs, and values that have helped form how we work with others. How were you treated by your parents? How were you taught to treat others at school or in the community? How were you held accountable when you did something we weren't supposed to? Were you supported or left on your own to handle difficult situations that arose?

These factors, along with your education and life experiences, help shape our self-esteem, identity, and sense of self, our level of security or insecurity, whether we need to be in more or less control of situations and people you work with, whether we have a need for power or not, whether we are driven to climb the corporate ladder or not, whether we are motivated by fear or trust, and whether we are reactive of proactive in work situations.

The Journey: The collaborative leadership journey provides an opportunity for you to explore your personal history for the purpose of understanding the source(s) of what drives, motivates, inspires, and frightens you. Have you had a significant personal emotional event that shaped who you are now? What is your passion in life, and where did it come from? What is your level of need for power, control, or authority in a work relationship, and why?

The Outcomes: On this journey, you will identify, consider, write down, and reflect on these and other questions, with the outcome being a clear statement about your assumptions, beliefs, and values about people at work, what motivates them, what builds trust, the role of respect and integrity in work relationships so that they can be their best selves, do their best work, and produce superior results. Another outcome is increased self-confidence, because you know where you came from and get to consciously choose how you wish to work with others.

2. Shifting Mindsets—From Power to Collaboration

The Challenge: The core challenge in the mindset shift is to move from hierarchical thinking that is embedded in us to collaborative thinking, the 4th Evolution. Old habits die hard. Hierarchical thinking is deeply embedded in how we have been educated and socialized, how we have come to view ourselves in an organizational setting, and how we get ahead in the world. We have described the Power Paradigm and hierarchical mind-set as the predominant leadership culture in most organizations. It is hard to escape. Senge talks about it, in the context of work he did with Chris Argyris, when he described the "the basic diseases of hierarchy" in *The Fifth Discipline,* which include an authoritarian organization that creates dependence, decision-making based on bureaucratic politics where the name of the game is getting ahead by making an impression, teams who practice skilled incompetence, blaming and shaming others for your mistakes, and basic mechanistic thinking.[17]

The Journey: It is difficult to escape this mental and behavioral model and change your assumptions, beliefs, values, behaviors, and leadership style. It can even be painful to try if you are working in a hierarchical organization. The collaborative leadership journey affords you an opportunity to see the impact of a power-based leadership style on others through 360 feedback. Your peers, direct reports, and possibly even your superiors will tell you how you are coming across, what impact your behavior is having them, how you are viewed, and whether you are effective. You get to clarify your core values, set your personal vision and mission, and see whether the ways you have been behaving toward others is how you now want to behave. Are your current 360 behaviors aligned with those values and your personal vision? How do you want to be viewed? What is the kind of work impact you want to have, and can you get there behaving the way you have been? Then you get to make a conscious choice about the direction you will take, in spite of where you work.

The Outcomes: I recall a senior leader at a leading consumer products company who read the chapter on collaborative leadership in my first book, *Transforming the Way We Work*,[18] followed the steps in the journey, and decided to leave the company and start her own business. Years later she wrote to tell me it was the best decision she had ever made. Even though she didn't make as much money, she said that for the first time in her life, she could be her authentic, genuine self and could sleep peacefully at night. Perhaps the most significant outcome of the journey is finding your true self. By opening up to feedback from those you work with, you get to choose to align how you work with your values, vision, and mission. You get to make a choice about the importance of healthy, collaborative relationships in your work life, rather than dominating and controlling others to get results. You come to understand that domination and control merely breed resistance, dependence and hostility, while a focus on relationships, support, and service increases influence, interdependence, and productive energy.

3. Ego and Arrogance—From Self to Self-Less

The Challenge: Perhaps one of the greatest challenges leaders face in making the transition from the need for power to the empowerment that comes from collaboration is to deal with their ego and sometimes their arrogance. Ego strength is essential for success in any organization. But it is of at least two kinds; one enables you to stand tall and strong for yourself and others and reflects positive self-confidence. The other type is negative and arrogant, where the world should revolve around me, myself, and I. "I am the smartest person in the room." "I have the knowledge, skills, and insights necessary to ensure our success." "I have the title, the power, and I am going to use them." For them it is about status, prestige, power, and position. We've all encountered people like this who claim to be leaders, but they disempower those around them, often hire "weaker" people so they can shine, and need to be the hero who saves the day when the organization has a problem. They are viewed as arrogant, self-centered, and political. The difficulty with ego and arrogance is that it often finds its origin in personal insecurity. Ego and arrogance are often compensatory behavior for low self-esteem and low self-confidence.

The Journey: For this type of leader, the shift to self-less leadership is difficult. It requires looking in the mirror and being brutally honest with themselves. With the collaborative leadership journey, the leader becomes aware of how they are perceived. They have coaching support to help them get to acknowledgement and acceptance of how they are behaving. The next step is taking full responsibility for their behavior and the impacts they are having on others. Again, coaching support is invaluable as the leader goes through this work. In some instances, being self-accountable and making amends to others are the essential next steps so that the leader can shift how others perceive them, especially among those who have been hurt by ego-driven, arrogant behavior. Once this is done, the leader is on the way to embracing a new way of being and working with others in the form of collaborative behavior.

The Outcomes: There are enormous rewards for the leader who chooses to work through these steps, not the least of which is high credibility with others and a more grounded sense of self. They choose to become more humble, connect with others and build trust-based relationships, and be self-less and of service to others. In serving others they build independence and interdependence among others, thereby gaining a type of influence. The self-less leader leads by principle, not politics or power. What matters is ownership, trust, and empowerment. They know that wolves lead their packs from behind, that geese fly in pairs and rotate the job of leading the flock, and learn the power of Lao Tzu's statement about those they work with, saying "we did it ourselves."

4. Power—From Control to Ownership

The Challenge: In the Power Paradigm, leaders use their authority to control what the workforce does and how they do it. We have seen that this approach is the predominant way in which most organizations are led, in spite of 21st Century realities. We have also seen that certain types of leaders need formal power and control to meet their personal needs, regardless of their impact on others. Formal power is something these leaders have. Control is something they do to others, often with very negative consequences. At work, power and control leaders are the funnel for decisions; control access of managers to key stakeholders; control the flow of critical business information; get too involved in the tactical and operational aspects of the organization; delegate, blame and shame others for their mistakes; and get angry when challenged.

The irony is that control is actually just an illusion. Productive energy is what the workforce *chooses* to give the organization. When the people feel controlled or micromanaged by their boss, productive energy goes down. It will increase the more they respect their leaders, feel trusted to do their jobs, and have ownership. There is no such thing as true control, just influence and motivation based on mutual respect.

The Journey: Leaders who believe they need formal power, authority, and control to get the job done have a challenging journey ahead of them. The steps include increase awareness through 360 feedback acknowledgement and acceptance with coaching support, taking responsibility, being self-accountable, and making amends. To truly make the shift to more collaborative leadership, two things need to happen. The first is to *let go*, which means letting go of the notion that success is about moving up the ladder; checking their assumptions, beliefs, and values about what motivates the workforce; building self-trust so that they can trust others to do their work; and taking more risks, learning new ways to work in groups and make decisions that rely on consensus rather than individual opinion.

If we cannot let go of the Power Paradigm, we cannot become collaborative. If we cling to power, we cannot empower others, and will eventually lose it. If we do not engage others in the critical decisions that affect the organization, we will lose all credibility.

The second thing that needs to happen is to *give up* the idea that power, authority, and control in the 21st Century are the most effective way to lead and manage. This means realizing that the only power leaders have is that which the workforce gives to them in the form of credibility, respect, and hard work. It means that in the 21st Century, leadership is through influence, facilitation, and service, not giving orders.

The Outcomes: When leaders have truly let go and given up the belief that power, control, and authority are the best way to lead, they open up potential for their own growth and development as a human being and professional. They unshackle themselves from assumptions that put distance between people, beliefs that undermine their own credibility, and values that are no longer relevant or appropriate in the 21st Century. By opening up to collaborative leadership, they can realize the full potential of the workforce through ownership, full engagement, and the creation of a collaborative leadership culture that empowers the human spirit.

5. Motivation—From Fear to Trust

The Challenge: Fear is one of the most powerful forces driving behavior in the workforce. They are afraid of getting fired, being written up or given negative feedback, losing their bonus or promotion, or making a mistake or failing. They may also be afraid of being embarrassed or humiliated or getting hurt in a relationship. All kinds of compensating behavior will be based on this complex of fears. Leaders who practice Power Paradigm leadership will operate in a way where fear is implicit, the subtext for their leadership. Fear is the predicate of the workplace culture, and it can be exacerbated by behavior seen as arrogant, insensitive, unempathetic, micromanaging, unethical, harassing, or bullying. Giving up or letting go of fear is perhaps one of the greater challenges for these leaders, because they may not know what to replace it with.

The Journey: These leaders need to understand why they need to use fear as the way they motivate, or demotivate, their workforce. Again, awareness through 360 degree feedback is an essential first step so they can then acknowledge and accept that this is how they are viewed. Second, they explore their own assumptions and beliefs about what motivates people to do their very best at work, coming to understand that fear actually creates resistance and resentment toward them. Then they explore the alternative motivator in a collaborative culture, which is trust, and explore the degree of self-trust they have. Self-trust is at the root of whether they will be able to trust others, and hence be able to let go of fear as their go-to strategy. By building trust into their vision and mission and seeing what kinds of behaviors they can show toward others, they are on the road to trust as their primary motivator.

The Outcomes: The transformation of a leader's motivators from fear to trust is truly a remarkable process. They are transformed as human beings, come from a place of abundance rather than scarcity, are appreciative and grateful toward others, see love as the basis for all positive human relationships, and view collaboration as the way they choose to lead.

6. Impatience and Reversion—From Frustration to Resilience

The Challenge: Even for the most committed, this journey can be frustrating, either because in their view it is "taking too long" or because the challenges seem insurmountable. This frustration can lead to impatience, and impatience to giving up. Giving up leads to a return to the old ways of doing things, or what I call reversion. Reversion may happen all at once; for example, when quarterly results don't meet expectations, they blame it on collaboration, and there is a demand for more control. Or it may happen a little at a time, as smaller challenges are encountered. Frustration and impatience can also happen when the leader is challenged by his or her superior, the board, or other stakeholders, as in, "Why are you doing this? What is the benefit for us as an organization?" There may be objections when one part of the organizations is working collaboratively while other parts are not. These culture wars can lead to some difficult conversations. At one Fortune 100 company I consulted with, the team was so successful with collaborative change that it got labeled "Team Alpha." They were shunned by their peers—"Who do they think they are?" When this dynamic happens, there is friction, which can result in reversion to the old way of working. The challenge for the leader on his or her collaborative journey is to withstand the pressure, to be resilient. This is merely another roadblock on the path. In the case of Team Alpha, they turned in an exceptional performance, which gave their leader a lot of latitude to make the case that collaboration was an effective way others could also explore.

The Journey: The journey from impatience and frustration to resilience and fidelity to the process is not as easy as you would think. Leaders can explore, through reflection and coaching, why it is they are getting frustrated. Is it because they have unrealistic time expectations? Is it because they would prefer to "fit in" with their peers and not buck the existing culture? Is it because they are motivated by the fear that their advancement opportunities in the organization may be negatively affected?

Leader can then go back to their personal vision, mission, and legacy to see if they are still true. If not, they may choose to modify them. If they are still true, then the conversation shifts to resilience and what it takes to have the grit and resolve, the discipline and will to see the effort through. It's a conscious choice at every step of the way.

The Outcomes: Resilience is a quality that is increasingly required to be able to navigate the turbulent waters of the 21st Century.[19] Collaborative leaders nurture this ability almost as a habit, knowing that it is grounded in what they believe, their values, vision, and mission. They will find this resolve in remembering their passion for their mission and realizing that temporal or transactional events will pass, but the longer arc of their actions will impact the rest of their professional careers and their reputations. Collaborative leaders do not cut and run or collapse when the going gets tough. They listen, observe, reflect, and redouble their efforts. Collaborative leaders never ever give up.

By way of summary, Table 5.1 presents the essence of the shift that is required to move from the power to the Collaboration Paradigm:

TABLE 5.1 *The Shift from the Power to the Collaboration Paradigm of Leadership*

DIMENSION	SHIFTING FROM POWER	TO COLLABORATIVE LEADERSHIP
PERSONAL HISTORY	Reaction	Pro-Action
SHIFTING MINDSETS	Power	Collaboration
EGO AND ARROGANCE	Self	Self-Less
POWER	Control	Ownership
MOTIVATION	Fear	Trust
DISCOUNTING AND DENIAL	Resistance	Acceptance
IMPATIENCE AND REVERSION	Frustration	Resilience

10 STEPS IN THE COLLABORATIVE LEADERSHIP JOURNEY

The ability to make effective choices and live an authentic life depends to a great extent on a capacity to be self-reflective. Self-awareness is the greatest asset people have for living fulfilling lives that provide a sense of direction and influence over what happens to them. If people do not understand their own feelings, fears, values, intentions, and patterns of behaviors, their lives can be like corks bobbing on the ocean.

—James W. Tamm and Ronald J. Luyet, *Radical Collaboration*[20]

The journey begins in a way that you can make effective choices and live an authentic life because you took the time to reflect, listen, and learn about who you truly are. It is from this exploration of your inner workings that you will define the ground you stand on. The act of reflection, in and of itself, can be the most significant think anyone can do to understand themselves better, to learn and grow so that their lives have meaning and their purpose is fulfilled.

There are ten steps in this journey, which generate a tremendous amount of data and insight so that you can craft your purpose, core values, mission, vision, and legacy (see figure 5.2). The steps are sequential. Throughout the process, reflect on what you have learned about you. Journal, explore, and if needed, get coaching support from someone who is certified by the International Coach Federation (ICF). Let's begin.

Step 1: Making a Conscious Choice

The first step is to make a conscious choice to begin the journey. Go into this process with your eyes wide open. Making a conscious choice to go on this journey means:

- Understanding what collaboration is all about and that this reflects the type of leader you would like to be
- Making a full commitment to this process, and staying the course is an investment in yourself that will have returns for the rest of your life

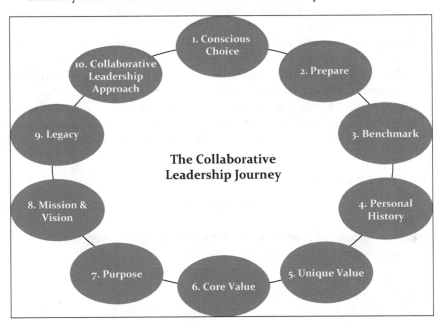

FIGURE 5.2 The Collaborative Leadership Journey.

- Looking in the mirror and being willing to tell yourself the unvarnished truth
- Having the highest level of personal integrity as you explore each dimension of who you are and how you will choose to lead
- Taking a leap of faith to become collaborative based on a fundamental belief in yourself
- Letting go of the past and crafting a new future that reflects your authentic self

Here is a select list of questions you might want to ask yourself as you ponder this choice:

- **Reflection:** Am I willing to regularly reflect on my behaviors, feelings, impacts on others, and other aspects of this journey? Am I willing to receive feedback from others, even if it is not what I want to hear or which may challenge my assumptions?
- **Your Leadership Paradigm:** How aligned am I with the Collaboration Paradigm of leadership? Am I prepared to make the shift from where I am now to become more collaborative? Do I have a passion to serve and support others, and to build relationships?
- **Character/Attributes:** Am I willing to tell myself the truth about my personal history and my assumptions and beliefs about people in the workplace? Do I know what my core values are? Do I want to clarify what my ethics are and create my moral compass? Do I want to build self-trust so that I can strengthen trust-based relationships at work?
- **Behaviors:** Am I prepared to practice collaborative behaviors and have a constructive impact on the lives of people I work with?
- **Roles:** Which collaborative leadership roles am I best suited to play right now? Which ones do I want to learn so that I can be more effective as a leader?
- **My Choice:** What do I see as the payoff/benefits for me to take this journey? What are the risks? If I begin it, I am prepared to continue it, or will the first challenge I encounter knock me off my stride? What will it take for me to succeed?

Actions You Can Take:

- Review Chapters 3 and 4 to understand what collaboration and collaborative leadership are.
- Review the questions above to see if this is a journey you wish to take.
- Make your decision and then celebrate yourself.

Step 2: Preparing for My Journey

If we're traveling to another country, we take time to plan for it, get our shots, renew our passports, and anticipate unforeseen circumstances. The same is true for this journey. Get prepared. Follow these steps. Hire a professional coach who is trained and skilled in the art, and get a journal where you can record your reflections during and after these ten steps. Whether your journal is paper or digital, it is important that you have a confidential place where you can record your most personal thoughts and feelings. A way of thinking about journaling and the reflective process is to find a time (15–45 minutes) during the day or week that best works for you, locate a quiet place where you will not be disturbed, and religiously go there. This may be a new habit, and like any new exercise, practice makes perfect. Make sure this time is sacrosanct, that you are not interrupted. Turn off all digital devices. Practice regularly.

Actions You Can Take

- Pick up a journal for your reflections, or create a secure space on your computer where you can record your thoughts.
- Identify where and when you will do your reflecting, preferably once a day or at least once a week.
- Identify an ICF-certified coach or someone who is objective, a mentor, and who will support and challenge you as you go through this process.

Step 3: Benchmarking My Leadership Style, Skills, and Behavior

The next step is to benchmark where you are in terms of your leadership style, your skills, and how others perceive you.

- **Discovering Your Leadership Style:** There are any number of tests you can take to determine your leadership style, but one of the most often used is the MBTI personality inventory. Based on the work of Swiss psychiatrist Carl Jung (1875–1961), the MBTI was developed by Isabel Briggs Myers and her mother, Katherine Briggs, in the 1940s.[21] The purpose of the MBTI was to make Jung's theory useful to people, a theory that basically says seemingly random behavior is actually quite orderly and consistent, and that there are basic differences between people based on their preferences.[22] There are 16 different personality types that are differentiated by these preferences: (1) Extrovert/Introvert, (2) Intuitive/Sensing, (3) Thinking/Feeling, and (4) Judging/Perceiving. Based on your preferences, which are determined by your answers to the questions asked in the MBTI instrument, you are assigned a letter in each pairing. There are also varying strengths of one's preferences. There is no right or wrong preference, merely different types, with the idea being that if we can shift from judging others because of their behaviors to understanding their type, we can strengthen our relationships with them by adapting and being more flexible. Like Robert Cooke's work on leadership cultures, the MBTI instrument has been proven to be statistically valid and reliable, and literally millions of people around the world have taken the instrument since it was first published in 1962.

FIGURE 5.3 The Enneagram.

Another instrument found to be helpful is called the *Enneagram*, which is a synthesis of a number of "ancient wisdom traditions" put together by Oscar Ichazo from Latin America into a system of nine different leadership styles, each with nine levels of an individual's development over time.[23] (See Figure 5.3.)

The Enneagram instrument is designed to increase self-awareness and understanding of both yourself and others. The nine different points on the circle represent distinct strategies, patterns of thinking, feeling, and acting that arise for a deeper, inner worldview. It is intended to help us become more successful in all of our relationships and understand ourselves and others better. In addition, "by identifying the psychological and emotional defenses specific to our type, the Enneagram creates opportunities for profound personal growth and healing."[24]

In my coaching experience, you can think of MBTI as your preferences and type at a single point in time, like an EKG gives you a reading on your heart; but the Enneagram reflects your entire life. When both are used as part of the style analysis, you have a powerful, validated sense of how you work best with others. They also strengthen your emotional intelligence by providing insight into how others work, how they make decisions, handle differences and conflicts, and what their preferences are for how to work with others.

- **Skills Assessment:** What are your strongest skills? Do you excel in working with teams? Or is it technical knowledge applied to a process or product? In a section of your journal, create a sheet for each of the following items: work, school, family, religion, social, community, political, financial, athletic, and cultural. On each sheet, in five-year increments, write down your specific accomplishments—things you actually did. For example, in the 15–20 age bracket under education, receiving Phi Beta Kappa would be a major achievement. These are things you have actually done, not feelings you had or things you think you should be able to do. These are concrete, specific accomplishments. It is your lifetime vitae in every aspect of your life. The reason for this assessment is to help build your actual skills competencies, which are part of your foundation, the ground you stand on, and contribute to your sense of self. Another reason is that shortly you will compare them against the list of skills needed for collaborative leadership.

Allow yourself some time to complete this step. It is often difficult to remember everything you did, so ask family and friends to help you remember. Once you have completed this diagnostic, look for patterns across the years and translate them into specific skills and competencies you have; for example, project oriented, organized, team leader, analytic, service to the community. Pull out the skills and capabilities you have that relate to the workplace.

In Chapter 4, Table 4.1, there are seven sets of principle-based collaborative behaviors, each with a specific set of skills. Match your competencies against this list of skills. Identify where there is alignment, and where there are gaps. Then prioritize the gaps based on where you have the least experience or achievements. This, then, becomes your agenda for building collaborative skills.

- **Behavioral Data—360 Degree Feedback:** To help you understand how your behaviors are perceived by others in the workplace, 360 degree feedback instruments can be used. Typically, a group of about 10 to 15 of your peers, superiors, and direct reports are asked to complete a valid and reliable instrument with anywhere from 100 to 250 questions that rate the leader on a range of behaviors. The behaviors tested will depend on the instrument used. The process is supposed to be confidential, with a report coming back to the leader with a range of scales and scores that is intended to help them understand how they are viewed by others. There are also comments made by the participants which are part of the report. They should be confidential.

  Another type of 360 is the qualitative feedback, where a trained interviewer and coach develops a set of questions to be asked of the 10 to 15 participants in a confidential interview. Interviewees are asked about the leader's strengths, their challenges, and the top issues they want the leader to work on. Once all the interviews have been conducted, that data is analyzed and summarized according to topics or issues for coaching. This is a completely confidential document. Only the issues these participants want the leader to focus on get reported out.

Once you have gathered all of this data, and have reflected on it in terms of your strengths challenges, you are now ready for the next step on your journey—understanding your personal history and the forces that have shaped you, your assumptions, beliefs, and values.

Actions You Can Take

- Take the MBTI personality test from the Myers and Briggs Foundation at https://www.myersbriggs.org/my-mbti-personality-type/take-the-mbti-instrument/. Explore the website for additional information about the MBTI.
- To interpret your results, read: David Keirsey, *Please Understand Me II: Temperament, Character, Intelligence* (Del Mar, CA: Prometheus Nemesis Book Co., 1998).
- Take the Enneagram personality test at: https://www.enneagraminstitute.com/. Navigate the site to find the test.
- To interpret your results, this book is by the people who developed the test: Don Richard Riso, Russ Hudson, *Personality Types: Using the Enneagram for Self-Discovery* (New York: Houghton Mifflin Harcourt Publishing, 1996).
- If you are already employed, ask your supervisor, human resources leader, or learning and development office for the opportunity to get 360 feedback as part of your professional development process.
- Get an ICF-certified coach to support you in interpreting all of this data.
- Actively reflect on what you have learned in your journal.
- Identify the three main things you want to work on over the next six months; set a goal and hold yourself accountable. Then take the next three things and repeat the process. Tackle only three things at a time.

Step 4: My Personal History

In this step, you get to explore your personal history in more detail to see how your upbringing has shaped your passion in life and affected how you view leadership. Each of us has a story to tell about where we came from, how we were brought up, big events that happened to us, and why we are the way we are. We have each been exposed to different behaviors and treatment which resulted in different levels of self-esteem, self-confidence, self-trust, and ability to trust others. We need to be aware of the forces that shaped who we are, not as a story that is descriptive, as interesting as that may be, but as a way to explain who we are now and how we got to our assumptions, beliefs, and values about working and leading others.

The goal of this step is to understand the source(s) of what drives, motivates, inspires, and frightens you. Have you had a significant personal emotional event that shaped who you are? What is your passion in life, and where did it come from? What is your level of need for power, control, or authority in a work relationship, and why? In this step of your journey, you get to dig deeper into your past to identify the forces that shaped who you are, and the events or life experiences that helped form your passion in life. Everyone has a passion, and in this step, we want to identify it since it is foundational for your professional career. Also, you will identify the positive forces that helped shape you, as well as those that may inhibit your success.

- **Exploring Your Past:** Here are some questions for you to consider, answer, and reflect on: How were you brought up? How did your parents raise you? What was important to them? How were you treated by your parents or your siblings? How were you taught to treat others at school or in the community? How were you held accountable when you did something you weren't supposed to do? How were you educated? Did you move around a lot? What were your parents' expectations of you? What happened when you did not meet their expectations? Who were other influential people in your life? What were key life experiences that helped you decide what you wanted to do with your life? In your journal, evaluate and reflect on what you are learning about yourself and what it all means for your approach to leadership.
- **Positive Forces:** Most of us have had positive things happen to us, positive people who have helped us see the world in an optimistic light, and experiences that have helped us move forward. Who were those people, events, and experiences that helped us think positively about ourselves and the world? Did you have a happy childhood? Was there stability and harmony in your home? Did you feel loved, honored, and respected? See if you can identify as many positive forces in your life as possible.
- **Inhibiting Forces:** Many of us were raised in families with one degree or another of dysfunction. Were you ever physically punished? Did you ever experience abuse of any kind? Did you witness abuse of any kind? Did you have any medical or health conditions that impacted your life? Were you ever bullied, harassed, or physically assaulted by students at school or others? Were you supported by your parents when this happened, or were you left to handle it yourself? Write down what you have experienced or witnessed, and how they have affected you. This step is very important because recognizing these events and acknowledging them actually empowers you. You may discover your hot buttons and where they came from. You can have great empathy for what is called your inner child, and that in turn helps you develop empathy for others.
- **Your Approach to Leadership:** For some people, this exploration can be a painful part of the process. It is critical to understand and embrace these pieces of your past that have helped shape who you are today. Based on all you have learned and reflected on, where are you now? What are your drivers? What motivates and inspires you? What are you most fearful of? What does all of this mean in terms of your assumptions and beliefs about people at work, your core values, and your approach to leadership? What does all of this mean in terms of your mission, vision, and legacy? We will explore these later in these steps.

Actions You Can Take

- In your journal, write down your life story as you have experienced it. Focus on the forces that most significantly impacted you—parents, siblings, relatives, education, medical/health, life experiences, especially the difficult ones, or spiritual experiences.

- Create a "Forces That Have Shaped Who I Am" sheet in your journal. Create two columns, "Positive Forces," and "Inhibiting Forces." Write them down, explaining what it was that happened and how it impacted you.
- Analyze what you have learned and see if you can summarize the three to seven things that most impacted you as you grew up and how they have shaped your view of the world.
- Specifically see how these people, events, and experiences shaped your assumptions about people in the workforce, your beliefs about what motivates them, your values, and your style of leadership.
- How have these people, events, and experiences shaped your views on collaboration and collaborative leadership?
- Review what you have learned with your coach or key support person.

Step 5: My Unique Gifts and Value

Each person has unique gifts that they bring to life and the workplace. This step is about discovering what they are and how they reflect the value you give to others. A gift is something that is unique to you, a talent, skill, passion, or interest that is unique to you. A gift is also something you give to others, particularly those with whom you work. It is a competency, an ability, a skill, or knowledge that you bring to the table that has special value for others.

What are your unique gifts? Is it physical, social, emotional, or intellectual? Is it focused on things, processes, or people? Is it a passion you have for a topic, issue, place, or activity that you simply have to do to feel fulfilled? Is there something you are fascinated by, curious about, or have a deep interest in, like molecular biology, entrepreneurship, climate change, or deep space that has captured your attention and your energy? Have you always been a leader of others in your life? Are you naturally intuitive? Do you have special technical expertise or special knowledge and experiences that can distinguish you? Once you have identified what your gifts are, how can they help others? What is it that you wish to bring to the workplace that can add value to the enterprise?

Actions You Can Take

- Reflect on steps 1 to 4 of this journey to help you determine where your passion is, what your innate capabilities are, where you excel, and what you are most interested in.
- Write down what your unique gifts are that you are bringing to your life and your work, and how you would like to use them to help others.

Step 6: Core Values and Moral Compass

To become a credible leader, you have to comprehend fully the deeply held beliefs—values, principles, standards, ethics, and ideals—that drive you. You have to freely and honestly choose the principles you will use to guide your decisions and actions. Then ... authentically communicate your beliefs in ways that uniquely represent who you are.

—James M. Kouzes and Barry Posner[25]

Whether for good or for ill, it is our core values and moral compass that guide us through life and inform our ethics, our beliefs, and how we treat others. This step in your journey is to give you an opportunity, after all the work you have done to this point, to choose your core values, define them, and then see how they help you create a moral compass that will guide you in life. Recall Stephen Covey's focus on building our character ethic: "There are basic principles of effective living, and that people can only experience true success and enduring happiness as they learn and integrate these principles into their basic character."[26] By identifying your core values, you will establish the foundation of how you choose to work with others. By living your values, you ensure that your work life will be governed by principle, rather than politics, power, or personality. By modeling your values to others, you build your credibility and ensure that a collaborative leadership culture is filled with integrity.

- **Self-Trust:** One of the most important core values for collaborative leadership is self-trust. It is critical because without it, it is next to impossible to trust others, and if individuals cannot do that as a leader, then they tend to revert to power, fear, and control in how they work with others. In Building *Trust at the Speed of Change,*[27] self-trust is defined as consisting of five values: self-respect, full responsibility and accountability, honor and dignity, integrity, and credibility, which are all part of the collaborative work ethic. Self-trust leads to self-confidence, and when you are confident, others you work with know it; it increases your credibility and respect with them. When you have self-trust, you will trust others to do their work, will not need to micromanage, and will empower them to be their best selves—because you are *your* best self.
- **Identify Your Core Values:** Kouzes and Posner have given us a clear set of questions about how to identify your core values:[28]

  o What do you stand for, and why?
  o What do you believe in, and why?
  o What brings you suffering, and why?
  o What makes you jump for joy, and why?
  o What keeps you awake at night, and why?
  o What is it you really care about, and why?
  o What do you want for your life, and why?

Answering these questions, in the context of all the work you have already done, will give you an idea of what is truly important to you, what you value in life. For some it is honesty and integrity, for others it is patience and persistence, while still others might say it is hard work or honor. Identify your own five to seven core values, define them, and see if they work in your own life and work. If not, reconsider them and identify values that do.

- **Create Your Personal Moral Compass:** We live in challenging ethical times, at all levels of our society, from the choices that doctors make on whether to prescribe opioid drugs, to the choices that Wall Street banks made in 2008 that resulted in the worst recession since 1929 and the Great Depression, to the corrupt practices of politicians who undermine the rule of law in American democracy, to the choices countries are not making to eliminate carbon dioxide from the atmosphere so we can save the planet from burning up. On top of that we also have global pandemics, enormous gaps in income between the super-rich and the poor, and police brutality and institutional racism—all present ethical and moral dilemmas. Leaders make choices about how to address these dilemmas based on their own moral compass.

Andrew Leigh has defined a moral compass as doing what's right, which stems from within us.[29] Kouzes and Posner talk about it in terms of moral leadership that calls us to a higher purpose:

> A personal creed gives you a point of reference for navigating the sometimes-stormy seas of organizational life. Without such a set of beliefs, your life has no rudder, and you're easily blown about by the winds of fashion. A credo that resolves competing beliefs also leads to personal integrity.[30]

In light of this, consider the elements a Personal moral compass in Table 5.2 as you develop your own. One way to bring your moral compass alive in your professional life is knowing when and how to use it. While you can look at a range of scenarios to see how it would apply, when it becomes particularly important is when your core values are challenged by an ethical dilemma. Where is your "red line," the line you will not cross no matter what; the line where you are willing to take a stand for what

TABLE 5.2 *Defining a Personal Moral Compass*

- It is based on a clear set of core values/principles.
- These values or principles are turned into specific behavior.
- Ethical behavior is a priority.
- Expectations are clear that there is ethical conduct.
- Ethical behaviors are practiced.
- There is self-accountability when ethical conduct is breached.

is right, no matter the cost? One example would be if you were an engineer at General Motors when a 57-cent switch could have prevented the loss of many lives, but leadership did nothing about it for over ten years. Or if you were the US government employee who blew the whistle on the government's failure to provide training or equipment for workers rescuing COVID-19 infected Americans in Japan to bring them home. Or what you do when the pharmaceutical company you work for increases the prices of lifesaving drugs by 500% in a year to the point that the people who need them cannot afford them. When would you take a stand even if it cost you your job? This is when you find out what you're made of and whether you truly own your values and your compass.

FIGURE 5.4 Moral Compass.

Actions You Can Take

- **Build Your Self-Trust:** Honestly answer whether you now trust yourself and why. Do you feel confident in your work and your relationships with others, and why? If so, how does it show up in others you work with? Are they highly motivated? How high is their productive energy? If not, what do you need to build it? Building and sustaining your self-trust is a key goal in this work.
- **Identify Your Core Values:** Once you have answered the questions posed by Kouzes and Posner, identify your five core values. Assess them in light of your answers to the questions above and your work in the first five steps of this journey. Then develop robust definitions for each value—definitions that are reflected in your own work and express what is most important to you. Own them.
- **Create Your Personal Moral Compass (Table 5.2):** Based on your core values, build your moral compass. Generate a set of scenarios where you can test it, ranging from minor transgressions or corner cutting in your organization, to "red line" situations as defined above. In each scenario, describe what you will do to honor your values.

Step 7: Discovering My Purpose

Man's search for meaning is the primary motivation in his [or her] life and not a "secondary rationalization" of instinctual drives. The meaning is unique and specific in that it must and can be fulfilled by him [or her] alone; only then does it achieve a significance which will satisfy his [or her] will to meaning.

—Viktor Frankl, *Man's Search for Meaning*[31]

At some point in your life, if you haven't already, you may ask yourself, "Why am I here on this planet? Why now? What is it I am supposed to be or do while I'm here?" What is your *raison d'etre*, your reason for being? Think of these questions as pointing toward your understanding of what your purpose is. As Senge points out, purpose is different from vision in the sense that purpose is a general heading, while vision is a destination; purpose is abstract, while vision is concrete; purpose is about being the best you can be, while vision is climbing Mount Everest.[32]

You may already know what your purpose is, in which case you are lucky and can move all the faster to making a difference in the lives of others. If you do not know, to get to your true purpose for being on this planet is going to take some time and a lot of reflection. It is not something that comes in a single reflection session, or in several. Often it percolates inside of you, and as you go through your life, it becomes increasingly clear. What can help are a couple questions: Based on your work so far, what are you most passionate about? What is it that drives you (e.g., empowering others, healing people, healing the planet, ridding the world of disease)? Your passion and drive are about the highest level of concerns, concerns that are emotional, that are central to who you authentically are, and that, if not part of your life, will leave you unfulfilled.

Actions You Can Take

- **Clues and Patterns:** Begin by reviewing all the work you have done already in your journal on Steps 1 to 6. Look for clues and patterns that may reveal elements of your purpose.
- **Read Viktor Frankl:** Read Viktor Frankl's book, *Man's Search for Meaning,* to see how he discovered his purpose in surviving the Nazi death camps at Auschwitz and Bergen-Belsen—a truly extraordinary story that led to his creating logotherapy as a life-deepening, existentialist therapy.
- **Identify Your Passion:** Answer the question about what drives you and what you are most passionate about, the thing that if you could not do it for the rest of your life, you would not find yourself fulfilled.
- **Reflect:** In your reflections keep this question top of mind and continue to write about it.
- **Be Patient:** It will come to you.

Step 8: My Mission and Vision

You go in the direction of your most dominant thought. Choose wisely for it is likely to come true.

—Edward M. Marshall, Ph.D.

You have explored your personal history, defined your core values, and written down you moral compass. You have pondered your life's purpose for why you are here on the planet, though you may not have an answer to it. Continue this journey with this step, because formulating your personal mission and vision statements may actually help you understand your purpose. It's an interactive and integrative process.

- **Your Personal Mission Statement:** Leadership teams will spend weeks developing their mission statements, but most of us do not have one. Your personal mission statement says who you are, what you do, who you serve, and next to your life's purpose, provides the next level down of clarity about what you're up to while on this planet. If your life's purpose is strategic, your mission is how you're going to realize it. Here is an example of a professional's mission statement:

  > *As a biomedical engineer, my mission is to heal the planet by creating lifesaving nanotechnologies that can cure cancer.*

- **Your Vision Statement:** Remember Senge's articulation of several characteristics of visions as being a destination, a picture of the future, concrete, and a significant goal like climbing Mount Everest.[33] Your vision can be both personal and professional, and typically has a ten-plus-year time frame, where your mission statement reflects your life's work and is long term. Vision statements can be renewed and upgraded as you go through your professional life. What is the concrete, major things you want to accomplish? Is it climbing Mount Everest? Or is it climbing the tallest peaks on each of seven continents? What is the purpose of doing either? How does this vision align with your mission, your life's purpose, and your passion? In our biomedical example, is your vision to cure all cancers, or is it the most aggressive cancer, or the one that kills the most people? Our engineer could write his vision this way:

  > *As a biomedical engineer, my vision is to provide cures to colon, pancreatic, and liver cancer within the next 15 years.*

At the end of the day, or the end of your life, how you have worked to realize your vision(s) will define your reputation and your legacy.

Action Steps You Can Take

- **Develop Your Mission Statement:**
  - Given your personal history, core values, and purpose, define your mission statement as who you are, what you do, and who you serve. Why is this your mission? What is important is that you capture the essence of your life's work.

- ○ Continue to refine it to the point that it is one to three sentences long; the shorter the better. For example, my mission statement is "To empower my students to be their best selves so they can do their best work."
- **Create Your Vision Statement:** Building on your mission statement, what is the concrete achievement you wish to make in the next ten years? It is not about whether it is realistic; it is about whether it truly matters.

Step 9: My Legacy

You are almost there. The last step before defining your new approach to leadership is articulating your legacy. This is what you leave behind when you depart this earth. It is what you are giving to others. For example, the biomedical engineer who achieves his or her mission and vision will have cured several kinds of cancer and further developed nanotechnologies so that they can be applied to other types of cancer, truly healing the planet. When Thomas Edison completed his 10,000th experiment and the result was the lightbulb, little did he know what his legacy would be—an electrified world. Sometimes we don't know what our legacies will be, so what we can do is chart a course using our values, purpose, mission, and vision that reflects who we authentically are and leaves the world a better place for our having been here.

Action Steps You Can Take

- **Define Your Legacy:** Articulating your legacy is not like crafting your mission or vision, though both of those clearly contribute to it. Legacy is not straight-line thinking. It's more organic. Edison was not sure he would electrify the world, just like Alexander Graham Bell did not realize iPhones would inhabit every corner of the planet. We don't always know what our legacy is going to be. We can't force it.
- **Determine Your Contribution:** You can consider the direction that your values, purpose, mission, and vision are taking you, and reflect on where you would like that to lead in terms of contributions you might make.
- **It Takes Time:** Realize that legacy work is organic and evolutionary and may take time to be revealed as you work toward it your entire professional life.

Step 10: My New Approach to Collaborative Leadership

You have arrived! Congratulations! This has taken quite a bit of time. It's been a lot of hard work, and you have perfected your habit of reflection. Now it's time to see what it all means in terms of your new understanding of collaborative leadership. Given all you have learned about yourself, what are your assumptions and beliefs now about people in the workforce? What will be your strongest attributes, your core behaviors, and the key roles you will have as a collaborative leader? What is your leadership philosophy now?

How will you sustain your journey? Remember, it's not over. Your next destination is personal mastery, which Senge defines this way: "It means approaching one's life as a creative work, living life from a creative as opposed to a reactive viewpoint."[34] He goes on to suggest that it is a discipline that gets integrated into your life, much as reflection is now. Discipline means the following:

- You continuously clarify what is important to you.
- Current reality is an ally, not an enemy.
- You have learned how to perceive and work with forces of change, rather than resist them.
- You are deeply inquisitive.
- You are connected to others and to life.
- You live in continuous learning mode.[35]

You will continue to learn and grow your entire life. Along the way, you will continue to reflect, gain new insights, coach and mentor others, be of service and support, and always help others be their best selves so they can do their best work and produce superior results.

CHAPTER CONCLUSION: EMPOWERING THE HUMAN SPIRIT THROUGH COLLABORATIVE LEADERSHIP

To become a leader, you must first become a human being.
—Confucius, 551–479 BCE

The journey to become a collaborative leader is indeed about revealing who you are as a human being, your essence, your reason for being on this planet, your assumptions and beliefs about those you work with, your core values and ethics in the form of a moral compass, your behaviors, skills, personal history, life experiences, and all the things that go into making you who you are. We know that when you build a house in an earthquake zone, flood plain, along the coasts, or anywhere that may be affected by the forces of nature, you must build a solid foundation that can withstand those events. If you shortcut this process, use the wrong kind of cement, or do not prepare the foundation properly, when you build the house on top of it, it will crack. When the first extreme weather event comes, it can be more easily destroyed. The same is true for your leadership. A solid collaborative leadership foundation means you invest the time to identify and define your values and ethics, come to understand, appreciate, and embrace your past, your drivers and motivators, your skills and capacities, and behavioral feedback from others. It becomes very difficult to navigate the turbulence of our high speed, volatile, complex, and uncertain world without being grounded in this foundation.

The collaborative leadership journey is designed to help you create, validate, and celebrate that foundation so that you become your true authentic self and are self-aware, self-trusting, self-confident, proactive, and ready to serve others. Recall our definition of this journey:

> *An inside-out journey of self-discovery, self-awareness, and reflection that helps you to define who you are as a human being and a professional, what you believe in, what you value, why you are here on this planet, and where you choose to go with the rest of your life. It is about your self-esteem, your sense of self-worth, and the ground you stand on. It is a journey with no destination but is about lifelong learning, growth, and development.*

When we have a strong foundation and solid ground to stand on, we can not only withstand the turbulence that is all around us but can also empower the human spirit. Because we now know who we are, have embraced our past, know our strengths and challenges, have worked through our ten-step journey, and have shifted how we choose to lead from power to collaboration, we will be able to fulfill the essential roles of collaborative leaders. We have become human, the best version of ourselves, and have become the leader who, in the words of Lao Tzu,

> *Is best when people barely know he/she exists, when his/her work is done, his/her aim fulfilled, they will say: we did it ourselves*

> —Lao Tzu, 6th Century BCE

CHAPTER REVIEW AND REFLECTIONS

Learning Objectives:

Let's reflect on the learning objectives for the chapter and summarize what we have learned:

- Understand what the collaborative leadership journey is and its benefits if you embrace the process.
- Consider who is likely not to take the journey.
- Discuss the challenges or barriers to becoming a collaborative leader and how they might be addressed.
- Consider what is involved in making a conscious choice to go on this journey.
- Review the steps in the collaborative leadership journey once you have made that choice.

Initial Questions Revisited, and for Reflection:

- *Do you now see yourself as a collaborative leader? In what ways ways (attributes, behaviors, and roles)?*
- *Why do you want to go on this journey? What are your greatest concerns? What do you see as the greatest potential benefits? Do the benefits outweigh the concerns?*
- *Given the challenges many people face, barriers they must navigate, and steps on the journey to becoming a collaborative leader, how will you address them? Are you prepared to invest the time?*
- *Are you ready to make a conscious choice to go on this journey?*
- *What steps in the journey do you see being the most challenging?*

ADDITIONAL READINGS

- DePree, Max. *Leadership Is an Art.* New York: Dell, 1989.
- Frankl, Viktor E. *Man's Search for Meaning.* Boston: Beacon Press, 2006.
- Kouzes, James, and Barry Posner. *The Leadership Challenge.* 6th ed. Hoboken, NJ: Wiley, 2017.
- Marshall, Edward M. *Building Trust at the Speed of Change.* New York: AMACOM Books, 2000; especially Chapter 7, "Leadership Trust and Integrity," pp. 134–161.
- Marshall, Edward M. *Transforming the Way We Work: The Power of the Collaborative Workplace.* New York: AMACOM Books, 1995; especially chap. 4, "Collaborative Leadership," pp. 68–86.
- Satir, Virginia. *The New People Making.* Atlanta, GA: Atlanta Book Company, 2009.

ENDNOTES

1 James M. Kouzes and Barry Z. Posner, *The Leadership Challenge* (San Francisco: Wiley, 2007), pp. 344, 346.
2 "#163, Stayer," *Forbes,* July 1, 2015, https://www.forbes.com/profile/stayer/#462d7e9b5a1c
3 Ralph Stayer, "How I Learned to Let My Workers Lead," *Harvard Business Review,* November–December, 1990.
4 Ibid., p. 1.
5 Ibid., pp. 1–2.
6 Ibid., p. 9.
7 Ibid.
8 Morten T. Hansen, *Collaboration* (Boston, MA: Harvard University Press, 2009), p. 165.
9 Stephen R. Covey, *The 7 Habits of Highly Effective People* (New York: Free Press, 1989).

10 Asad Meah, "47 Inspirational Jeff Bezos Quotes on Success," https://www.awakenthegreatnesswithin.com/47-inspirational-jeff-bezos-quotes-on-success/

11 The Myers and Briggs Foundation provides a wealth of information on the MBTI, which can be found at this website: https://www.myersbriggs.org/my-mbti-personality-type/mbti-basics/home.htm?bhcp=1

12 Peter M. Senge, *The Fifth Discipline* (New York: Currency, 2006).

13 Jim Collins, *Good to Great* (New York: HarperCollins, 2001).

14 Senge, op. cit., pp. 136–162.

15 Demetrios Gianniris, "The Millennial Arrival and the Evolution of the Modern Workplace," *Forbes*, January 25, 2018.

16 Bill George, Peter Sims, Andrew N. McLean, and Diana Mayer, "Discovering Your Authentic Leadership," *Harvard Business Review,* February 2007, p. 2 on life stories; Bill George's 'Authentic Leadership': Passion Comes from People's Life Stories, Knowledge @ Wharton, March 28, 2007, https://knowledge.wharton.upenn.edu/article/bill-georges-authentic-leadership-passion-comes-from-peoples-life-stories/

17 Senge, *The Fifth Discipline,* pp. 171–174.

18 Edward M. Marshall, *Transforming the Way We Work: The Power of the Collaborative Workplace* (New York: AMACOM Books, 1995), pp. 68–86.

19 Rick Hanson, *Resilient* (New York: Harmony Books, 2018); a neuroscientist, Hanson has developed a comprehensive way to think about dealing with rapid organizational change.

20 James W. Tamm and Ronald J. Luyet, *Radical Collaboration* (New York: HarperCollins, 2004), p. 107.

21 Carl Jung, *The Collected Works of C.G. Jung, V. 6, Personality Types,* revision by R. F. C. Hull (Princeton, NJ: Princeton University Press, 1971).

22 The Myers and Briggs Foundation website provides a helpful overview of the MBTI; reference also *MBTI® Manual: A Guide to the Development and Use of the Myers-Briggs Type Indicator®*; both the overview and the MBTI instrument can be found at: https://www.myersbriggs.org/my-mbti-personality-type/mbti-basics/

23 Don Richard Riso, *Personality Types* (New York: Houghton Mifflin Harcourt, 1996); Enneagram Institute, *The Traditional Enneagram,* https://www.enneagraminstitute.com/the-traditional-enneagram

24 *A Guide to the Enneagram and the Nine Types, 2007-2017,* https://www.enneagramworldwide.com/wp-content/uploads/2014/01/Enneagram-Guide.pdf

25 James M. Kouzes and Barry Posner, *The Leadership Challenge* (San Francisco: Jossey-Bass, 2007), p. 48.

26 Stephen R. Covey, *The 7 Habits of Highly Effective People* (New York: Free Press, 1989), p. 18.

27 Edward M. Marshall, *Building Trust at the Speed of Change* (New York: AMACOM Books, 2000), pp. 44–63.

28 Kouzes and Posner, op. cit., pp. 69–70.

29 Andrew Leigh, *Ethical Leadership* (London: Kogan Page, 2013), p. 40.

30 Kouzes and Posner, op. cit., pp. 345–346.

31 Viktor E. Frankl, *Man's Search for Meaning* (Boston, MA: Beacon Press, 2006), 108–109; I have added [or her] to reflect that both men and women search for meaning in their lives. On a personal note, I had the good fortune to meet Dr. Frankl in person while an exchange student at the University of Vienna, Austria, and had the opportunity to watch him in clinic as he worked with patients using his therapeutic technique called "logotherapy." He was an exceptional human being, and his work is being carried on around the world.

32 Senge, *The Fifth Discipline*, p. 138.

33 Ibid.

34 Ibid., pp. 131–133.

35 Ibid.

Figure Credits

CHAPTER SIX

Collaborative Leadership Skills

Leadership is an identifiable set of skills and abilities that are available to all of us.

—James Kouzes and Barry Posner[1]

*I*T WAS THE *learning team's regular Thursday meeting time. It was raining so they met in a library conference room to talk through this week's assignment. They had begun their collaborative leadership journeys and were ready to learn about leading others. But still something else was needed. Ana captured the sentiments of the group when she said, "I'm ready to go, but this all feels so new. I thought I was collaborating with others in the past, but now I know there's a whole lot more to it. I need some skills, but am not sure which ones are the right ones." Priyanka built on Ana's observation, "That's right, Ana. I did too—I'm on social media every day, but now I know there's so much more to what it means to lead collaboratively." Morare added, "We're already doing a great job on this team. We're giving each other room to share our thoughts and concerns. At each meeting, a different one of us is facilitating. We've got a consensus decision-making process. I'm curious about what other skills I need to master collaborative leadership."*

Hanyue was also excited to learn about these skills and wanted to know what they were and how they related to the seven principles of the Collaboration Paradigm. It was time to dig in. They opened up their assignment to see these questions for reflection:

- *What types of challenges do collaborative leaders face in companies as they work to create collaborative cultures?*
- *What are the collaborative leadership skills that will help me navigate these challenges in a way that honors my values and commitment to empowering the workforce?*
- *How do I become a "master" of collaboration so that I can help others and transform any leadership culture I enter?*

Learning Objectives

By the end of this chapter, you will:

- Understand the *context* in which collaborative leadership skills will be used, as well as some of the key challenges collaborative leaders will face
- Learn the *framework* that connects collaborative leadership skills to the seven principles of collaboration, as well as the attributes, behaviors, and roles of collaborative leaders
- Understand the *principle-based collaborative leadership skills* that will empower the workforce to be their best selves, do their best work, and produce superior results
- Review the *phases involved in the process* of making these skills your own—learning, practicing, reflecting, mastery, and empowering others

The Main of Point of This Chapter

Collaborative leadership is not about power and control, telling people what to do and then finding them doing something wrong. Collaborative leadership is about building trust-based relationships, ensuring psychological safety, giving people ownership over the values, vision, mission, strategy, and their own jobs. It is about influencing, facilitating, engaging, and empowering them; designing and facilitating collaborative meetings; forming and developing collaborative teams; and building workplace cultures that honor the human spirit. It's about behaving in a way that is aligned with the seven principles of collaboration, walking the talk, and mastering the skills that will empower others. To this end, there are seven sets of skills collaborative leaders need to be successful, each of which is tied to one of the seven principles.

For the new collaborative leader, your ability to learn, practice, and master collaborative leadership skills will enable you to empower the workforce to be their best selves so they can do their best work. In the face of many organizational challenges, however, it also takes courage, persistence, a firm belief in yourself, and the use of collaborative leadership skills to ensure success. You will find yourself in situations where there is fear, distrust, disempowerment, and dysfunction. These skills will enable you not only to navigate them and achieve results but also to build a collaborative leadership culture among the people you are leading. The goal of using these skills is to build a culture of psychological safety, ownership, and trust.

Here are some key points to consider for this next step of the journey:

- **Beyond Training:** Collaborative leadership skills are not about techniques or tools that you put in your tool kit. There are all kinds of workshops for that. These skills are grounded in a deep faith in the people you work with, and their desire to transform the workplace from a culture of fear to one of trust.

- **All Skills Are Not Created Equal:** Among the seven sets of principle-based collaborative leadership skills, some are more critical than others. Central to all collaborative work is the art of facilitation that empowers others to own their meetings, teams, projects, and results. Helping teams build true consensus is the turnkey to help team members work through their differences with each other. Being ethical in all one's actions is essential to credibility. Being self-aware enables you to stop and reflect on your own behavior, and make the necessary course corrections. Active listening is essential for demonstrating empathy toward others, as well as being a good coach. People problem-solving skills ensure that even the thorniest of problems can be addressed.
- **Mastery:** The ultimate goal is mastery of all seven sets of skills so that you can not only empower the people you work with and create a collaborative leadership culture but also teach others how to master these skills. It takes time to learn, practice, and master these skills, so it is important to be patient, open, persistent, and curious and to embrace the process that will empower you and others to create workplaces that honor the human spirit, and get real work done.

CHALLENGES FACING COLLABORATIVE LEADERS

Because the predominant leadership culture is still the Power Paradigm, collaborative leadership is not for the faint of heart. The structure of most companies is still hierarchical. Some companies that are more enlightened and realize that the "people factor" is important. But it is important for the collaborative leader to understand that underneath all of the slogans and positive vision statements about how important people are, is a culture driven by power, fear, and control.

SIDE BOX 6.1.

The new CIO of a major Silicon Valley tech firm joined the company with much fanfare. He had a reputation for being collaborative, having great people skills, and solid business acumen. When he joined the company, his first 100 days involved meeting the workforce on four continents. He got rave reviews for his authenticity and humanity and discovered that they had been treated terribly by the former command-and-control CIO. He discovered that people were being punished for minor infractions of company rules, while at the same time sexual harassment and ethical violations by technically important managers went unaddressed. It was an unsafe and fearful work environment, especially for women.

The new CIO decided to transform the culture, to become a collaborative leadership culture, even though the larger corporate culture was power-based. He believed that if his organization could become collaborative and produce results, others in the company might follow. He was wrong. Within a year, he got pushback from other leaders on the Executive Team. He even got pushback from two of his direct reports. The former

SIDE BOX 6.1 (CONTINUED).

acting CIO was still in the organization, still had a budget, and refused to recognize the authority of the new CIO, undermining him at every step. Efforts by the new CIO to rein in this former leader failed because he had strong relationships with several members of the Executive Team and used them to challenge the new CIO's cultural and business vision. This situation was untenable. It did not take long before there was a tense, difficult conversation with the CEO. The former leader was terminated, and the culture change process proceeded.

It took courage for the new CIO to challenge the prevailing leadership culture, and it took considerable skill to navigate this transition (see Side Box 6.1). He had mastered the skills of facilitation, active listening, building ownership, consensus decision-making, giving feedback, and having difficult conversations. Most importantly, he was self-aware, made course corrections, demonstrated empathy toward others, even those who challenged him, and empowered his workforce to be their best selves, do their best work, and produce superior results.

The point of this story is that collaborative leaders and managers face a number of challenges and barriers to being collaborative. But because of the inside-out journey, collaborative leaders will have the strength to withstand the pressures of organizations that are not collaborative. With the skills discussed below, you will be able to navigate the challenges and barriers you will encounter.

Challenges Collaborative Leaders May Face

What are these challenges? You will likely encounter one or more of the following:

- **Cultural Forces:** The predominant culture in most companies is the Power Paradigm, which is either passive/defensive or aggressive/defensive, is highly political, siloed, and has many subcultures. The power of this culture can sometimes feel overwhelming. You may feel like a salmon swimming upstream. Sometimes you may find yourself saying, "If you can't beat them, join them." Don't. Remember the journey you have been on, your vision for the type of workplace you wish work in, and your commitment to the people you work with to empower them to work collaboratively.
- **Self-Inflicted Wounds:** We all make mistakes or have doubts about our ability to work collaboratively, especially when we are just beginning. Some of these self-inflicted wounds that can derail the collaborative leader include fear of failure, the inability to let go of old beliefs about the workforce,

not being sufficiently self-aware to self-correct, being inflexible when faced with resistance, or reverting to old behavior under pressure. In these situations, it is important to revisit the collaborative leadership journey, to understand the root causes of your behavior, regain trust by being self-accountable, and then recommit and redouble your efforts.

- **Leadership Dynamics:** Like our high-tech CIO, there are significant political and power dynamics within the leadership ecosystem. Unless you are the CEO, you may face a hostile boss who does not agree with your collaborative approach to leading others or peers who are ambitious and are competing for higher positions. Some peers may be jealous of you, your reputation, or your skills and seek to undermine you. Bullies will try to intimidate you. There are also those who are intolerant, naysayers or negativists who are always critical of someone trying to do new things.

- **Workforce-Leadership Dynamics:** The workforce-leadership dynamic is a very potent force in any organization. If you are a collaborative leader, you may experience leadership who snuff out workforce motivation by imposing their will on them; a lack of respect by the workforce for leadership who are not credible; workforce fear of retribution if they speak truth to power; distrust that comes when leaders do not walk the talk, provide conflicting signals, or behave in ways that demonstrate a lack of integrity; a failure by leadership to engage the workforce, ask for their opinions, or to be transparent; or leadership impatience with collaborative processes.

- **Team Dynamics:** There are all kinds of dynamics that happen in teams, especially when they are operating in a competitive, power-based work culture. Among the dynamics are broken trust between two or more members; walking on eggshells for fear of upsetting a member; feeling it's not psychologically safe to speak up; competition for control; backstabbing or rumor mills that assassinate someone's reputation; feuds or disputes that insist you take sides; bullies who use their power to get their way; people who bring their personal issues or family dysfunction into the workplace; people who tell you to slow down; public attacks, sarcasm, and opposition in meetings.

- **Business Challenges:** Because you are helping lead or manage an enterprise, there are also business challenges you will encounter that impact your ability to lead collaboratively: poor quarterly business results that require cutting back on collaborative projects; a disruptive new competitor that results in a reallocation of business and budget priorities; a merger or acquisition that threatens people's jobs or the stability of the business; the latest "bright, shiny object" that captures the attention of an executive, resulting in an organizational change; reorganizations that result in members of your workforce being moved to new roles against their will; a rollout failure that makes your group look bad; reengineering of business processes that requires significant changes in how work gets done; and the RIF, a reduction in force, that gets announced by email.

Strategies Collaborative Leaders Can Use to Meet These Challenges

When confronted with these challenges, what kinds of strategies can help you survive and thrive collaboratively in this kind of work culture? Here are several you might consider:

- **Don't Quit—Stay the Course:** It takes courage, will, self-discipline, and persistence to lead culture change. Be the change you want to see. Reflect. Actively listen. Engage others to find a path forward.

- **Gain Perspective:** Take a step back from daily activities to see the big picture. Use your reflection time to describe what is going on in your workplace and how it is affecting you and others, and brainstorm how you want to use collaboration to make a difference. This is transcending the current reality.

- **Be True to Yourself:** You know who you are, your values, vision, and mission. You are grounded, and as long as you come from that place and apply your collaborative leadership skills, you will be fine. Often rejection or criticism is coming from people who are less sure of themselves or feel threatened. Use empathy, kindness, and your genuine desire to connect and listen, and you may find that they make a shift in their attitudes.

- **Honor the 7 Principles:** If you meet force with force, the outcome will be counterproductive. Instead, come from the 7 Principles of the Collaborative Work Ethic. It's about ownership, trust, respect, and integrity. If you come from the place of acceptance of the other's fear or concerns, you have the opportunity to have a productive dialogue.

- **Let Go: What you Resist Persists:** Be willing to "let go." Sometimes it is not possible to find a solution. What you resist often persists. Sometimes dialogue is not the language others understand. You can use the power of your letting go to engage your colleague and, at the proper time, come back to have a productive conversation.

- **Stay in Relationship:** You get to be right or in relationship. Engage, listen, coach, cocreate solutions, and if necessary, have a difficult conversation.

- **Learn to Dance:** Operating in a power-based organization often requires you to know how to "dance" with that culture. This means being flexible, agile, and patient. Behavioral change does not happen in a straight line. Remember the parable of the tortoise and the hare—slow and steady wins the race.

- **Respond, Don't React:** Sometimes, in the heat of the moment, we feel we have to react to what the other is saying. We don't. Remember your grounding. Be reflective. Consider what the other is saying, where it may be coming from, and then respond with empathy.

- **When in Doubt, Give Them Ownership:** You will find yourself in situations where you are not sure what approach to take. In collaboration, your failsafe is to give your colleagues or team ownership over the issue. What would they like to do? What do they think the options might be? What would they like the results to be? What are the criteria for making a decision? Remember that people take care of what they own. Giving others ownership means you're not advocating for a position; you are facilitating the team, and trusting them to come up with the answer.

- **Come From Service:** Often we can get invested in a result, a tool, or a process, and forget that at the end of the day, it's about them. Leadership is about serving others, so that when their work is done, they own it.
- **Revisit and Recommit:** In some situations, it is important to revisit your collaborative leadership journey, understand the root causes of your behavior, regain trust by being self-accountable, and then recommit.
- **Depart:** Sometimes, the culture of the organization is so toxic or unhealthy that the only option is to leave the situation or job. You first need to honor yourself and your values, well-being, physical health, and family. You tried to make it work. You did your best, but the culture of this organization is simply not ready for collaboration.
- **Become a Master:** Your ultimate goal as a collaborative leader is mastery. First learn the skills, then practice them so much that you become a master. Once you are a master, you train others, and they in turn will empower and train those they work with. Think of yourself as a pebble in the pond, and that your work has a ripple effect across your organization and in all of your relationships both inside and outside of work.

A FRAMEWORK FOR COLLABORATIVE LEADERSHIP SKILLS

Here is framework for understanding what collaborative leadership skills are and how they are connected to the Collaboration Paradigm of leadership. They are tied to each of the *7 Principles of the Collaborative Work Ethic* and will enable you to serve and empower others.

First, let's define what is meant by a *skill*. *Merriam-Webster* defines it as "the ability to use one's knowledge effectively in execution or performance; a learned power of doing something competently."[2]

For collaborative leaders, this means they have the knowledge and aptitude to implement collaborative behaviors, processes, or specific tools for the purpose of empowering others to be their best selves so they can do their best work. Second, these skills have been identified as critical to being an effective collaborative leader based on the following criteria, where each skill reflects the beliefs and assumptions of the Collaboration Paradigm about how to empower those we work with, reflects one of the seven principles of collaboration, aligns with collaborative leadership attributes, and implements one or more collaborative leadership behaviors (Table 6.1).

TABLE 6.1 *Collaborative Leadership Skills*

COLLABORATIVE PRINCIPLE	COLLABORATIVE BEHAVIORS	KEY COLLABORATIVE LEADERSHIP SKILLS
Trust: What we value most in ourselves and each other; measure of confidence in the character of self and others; faith; rejects fear as a motivator	Puts relationship first Optimistic and inspiring Aligning Transparent and confidential Builds trust in others; is trustworthy Shows humility	**Overall Goal: To build relationship, credibility and trust with the workforce through:** Envisioning the future; aligning the workforce; transparency
Ownership: People take care of what they own; a commitment to others owning their work and the direction of the organization	Facilitative Connects with and engages others Builds a "We" culture Sponsors team and other processes Empowers others to be their best selves and do their best work	**Overall Goal: To build ownership of the vision, mission, values, strategy, work, and change through:** Facilitation; sponsorship; engagement; meetings, teams, processes, change; preventions and interventions; building true consensus
Integrity and Ethics: Operating on principle; walks the talk; credible; adheres to a code of moral values	Ethical above reproach; makes ethical decisions Creates ethical culture Walks the talk Practices the seven principles of collaboration Ensures safety of the workforce—physical, emotional, psychological	**Overall Goal: To ensure the highest integrity and ethics through:** Ensuring ethical behavior across the organization; personal moral code; sets the moral tone for the organization; protecting psychological safety of the workforce
Honor: Faithful stewardship of values, ethics, and the culture	Honors commitments Courageous Self-disciplined; willpower; never quits Consistent application of collaborative principles Stewardship of the culture, organization, and community	**Overall Goal: To provide faithful stewardship of the ethics, culture, and organization through:** Self-awareness and disciplined reflection; Chief cultural officer, the steward of the collaborative leadership culture
Mutual Respect: Building the self-esteem of each individual, team or group; operates with high emotional intelligence; creates a culture of respect	Emotionally intelligent; empathic toward others Actively connects and listens to others Ensures four-way communications Nurtures and supports others Acknowledges and appreciates others	**Overall Goal: To build mutual respect across the organization through:** Showing up, being present, and connecting; showing empathy through active listening; good questions; dialogue; coaching; four-way communications; nurturing and acknowledgement; appreciation

(Continued)

TABLE 6.1 *Collaborative Leadership Skills (Continued)*

Full Responsibility: Responsible for self and others, the meeting, team, process, project, organization, community	Learning Adaptive Stewardship of the hopes, dreams, and aspirations of the workforce Ensures effectiveness, efficiency, and results	**Overall Goal:** To demonstrate **full responsibility for the success of the workforce and the organization through:** Motivating the workforce People problem solving
Accountability: Holds self and others accountable for behavior and results	Self-aware and reflective Holds self-accountable Holds others accountable	**Overall Goal:** **To ensure there is accountability through:** Giving and receiving feedback; conducting difficult conversations

CRITICAL COLLABORATIVE LEADERSHIP SKILLS

Our purpose here is to describe seven sets of collaborative leadership skills that can be used to empower the workforce. Within each set of skills, there are specific collaborative tools that can be used at the discretion of the leader. Some are used more than others—for example, facilitation is used almost constantly, while conducting a difficult conversation is not—but both are essential skills. For each of the skills, we will define it, discuss why it is so critical, and explain what the skill involves and when to use it.

Skill Set 1: The Principle of Trust

Trust is the fundamental building block in human relationships. It is at the root of how we treat each other. It is a principle that governs how we perceive ourselves, and how others see us. Without trust, our relationships become merely transactions. With trust, there is the potential for deep collaboration. Most of us enter our relationships with others somewhere along a continuum which reflects the degree of trust we have in others. Some people begin from a position of assumed trust, faith that there is already credibility and integrity; trust is given without having to be earned. For others, trust must be earned over time, and is proven by one's deeds matching their words. With breaches of trust, much work must be done to earn it back.

A primary goal of the collaborative leader is to build trust-based relationships in the workforce, through two key skills: (1) Envisioning the future and aligning the workforce and (2) Transparency.

Skill: Envisioning the Future and Aligning the Workforce

- **Definition of the Skill:** Kouzes and Posner helped us understand that *inspiring a shared vision* was one of the five core practices of leadership:[3] leaders envision exciting and ennobling possibilities, enlist others in a common vision, breathe life into the hopes and dreams of others, forge a unity of purpose by showing how the vision is for the common good, and stir the fire of passion in others. This means that collaborative leaders at any level of an organization will articulate the vision and mission of the entity in a way that reflects market realities, as well as the hopes, aspirations, dreams, and expectations of the workforce. Leaders then engage their stakeholders and align them around the vision and direction of the organization.

- **Why This Skill is So Critical:** To trust leadership, the workforce needs clarity on where they are headed and why they are doing what they're doing, and to give them a sense of meaning in their work lives. They need to be engaged and feel a sense of ownership of the organization's vision. Without that ownership, motivation and productive energy will decline and the workforce will see themselves as mere cogs in the machinery.
- **What This Skill Involves:** Setting the direction of the organization is not done by one person or a small group of people who then announce it to the workforce. This skill involves a high degree of engagement of key stakeholders across the organization.
- **When to Use This Skill:** Collaborative leaders typically use this skill whenever they have taken over a new position in an organization, business unit, or team. It is the next step after leaders get to know their workforce and build an initial level of trust and credibility.

Skill: *Transparency of Operations*

According to Clive Thompson, who wrote an article called "The See-Through CEO" in *Wired,* the 92+ million Millennials in the US workforce expect open access to information: "For them, authenticity comes from online exposure. It's hard to trust anyone who doesn't list their dreams and fears on Facebook".[4] Watson Wyatt found that there was a direct link between high levels of engagement and the degree of transparency. 90% of highly engaged workers said their immediate supervisors kept them involved about management decisions, vs. 24% of the low-engagement workers. 85% of highly engaged workers said their company did a good job of seeking their opinions, vs. 7% of the low-engagement workers.[5] Deloitte found that 46% of the people in their workplace survey said that a lack of transparent leadership communication would drive them to seek new employment.[6] Benko and Anderson suggest that we now live in "glass houses," and that leaders now are not the *deliverers* of information, but are the *facilitators* of it.[7]

- **Definition of the Skill:** Transparency is a standard of openness in the organization; no more smoke-filled rooms or conversations behind closed doors found in companies run by the Power Paradigm; accessibility to information about the organization, its operations, decision-making processes, finances, strategy, and direction. It involves engagement of the workforce, and there is accountability.

- **Why This Skill is So Critical:** Transparency builds workforce trust in, and strengthens the credibility of, leadership. As Benko and Anderson point out, transparency strengthens authenticity, improves organizational effectiveness, and raises performance by building trust.[8]
- **What This Skill Involves:** Transparency skill is the ability of leaders to demonstrate that the organization and its processes are open to scrutiny, that it is in effect open book. It is about the workforce knowing what is happening and being able to contribute their intellect and insights to organizational processes, knowledge development, decision-making, and problem solving.
- **When to Use This Skill:** It should be practiced by all leaders and managers all of the time. There are specific situations where an increased level of transparency is needed, such as major organizational changes.

Skill Set 2: The Principle of Ownership

Ownership is the central principle that distinguishes collaboration from any other leadership paradigm. People take care of what they own. If individuals are given ownership of their jobs, rather than just being given a set of roles and responsibilities, they will perform them excellently. If teams own their work, they will be more willing to be held accountable for the results. Consensus decision-making is how team members create ownership of their work. In a collaborative leadership culture, ownership transforms how people think about themselves, their work, their teams, and their organizations. With ownership comes high levels of productive energy.

An essential goal of the collaborative leader is to build ownership, by the workforce, of the vision, mission, values, strategy, work, and any changes by employing two key leadership skills: (1) Empowering the workforce through the *facilitation* of relationships, processes, teams, and change; and (2) Building *true consensus*, particularly in decision-making.

Skill: Facilitation of Teams, Meetings, and Change Initiatives

Collaborative leaders have a primary commitment to serve and empower the workforce. They don't tell workforce what the decisions are; they ask them for their input before decisions are reached. They don't issue commands; they engage and build ownership. The core skill to empower teams, groups, and organizations is facilitation. As Kouzes and Posner suggest in their 4th leadership practice, Enabling Others to Act, collaborative leaders give power away, which strengthens everyone's capacity to deliver on their commitments. They include rather than exclude, which gives people a sense of ownership.[9] Collaborative leaders facilitate the development of trust-based relationships among those they work with, and facilitate the engagement of the workforce in aligning on the organization's values, vision, mission, and strategy. They ensure that facilitation becomes central to the leadership culture. They develop collaborative teams, ensure that collaborative meetings are facilitated by independent, highly trained professionals, and facilitate organizational change.

The central point is that engagement is a process, facilitation is the skill that enables it, and ownership and trust among those facilitated is the outcome. They are inextricably interconnected.

- **Definition of the Skill:** Schuman defines facilitation this way: "A facilitator helps a group to work collaboratively by focusing on the process of how the participants work together ... they are not participants, have no authority to impose any action on the group, and have no vested interest in the outcome."[10] Some see facilitation merely as a technique that can help them run meetings or teams. In a collaborative leadership culture, facilitation is a way of being and a way of working. It is an integral part of the collaborative philosophy—the belief system that the workforce is competent, has gifts they are willingly to give to the organization, and the value system where respect for and trust in the capabilities of each individual is central. To empower the workforce, facilitation is both a skill and an art form.
- **Why This Skill is So Critical:** Facilitation is the primary way the workforce is empowered, through which engagement and motivation of the workforce occurs, and by which ownership and trust are created. Without committed and skilled facilitators across the organization, there can be no collaborative leadership culture.
- **What This Skill Involves:** Facilitation requires a complete transformation of those old ways of working so that the leader serves the workforce, that "we" are in this together, and the leader's role is to empower them to be their best selves. It involves a commitment to this philosophy, an investment in learning collaborative facilitation, lots of practice and reflection, and a commitment to continuous learning.
- **When to Use This Skill:** It is used all the time by leaders, managers, and trained team and meeting facilitators. It is the means by which alignment occurs with the values, vision, mission, and strategy of the organization. It is how four-way communications happen, how meetings are designed and facilitated, how collaborative teams are formed and developed, how business and change processes are implemented, and how stakeholders are engaged to ensure their ownership of the outcomes.

Skill: Building 100% True Consensus, No Reservations—the Gold Standard of Collaboration

There are several schools of thought about the idea of achieving *100% true consensus* on decisions:

1. **Anti-Groupthink:** This school of thought agrees with McDermott and Hall that consensus is, "a process that seeks to eliminate differences by getting everyone to agree." They go on to say that "consensus is actually an enemy of collaboration."[11]

2. **Expansive:** Peter Senge suggests there are two types of consensus: (a) Focusing down consensus that seeks the common denominator in multiple individual views, and (b) Opening up consensus that seeks a picture larger than any one person's point of view.[12]

3. **Synergy:** This school of thought sees teams making better decisions than individuals most of the time, and that by working through differences within a team or group, not only does everyone benefit by increased levels of knowledge and understanding, but everyone's viewpoint is respected, and trust is built because everyone owns the decision. The team is a "We," operating collaboratively.

- **Definition of the Skill:** Building 100% true consensus is the facilitated process teams use to make decisions that are primarily strategic or tactical. True consensus means 100% agreement, no reservations and that teams work through their differences to build a shared understanding, rather than sweeping their differences under the carpet. True consensus builds high trust, ownership, full responsibility, and accountability among team members. It means everyone's point of view is considered.

- **Why This Skill is So Critical:** Without trust, relationships and teams will not work effectively. Without ownership of a process or a decision, trust cannot be effectively generated. Building 100% true consensus is the mechanism, the way in which ownership is built so that trust, synergy, and superior results are achieved. True consensus is the heartbeat of a team's work and collaborative leadership culture.

- **What This Skill Involves:** There are six primary decision-making rules for individuals, groups, and teams: One person decides; minority rule (< 50%); majority rule (50% +1); super majority (80%); "can-live-with" consensus (81–99%); and true consensus, no reservations (100%). When asked which decision-making rule they would prefer, most teams say "can-live-with" consensus, because for the most part, people have not learned how to work through their differences. When it comes to strategic decisions that affect the future of everyone on the team and the organization, then teams will want true consensus because no one wants to be left out of the decision-making process. No one wants to have their views ignored by the other members of the team. At the end of the day, it is about respecting each and every member of the team, their intellect and input, and moving away from "might makes right" and toward an inclusive process where everyone's views are heard and respected.

- **When to Use This Skill:** Attaining 100% true consensus is most often used as the decision rule for strategic decisions, and sometimes tactical, or what one client called a "thorny tactical" decision where there needed to be full team agreement.

Skill Set 3: The Principle of Integrity and Ethics

Merriam-Webster defines integrity as the "firm adherence to a code of moral values."[13] Put another way, leaders are seen as having high integrity when their actions match their words as well as their intent, or what is commonly referred to as walking-the-talk. If the leader is viewed as being honorable, respectful, responsible, and accountable, there is a greater likelihood of high integrity and being considered ethical. If the leader lies, cheats, steals, manipulates, intimidates, or harasses, this is a breach of integrity and a violation of ethical conduct. Collaborative leaders consistently demonstrate the highest standard of integrity—**above reproach**.

Merriam-Webster defines ethics as a "set of moral principles, a theory or system of moral values ... the principles of conduct governing an individual or a group, and a guiding philosophy".[14] One's integrity is at the core of their ethical code and conduct. Ethical conduct is an essential condition for a collaborative leadership culture that is built on trust, honor, dignity, respect, and accountability. Ethical leaders can be counted on to do the right thing when faced with difficult choices. Ethical leaders will put acting with integrity above their self-interest. They will always do what is best for the organization rather than any special interest.

An essential goal of the collaborative leader, then, is to ensure the highest integrity and ethics across the organization by developing these two key collaborative leadership skills: (1) Ensuring ethical behavior across the organization and (2) Protecting the psychological, physical, and emotional safety of the workforce.

Skill: Ensure Ethical Behavior across the Organization

We live in a world where ethical leadership behaviors are under assault by levels of corruption and misconduct in corporations, governments, and nonprofits. Unethical behavior undermines the credibility and legitimacy of their leadership. Without ethical conduct, there is no trust. Without trust, it is impossible to lead.

- **Definition of the Skill:** Ethical leaders are responsible for creating ethical leadership cultures that have five key elements:[15]

  - Ethical leaders set the right tone for the organization and model ethical conduct; leaders can be trusted to do the right thing.
  - Supervisors reinforce the ethical tone and also model ethical conduct.
  - Peers talk about the importance of ethics and support each other in doing the right thing.
  - Ethical values are embedded in the organization—it's how things are done.
  - There are formal rules and structures to govern and guide all stakeholders.

- **Why this Skill is So Critical:** Without ethical conduct, leadership cannot be trusted. Without ethical behavior, there is no credibility and the moral foundation of the organization is compromised, undermining any possibility of collaboration.

- **What This Skill Involves:**
  - Leadership makes a clear commitment, based on core values, to conduct itself in accordance with the highest ethical standard with a standard of being above reproach.
  - Leadership turns the ethical commitment into a personal moral code that is shared with superiors, peers, and direct reports.
  - An ethical system is created in the organization, linking commitments to policy, practices, standards, implementation, and accountability.
  - Leadership maintains a consistent process of self-reflection where that code is evaluated against actual conduct, and if necessary, adjustments in behavior are made.
  - Collaborative leaders hold themselves accountable to others when there is an ethics/personal moral code violation.

- **When to Use This Skill:** Ethical leadership is a way of life that is consistent with the seven principles of collaboration. Ethical conduct is a 24/7/365 commitment, both inside and outside the workplace.

Skill: Protect the Psychological Safety of the Workforce

When people are fearful, they are less likely to speak up, especially if they are concerned about issues of unethical conduct or when there is a breach of integrity. This is especially true in leadership cultures based on power, fear, and control. If you speak up you could lose your job, or like Susan Fowler, become a pariah who is passed around or avoided. I have even seen a senior leader at one Fortune 100 company get "banished" to a developing country because he spoke up at leadership meetings about things the boss did not want to hear.

Conversely, when there is psychological safety, the workforce is significantly more productive. Google found that psychological safety was the single most important factor in high performing teams.[18] Gallup, in a 2017 poll, found that only 30% of workers felt their opinions

---

SIDE BOX 6.2: SUSAN FOWLER'S EXPERIENCE AT UBER

Most of us now know the story of Susan Fowler, an engineer at Uber, who on February 19, 2017, published a scathing blog post that called out the leadership of Uber, led then by Travis Kalanick, for unmitigated sexual harassment at the level of the company's culture.[16] She described how she was persistently propositioned by her supervisor shortly after coming to the company, took screenshots of his messages to human resources, and was rebuffed by HR. His behavior was excused, and she was told to go find another team or put up with his behavior. She left and joined another team. Her path in the company was obstructed by management because of trumped-up "performance" problems, when what she had done was speak truth to power. Clearly, it was not a safe place to work—psychologically, physically, or emotionally. After a year, she left the company for another position.

Fowler's blog post made big headlines, and she became a *cause celebre*, even helping accelerate the #MeToo movement. The board of directors, led by Ariana Huffington, realized it had a significant public

SIDE BOX 6.2: (CONTINUED)

relations, leadership, and business issue. On February 20, 2017, they hired former US Attorney General Eric Holder to conduct an investigation. Holder's June report showed that sexual misconduct and racial discrimination were systemic and rampant across Uber. He found 215 cases of workplace violations—47 were sexual harassment; 54 were racial discrimination. His report made a range of recommendations to change Uber's system, including redesigning its culture.[17] It was not long before the CEO resigned, though he still remains on the board. Other senior executives either left or were fired. Uber quickly lost $17 billion in value along with market share. There are consequences when company cultures and leadership violate basic ethics and human decency.

mattered in their organizations. When it was doubled to 60%, there was 27% less turnover, 40% fewer physical safety incidents, and a 12% increase in productivity.[19]

- **Definition of the Skill:** Harvard's Amy Edmundson defines psychological safety as a "climate in which speaking up is enabled and expected."[20] She goes on to say, that in a psychologically safe workplace, "people are comfortable expressing and being themselves," are comfortable sharing concerns and mistakes without fear of retribution, blame, or humiliation."[21] This safety is also about physical and emotional safety. Workers are safe from physical harm and are free from sexual harassment, bullying, racial discrimination, or discrimination of any kind. This collaborative leadership skill, then, is the ability to create a workplace that is free from fear.

- **Why This Skill is So Critical:** As noted in the Gallup study, when the workplace is safe, there is greater productivity, less turnover, and fewer accidents. There is also greater willingness to take risks, make mistakes, learn, and grow. Innovation is the result. When the workplace is psychologically, physically, and emotionally safe, there is higher trust, ownership, responsibility, and willingness to be accountable.

- **What This Skill Involves:** Edmundson has suggested three key goals for this skill:[22]

  – Creating shared expectations and meaning

  – Building confidence that people's voices are welcome

  – Maintaining an orientation toward continuous learning

- **When to Use This Skill:** It is essential that collaborative leaders create a workplace free from fear at all times.

Skill Set 4: The Collaborative Principle of Honor

Semper Fidelis, which means "always faithful," is the US Marine Corps motto, which reflects a code of honor among soldiers. It is their bond, their word, their commitment to one another. It means something to be a Marine. For a collaborative leader, honor is a mark of distinction, their reputation, and the regard which others have for us. To be honorable means the leader has high integrity and can be counted on. In a collaborative workplace, the leader honors their commitments and agreements so that others can count on them, trust them, and depend on them. *Merriam-Webster* defines *honor* in the context of leadership as integrity.[23]

Honor happens at two levels: At the individual level, being an honorable collaborative leader is also about being true to one's core values and principles, as well as being one's authentic self. In the team or organization, the collaborative leader protects the core principles of the culture and demonstrates integrity above reproach.

The essential goal of the collaborative leader is to provide faithful stewardship of the ethics, culture and organization through (1) Individually, being self-aware through disciplined reflection, and (2) Organizationally, being the Chief Cultural Officer, the steward of the collaborative leadership culture.

Skill: Self-Awareness through Disciplined Reflection

- **Definition of the Skill:** Goleman defines self-awareness as "the ability to recognize and understand your moods, emotions, and drives, as well as their effect on others." He noted four signs of self-awareness as candor, realistic self-assessment, self-confidence, and a self-deprecating sense of humor.[24]
- **Why This Skill is So Critical:** To be trusted by others, it is essential that the collaborative leader practice disciplined self-reflection for the purpose of being and remaining self-aware. Being disciplined means regularly engaging in a process of mindful reflection on their own behavior, situations they have encountered, their own behavior, and how they will move forward.
- **What This Skill Involves:** Commitment and self-discipline are the two most important ingredients. Even if a commitment is made to reflect on a regular basis, without the self-discipline to do so, it will be less likely to happen. This is not a practice that is a "nice to have" or a "want to have." It is a "must have," to remain grounded in your values and the principles of collaboration. Without regular mindful reflection, it is much easier to become reactive to events, rather than responsive.
- **When to Use This Skill:** Preferably daily, but no less than weekly. The frequency is essential to remain grounded in a very fast-paced work world.

Skill: Chief Cultural Officer and Steward

- **Definition of the Skill:** In Robert Greenleaf's work on servant leadership, he cites stewardship as one of the ten characteristics, which involves holding the institutions in trust for the greater good of society, serving the needs of others, and being open and persuasive, not controlling.[25] In a collaborative leadership culture, the stewardship role is fulfilled by the collaborative leader, whose job it is to keep their eye on and protect the organization's collaborative culture.[26]

- **Why This Skill is So Critical:** There needs to be at least one person in the C-suite who has their eye on the collaborative culture at all times. It is also the responsibility of every leader and manager across the organization to be a steward of the collaborative culture. They can be the chief cultural officers within their own units or teams and in this way cultivate a shared sense of responsibility.
- **What This Skill Involves:** There must be both alignment and credibility among senior leaders. They also need to be deeply respected by other leaders across the organization since it is only through relationship and influence that they can perform their responsibilities.
- **When to Use This Skill:** Chief cultural officers implement a more proactive, high engagement and ownership strategy to keep the collaborative culture alive, but remain vigilant for any breaches and put interventions in place to address them.

Skill Set 5: The Collaborative Principle of Mutual Respect

The collaborative principle of mutual respect has three components to it:

- **Self-Respect:** This is about one's self-esteem, the regard that I have for myself, self-confidence, competence, self-trust, and sense of purpose. In a collaborative leadership culture, high self-respect enables us to respect others.
- **Respecting Others:** This means we have the highest regard for others, without any consideration of their gender, race, color, religion, culture, country of origin, sexual orientation, or disability.
- **Leadership Culture of Respect:** A culture that honors the dignity, competencies, and gifts that each person brings to the workplace. It values each person for who they are and where they are in their growth and development, invests in their continued development, appreciates and acknowledges their contributions, and empowers them to be their best selves and to do their best work.

The essential goal of the collaborative leader in this principle is to build mutual respect across the organization through applying the following skills: (1) Showing up and being present, (2) Showing empathy, (3) Coaching, (4) 4-way communications, and (5) Nurturing and acknowledgment.

Skill: Showing Up, Being Present, and Connecting

- **Definition of the Skill:** It is said that showing up for others is 90% of the relationship. This means being present both physically and emotionally. It means being available, open, and ready to listen and support. It means not being distracted, but being focused on the individuals or the team that the leader is working with. Finally, it means connecting with individuals or team members—recognizing their presence, their hopes and expectations, and their needs.

- **Why This Skill is So Critical:** A collaborative leader's credibility is tied to the ability to build trust-based relationships. To do so, in part, requires them to show up, be present, and connecting. It is about demonstrating one's humanity and authenticity.
- **What This Skill Involves:** It is self-defining—it literally involves showing up at work, at team meetings, in engagements of all kinds. It is not hovering or micromanaging, but being open and available.
- **When to Use This Skill:** For a collaborative leader, showing up, being present and connecting is a constant process, whether it is at a kick-off event, a department-wide "all-hands" meeting, or a host of other meetings and processes.

Skill: *Showing Empathy, Active Listening, and Dialogue*

- **Definition of the Skill:** Empathy, active listening, and dialogue have been put together under the principle of mutual respect because they are interconnected. If you are actively listening to another human being, you are empathizing; when you are in a dialogue with others, you are actively listening.
- **Why These Skills Are So Important:** The ability to build high trust relationships as well as psychological safety is built on a collaborative leader's emotional intelligence, especially their empathy toward others, their ability to be open, actively listen and validate what others are saying, and to create an open dialogue where it is safe to speak truth to power.
- **What These Skills Involve:**

  ○ **Empathy:** Goleman defines empathy as the ability to understand the emotional makeup of other people and then treating them respectfully.[27] It's walking a mile in the other's shoes, looking at the world from their perspective as best you can, and showing appreciation for their circumstances as they describe them. It's giving them the benefit of the doubt and being as optimistic as possible. Empathy Involves the ability to disconnect from one's own judgments or positions about another person or situation, to ask good questions that demonstrate true caring and appreciation for the challenges the other is experiencing.

  ○ **Active Listening:** Empathy involves active listening where we listen to others with our ears, head, and heart. Active listening involves suspending one's own point of view about the situation, looking the other person in the eye, watching nonverbal communication cues, hearing what is "behind" what is being said, reflecting back to the individual what you heard to *their* satisfaction.

- ○ **Dialogue:** Dialogue, as distinct from discussion, is about assuming that many people have part of the answer to a particular issue. Chrislip suggests that in collaborative workplaces, dialogue has participants working together toward a common understanding, creating common ground.[28] Senge suggests that it is a "free flow of meaning between people."[29] Collaborative leaders are focused on building deep, trust-based relationships where the workforce is empowered to own their jobs, projects, processes, as well as the values, vision, and mission of the organization. To do so requires building mutual respect, which is created by empathizing, actively listening, and engaging others in meaningful dialogue, which involves opening up one's mind, opening up the space for team members and others to consider the issue at hand, exploring together variables and options, and then helping the group come to a resolution on how to address the situation.

- **When to Use These Skills:**

  - ○ This integrated set of skills is an attitude, an orientation—they are used all the time.
  - ○ They are especially important in brainstorming, coaching, feedback, or difficult conversation situations.

Skill: Coaching for High Performance

- **Definition of the Skill:** The International Coach Federation (ICF) defines *coaching* as "partnering with the client in a thought-provoking and creative process that inspires them to maximize their personal and professional potential."[30] Goldsmith and Lyons suggest four elements of a definition of coaching: A behavior approach of mutual benefit; not a technique or a one-time event; establishes healthy relationships; and can be transformational.[31]
- **Why This Skill is So Critical:** Coaching is a critical skill for collaborative leaders because it redefines their relationship with the workforce from being a boss to that of facilitator and coach. It enables the leader to empower the workforce, to build ownership and to focus on the individual's or team's development.
- **What This Skill Involves:** According to the ICF, coaching involves 11 core competencies: meet the ethical guidelines and professional standards, establish the coaching agreement, establish trust and intimacy with the client, demonstrate coaching presence, demonstrate active listening, ask powerful questions, be direct, create awareness, design actions, plan and set goals, and manage progress and accountability.[32]
- **When to Use This Skill:** Coaching can be used both directly and indirectly. If used directly, it is explicit, as in a coaching session where both parties

understand what is happening. It can also be used indirectly, as in having a coaching attitude of asking good questions, actively listening, reflecting, and empowering others to take ownership of the issue and its solution. Along with facilitation, coaching is one of the most critical collaborative leadership skills.

Skill: Four-Way Communications

- **Definition of the Skill:** In the Power Paradigm, communications are one-way, from the top to the bottom. In the People and Principle Paradigms, communications are two-way, where the front line gives feedback to management. In the Collaboration Paradigm, communications are four-way, from top to bottom, bottom to top, and side to side.
- **Why This Skill is So Critical:** In order to achieve alignment and ownership of an organization's vision and mission, there is a four-way communication process that ensures all members of the workforce are heard, and there is a complete feedback loop.
- **What This Skill Involves:** Four-way communications do not involve the public relations function of a company, where talking points are massaged for workforce consumption. Instead, senior leadership makes a firm commitment to the value of four-way communications, creates the infrastructure so it can happen, and follows through on it. If there is reversion and senior leaders back down on this commitment, it will undermine their credibility. Honoring it helps transform the leadership culture of the organization.
- **When to Use This Skill:** This skill is used constantly by all levels of management in an organization, and especially prior to any major organizational changes.

Skill: Nurturing and Acknowledgement

- **Definition of the Skill:** Kouzes and Posner's fifth leadership practice is to *encourage the heart.* This involves genuine acts of caring to uplift the spirits of the workforce, recognition of contributions, and appreciation of everyone and celebrating values and victories.[33] Collaborative leaders come from a place of nurturing and support for the people, showing them deep respect and appreciation for their hard work and contributions.
- **Why This Skill is So Critical:** In the People, Principle, and Collaboration Paradigms, there is a recognition that the workforce is made up of human beings with hearts, needs, aspirations, hopes, fears, and expectations. They recognize the psychological need of the workforce to be appreciated.
- **What This Skill Involves:** Nurturing behavior involves a high degree of empathy by the leader, as well as appreciation for how hard the people are working, the gifts and skills they bring to the task at hand, their commitment, their

productive energy, and their dedication to the success of the organization. It also involves a high degree of authenticity on the part of the leader. When they acknowledge or appreciate one or more members of the workforce, it is coming from their hearts.

- **When to Use This Skill:** Frequently and often, but not so often it can be considered disingenuous. Nurturing behavior is not a "one and done" skill either. Collaborative leaders learn both the art and the skill of when and how to authentically acknowledge and appreciate the people they work with, knowing that the workforce craves knowing that they are appreciated, are doing good work, and matter.

Skill Set 6: The Principle of Full Responsibility

The sixth principle of collaboration is full responsibility, which has two components: being responsible for yourself and being responsible to others.

- **Being Fully Responsible for Myself:** This means that leaders own and are responsible and accountable for the assumptions they make, the beliefs they hold, their attitudes toward others, and their behaviors and actions. It means they are willing to be held accountable and are open to receiving feedback and to modifying their behaviors. It means they are trustworthy and a person of integrity.
- **Being Fully Responsible to Others:** This means they care about their colleagues, team members, and the organization; are aware of issues or problems that may be obstacles to the effectiveness of others; and will show up, speak up, and step up to address them.

The essential goal of the collaborative leader in this principle is to apply these two skills: (1) Motivating the workforce and (2) People problem solving.

Skill: Motivating the Workforce

- **Definition of The Skill:** The workforce can be motivated either by extrinsic or intrinsic rewards. Extrinsic rewards are things like salary, benefits, stock options, and car washes. These rewards are far less important to the workforce than intrinsic rewards, which Thomas has defined as intrinsic motivation:[34]

  - A sense of meaningfulness, that what you are doing is worth your time and energy; that your purpose matters in the larger scheme of things
  - A sense of choice, the opportunity to use your own judgment to do the things that make sense to you
  - A sense of competence, that you are accomplishing things and are doing good, high quality work
  - A sense of progress, that your work is moving forward

- **Why This Skill is So Critical:** People need to know that they matter, that they are contributing to something that will make a difference, and that they can find meaning in their work. Collaborative leaders motivate the workforce by connecting the work of the organization to the need for purpose and meaning. This is how productive energy is generated, how top talent is recruited and retained, and how people will be able to be their best selves and do their best work.
- **What This Skill Involves:** Collaborative leaders must deeply appreciate the significant differences between extrinsic and intrinsic rewards. While all workers need salaries and benefits, collaborative leaders will focus on how they will engage the creative and innovative capabilities of the workforce by focusing on their need to have purpose, have meaning, and to make a difference.
- **When to Use This Skill:** A focus on intrinsic motivation needs to be people policy for every collaborative organization. In addition, in coaching and developing individuals and teams, it is critical to connect individual aspirations and team missions with a higher purpose, so that people realize that everything they do is making a difference.

Skill: People Problem-Solving

- **Definition of The Skill:** Every team and organization will experience a wide range of people problems from performance issues, interpersonal conflict, responsibility and accountability breakdowns, dysfunctional behavior, unethical conduct, and many others. Some of these people problems are short term, while others develop over a longer time period. Some of these problems are smaller than others, some have limited negative impacts, while others may threaten the organization's survival. Each people problem can affect the morale or performance of the organization, a team, production schedules, budgets, quality, and customers.
- **Why This Skill is So Critical:** Wong has argued that behavior is the most important determinant of a team's success, so being able to resolve people's behavioral problems becomes critical to the organization's success.[35] Solving these problems quickly becomes an imperative for collaborative leaders who honor the principle of full responsibility. They can't be swept under the carpet. They must be addressed head on. Failure to address these people problems can result in serious consequences for individuals, teams, business units, or the organization overall.
- **What This Skill Involves:** The literature on people problem-solving is rather sparse, even though people problems are, as Wong points out, the most essential ingredient to a team's and organization's success. Most of the problem-solving literature is focused on business problems, are content or strategy-oriented, and does not incorporate the importance of an organization's leadership culture as the context for how problems get resolved. The model shown in Figure 6.1 reflects over 30 years of experience in working with

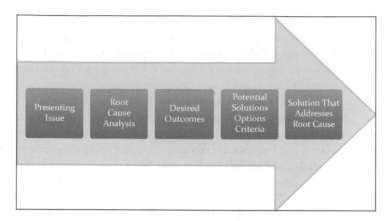

FIGURE 6.1 Collaborative People Problem-Solving Method.

individuals, teams and companies of all kinds as they struggled to solve their people issues. There are five parts to it:

○ **Presenting Issue:** The presenting people issue is *never* the real issue. I once had a client who said his third-shift workers were stealing medical supplies, so he decided to increase security and offer the workers incentives. Research discovered that the real problem was that the workers had a strict command-and-control, micromanaging supervisor, they were working three jobs to make ends meet, and needed an hourly rate increase and a supervisor who was more collaborative.

○ **Root Cause Analysis:** To get at the real problem, there must be a root cause analysis to truly understand the issue. The rule of "five whys" can be used to get to the root cause. By the time you get to the fifth "why," the real reason for the behavior or conduct will be discovered. Often it is rooted in the individual's background, previous experiences or some pain or hurt they have experienced.

○ **Desired Outcomes:** It is important to be clear about the outcomes desired from the problem resolution. They need to be clear and specific.

○ **Potential Solutions, Options, and Criteria:** Based on the real root cause(s) of the presenting problem, and the desired outcomes of the process, the team or coach can brainstorm possible solutions, narrow those options to several, and then establish the criteria by which the solution will be selected.

○ **Solution That Addresses the Root Cause:** Using the criteria the coach/team have agreed on, one of the options is selected. The test of the validity of the solution will be whether it resolves the presenting problem. If it is not resolved, then the process is repeated.

- **When to Use This Skill:** This method should be used whenever there is a difficult, challenging, or seemingly intractable people problem. This method is different from the difficult conversations tool to be discussed in the next set of skills. It can be used in the moment when teams encounter a people obstacle or barrier to their progress. It can also be used by coaches of individual workers as a way of helping them develop, learn, and grow.

Skill Set 7: The Principle of Accountability

The seventh principle for a collaborative leadership cultures is accountability, and there are two types of accountability: self-accountability and holding others accountable.

- **Self-Accountability:** In the Power Paradigm, people avoid "getting caught," or they use the mantra "ask for forgiveness, not for permission." In a collaborative leadership culture, the focus is on "owning up" to your mistakes, or what I call the Blue Angels Principle.[36] This US Navy precision flying team flies six F/A-18 Hornet jets at 700 mph, often at 18-inch wing separation through hundreds of acrobatic maneuvers in a 45-minute air show. Mistakes can be fatal, so if you make a mistake, everyone knows it. This principle says that if you make a mistake, you own up to it, learn from it, and commit to it never happening again. In a collaborative leadership culture, this idea of self-accountability is very powerful; it strengthens trust because people can count on you to own up. It's not about getting caught, it's about getting better.
- **Holding Others Accountable:** In a collaborative leadership culture, this is where the rubber hits the road. You can run but you cannot hide. We are accountable to each other. This means we hold each other to the highest standards of collaborative and ethical conduct, not from a place of authority or control but from a place of compassion, growth, and development. If someone on our team, in the organization, or in leadership is consistently behaving badly and will not change, even after an empathic exploration of causes and even difficult conversations, that individual can be terminated. If there is an ethical breach, there should be a zero tolerance standard of immediate dismissal.

The essential goal of the collaborative leader is to implement this principle across the organization by applying these two skills: (1) Giving and receiving feedback and (2) Conducting difficult conversations.

Skill: Giving and Receiving Feedback

- **Definition of the Skill:** Seashore et al. define feedback as information about past behavior delivered in the present, which may influence future behavior.[37] It is data about one's behavior, as perceived by another person, who shares that information in a way that can be heard and that can strengthen the relationship.

- **Why This Skill is So Critical:** Without effective feedback, a collaborative enterprise will have its progress stifled. As Seashore et al. point out, "Feedback in the workplace is fundamental for helping those who wish to improve their performance, reach an objective, or avoid unpleasant reactions to their efforts."[38] Feedback is an essential communication function in a collaborative leadership culture that enables people to build trust, mutual respect and understanding, and promotes constructive action that moves the team and organization forward.
- **What This Skill Involves:** It involves one person giving and a second person receiving feedback. But it is far more complex than that. Virginia Satir, who developed family systems therapy, developed an interaction model that helps us understand the psychology of giving and receiving feedback. There are seven steps:[39] (1) Message sent elicits (2) Meaning, which triggers (3) Feelings about the meaning, which activates (4) Feelings about the feelings, which evokes (5) Defenses such as denying, ignoring, or projecting, which requires (6) Rules for commenting, which directs (7) A response, which is congruent or incongruent (true/untrue). It is important to understand that one's perceptual screens will be the lens through which feedback information is sent and received. It becomes critical that the person giving feedback use empathy to understand and appreciate the complexity of the process, and that the receiver of feedback self-regulate to reduce levels of defensiveness, so that the process can be constructive. It's a two-way exchange.
- **When to Use This Skill:** Giving and receiving feedback can be involuntary or voluntary. Seashore et al. point to several key understandings about when feedback occurs:[40]

  - Even when requested, feedback describes the giver more than the receiver.
  - Feedback is best done when it is invited or asked for.
  - For feedback to be effective, there must be an agreement about the type of feedback being requested.
  - Feedback is a collaborative process that is constant and is an interaction between two or more people.

Skill: *Conducting Difficult Conversations*

- **Definition of The Skill:** Stone et al. define a difficult conversation as "anything you find it hard to talk about."[41]
- **Why This Skill is So Critical:** In difficult conversations there is no blaming, shaming, projection, or intimidation. It's not about power, it's about relationship. It's about finding a shared understanding that respects the viewpoints of each person. One person does not have "the truth" or power over the other person. It also creates the context where shared problem solving can occur.

- **What This Skill Involves:** There are two ways of thinking about difficult conversations:
  - **The Three Conversations:** Stone et al., who point out that every difficult conversation has three parts to it:[42]
    - The "what happened" conversation, which involves a disagreement, who said what, and who's to blame.
    - The "feelings" conversation, which has to do with whether my feelings are valid or appropriate, whether I should acknowledge or deny them, and what I should do with the other person's feelings.
    - The "identity" conversation, which is the internal conversation we have about whether we are competent or incompetent, worthy of love or not.
  - **What's So, So What, Now What:** The second approach comes from the human potential movement and is an upgraded version of these three conversations, which include:
    - The "What's So" conversation is factual; there are no "you" statements, which blame or accuse the other.
    - The "So What" conversation involves feelings about what happened, expressed as "I" statements.
    - The "Now What" conversation involves both parties talking about where they go from there; they use "We" statements and focus on solutions.
- **When to Use This Skill:** This is not a coaching conversation, nor is it a giving and receiving feedback conversation, though it certainly reflects elements of both. The what's so, so what, now what tool is used by the collaborative leader when the situation has escalated beyond coaching or feedback. The individual may need to be held accountable for inappropriate behavior, dysfunctional behavior, disruptive interpersonal relations with another or in a team, or when they present as an obstacle to a team's progress. It is typically used when the team itself is not able to resolve it through their operating agreements. It is also often the last step before dismissing the individual from the organization.

LEARNING COLLABORATIVE LEADERSHIP SKILLS

Becoming skilled as a collaborative leader is going to take some time. This section of the chapter will describe the five phases in the process of making these skills your own—learning, practicing, reflecting, mastery, and empowering others.

- **Phase 1: Learning:**
  - **People Lab:** In the learning phase, consider this process as a "people lab," where you get to explore, understand, and appreciate what is involved in achieving mastery as a collaborative leader.

- ○ **Rationale:** It is important to review your collaborative leadership journey to reflect on why you took the journey, and why it is so important for you to learn a new set of skills.
- ○ **Understand:** The cognitive part of the learning phase involves learning about each of the skills, starting with the seven sets of skills identified above. What is the reason for each of the skills, what is involved from a behavioral standpoint, and what kinds of changes you may need to make to be successful at the skill.
- ○ **Prioritize:** Identify the top three to five skills you need to learn first; understand why you have chosen each skill. As a suggestion, start with reflection and facilitation.
- ○ **Specialized Training:** There are many resources available for specialized training. Many, however, are "technique" oriented training and may not reflect the collaborative value set.

- **Phase 2: Practicing:** As the saying goes, "How do you get to Carnegie Hall? Practice, practice, practice." The only way to achieve mastery and be able to train and empower others is if you practice each skill regularly. Start your disciplined reflection skill right away, and do it daily. For the facilitation skill, once you are trained, find or create opportunities to practice at work, with friends, or your family.
- **Phase 3: Reflecting:** Reflect not only on your practice of each skill by yourself but also to get a practice partner to work with and give you feedback. A tool you can use as you debrief your practicing a skill is: what worked, where to improve, impact. What did you do that worked, what was the impact of your work on others, where do you need to improve, and what was the impact on others of where you did not do as well?
- **Phase 4: Mastery:** Mastery is a goal rather than a destination. You will always be striving to be a master of each of the skills.
- **Phase 5: Empowering Others:** There is a threshold of collaborative skill competence you will achieve relatively quickly, where you feel confident enough to begin teaching others.

CHAPTER CONCLUSION: COLLABORATIVE SKILLS CREATE COLLABORATIVE LEADERSHIP CULTURES

As a prospective collaborative leader, you have come a very long way. You understand the evolution of leadership paradigms, from Power to People to Principle to Collaboration. You understand the core beliefs and principles of a collaborative leadership culture and the attributes and behaviors of a collaborative leader. You have courageously gone on your collaborative leadership journey and come out on the other side ready to learn the skills that are essential to empowering others to be their best selves and to do their best work.

The organizational terrain for collaborative leaders is incredibly challenging. The predominant leadership culture even now is the Power Paradigm. To begin practicing collaborative skills in this environment can be challenging. If problems get solved, however, and people are honored by the process, even in this hostile climate, it is possible to make gains on the collaboration front. Particularly hopeful is that when teams get a taste of what it feels like to own how they work with each other, and how they work together to solve problems, they become ambassadors for change within that organization. A range of strategies was suggested to help cope with these organizational challenges, not the least of which is to be true to your beliefs about how people should be treated in the workplace, never quit, always persist, and look for whatever opportunities to empower people that may exist.

To make the creation of a collaborative leadership culture real, leadership skills were identified, each tied to the implementation of one of the 7 Principles of the Collaborative Work Ethic. We defined each of the skills, connected them to the work of other scholars and practitioners, demonstrated their relevance to the creation of a collaborative leadership culture, described what they involved, and framed them in the context of a five-phase process that leads to mastery and the empowerment of others to use them.

The main point of this chapter was this: Collaborative leadership is not about power and control, telling people what to do and then finding them doing something wrong. Collaborative leadership is about building trust-based relationships, giving people ownership over the values, vision, mission, strategy, and their own jobs. It is about influencing, facilitating, engaging, and empowering them; designing and facilitating collaborative meetings; forming and developing collaborative teams; and building workplace cultures that honor the human spirit. It's about behaving in a way that is aligned with the seven principles of collaboration, walking the talk, and mastering the skills that will empower others. What can be particularly helpful, and what can give the collaborative leader a boost, is the power that comes when collaborative teams are created and developed, which is the subject of our next chapter.

CHAPTER REVIEW AND REFLECTIONS

Learning Objectives:
Let's reflect on the learning objectives for the chapter and summarize what we have learned:

- Understand the *context* in which collaborative leadership skills will be used, as well as some of the key barriers or challenges collaborative leaders will face.

- Learn the *framework* that connects collaborative leadership skills to the seven principles of collaboration, as well as the attributes, behaviors, and roles of collaborative leaders.
- Understand the *principle-based collaborative leadership skills* that will empower the workforce to be their best selves, do their best work, and produce high performance and sustainable results.
- Review the *phases involved in the process* of making these skills your own—learning, practicing, reflecting, mastery, and empowering others.

Initial Questions Revisited, and For Reflection:

- *Given the challenges that collaborative leaders face in companies, are you prepared to move forward?*
- *Which collaborative leadership skills will be most helpful for you as you navigate these challenges in a way that honors your values and commitment to empowering the workforce?*
- *Are you ready to practice, practice, practice to become a "master" of collaboration so that you can help others and transform any leadership culture you enter?*

ADDITIONAL READINGS

- Goldsmith, Marshall. *What Got You Here Won't Get You There.* White Plains, NY: Disney Hyperion, 2007.
- Goldsmith, Marshall, and Laurence Lyons, eds. *Coaching for Leadership.* 2nd ed. San Francisco: Pfeiffer. 2006.
- Satir, Virginia. *The New Peoplemaking.* Mountain View, CA: Science and Behavior Books, 1988.
- Seashore, Charles N., Edith W. Seashore, and Gerald M. Weinberg. *What Did You Say? The Art of Giving and Receiving Feedback.* Columbia, MD: Bingham House Books, 2003.
- Stone, Douglas, Bruce Patton, and Sheila Heen. *Conducting Difficult Conversations: How to Discuss What Matters Most.* New York: Penguin Books, 2010.

ENDNOTES

1 James M. Kouzes and Barry Z. Posner, *The Leadership Challenge*, 6th ed. (Hoboken, NJ: Wiley, 2017).
2 *Merriam-Webster,* https://www.merriam-webster.com/dictionary/skill

3   James M. Kouzes and Barry Z. Posner, *The Leadership Challenge* (Hoboken, NJ: Wiley, 2017), pp. 95–116.

4   Clive Thompson, "The See-Through CEO," *Wired*, March, 2007, quoted in Cathleen Benko and Molly Anderson, "Lattice Ways to Participate," in *Creating a Company Culture of Collaboration and Transparency* (Boston, MA: Harvard Business Review Press, 2010), p. 11.

5   Watson Wyatt, *Driving Business Results through Continuous Engagement*, Watson Wyatt Worldwide, Arlington, VA, 2009, quoted in Benko and Anderson, ibid., p. 13.

6   Deloitte Consulting, "Trust in the Workplace: 2010 Ethics and Workplace Survey," 2010, https://docplayer.net/13107004-Trust-in-the-workplace-2010-ethics-workplace-survey.html

7   Benko and Anderson, op. cit., p. 11–13.

8   Benko and Anderson, ibid., p. 15.

9   Kouzes and Posner, op. cit., pp. 193–244.

10 Sandor P. Schuman, "The Role of Facilitation in Collaborative Groups," Executive Decision Services, 1999, http://www.exedes.com/articles/Role-of-Facilitation-in-Collaboration.pdf

11 Ian McDermott and L. Michael Hall, *The Collaborative Leader* (Williston, VT: Crown House, 2016), p. 98.

12 Peter Senge, *The Fifth Discipline* (New York: Currency, 2006), pp. 231–232.

13 https://www.merriam-webster.com/dictionary/integrity

14 https://www.merriam-webster.com/dictionary/ethics

15 Andrew Leigh, *Ethical Leadership* (London: Kogan Page, 2013), p. 46.

16 Susan J. Fowler, "Reflecting on One Very, Very Strange Year at Uber," February 19, 2017, a blogpost, https://www.susanjfowler.com/blog/2017/2/19/reflecting-on-one-very-strange-year-at-uber; see also Emily Chang, *Brotopia* (New York: Penguin Random House, 2018), pp. 105–134.

17 "Uber Report: Eric Holder's Recommendations for Change," *New York Times*, June 13, 2017; Eric Holder, *The Holder Report*, (Washington, DC, Covington and Burling, 2017).

18 Amy C. Edmundson, "The Importance of Psychological Safety," *Human Resources*, December 4, 2018, p. 1.

19 Gallup, *State of the American Workplace Report* (Washington, DC: Gallup, 2017), 112; cited in Amy C. Edmundson, *The Fearless Organization* (Hoboken, NJ: Wiley, 2019), pp. xv–xvi.

20 Amy C. Edmundson, op. cit., p. 2.

21 Amy C. Edmundson, *The Fearless Organization*, op. cit., p. xv–xvi.

22 Ibid., p. 159.

23 https://www.merriam-webster.com/dictionary/honor

24 Daniel Goleman, "What Makes a Leader?," *Harvard Business Review, Best of 1998*, January 2004, pp. 4–6.

25 Larry Spears, "The Understand and Practices of Servant Leadership," presentation at Servant Leadership Research Roundtable, Greenleaf Center for Servant Leadership, Regent University School of Leadership Studies, Virginia Beach, VA, August, 2005.

26 See Shelley DuBois, "The Rise of the Chief Culture Officer," *Fortune*, July 30, 2012, https://fortune.com/2012/07/30/the-rise-of-the-chief-culture-officer/; and Blake Morgan, "Chief Culture Office and Chief Customer Officer: A Winning Combination," *Forbes*, January 16, 2018, https://www.forbes.com/sites/blakemorgan/2018/01/16/chief-culture-officer-and-chief-customer-officer-a-winning-combination/#51ef12903ab1

27 Goleman, op. cit., pp. 4–10.

28 David D. Chrislip, *Collaborative Leadership Fieldbook* (San Francisco: Jossey-Bass, 2002), pp. 96–98.

29 Senge, *The Fifth Discipline*, p. 223.

30 "ICF Definition of Coaching and Core Competencies," https://coachfederation.org/about#:~:text=ICF%20defines%20coaching%20as%20partnering,their%20personal%20and%20professional%20potential

31 Marshall Goldsmith and Laurence S. Lyons, eds. *Coaching for Leadership*, 2ⁿᵈ ed. (San Francisco: Pfeiffer, 2006), p. xx.

32 ICF, op.cit.

33 Kouzes and Posner, op. cit., pp. 245–294.

34 Kenneth Thomas, "Four Intrinsic Rewards," Chapter 4, in *Intrinsic Motivation at Work*, 2ⁿᵈ ed. (Oakland, CA: Barrett-Koehler), pp. 47–59.

35 Zachary Wong, *The Eight Essential People Skills for Project Management* (Oakland, CA: Barrett-Koehler, 2018), p. 23.

36 https://www.blueangels.navy.mil/

37 Charles N. Seashore, Edith W. Seashore, and Gerald M. Weinberg, *What Did You Say? The Art of Giving and Receiving Feedback* (Columbia, MD: Bingham House Books, 2003), p. 3.

38 Ibid., p. 7.

39 Ibid., p. 19; see also Virginia Satir, *The New Peoplemaking* (Mountain View, CA: Science and Behavior Books, 1988).

40 Seashore et al., op. cit., pp. 25–40, 76, 91.

41 Douglas Stone, Bruce Patton, and Sheila Heen, *Conducting Difficult Conversations: How to Discuss What Matters Most* (New York: Penguin Books, 2010), p. xxvii.

42 Ibid., pp. 7–8.

Collaborative Teams

CHAPTER SEVEN

Collaborative Teams:

THE DRIVERS OF TRANSFORMATION

Remember teamwork begins by building trust.

—Patrick Lencioni, *The Five Dysfunctions of a Team*

*T*HE LEARNING *team had scheduled an extended meeting time because they knew the critical importance of their dialogue and assignments this week—collaborative teams. Hanyue had arranged to have the meeting at his apartment, where the team members brought food from their countries to have for dinner. It was Priyanka's turn to facilitate, so she reviewed the agenda and desired results with the team and asked for upgrades to build ownership of the meeting. Linda started by appreciating the team for all the hard work they had done and shared her concern she wasn't doing enough to support the team. Morare encouraged her, "You have always been a strong contributor to our work, and your insights into how people work best together have helped me become more empathic. Thank you." Linda smiled and relaxed. Priyanka deftly shifted the conversation to their assignment on collaborative teams. Ana was frustrated. "We've been a collaborative team for at least six weeks now. Why do we need to read an entire chapter on this topic?" Hanyue, who had been quiet up until now, tried to help. "We went through an abbreviated form of collaborative team governance, but I know there has to be more to it. This approach to team development didn't appear out of thin air. I want to understand more about the theory and implementation of this approach." Priyanka intervened and asked them to look at the questions for their reflection as they read this chapter:*

- *How does a collaborative team reflect the Collaboration Paradigm of leadership, and how is it different from the more traditional, power-based approach to teams?*
- *What makes the Collaborative Team Governance Process unique and different from the traditional approaches?*

208 | Leadership's 4th Evolution

- *Do I believe 100% true consensus on decisions is possible? What is the process for achieving it, and why is it so important?*
- *If I decide to master the skills necessary to form and manage a collaborative team, what kinds of challenges will I face in facilitating them?*

LEARNING OBJECTIVES

By the end of this chapter, you will:

- Understand the evolution of 20th Century organizational teams and their development
- Learn about the leadership, culture, processes, and structure of 21st Century collaborative teams from a systems perspective
- Understand the power of 100% true consensus as a decision-making rule for people and work processes
- Dig deeper into what makes collaborative teams unique, their governance process, and the 7 steps of forming a collaborative team
- Identify the central challenges facing collaborative teams and how they can be addressed to ensure effectiveness

THE MAIN POINT OF THIS CHAPTER

Imagine this scenario: A new technology product team of 12 very skilled individuals assembled in Conference Room 403 at 8:00 a.m. We'll call them Team Delta. No one is very sure what it is all about, but they each had gotten an email from the Chief Operations Officer (COO) to show up and be ready to work. The team leader walks in five minutes late, sits at the head of the table, and then puts the agenda for the meeting up on a screen—a list of ten topics he wants to cover at the meeting. He starts out by introducing himself, gives his title, and explains what he had been asked to do by the COO. He informs them that this is a very critical team, identifies their task and their timeline, and then says, "We have very little time, so let's get to work." You can see the confusion on people's faces, but they know better than to challenge the COO's emissary. There could be consequences that aren't good for anyone's career. So the team gets started. Three weeks later, at their next meeting, only nine members show up. They had "work conflicts." Updates that were due did not get delivered. The team leader is furious and makes his feelings known to the team. Afterward, he hunts the three down and gives them an ultimatum. A month later there's another update meeting. This time, half the team has other things to do and does not show. This time, the team leader cancels the meeting and heads to the COO's office. It's not a pretty picture. The COO came to the next meeting, and his sharply worded emails to the six recalcitrant members had them show up as well, though reluctantly. They were tired of being bullied and micromanaged by the team leader. Now the project is behind schedule, the team is in disarray, morale is in the tank, and the whole team is on a forced march to complete the work product, which they did. Needless to say, the team failed, the team leader failed, and the resulting product, which was late, was not of very high quality.

Team Delta's experience is, unfortunately, the experience of most teams that are in the Power Paradigm, where the focus is on control and results, rather than on people and trust, the team's culture, and how they're going to work together. This is a results-over-relationship approach. The team development approach they were using was Tuckman's "forming-storming-norming-performing" model.[1] Delta, however, got what many leaders have called "storming-storming-storming-nonperforming."

Teams are how we get work done in the 21st Century. The 20th Century storming model for teamwork is no longer effective in our digital, globally interconnected, and uncertain world. In the 21st Century, teams work virtually, and members are culturally diverse, work in different time zones, and are largely Millennial. They need to feel psychologically safe and want to own their team processes. Trust is the glue that holds them together.

The 4th Evolution of teamwork, Collaborative Teams, honors the power of a team's culture, creates psychological safety by front-loading the process, where team members agree on how they will work together, which results in high trust and greater team effectiveness. The Collaborative Team Governance Process has two steps—norming and performing. It puts relationship first and translates their shared values and beliefs into agreements adopted by 100% true consensus, no reservations. Collaborative teams are about "We", not "Me". They require individuals to put the good of the team ahead of their individual interests so that the team can empower each member to be their best self so they can do their best work. This is done by giving team members ownership of how they will work together, ownership based on true consensus decision-making, which in turn builds high levels of trust, responsibility, and accountability. As a result, collaborative teams are more productive, creative, faster, and have higher quality outcomes.

Let's revisit Team Delta from a collaborative team perspective. The COO sends out a note to the 12 team members and shares with them the mission and intent of the team project. He compliments them on their technical expertise and tells them they are essential to the success of the project. He lets them know there is a team facilitator who will be contacting them about the upcoming kick-off meeting, which he will attend. The next day, the facilitator sends an email to each team member asking them for 30 minutes to discuss the project to get to know them, and to get their input into the kick-off meeting agenda. Over the next few days, all team members have 1:1 meetings with the facilitator. The kick-off meeting agenda is sent to them two days ahead of time. At the kick-off meeting, the COO starts it off by welcoming all team members, discusses the mission of the team and where it fits into the company's overall strategy, and then turns it over to the facilitator who shares the results of the 1:1 meetings with the full team. Confidentiality has been maintained. Then the facilitator introduces the team to the Collaborative Team Governance Process where they will create the team Operating Agreements and Team Charter. Over the next two days, the team completes this up-front relationship-building work. Everyone is on board, owns the Agreements and Charter, 100% true consensus, no reservations, and they get to work. Everyone is clear about who is responsible for what, and over the next few weeks, the project is completed, ahead of schedule and under budget. The quality is exceptional, the COO is ecstatic, and the team members celebrate their accomplishment and each other.

This represents the 4ᵗʰ Evolution of teamwork, Collaborative Teams, which is the primary focus of this chapter. We will consider Collaborative Teams from a systems perspective. Third, we will explore why 100% true consensus, no reservations, as a decision-making rule, is the gold standard for building trust, mutual respect, and accountability. Fourth, we will walk through the steps of the Collaborative Team Governance Process and then consider some of the organizational challenges you may facing being a facilitative leader of collaborative teams.

HOW WE GOT HERE: THE EVOLUTION OF TEAMING

The fundamental fact of man's capacity to collaborate with his fellows in the face-to-face group will survive the fads and one day be recognized.

—Douglas McGregor, 1960

All teams are not created equal. Just because someone calls a group a team doesn't make it so. The idealized notion of a team is one of high trust, synergy, and learning, where the team members are excited about their work, own it, have agreed-upon ways to work with each other, and produce superior results. This is a description of a *collaborative team*. Unfortunately, most teams operate more like Team Delta. How did we get here? How did team development evolve from the power to the Collaboration Paradigm?

20ᵗʰ Century Teaming: Key Thinkers

Over the past sixty years, there has been an evolution in our thinking and practice about how small groups work effectively. There are 5 key thinkers who have been instrumental in helping us understand the power of teams as units of work and change in an organization. The emergence of the 4ᵗʰ Evolution of teams, Collaborative Teams, has been the natural culmination of all we have learned since Douglas McGregor first introduced us to teamwork in 1960.

Douglas McGregor: Importance of Teamwork

It was Douglas McGregor, the primary author of the People Paradigm of leadership, who got us to start thinking seriously about teamwork and understand the power of groups in an organizational setting:

> We cannot hope much longer to operate the complex, interdependent, collaborative enterprise which is the modern industrial company on the completely unrealistic premise that it consists of individual relationships.[2]

McGregor was particularly concerned about the relationship between individuals and groups in a corporate setting and whether the two were antithetical or complimentary to each other. He concluded that they could not only coexist but needed each other. He then focused on what it takes for teams to be effective and cites a number of factors:[3]

- The atmosphere of the team is informal, comfortable, and relaxed; people are involved and interested.
- There is a lot of discussion in which almost everyone participates.
- The task of the team is well understood and accepted by the members.
- The members listen to each other; people are not afraid to put for a creative thought.
- There is disagreement; the team does not avoid conflict; there is careful examination and resolution of the differences.
- Most decisions are reached by a "kind of consensus" in which it is clear everyone is in general agreement and willing to go along.
- People express their feelings; few hidden agendas.
- People accept assignments.
- The chair of the team does not dominate it; leadership shifts from time to time depending on circumstances.
- The team is self-aware and reflects on its own operations.

McGregor did not believe that a team's effectiveness depended on the leader. He argued that the research "indicates quite clearly that skillful and sensitive membership behavior is the real clue to effective group operation."[4]

Bruce Tuckman: Stages of Group Development

In 1965 Bruce Tuckman published an article on team development that became perhaps a popular way in which teams were formed. Remember Team Delta? It was grounded in Tuckman's model which is important to understand because of what we have learned about team behavior as a result of companies still using this 20th Century, power-based approach.

Tuckman developed a theoretical model, based on considerable research, which argued there are five stages in a team's development:[5]

1. **Forming:** Members are learning the task and about each other.
2. **Storming:** There is group conflict as members confront and criticize each other and the approach they are taking on the task. There is a lack of clarity on roles and responsibilities, operational rules and procedures, and individual need for recognition of their skills. Members search for their identity, and often have challenges navigating this stage.
3. **Norming:** Members start to resolve their issues and develop social agreements; they begin to recognize their interdependence, develop cohesion, and agree on group norms to help them function effectively in the future.
4. **Performing:** The group has sorted out its social structure and understands its goals and roles.
5. **Adjourning:** The team has rituals for closing down where there is some celebration of their success.

It is important to remind ourselves that Tuckman's model is theoretical. In fact, in an essay he wrote in 1977, he concludes a review of the literature by saying: "It is noteworthy that since 1965 there have been few studies that report empirical data concerning the stages of group development."[6]

My field research over several decades, working with hundreds of teams, found Tuckman's model has become the way in which many corporations have formed teams, in large part because there has been no alternative. The consequences have been severe. Whenever I started working with a new team, members were skeptical about "yet another program-of-the-month" approach. They had the scars of failed teams, and had a right to be skeptical.

In 4th Evolution Collaborative Teams, we built on the lessons learned from the Tuckman model in one very significant way. His model has "norming" as the 3rd stage of team development. In Collaborative Teams, norming is the 1st stage, because the culture of the team drives behavior, and before the team can effectively function, they must first agree on how they are going to work together, enabling them to build ownership and trust. This is the principle of culture-first, content last.

Senge: Team Learning
In 1990 Peter Senge gave us a model of team development that was years ahead of its time: team learning.[7] Senge saw team learning as a discipline within which teams could become their most effective, as "the process of aligning and developing the capacity of a team to create the results its members truly desired. It builds on the discipline of developing a shared vision. It also builds on personal mastery."[8]

He saw team learning as having three critical components: (1) The need to think insightfully about complex issues, (2) The need for innovative, coordinated action, and (3) The role of team members on other teams helping them foster team learning as well.[9] According to Senge, teams need to learn how to deal with powerful forces that oppose productive dialogue, specifically "defensive routines."[10] Think about the passive/defensive or aggressive/defensive leadership cultures discussed in Chapter 2. When a team feels empowered to learn, dialogue, challenge, and take risks but is surrounded by a leadership culture that practices control, fear, intimidation, or retribution, it becomes essential for teams to know how to function and maintain their learning character. Among the practices that are encouraged to promote learning are the following:[11]

- **Dialogue and Discussion:** Dialogue is an open exploration of ideas between people, where they suspend their assumptions, are facilitated, and where they regard each other as colleagues; discussion, on the other hand, is where the purpose is for one person to win over another by being more persuasive.
- **Consensus:** There are two types, one that is "opening up" that seeks a shared view larger than any individual, and a "looking out" approach where everyone tries to see their viewpoint though the eyes of another so they see something new.
- **Dealing With Conflict and Defensive Routines:** *"To retain their power, defensive routines must remain undiscussable. Teams stay stuck in their defensive routines only when they pretend that they don't have any ... that everything is all right, and that they can say 'anything.'"*[12] Basically, teams need to self-disclose and get out of denial about their own defensiveness, and use the skills of reflection and mutual inquiry to understand underlying assumptions and reasoning—remember Schein's "cultural DNA"?
- **Practice:** Team learning is a skill that must be practiced and mastered; dialogue becomes a crucial tool, as is the creation of a shared language.

There is a lot of wisdom here for Collaborative Teams in terms of what it means to be a dynamic, open, learning team. First is the focus on the dynamics of group learning, practice, and mastery. Second is the recognition of the reality that most collaborative teams will find themselves embedded in defensive leadership cultures, and will need to develop coping mechanisms so they can honor their values. Third is the essential role that dialogue has as a tool for leveraging their collective intelligence of all members of the team so they can sustain their collaborative culture, resolve conflicts, and solve problems. Finally, Senge builds on McGregor's mention of consensus as a realistic decision-making tool that will help align team members around critical decisions.

Katzenbach: The Wisdom of Teams
In 1993 Katzenbach and Smith wrote *The Wisdom of Teams*, which focuses on key factors for teams to be high performing.[13] They argue that teams and hierarchy are

compatible, and essentially provide a road map for command-and-control leaders on how to create high performance teams. They note that high performance teams are extremely rare due to a lack of commitment by the members to one another, teams are the best way to integrate across hierarchical boundaries, the wisdom of teams lies in its disciplined pursuit of performance, and organizational leaders can foster team performance best by building a strong performance ethic, rather than by establishing a team-promoting environment alone.[14]

The belief system inherent in their performance-driven approach to team development is that the individual's needs, skills, and experiences are subordinated to the achievement of the organization's performance objectives. They fail to understand that the most effective way to achieve high performance is by building a team culture of psychological, safety, ownership, and trust that respects the gifts and talents of each and every individual. They understand the problem of getting workforce commitment, but fail to provide a process by which to achieve it. Finally, they assert, quite boldly, *"Those who see teams as a replacement for hierarchy are missing the true potential of teams."*[15]

To the contrary. The true potential of teams and their members is realized when they own the values, vision, and mission of the team, own the agreements which will govern how they work, own the task, and feel safe enough to challenge the status quo, take risks, make mistakes, learn, and grow. This cannot be done in a power culture that is only focused on output rather than the development of the people. In effect, Katzenbach's approach to team development is Taylor revisited—just with a different mechanism for controlling the workforce.

Lencioni: The Five Dysfunctions of a Team[16]

In another important book on teams and team development, Patrick Lencioni wrote *The Five Dysfunctions of a Team*, in which he chronicles five reasons why teams do not work well. In Lencioni's work, based on his consulting with many CEOs and their leadership teams, he found two significant overall findings: (1) Genuine teamwork is illusive in most organizations, and (2) "[O]rganizations fail to achieve teamwork because they unknowingly fall prey to five natural but dangerous pitfalls":[17]

1. There is an absence of trust among team members due to an unwillingness by members to be vulnerable in the group.
2. There is a failure to build trust, as well as a fear of conflict, resulting in veiled discussions and guarded comments.
3. There is a lack of healthy conflict, resulting in a lack of commitment and buy-in to decisions, though agreement may be faked in meetings.
4. This lack of buy-in and commitment leads to avoidance of accountability, either for oneself or for holding others accountable.

5. The failure of accountability creates an environment where there is inattention to results because individuals put their own goals above the collective goals of the team.

A functional team has the opposite set of characteristics, where members trust each other, engage in unfiltered conflict around ideas, commit to decisions and plans of action, hold one another accountable for delivering against those plans, and focus on the achievement of collective results.

The most important dysfunction, at the root of team ineffectiveness, is the absence of trust, a core principle of the Collaboration Paradigm. Lencioni defines team trust as "the confidence among team members that their peers' intentions are good, and that there is no reason to be protective or careful around the group."[18]

He goes on to say that the way you overcome this lack of trust is by conducting a series of team exercises, even experiential exercises, behavioral style analysis, and 360 feedback. The premise of his approach is that by getting to know each other better both descriptively and in team experiences, they will learn to trust each other.

I could not agree more with Lencioni that trust is at the core of what makes a team successful. Where this work in collaborative teams has built on his platform is in how you actually build trust. I suspect that he may not have intended this, but this trust premise, in my experience, found its way to outdoor team exercises like trust falls or even Outward Bound–type experiences. In my consulting work, I found that what they learned over a weekend simply could not be transferred to how they worked with each other in the office.

The realities of the 21st Century require a deepening of the trust premise that is embedded in a nuanced approach to team formation, governance, and development. We live in a world that is volatile, uncertain, and complex, a world where organizations are global, diverse, technologically and data driven, and populated by Millennials. The traditional approaches to teamwork in a hierarchical culture no longer apply.

COLLABORATIVE TEAMS: A SYSTEMS APPROACH

Collaboration is multiplication.

—John C. Maxwell[19]

It all began in Texas in 1989. I had just started my new management consulting firm and had gotten an opportunity to work in the information technology function at DuPont, based in Wilmington, Delaware. I started working with my sponsor's leadership team and then he then sent me to work with three senior managers in Houston, Texas. Because of increased competition from Dow Chemical, my sponsor needed to cut costs in the Texas operation fairly drastically, and charged these three leaders with the task of integrating their three organizations into one integrated supplier of information systems. Further, he said that if this didn't work out, he might have to outsource their function.

There was a problem, though. These three leaders did not get along. Two of them were from competing plants. They provided the same services to the petrochemicals business but had different computing and internal management systems. In addition, a third organization in Houston was part of the package, a sales organization that had a third type of computing system as well as a different customer base. They were not wild about integrating. In six months? More likely this would take six years.

I flew to Houston to meet these leaders at the airport Marriott. I had been warned they "ate consultants for breakfast." When I got to the meeting room at 7:30 a.m., they were already there. As soon as I walked in, one leader barked out, "Who are you and why ought we to listen to you?" OK. Game on. My response was, "Good morning. Would you mind if I got a cup of coffee first?" I needed time to figure out what I was going to say. When I got to my seat I said, "You don't have to. In fact, I can turn right around and get back on a plane to my family." To make a long story short, we ended up having a very productive first day, followed by a second, followed by 18 months of deep work transforming the leadership culture, processes, and structure of these three organizations, integrating them into a unified supplier of information systems. More importantly, we co-created a collaborative, team-based culture that won a national competition run by the Association for Talent Development. It was their first-ever *Excellence in Organization Development Award*, which was given to the entire team and my company to celebrate their achievement.

Why did we win? The evaluators said that they had interviewed workers at every level of the organization and were impressed that no matter who they spoke with, they all said the same thing about the value of collaboration, their teamwork, and the mission and vision of the organization. This is called ownership and alignment.

After the first Houston meeting, the work began with the information systems leadership team. At our next meeting in Orange, Texas at the DuPont plant, as facilitator of the process my first question was, "What do you need as a team in order to work together to meet the strategic challenge that you have been given by Wilmington?" From that moment on, we co-created what is being described in this chapter as the Collaborative Team Governance Process. How were they going to work together was the first question. The first step was to clarify the principles and values they wanted to drive the organization's behavior. Based on those core values, we created a set of Operating Agreements they agreed to by 100% true consensus, no reservations. To achieve that level of consensus, they had to work through their differences with each other. It wasn't easy at first. They had a bias for action, and working through interpersonal differences was uncomfortable. They persisted and did an excellent job, followed by the creation of the Team Charter. After that we tackled the integration challenge, which required a deconstruction of the existing organization and its work processes, and rebuilt it from the ground up with a flatter, team-based framework. Business processes were simplified. Layers of management were removed. The span of control went from 1:5 to 1:50. The performance management system went from a forced ranking process to a team-based performance system that rewarded individual, team, and organizational performance. Customer satisfaction ratings went up by 60% in the first nine months. Their costs went down by 34%. Safety performance dramatically improved. And then, to build internal self-sufficiency, 10% of the workforce was trained in how to facilitate a meeting, 5% was trained in how to facilitate the Collaborative Team Governance Process, and the leadership took responsibility for maintaining the culture. All in 18 months, not 6 years.

At our last meeting, when I asked them who their leader was going to be going forward. They immediately said, in unison, "We are the leader." They had mastered situational and facilitative leadership. The bottom line of this case study in collaborative transformation is the *ownership principle*—that people take care of what they own. The early foundations of Collaborative Teams—100% consensus decisions, ownership, trust and accountability—came from the roll-up-your-sleeves pragmatism of 11 amazing human beings who struggled with this journey, and discovered their authentic selves, their integrity, and each other. More than three decades later, this organization has sustained its collaborative culture.

Over those 30 years, I continued to evolve this basic formula, applying it in executive, senior leadership, and management teams focused on solving critical business issues of all kinds, from information technology integrations, mergers/acquisitions, and reorganizations, to cross-functional and cross-national projects, business process redesign efforts, and cultural transformations. In every instance, the team was the unit of organizational transformation. And what made that possible was the ownership that was created by the Collaborative Team Governance Process, to which we now turn, using the Collaboration Systems model to help us build out what it truly means to be a collaborative team. But before we do, there is one more cornerstone for collaborative teams.

Psychological Safety: A Precondition for True Collaboration in Teams

Collaborative Teams cannot function effectively unless its members feel psychologically safe—able to be vulnerable, speak truth to power without fear of retribution, and take risks and make mistakes in an environment of learning and development. It means freedom from fear of sexual harassment, physical assault, and discrimination of any kind, bullying, micromanagement or intimidation. Since 1990 leaders have become increasingly aware of the importance of creating workplace cultures that are psychologically safe, but there is still a long way to go. Let's consider three key thinkers who have done the research that statistically documents this finding.

- **William Kahn:** In 1990 Kahn's research focused on the psychological conditions for workforce engagement or disengagement in the workplace. One of the critical factors for engagement was psychological safety, which he defined as the "sense of being able to show and employ self without fear of negative consequences to self-image, status, or career."[20] When workers feel psychologically safe, he pointed out, they feel their situation is trustworthy, secure, predictable, and clear in terms of behavioral consequences. In interpersonal relationships, there is support, trust, openness and lack of a threat. Managers demonstrate behaviors that show support, consistency, trust, and competence.

- **Amy Edmundson:** Edmundson's work in psychological safety, from hospital teams to the corporate workplace, has accelerated our understanding not only of what it is, but why it is so critical to workers. In her 2019 book, *The Fearless Organization,* she bottom-lines her work with this recognition of the critical role psychological safety plays in the 21st Century organization:

  > *For an organization to truly thrive in a world where innovation can make the difference between success and failure, it is not enough to hire smart, motivate people. They must also feel psychologically safe.*[21]

  In a workplace culture where people feel safe, they are not hindered by interpersonal fear; share their concerns and mistakes without fear of embarrassment or retribution; are confident they can speak up and won't be humiliated, ignored, or blamed; and tend to trust and respect their colleagues.[22]

- **O. C. Tanner:** In late 2019 the O. C. Tanner Institute, with Human Synergistics International, published their 2nd annual *Global Culture Report* that represents the results of a research study involving more than 20,000 workers and leaders across the world on the health of workplace cultures. The bottom line of their report is that "a new approach to employee experience and workplace culture is needed."[23] Of particular note for this chapter is their finding on psychological safety in the workplace as it relates to teams. Their research found that teams thrive when they have a strong sense of autonomy and psychological safety, that when employees feel safe, there is a 347% increase in the probability of highly engaged employees, a 277% increase in the probability of a highly rated employee experience, a 154% increase in great work, and a 33% decrease in moderate-to-severe burnout.[24]

Collaborative teams create a work environment where people feel psychologically safe and where these results can be achieved. Let us consider the how of collaborative teams: their infrastructure. To do this we will first define what we mean by a collaborative team and then provide an overview from a systems perspective—leadership, culture, processes, and structure.

Defining a Collaborative Team, the 4ᵗʰ Evolution

Successful teamwork is the ability to work together toward a common vision ... It is the fuel that allows common people to attain uncommon results.

—Andrew Carnegie[25]

We know that teams are how we get work done in the 21st Century. There are all kinds of teams ranging from leadership, management, project or product, departmental, cross-functional, self-directed, and virtual teams to "tiger" teams for specialized challenges. But just because you call it a team doesn't make it one. As we have seen, if teams apply Tuckman's model, more often than not end up just storming and not-performing.

The 4ᵗʰ Evolution of teams is the Collaborative Team, which McGregor predicted six decades ago. It has taken us the last 40 years to determine the cornerstones of Collaborative Teams, the 7 Principles of the Collaborative Work Ethic, to build and test a culture-first implementation methodology known as the Collaborative Team Governance Process, and to develop a formula for Collaborative Team success:

- A culture of *psychological safety* where people are free to express their points of view without fear of retribution
- The importance of *listening* to each other, *dialogue,* and *full expression* of viewpoints
- The importance of *100% consensus* as a decision-making agreement
- The critical role of disagreement within the team and a focus on *resolution of those disagreements*
- The *rotation* of team leadership, as we have learned from "Lessons From The Geese"[26]
- The importance of being self-aware, reflecting on its own process, and making adjustments

Based on this formula, a Collaborative Team is defined as:

A psychologically safe space where team members own their team's governance for how they will work together, their vision and mission, and create trust-based relationships where members are empowered to be their best selves so they can do their best work and achieve superior results.

What Makes Collaborative Teams Unique

We are standing on the shoulders of giants, the leading thinkers, researchers, and practitioners who came before us and helped build the conceptual and methodological foundations that are the basis for collaborative teams. All teams have members, leadership, missions they must fulfill and tasks they must achieve. But as we have seen with Tuckman's approach, there needs to be a principle-based process for achieving a higher level of cohesion, trust, and credibility on the front end of team development so that the team can be effective. Tuckman taught us the importance of front-loading the norming step of the process. We learned from Katzenbach and Smith that while collaborative teams can survive within a hierarchical structure, from a principles perspective, they are incompatible with hierarchy. From McGregor we developed a rigorous and effective way to implement consensus decision-making, and the importance of self-awareness and rotating the leadership/facilitator role in a team. Senge reinforced the importance of consensus decision-making, and we adopted the importance of creating a learning environment—one Edmundson would consider to be psychologically safe. Finally, from Lencioni, we adopted the critical importance of trust-based relationships, the importance of buy-in/ownership, accountability, and producing results.

Based on several decades where I facilitated the development of hundreds of Collaborative Teams, I learned there are 8 elements that make them unique and different from any other kind of team:

- **Culture-First:** Collaborative Teams start with building strong, trust-based relationships, because the *how* teams are going to work together must precede the *what* they are going to do, otherwise they follow the Tuckman storming-non-performing model. Culture-first means that the principles, values, beliefs, and hopes of the team members drive team behavior and performance. There is alignment and shared ownership of those principles and beliefs, which are then translated into Operating Agreements they adopt 100% for how they will work together.
- **Front-Loaded and Intentional:** The formation of Collaborative Teams is front-loaded and intentional. Team governance is literally the *first* thing a team does before it focuses on task so that everyone on the team is playing by the same rules. It is intentional because we have learned that only when teams are empowered, own the process, and achieve a high level of trust can there be exceptional results.
- **Principle-Based:** Collaborative Teams are based on the 7 Principles of the Collaborative Work Ethic, where every action or decision is based on principle.
- **Psychologically Safe:** Collaborative Teams are safe work spaces where members are free from the fear of retribution, humiliation, harassment, discrimination, or other behaviors that demean the human spirit. The Collaborative Team culture is grounded in principle, led by self-aware and empathic leaders and facilitators, where violations of this safety are dealt with decisively.

- **Ownership—the Key to Trust:** What makes Collaborative Teams unique is their focus on the principle of ownership—that team members own the values and principles that govern the team, the Agreements for how they will work with each other, the Charter that turns their mission into action, their roles and responsibilities, and the action plan that produces results. As a result of this ownership, there is high trust, mutual respect, honor, full responsibility, and accountability.
- **A 100% True Consensus, No Reservations:** It is when teams reach 100% true consensus on strategic and sometimes tactical decisions that the teams achieve full ownership. The bottom line of consensus for a team is *working through dissensus*—their disagreements with each other. Teams' members are diverse, culturally disparate, and come from different backgrounds, experiences, and expectations. They are going to disagree. The Collaborative Team Governance Process provides a way for team members to respect each other's differences while working through them to achieve 100% true consensus, no reservations and full ownership.
- **Empowerment:** Collaborative Teams empower each individual to be their best self so they can do their best work, and enable team synergy, where the whole is greater than the sum of its parts.
- **Real-Work-in-Real-Time:** Because most team members are busy and have little patience for process, Collaborative Teams are formed and chartered around real-work challenges that the team needs to address in a unified way.

Leadership of Collaborative Teams

There are three types of leadership roles in a collaborative team:

- **The Sponsor:** Collaborative Teams have executive sponsors with responsibility to ensure the team has the support and resources needed to get the job done. When a Collaborative Team is created by a leadership or management team, someone on that team takes on this responsibility. The sponsor also ensures there is a free flow of communications between the team and leadership, and provides air cover and support for the team when there are disagreements with leadership. According to Gratton and Erickson, sponsors can do a number of things to build and support collaborative teams, including modeling collaborative behavior, mentoring and coaching, supporting a strong sense of community, and assigning team leaders who are both task and relationship oriented.[27]
- **The Facilitative Leader:** Leaders have a primary commitment to serve and empower the workforce. They don't issue commands; they engage, ask questions, actively listen, reflect and validate, and build ownership, all through facilitation. They are objective, protect the team's process, ensure psychological

safety, make sure team meetings are run collaboratively, and work to ensure that the Team Charter and mission are achieved. This role gets rotated among the team members on a regular basis (e.g., every 3 to 6 months) so that everyone has the opportunity to facilitate the team. Facilitative leaders also have responsibility between meetings to support team members, ensure that they are honoring their agreements, and ensure that action items are being completed on time.

- **The Resource:** External or internal experts who have specific content or process knowledge are often invited into a team. They provide leadership in the sense that for a short period of time, what they know gives the team direction.

Collaborative Team Life Cycle

Collaborative teams have a number of processes that help define it and determine its effectiveness. Most teams will go through 3 to 4 phases in their life cycle, including: 1) Formation, when they are created; 2) Management and development, where teams learn and grow over time; 3) Self-renewal, when the team has changed enough that they need to revisit their collaborative team governance agreements; and 4) Sunsetting, when the team goes out of business and members celebrate each other and their successes.

Collaborative Team Meetings

Meetings are how most Collaborative Teams get their work done. They are facilitated group dialogue, problem-solving, and decision-making work sessions that are based on the principle of ownership. Everyone owns the meeting, are results-driven, and are focused on helping the team achieve its tasks and mission. There are 5 meeting roles, including the team's executive sponsor, the facilitator, recorder, external resources/experts, and the members themselves. Each meeting has a design, which is different from a meeting agenda in that it is not just a list of topics, like Team Delta had, but are Desired Results which the facilitator and team members co-create to achieve the team's mission and tasks. These designs are delivered to team members 2 to 3 days in advance of the meeting so that all members will be prepared, and are owned by the members.

Collaborative Meeting Tools

There are 6 key meeting tools facilitators use to keep the meeting on track. They include: (1) Meeting rules for how people will treat each other in the meeting; for example, one person talking at a time, no phones or laptops, and no side conversations; (2) A Meeting Road Map of topics so that the team can see their progress during the meeting; (3) A Decisions Reached list of the specific decisions reached by the team; (4) An Issues for Future Discussion list to prevent the team members from going down rabbit holes on issues not germane to the meeting, but are scheduled for future meetings; (5) The Action Plan list of who is going to do what by when; and (6) The

Meeting Memory, which is a written record of what was discussed at the meeting, what decisions were reached, what issues remain to be discussed, and what action steps the team will take to achieve its mission.

Collaborative Meeting Logistics

We often underestimate the importance of meeting logistics until we have breakdowns that threaten the process. A rule of thumb is that everything is set up well in advance of the actual meeting so that the members can focus on the work of the meeting. To do so, the facilitator considers the meeting schedule, where times are set in advance by all members; the meeting's location, making sure it is scheduled, available, and meets the needs of the members; if there is a virtual meeting, the facilitator selects a technology platform like Zoom that will work for the team and makes sure it is set up well before the meeting begins; and finally, the facilitator must plan the implementation of the meeting well in advance.

Collaborative Meeting Interventions

Meetings never go as planned. As a collaborative meeting facilitator, you must be prepared to handle any type of situation. Here are 6 of the more common ones: 1) Late/no attendance, where members show up late or not at all; the intervention is to have an offline conversation with them to find out why; if they are repeatedly late or not in attendance, they are held accountable by the team; 2) Violating meeting rules, which results in the facilitator having an offline conversation to address the issue; repeated violations result in holding them accountable; 3) Often there are dominating members who like to monopolize the conversation; the facilitator deftly segues that member's comments into a general conversation by asking others their views on the topic. if the member continues to dominate, an offline conversation can help them understand the impact of their behavior on others; 4) If the team runs out of time in its deliberations on a given decision, the facilitator negotiates an additional time block for the team to continue the conversation; 5) If the team gets deadlocked and cannot reach a true consensus agreement, the facilitator helps the team understand the root causes of the disagreement and work through them until there is a resolution; and 6) Sometimes members may have differences outside of the meeting or other conflicts that can bleed into how the team meeting is run; if it happens in the room, it gets resolved in the room because the entire team is impacted; it may also require offline work.

Team Dynamics and Work Processes

Effective collaborative team performance involves 3 basic types of processes: 1) People processes, where teams complete Collaborative Team Governance, engage key stakeholders, ensure there are effective communications, conduct internal performance reviews, and celebrate successes; 2) Work processes, where Collaborative Teams work to achieve their mission through team meetings, brainstorming, joint problem-solving, making decisions, working with other teams, working across silos, and dealing with critical business challenges; and 3) Internal team dynamics that may involve interpersonal differences and even conflicts; collaborative team dynamics involve being empathic, actively listening to each other, getting to the root cause of the differences, and working toward a resolution all can agree to.

Building Self-Sufficiency

To sustain a Collaborative Team, the organization's collaborative leadership culture, and to help it navigate organizational change, it is critical to build the internal capability and the skill sets of a number of members of the workforce. There are 3 levels of skills development that are essential: 1) The Collaborative Meeting Facilitator, where members learn how to design and facilitate a collaborative team meeting, learn small group dynamics, process management, and preventions and interventions; 2) The Collaborative Team Facilitator, where members learn how to facilitate the Collaborative Team Governance Process, which requires the facilitator to be self-aware and reflective, know their hot buttons, and have an intervention plan for resolving team issues; and 3) The Collaborative ChangeMaster, where members have already qualified as meeting and governance facilitators. Their primary purpose is to keep their eye on the change ball. Because every organization is going through some form of change, ChangeMasters are, in effect, collaborative organization development consultants, and their role is to ensure that change processes are owned by the workforce and to address change challenges as they show up.

Collaborative Team Structure/Design

Collaborative Teams are flat with their structures represented by the circle. In human relationships, circles are a symbol of unity, equality, and strength. In Collaborative Team meetings, it is best if members sit in a circle. There is no head of the table. If virtual and working on Zoom, note that all the photo boxes are the same size. No matter where you sit in the circle, or where you are in the Zoom space, you are equal to everyone else, regardless of your title. It levels the playing field, and it increases respect because every member's opinion matters. In addition, circles symbolize that those in the circle are collectively responsible for what happens there.

At the organizational level, the design of the organization is also flat, with the strategic or executive leadership team in the center, and functional, project, management, cross-functional, or virtual teams radiating out from the center. Each team is connected to the executive leadership team through team sponsors to ensure effective internal communications, and organizational alignment. In each case there is a sponsor link back to the executive leadership team. Figure 7.1 shows an example of this kind of structure.

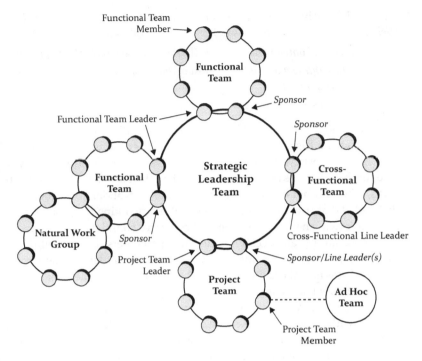

FIGURE 7.1 The Structure of a Collaborative Organization.

THE CRITICAL ROLE OF 100% TRUE CONSENSUS, NO RESERVATIONS

There is perhaps no more controversial construct in Collaboration Teams than the idea that their members can reach 100% true consensus, no reservations decisions, the gold standard for Collaborative Team decision-making. Our purpose here is to clarify what this standard is, how it contrasts with other notions of consensus, why it is so critical to the development of a collaborative leadership culture, and how it actually can be achieved.

Four Misconceptions about Consensus Decision-Making

- **<u>Unanimity?</u>** In *How Google Works*, Schmidt and Rosenberg define consensus as "to think or feel together. Note that this implies nothing about unanimity; consensus is not about getting everyone to agree. Instead, it's about coming to the best idea for the company and rallying around it."[28] With all due respect for Google's authors, consensus is indeed about unanimity. In fact, *Merriam-Webster* is crystal clear on this point, with the following definition:[29]

> *1a: General agreement: UNANIMITY; the consensus of their opinion*
> *b: The judgment arrived at by most of those concerned; the consensus was to go ahead*
> *2: Group solidarity in sentiment and belief*

- **It's Not Possible:** This belief is widely held that a diverse group of people who work on a team together cannot possibly reach a consensus. I encountered this position in almost every team I worked with. When I drilled down into why they held this belief, it was typically because 1) They had never seen it happen before, and 2) They did not know how to do it. I have seen about 500 teams overcome their belief that true consensus is not possible by working the process, and when they achieve it, there is a new sense of collective confidence, trust, ownership, full responsibility, and accountability. Team members tend to sell themselves short simply because they don't know how to reach this level of agreement. The key to success is in the facilitator's own belief it can be reached and in his or her skill in helping team members realize it.

- **"Can Live With" Consensus:** Another misconception is that consensus is a "can live with" agreement. Susskind argues in his article on consensus-building techniques that there is a five-step process for achieving it: convening the group, clarifying responsibilities, brainstorming, reaching a decision, and implementing it. In the reaching a decision step, he states: "At the final scheduled meeting, the facilitator asks team members whether they can no live with the package they have taken back to constituents for review and comment."[30]

  A "can live with" consensus is a false consensus that leaves team members with a "trap door" through which they can escape full responsibility for the decision and their disagreement with it. In effect, they get to hide. If a team is provided a trap door, someone is going to use it, and the team will never know whether that person truly owns the decision—that is, until the decision results in a bad outcome. Then that person often will say, "I told you so." Without full ownership, there is no full responsibility or accountability for the decision. Even worse is the lack of trust and mutual respect that results when team members cannot fully count on their colleagues to be all in.

- **Striving and Tie-Breakers:** A fourth misconception about true consensus is that a team should "strive" for consensus, and if there is still disagreement after considerable discussion, then the decision should be escalated to the senior leader, who will break the tie. Google's Schmidt and Rosenberg argue for this approach when they say that there has to be a deadline and a decision-maker who is ultimately responsible for the decision: "People can debate for hours, a time sink that often ends in mediocre compromise and always incurs a heft opportunity cost."[31] At this point, the decision-maker steps in to break the tie.

This is another form of false consensus. If the team members know, from the beginning, that their deliberations will be cut short by whatever artificial deadlines are set by their boss, and that the boss will serve as the tie-breaker, they never have to fully debate the issues, air their differences, or take full responsibility for the decision. This approach to consensus makes the team members dependent on the boss, disempowers them, and undermines any sense of team ownership of and accountability for the decisions.

- **"Groupthink":** General George S. Patton is widely quoted as having said, "If everyone is thinking alike, then somebody isn't thinking."[32] Some people have criticized the idea of consensus by calling it "groupthink," that everyone has to think alike, implying that there cannot be any disagreement. Perhaps there is a fear by leaders such as Patton that people could actually achieve unanimity in their decision-making process.

  Again, this is a misunderstanding of what is involved in reaching true consensus. Consensus is really about *dissensus*, which *Merriam-Webster* defines as a difference of opinion.[33] A team will reach its 100% true consensus, no reservations decision by considering all points of view, ranging from minor disagreements to major ones. Disagreements are expected and welcomed in the decision-making process, for it is the process of working *through* those disagreements that makes the team bond stronger, the ownership greater, the decision better, the trust deeper, and the accountability assured.

The Power of 100% True Consensus, No Reservations

When a team is making a decision, there are typically 6 rules from which they can choose: 1) One person decides; 2) Minority rule (<50%); 3) Majority rule (50%+1); 4) Super majority (80%); 5) "Can live with" (90%); 6) True consensus, no reservations (100%). Most teams will choose "can live with" consensus as their decision-making rule. If they do, after 4 to 6 months of trying it and finding it does not work out due to a lack of ownership, they will often move to true consensus. Teams choosing 100% consensus typically apply it in making strategic decisions that affect the direction, mission, or objectives of the team vs. tactical or operational decisions.

There are several reasons that 100% true consensus, no reservations is the gold standard for collaborative team decision-making:

- **Working Through Differences:** It requires the team to commit to working through their differences, even if it takes longer than the deadlines they face. They realize that their unity will be tested by their superiors, subordinates, and other teams, and that if there is even a crack in that unity, it can be exploited to undermine the team's work.

- **Respect and Ownership:** This rule sets a critical boundary for team members that they must respect everyone's point of view, that they cannot proceed until all views are heard and everyone buys into the decision.
- **Honor and Accountability:** This gold standard means that every member can trust their colleagues to honor the decision when they leave the meeting, and that they will be accountable for implementing and upholding the decision, especially important in virtual teams.
- **Synergy and Shared Humanity:** It is a powerful feeling to know that you have been heard, your views have been respected, that you have deepened your understanding of the views of your teammates, deepened your respect for who they are and what they bring to the team. This is what synergy is truly about. It's not a transactional process. It is a profound engagement of our shared humanity.
- *Ubuntu* **and "We":** *Ubuntu* is a belief system I learned while working with South Africans. They taught me that it means "I am, because we are." This is the true power for 100% true consensus, no reservations—it creates a "We".

Achieving the 100% True Consensus, No Reservations Agreement

The first time a team grapples with coming to 100% true consensus, no reservations on a decision is perhaps the most difficult one. It's new territory. Typically, there are no members of the team who have worked this way before. It's *the culture shift, from the Power Paradigm to Collaboration*; from fear to trust; from dependence to interdependence; from disempowerment to self-empowerment. So they struggle and need to be facilitated by a skillful, trained, objective facilitator who understands small group dynamics and the Collaborative Team Governance Process.

A senior leadership team at a Fortune 100 company was able to cut their decision-making time by 60% as a result of this process. Where once it took a full day for this team to make three strategic decisions, because they argued from their positions on each one, now they were able to make ten strategic decisions in a half day because they had a clear, agreed-upon, decision-making agreement. This is the power of having a front-loaded, culture-first norming process as the first thing a team does—*how* before *what*.

THE COLLABORATIVE TEAM GOVERNANCE PROCESS

From that very first experience of co-creating a Collaborative Team in the Gulf Coast of Texas in 1989, and continuing to apply, improve, and implement the Collaborative Team Governance Process over the next three decades, I experienced profound transformations of individual behavior, team behavior, interpersonal relationships, and team performance. I learned that this process taps into the deep desire people have to truly collaborate with each other. They just don't know how. Every team I worked with was in a hierarchical, power-based, control-oriented, and fear-driven leadership culture. It took great courage for these team members, for whom I have the deepest respect, to take a leap of faith to try this process. And when they completed it, the team leader spoke for them all: "I can't believe we worked that other way for so long."

The Collaborative Team Governance Process is the vehicle for the cultural transformation of a team which enables them to move from the Power to the Collaboration Paradigm in a matter of a few days. Let's define what this process and then describe the 7 steps involved in its implementation.

Defining the Collaborative Team Governance Process

Team members need to have a shared set of rules for how they are going to work together, and they all need to agree to those rules, or what we call Operating Agreements, so that everyone on the team agrees with how they will work with each other. Each member joining a team comes with their own values, beliefs, assumptions, expectations, and rules for how they have operated before on other teams. If you have nine members of a team each playing by their own rules, there is going to be chaos, or storming behavior. So our definition of the Collaborative Team Governance Process is this:

> It is a culture-first, principle-based, front-loaded approach to the development of a team's governance where members agree by 100% true consensus, no reservations to a set of Operating Agreements for how the team members will work with each other, a Team Charter defining the mission and responsibilities, and a team Action Plan that defines how the team will achieve its mission.

The core benefit of this process is that team members own every aspect of their team's leadership, culture, process, and structure. They deeply trust and respect each other. They behave ethically and with the highest integrity. They are fully responsible for the work of the team and are willing to hold themselves accountable. But even more important is that as a result of this process, they become a "We" in the psychologically safe place they have created, they discover who they are as human beings, are able to make themselves vulnerable, allow themselves to take risks, innovate, and learn, and in the process become the best version of themselves, forming deep, trusting relationships with their teammates. They move beyond transactions, power, and fear, to transformational relationships based safety, ownership, and trust.

The 7 Steps of the Collaborative Team Governance Process

There are 7 steps involved in implementing the Collaborative Team Governance Process:

Step 1: Decision to Form a Collaborative Team: The typical first step in this process is for a sponsor, usually a senior leader, to decide that given a critical issue facing the organization, that a team must be created to address that issue. It may be a drop in revenues, loss of a major customer, a new strategic direction, or a major change initiative. There is sufficient "pain" that leadership is willing to invest the team's time to resolve it. The leader, who becomes the sponsor, decides to take the team through Collaborative Team Governance so that it can more effectively and quickly address the issue. A second kind of situation is in the normal course of business, when a leader decides to transform the culture of their team or organization, and Collaborative Team Governance is the means to do that.

Step 2: Facilitator Selection: Objective, trained facilitators are absolutely essential to the success of the process. Typically, Collaborative Team Governance facilitators are third parties, often outside consultants. They cannot be a member of the team, and certainly not the team leader. They are respected, self-aware, skilled in small group work, believe in collaborative principles, and fundamentally believe that 100% true consensus, no reservations can be achieved. If they do not believe it is possible, they should not be asked to facilitate this process because it will backfire. Once selected, the facilitator meets with the sponsor to achieve alignment on the mission and responsibilities of the team.

Step 3: Discovery and Report for the Team: The facilitator's next step is to conduct an in depth discovery process. This involves three steps: (1) Contextual research involves getting to know the business, its context, people and offerings, and a wide range of documentation is reviewed; (2) There are interviews with members in a one-to-one confidential setting, providing a range of perspectives on the organization, the team, its members, and internal dynamics; and (3) A discovery report is prepared that summarizes all of the data covered, protects the confidentiality of the team members' comments, and provides a potential path forward to begin addressing the priority issues.

Step 4: Kick-Off Meeting and Rules for Success: It's time to have the kick-off meeting, where the facilitator presents the discovery report, the team processes the results, a decision is reached as to whether to proceed with the recommended process, and priorities are established. If the team decides to move forward, they are introduced to the Collaborative Team Governance Process and are invited to agree to the 7 Rules for Success, rules that have been found, over time, to be essential for this process: (1) 100% attendance; (2) 100% participation; (3) 100% true consensus, no reservations on all Operating Agreements and Team Charters; (4) Leave no stone unturned, which means members agree to raise any questions or reservations they may have; (5) Stick to your guns, which means that if you believe in something strongly, articulate our position; (6) Listen with your ears, eyes, and your heart, which means being empathic and actively listening for understanding; and (7) Stay until done, which means members agree to finish the process, no matter how long it takes.

Step 5: Team Operating Agreements: *Operating agreements are the conscious choices team members make, by 100% true consensus, no reservations, for how they will work with each other.* There are 14 Operating Agreements, which evolved over several decades, responding to what teams said they needed to be most effective (see

Leadership Team Operating Agreements: Starting to Create a Collaborative Operating System

FIGURE 7.2   A Team's Collaborative Operating Agreements.

Figure 7.2). Each agreement consists of a set of distinctions that the facilitator identifies and helps the team work through to a decision. For example, in the decision-making agreement, the 6 rules for making a decision are a distinction. Another one is the difference between strategic, tactical, and operational decisions. A third is the domains of decision-making: the team as a whole, the sponsor, and individual members. Most teams will need the following agreements: decision-making, disagreements, confidentiality, intention, team operations, attendance, communications, listening/feedback, conflict resolution, accountability, and amendments. It is also important for the teams to decide how they are going to sustain the agreements and their team culture.

Step 6: Collaborative Team Charters: Once the Operating Agreements have been agreed to 100% true consensus, no reservations, the team then focuses on its Charter. There are several components to this document, starting with the sponsor's charge to the team which includes the deliverables, time frame, and boundary conditions for the work to be done. To create its mission statement, the team identifies all its stakeholders and their interests in the team doing its work excellently. In addition, they create a communications plan for how often they will engage these stakeholders. Next, the mission statement is prepared around who they are, who they serve, and what they do as a team. There are boundary conditions for most teams, which may include budget, timeline, and other constraints. Finally, there is a work plan that will produce the deliverables expected.

Step 7: Completion of Governance: The last step in the process is getting a final 100% true consensus, no reservations agreement to the Operating Agreements and Charter. If the team has done its work up until this point, this should not take long. Then the team celebrates its achievement with some kind of event outside of work. It is really important, after all this work that the members are acknowledged for their hard work and success.

5 KEY COLLABORATIVE TEAM CHALLENGES

Even the most robust of Collaborative Teams, after it is formed, runs into any number of challenges to its continued viability, challenges that can undermine the collaborative culture and trust among team members.

- **Complex Organizations and Collaboration to the 10th Power:** Gratton and Erickson found that in complex, virtual corporations, large teams present a "collaboration conundrum," where "large" is defined as more than 20. They note that corporate teams have increased in size, up to 100, often to ensure that all key stakeholders are involved, and that at this size the level of collaboration decreases.[34] The challenge is to keep a high level of ownership and collaboration across a large global organization. There is a collaborative solution, which is 105th power. Since the optimal size of a collaborative team is seven to ten, and when formed they have a very high level of ownership over their processes, the members become ambassadors for collaboration. If each member of a ten-person team empowers a team to become collaborative through the governance process, that is 100 teams; multiply that by ten four more times and you can empower a company of 100,000 members to become a collaborative leadership culture within a relatively short time. The 100% consensus ownership principle is central to the ability to achieve this cultural transformation, even if they are virtual.

- **Working Across Silos:** Most organizations are highly siloed by function and are working in a hierarchical corporate structure. In this culture there is a high degree of isolation of one function from another, leading to what the zoologist Desmond Morris called the territorial imperative.[35] Human beings have this need to claim and protect territory. In organizations this is the silo, the function, and sometimes the team. We will defend that territory. It's tribal. It's very real. Collaboration does offer a better way to lead and manage. It starts at the top of the organization, where the motto is to *collaborate inside to compete outside*. First, senior leadership completes the collaborative team governance process, builds a high level of trust and mutual respect, and aligns their functional, departmental, or business unit missions with the vision, mission, and strategy of the organization. Second, senior leadership sets the expectation that everyone in the organization will work collaboratively. They provide the support, opportunities, and resources for leaders, managers and teams at every level to complete the governance process, and to build internal facilitation capability. Third, each senior leader has the responsibility to ensure that health and well-being of the collaborative culture within their departments or business units. They measure the health of the culture using a collaborative culture assessment instrument to benchmark the culture and progress over time to assess progress.

- **Cultural Islands:** Managers on the front lines of an organization may want to create collaborative teams within their sphere of influence. Once created, these teams may realize they are cultural islands in a sea of hierarchy and behave differently, and sometimes find it difficult to navigate their organizational terrain. They can feel isolated and alone. Others may withhold information, start rumors, or otherwise make their lives difficult.

  The key choice for the collaborative team is to become proactive. They can share their team experiences, continue to produce outstanding results, and offer their facilitation services to help other teams to design and run their meetings. By doing this, the collaborators become ambassadors for change in a way that adds significant value to the organization. They can also offer to train others on collaborative meetings.

- **Maintaining Team Trust:** After a period of time, a team that has completed governance may experience members who take the team's collaborative processes for granted. Sometimes, this shows up as people breaking agreements or key decisions not being honored. Or it might be that members of the team have a significant breakdown in their relationship. Sometimes, there are external factors that create stress and pressure as a result of disruptions, poor financial performance, or significant change in the organization.

  How can a collaborative team culture of trust be maintained over time? First, team members need to be aware that over time there may be some erosion of their culture. Second, they can regularly monitor the health of their culture through team feedback sessions. Third, they should regularly review their Operating Agreements to see if they need to be upgraded or revised. Fourth, there can be coaching and feedback sessions with difficult team members. Like a marriage, the collaborative culture of a team must be consciously and consistently renewed.

- **Working Globally and Virtually:** According to Gallup and the Bureau of Labor Statistics, as of 2015, 22% of Americans work from home, while almost 50% work virtually.[36] As a result of the Covid-19 pandemic, it is even more. Our teams work globally, across different time zones, with members coming from different cultures with different languages, customs, and behaviors. They end up working virtually with teammates on the other side of the planet, oftentimes not ever having met in person or having the opportunity to develop trust or mutual respect. They are put onto a team because of a skill or subject matter expertise. They use a wide variety of technology platforms intended to give them a way to communicate, solve problems, and make decisions. What could possibly go wrong?

According to Dhawan and Chamorro-Premuzic, there are three kinds of distance that occur in remote collaboration: (1) Physical, in terms of place and time; (2) Operational, in terms of team size, bandwidth, and skill levels; and (3) Affinity, in terms of values, trust, and interdependency.[37] I would add a fourth type of distance, cultural, in terms of different customs, habits, behaviors, expectations, and perceptions that team members have.

Neeley makes the point that these global, cross-cultural, virtual teams may have identity issues and a mismatch of perceptions.[38] Because people define themselves in by any number of variables—like age, gender, ethnicity, religion, political ties and sexual orientation—there is considerable room for misperception, miscommunication, and misunderstanding, which can lead to significant breakdowns in trust, ownership, and performance. He suggests three strategies: (1) For fluent speakers to dial down their dominance, in terms of the pace of speaking, not dominating a conversation, and active listening; (2) For less fluent speakers to dial up engagement, in terms of refraining from reverting to their native language, asking if others understand them, and resisting withdrawal from the conversation; and (3) For team leaders to increase inclusion in terms of balancing speaking and listening, drawing contributions of all team members, and soliciting participation from less fluent speakers.39

These strategies are helpful in transactional meetings. But for Collaborative Teams and meetings, the most important thing they can do is their Collaborative Team Governance Process. I have implemented this process with teams on five continents and found that collaborative governance has a leveling effect. You may recall from Cooke's work on constructive/collaborative cultures that his sample of over 4 million people around the globe preferred to work in collaborative leadership cultures.[40] By creating their Collaborative Team Governance Process, their needs for psychological safety, mutual respect, trust and ownership can be met, which creates a platform for vulnerability, engagement, mutual understanding, effective problem-solving, and conflict resolution.

For the ongoing health of global and virtual teams, they also need to implement some of the processes recommended above with cultural measurement, regular feedback, and periodic review of their governance documents to sustain their effectiveness.

CHAPTER CONCLUSION: THE 4TH EVOLUTION— COLLABORATIVE TEAMS

As a collaborative leader, your organization is undoubtedly experiencing a maelstrom of change in this volatile, uncertain, and complex world. Where can you go to find some semblance of stability, focus, and purpose? Teams are today's home base, the place where we can find identity, connection, trust, psychological safety, and a shared vision and mission. We know that teams are the primary unit of organizational change in the 21st Century. They are how we get work done. The question, then, is how people will work together in those teams.

The history of teams is littered with failed efforts of people trying to figure out how to answer this question. For decades, the approaches to teaming organizations used were implemented largely within the predominant Power Paradigm of leadership. Teams were task driven, with leaders who were told to produce specific outcomes within a specific time frame and budget. Some business leaders began to experiment with self-directed teams, autonomous teams, and team-based management. Many organizations adopted Tuckman's approach of "forming-storming-norming" and hopefully performing, which was never empirically tested. Typically, the team process ended up more like "storming-storming-nonperforming." Members became disillusioned because of the wasted energy, time, and resources, all because they didn't know how to work together collaboratively. It makes no sense to continue using this 20th Century approach when there is a more successful alternative—the 4th Evolution: Collaborative Teams.

In the development of the methodology for creating Collaborative Teams, we have stood on the shoulders of giants, the first of whom is Douglas McGregor. We can recall that in 1960 he made a prophetic statement: *"The fundamental fact of man's capacity to collaborate with his fellows in the face-to-face group will survive the fads and one day be recognized."*[41]

That day is today!

McGregor, Senge, Lencioni, Covey, and Edmundson all helped build the cornerstones for a robust approach to Collaborative Teams. They helped us understand the critical importance of working in teams and making decisions by consensus, team learning, trust and ownership, principle-based behavior and psychological safety, all of which were integrated into the Collaborative Team Governance Process, which is at the heart of the 4th Evolution. The most important of these cornerstones is the role of the members' ownership of the team, its culture and work processes, and how 100% true consensus, no reservations as a decision-making rule helps teams work through their differences. Team development essentially shifted away from a power-based, transactional or mechanistic approach to work and toward a principle-based, relational and holistic approach to empowering team members to be their best selves so they can do their best work and produce superior results.

McGregor would be proud to know that his prediction has finally come true. Collaborative Teams are now the way that the Collaboration Paradigm, the 4th Evolution of leadership, can be implemented in organizations. They are the *how* collaboration is applied in everyday work life and how work can be transformed. Collaborative Teams are about "We", not "Me", about *ubuntu*.

CHAPTER REVIEW AND REFLECTIONS

Learning Objectives:
Let's reflect on the learning objectives for the chapter and summarize what we have learned:

- Understand the evolution of 20th Century organizational teams and their development.
- Learn about the leadership, culture, processes, and structure of 21st Century collaborative teams from a systems perspective.
- Understand the power of 100% true consensus as a decision-making rule for people and work processes.
- Dig deeper into what makes collaborative teams unique, their governance process, and the 7 steps of forming a collaborative team.
- Identify the central challenges facing collaborative teams and how they can be addressed to ensure effectiveness.

Initial Questions Revisited, and for Reflection:

- *Now that you understand what a collaborative team is, are you ready to facilitate teams in your organization?*
- *Do you understand the steps of the Collaborative Team Governance Process and what makes this process unique and more successful than other team development processes?*
- *Do you believe that 100% true consensus decision-making is possible? Do you now see how critical this level of ownership is to building psychological safety and trust?*
- *Now that you're going to be a collaborative leader, are you ready to meet the kinds of challenges you may face in addressing them?*

ADDITIONAL READINGS

- Edmundson, Amy. *The Fearless Organization*. Hoboken, NJ: Wiley, 2019.
- Lencioni, Patrick. *The Five Dysfunctions of a Team*. San Francisco: Jossey-Bass, 2002.
- Marshall, Edward M. *Transforming the Way We Work: The Power of the Collaborative Workplace*. New York: AMACOM Books, 1995.
- Senge, Peter M. "Team Learning." Chap. 11 in *The Fifth Discipline*. New York: Currency, 2006, pp. 216–252.

ENDNOTES

1 Bruce Tuckman and Mary Ann Jensen, "Stages of Small-Group Development Revisited," *Organization and Management,* Sage Publications, Inc., *Journals,* December 1977, pp. 427–429.
2 Ibid.
3 Ibid., pp. 315–317.
4 Ibid., p. 321.
5 Bruce W. Tuckman, "Developmental Sequence in Small Groups," *Psychological Bulletin* 1965, Vol. 63, No. 6, pp. 384–399.
6 Bruce W. Tuckman and Mary Ann C. Jensen, op. cit., pp. 419–427.
7 Peter M. Senge, *The Fifth Discipline* (New York: Currency, 2006), pp. 216–252.
8 Ibid., p. 218.
9 Ibid., p. 219.
10 Ibid., p. 220.
11 Ibid., pp. 221–252.
12 Ibid., p. 238.
13 Jon R. Katzenbach and Douglas K. Smith, *The Wisdom of Teams* (Boston: Harvard Business Review Press, 1993).
14 Ibid., pp. xvii–xviii, pp. 4–8.
15 Ibid., p. xvii.
16 Patrick Lencioni, *The Five Dysfunctions of a Team* (San Francisco: Jossey-Bass, 2002).
17 Ibid., p. 187–190.
18 Ibid., pp. 195–201.
19 John C. Maxwell, *The 17 Essential Qualities of a Team Player* (Nashville, TN: Thomas Nelson Publishers, 2002), p. 10.
20 William A. Kahn, "Psychological Conditions of Personal Engagement and Disengagement at Work," *Academy of Management Journal* (Dec., 1990) Vol. 33, No. 4, p. 705.
21 Amy Edmundson, *The Fearless Organization* (Hoboken, NJ: Wiley, 2019), p. xiv.
22 Ibid., p. xvi.

23   O. C. Tanner Institute, *2020 Global Culture Report* (Salt Lake City, UT: O. C. Tanner Institute), p. 2.

24   Ibid., p. 117.

25   https://www.goodreads.com/quotes/251192-teamwork-is-the-ability-to-work-together-toward-a-common

26   Dr. Robert McNeish, "Lessons From The Geese," Baltimore, MD, 1972, https://transformation-center.org/wp-content/uploads/2015/03/Lessons_From_The_Geese1.pdf

27   Lynda Gratton and Tamara J. Erickson, "Eight Ways to Build Collaborative Teams," in *On Teams* (Boston, MA: Harvard Business Publishing, 2013), p. 67.

28   Eric Schmidt and Jonathan Rosenberg, *How Google Works* (New York: Grand Central Publishing, 2017), p. 154.

29   https://www.merriam-webster.com/dictionary/consensus

30   Lawrence Susskind, "Breaking Robert's Rules: Consensus-Building Techniques for Group Decision-Making," *Negotiation*, May 1, 2005, p. 5.

31   Schmidt and Rosenberg, op. cit., p. 156.

32   Ibid., p. 154.

33   https://www.merriam-webster.com/dictionary/dissensus

34   Lynda Gratton and Tamara J. Erickson, "Eight Ways to Build Collaborative Teams," *Harvard Business Review*, November, 2007, p. 5.

35   Desmond Morris, *The Naked Ape* (New York: Dell, 1967).

36   Erica Dhawan and Tomas Chamorro-Premuzic, "How to Collaborate Effectively If Your Team Is Remote," *Harvard Business Review*, February 27, 2018, p. 3.

37   Ibid.

38   Tsedal Neeley, "Global Teams That Work," *Harvard Business Review*, October, 2015, p. 7.

39   Ibid.

40   Human Synergistics and Center for Applied Research, *Organizational Culture Inventory, OCI®: Interpretation and Development Guide* (Plymouth, MI: Human Synergistics/Center for Applied Research, 2009); see also Janel L. Szumal and Robert A. Cooke, *Creating Constructive Cultures* (Plymouth, MI: Human Synergistics International, 2019).

41   McGregor, op. cit., p. 324.

Figure Credits

Fig. 7.1: Edward M. Marshall, "The Structure of a Collaborative Organization," Transforming the Way We Work: The Power of the Collaborative Workplace, p. 113, AMACOM Books, 1995.

Fig. 7.2: Copyright © 2010 by The Marshall Group, LLC. Reprinted with permission.

PART IV

Collaborative
Organizational Change

239

CHAPTER EIGHT

The Human Side of Organizational Change

*Nothing so undermines organizational change as the
failure to think through the losses people face.*

—William Bridges, *Managing Transitions*

*I*T WAS *Morare's turn to facilitate the team's session on organizational change. He was eager to dialogue with the team because in his internship he had witnessed the human impacts of a disastrous change process in that company. Everyone gathered in a library conference room. There was good-natured banter as they waited for Linda to join after her job interview. When she arrived, Morare opened with his story about watching how this company's reorganization affected his teammates. He found one of his teammates huddled in his cubicle with his head down on his desk, wondering what he was going to do now that his job had been eliminated. Others were angry at management for a total lack of involvement in any aspect of the change process. Hanyue wondered out loud, "Why did they not engage the workforce? Don't they understand how this will impact their trust of management?" Ana jumped in to share that in her experience in information technology, senior leadership demonstrated a very negative attitude toward any workforce engagement. They believed that if the workers knew what was being discussed, they might leave the company. She then pointed out that it was precisely because of this failure to engage that she saw five senior engineers, with a combined 45 years of experience, leave. Priyanka was curious about how leaders got to the point that change processes would ignore the human factor. She knew rapid change was never going to stop and expressed hope that there was a better way. She brought out the study questions for the reading and put them on the flip chart in the room:*

- *How do you see organizational change as an intensely human endeavor?*
- *What is the context for organizational change? Why must organizations change how they work?*
- *How did we get to this place where most change processes fail? Who were the key thinkers, and how did they contribute to the development of the Collaborative Method?*
- *What types of organizational change have been used in the past, and how have they contributed to the development of the 4th Evolution of organizational change, the Collaborative Method?*
- *What have been the human impacts of these change methods on the workforce?*

LEARNING OBJECTIVES

By the end of this chapter, you will:

- Understand that organizational change is an intensely human endeavor that involves the hopes, dreams, and aspirations of the workforce, that they are on the front lines of implementing the change, and that because they will be directly affected by the change, they have the right to own the change process
- Understand the context for organizational change, its velocity, and its impact on organizations
- Learn how key influential thinkers helped shape the field of organizational change and contributed to the development of the Collaborative Method
- Discover the traditional approaches to organizational change—structure first, process based, and digitally driven—and why most initiatives fail
- Understand the human impacts of these traditional approaches to organizational change

THE MAIN POINT OF THIS CHAPTER

The executive team was pondering how they were going to meet a disruptive technology challenge from a competitor. They knew they had to make some significant changes. The CEO said, "If we expect to beat our competition in this rapidly changing market, we're going to have to reduce headcount, rationalize and simplify our supply chain processes, and install a new information technology system. This will need to happen this next year, but let's keep this to ourselves. We will announce it at the right time. I don't want our best people heading for the exits before we're ready."

Headcount? Really? These are living, breathing human beings they're talking about. In my experience, this is how some leaders talk about their workforces when they're going through significant change. *Organizational change is an intensely human endeavor.* It is not just about structure or process, value generation, efficiency, or headcount reduction. Organizational change is about the hopes and aspirations of the workforce, their careers, families, and communities. It requires the input of all affected, especially those on the front lines, because organizational change threatens the stability of their lives.

Everyone knows that the world is changing rapidly, that global competition is fierce, and that technological disruptions are occurring at an increasing rate. We also know that there is no longer such a thing as a job for life, a 20th Century antique. People change jobs every two to three years. But when leaders who believe in the Power Paradigm assume their workforces should not be involved in the change process and exercise their power to exclude them, there is going to be a human reaction, typically resistance, anger, resentment, and distrust toward leadership. In fact, the lack of ownership of change initiatives by those impacted by them is one of the two main reasons there is a 70+% failure rate among traditional change methods. The other reason is a lack of consistent leadership involvement.[1] Because organizational change is often a threat to the survival of workers, if they don't own it, and leadership gets distracted by the next bright shiny object, it is likely to fail.

There is another approach to change that is principled, honors the human spirit, is ethical, is transparent, and engages the hearts, minds, and productive energy of the workforce. The Collaboration Paradigm's approach to organizational change is called the *Collaborative Method*, the 4th Evolution.[2] The fundamental premise of this method is that organizational change is an intensely human endeavor, and that to be successful, the change method must be culture driven, people centric, and owned by the workforce. The workforce not only needs to understand why they have to change, they must believe in it, align with it, and own its implementation. It is their right.

In this chapter, we will learn about the rapidly changing external environment that is forcing organizations to change how they work. We will then review the key thinkers about organization development and change who have helped frame the Collaborative Method. We will explore the three primary methods for organizational change that have dominated the 20th and early 21st Centuries, followed by an exploration of the human impacts of change. Based on this analysis, we will propose a workers bill of rights in organizational change as a way of saying that leadership cannot succeed in a change initiative without the people owning it, followed by a description, in Chapter 9, of how the Collaborative Method honors those rights.

THE CONTEXT FOR ORGANIZATIONAL CHANGE

Nothing endures but change.

—Heraclitus[3]

In his book *Technology vs. Humanity,* futurist Gerd Leonhard helps us understand that the world as we know it now is in the process of a dramatic transformation due to megashifts that will "trigger a tsunami of disruption and change, potentially equating to a mass extinction event for much of the existing global commerce infrastructure."[4] Among the ten megashifts he has identified are the following:[5]

- **Digitization:** Everything that can be digitized, will be.
- **Mobilization and Mediazation:** Next-to-limitless connectivity and computational capability will become the new normal.
- **Disintermediation:** There will be disruption by cutting out the middle man and going direct.
- **Transformation:** It will be the number one priority for most companies and organizations as exponential technological change impacts them across the board.
- **Automation:** This is the key to hyper-efficiency because it makes it possible to substitute machines for humans.
- **Virtualization:** This is the idea of creating a nonphysical, digital version of something, such as cloud computing.
- **Robotization:** Robots are going to be absolutely everywhere, like it or not.

Their combined impact on humanity will be a loss of human control, the near total disruption of the world as we know it, and certainly the disruption of today's business, nonprofit, and civil society organizations, as well as the way we lead them. Leonhard argues that these "megashifts are different from technological forces; when combined they create a perfect storm for humanity," and goes on to say:

> As we head into exponential change, we must also collaborate to address ethics, culture and values. Otherwise, it is certain that technology will gradually then suddenly become the purpose of our lives, rather than the tool to discover the purpose.[6]

The Velocity of Change

The acceleration of technological advancement over the next 30 years is an example of what Leonhard was talking about. The Emerging Future organization provides us with a graphic perspective on where we are now, in 2020 (see Figure 8.1), and where we will be in 2050, when they predict we will be a billion times more advanced.[7] According to this organization, by the early 2040s "the rapid pace of improved changes

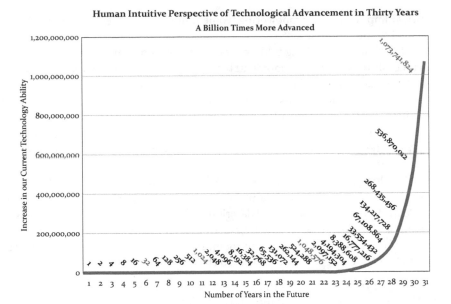

FIGURE 8.1 The Rate of Technological Advancement in 30 years.

will be hundreds of millions of times faster than today. ... The only way humans will be able to keep up ... will be with virtual assistants and computers inside us."[8]

The question we must consider is whether human beings have the capacity to adapt to all this change. What will be its impact on our organizations, leadership cultures, and our relationships with each other?

How will we as human beings cope with all of this change? We're way beyond the ideas of being agile and adaptive. We need a comprehensive, systems approach to understanding how our organizations function, and we need a leadership culture that respects the abilities of its workforce to respond to these inevitable disruptions.

The Transformation of Industry

As a consequence, this technological transformation, industries are also being transformed. Ross, in *The Industries of the Future,* helps us understand how technological changes like big data and robots are shaping the future of business and markets, as well as the organizations and their workers. He points to cutting-edge advances in artificial intelligence and machine learning, dramatic advances in life sciences that will allow people to live longer, healthier lives, the uneven distribution of wealth they will produce, leaving those who are behind today even further behind, the weaponization of code and subsequent cybersecurity threats, the expansion of big data, and the critical importance of empowering women, integrating them economically and politically into our companies.[9]

In 2018 Deloitte Consulting told us about Industry 4.0, which goes beyond Leonhard's megashifts and is a developmental stage in the organization and management of the value chain process involved in manufacturing.[10] Their research showed several key characteristics of this evolution, including vertical networking of smart production systems and networking of smart logistics, production, and marketing; horizontal integration and cooperation through global value-creation networks; and through-engineering the entire product life cycle across the entire value chain.[11]

Volatility, Uncertainty, Complexity and Ambiguity

The term *VUCA* (volatility, uncertainty, complexity, and ambiguity) originated with the US Army War College as a way of describing the world after the Cold War with the Soviet Union (1990s).[12] In subsequent years it was adopted by business to help explain the major forces that were impacting them. In 2016 the Strategic Agility Institute issued its first VUCA report, which defined these terms:[13]

- **Volatility:** An increase in the pace or rate of change
- **Uncertainty:** Unpredictability about the future
- **Complexity:** Having interconnected parts or variables
- **Ambiguity:** Lack of clarity about the meaning or trends of events

They surveyed close to 300 business leaders across a range of industries in terms of the speed at which VUCA was impacting them and found that on a scale of 0–100, their VUCA Index was 69.57 in terms of the expected level of future turbulence.[14]

Globalization

In 2017 McKinsey & Company helped us understand how globalization was impacting our world and organizations. The bottom line of their analysis of nine different global trends was that "growth is shifting, disruption is accelerating, and societal tensions are rising."[15] They grouped the nine trends into three buckets, or what they called "crucibles":

- **Global Growth Shifts:** The globalization of digital products and services that is surging while traditional trade and financial flows have stalled; growth dynamics have shifted from countries to regions.
- **Accelerating Industry Disruptions:** Digitization, machine learning, and the life sciences are combining to redefine what companies do; the terms of competition are changing as we experience a business ecosystem revolution.
- **New Societal Deal:** We must protect ourselves from the dark side of malevolent actors, including cybercriminals and terrorists; more collaboration is needed between business and government to accelerate growth for all.

Global Climate Change: The Threat of Mass Extinction

In January 2019 the United Nations Intergovernmental Panel on Climate Change warned us that the planet has until 2030 to reduce the level of greenhouse gas emissions to 1.5° Celsius above preindustrial levels, or we will face catastrophic consequences, with a disproportionate share of those negative consequences impacting the poorest of us.[16] As of early 2020, the planet was already at 1.2°C and rising. We are already experiencing extreme weather events, from catastrophic fires in Australia and California, to the melting of both polar ice caps, and a recent report that Indonesia has to move its capital from Jakarta to the island of Borneo due to rising sea levels.[17] Species of plants are disappearing; animals are going extinct; warming waters are killing the Great Barrier Reef off of Australia; and drought, famine, and the inability to grow food are causing mass migrations that will only get more intense with time. All of us are facing the existential threat of mass extinction in the next 100 years.

To bring the reality of this home, on November 6, 2019, 11,258 scientists from 153 countries, who felt a moral obligation to speak up, gave the world a grim warning: that there will be untold suffering caused by climate change unless humanity drastically changes its ways. They said these changes must be in six areas: energy, short-lived pollutants, ecosystems, food, ending extraction behavior, and population control.[18] Even as the polar ice caps are melting at faster and faster rates, and up to 10 feet (3 meters) of sea level rise threatens hundreds of millions of people around the world by the end of this century, the consequences of global climate change are still beyond anything we can now imagine.

The Demographic Shift

The world we have been describing is one that our learning team and close to 2 billion Millennials and 2 billion Gen Zers around the world are inheriting, one that poses enormous challenges in terms of how they can lead 21st Century organizations. They represent a very potent force for change in our organizations, not only because they now dominate the global workforce but also because of what they expect in terms of leadership cultures.

We are witnessing a fundamental shift in the character of the workforce as well. As the generation of workers born after World War II age out and retire, organizations around the world are now populated by Millennials. According to the Pew Research Center, as of 2017 in the United States, 56% are Millennials.[19] In the global workforce, by 2020 fully 75% were expected to be Millennials.[20] They have very specific expectations about the type of workplace they want to be in at the same time they remain increasingly skeptical about business, leadership, and their own futures. They want more collaboration in the workplace and substantially more flexibility, independence, and autonomy.[21]

All is not well, however. According to an annual global Millennial survey of 13,416 individuals across 42 countries, conducted by Deloitte, this is a generation disrupted, where all the accelerated technological change leaves them feeling unsettled about their future. They are skeptical about business' motives, with 49% of the participants saying they would like to quit their jobs. They have a love-hate relationship with technology, with 71% feeling positive about their personal digital devices and social media, though 64% said they would be healthier if they spent less time on them. At the same time, 79% being concerned they will be victims of online fraud.[22] They want their work to be purpose driven, inventive, flexible, with no silos and greater collaboration.[23] This demographic wave of clear expectations is colliding not only with the inability of Power Paradigm leaders to change fast enough, but also with the realities of a dramatically changing world around them. They are extremely comfortable with and can adapt to technological advancements, but the inability of organizational leadership to change the culture fast enough does not bode well for many businesses and nonprofits. They will simply move on.

HOW WE GOT HERE: KEY THINKERS SHAPING ORGANIZATIONAL CHANGE

All forms of learning and change start with some form of dissatisfaction or frustration.

—Edgar H. Schein[24]

The field of organizational change has been evolving since the 1950s, influenced deeply by five key thinkers. Each one of their theories provide critical grounding that helped shape the 4th Evolution of organizational change methodology, the *Collaborative Method*.

Kurt Lewin: Field Theory, Group Dynamics and Organization Development

Kurt Lewin was a German Jew born in 1890 who fled to the United States in 1933 to escape the Nazi death camps. He taught at Cornell and the University of Iowa and then led the Research Center for Group Dynamics at MIT. He helped found the Tavistock Institute of Human Relations in the United Kingdom and the National Training Laboratories in Bethel, Maine, a founding institution for organization development. Lewin was the intellectual father of contemporary theories of applied behavioral science, action research, and planned change and was a humanitarian who believed the human condition could be improved through the resolution of social conflict, particularly for minority and disadvantaged people.[25]

For us to understand Lewin's approach to organizational change, we need to first understand three key elements of his work. His unifying theme was the idea that "the group to which an individual belongs is the ground for his perceptions, his feelings and his actions."[26] This theme found expressions in field theory, group dynamics, and planned change. In field theory, there are three important aspects:[27]

- It understands group behavior is the context of the "field" in which the behavior takes place—like an organization or a team.
- According to this theory, "group behavior is an intricate set of symbolic interactions and forces that not only affect group structure, but also modify individual behavior" and how we act as individuals in the workplace.
- If there is behavioral change, it results from what is going on in the workplace.

Lewin's second major contribution to organizational change was group dynamics, which argues that group (team), rather than individual, behavior should be the main focus of change. Further, he posits that we should concentrate on group norms, roles, interactions, and socialization processes, and that group dynamics are about what is going on in those groups.[28] Finally, he gave us planned change, a three-step model known as "freeze-unfreeze-refreeze":[29]

- **Step 1: Unfreezing:** For there to be change, the equilibrium in human behavior has to be destabilized (unfrozen) before old behavior can be unlearned and new behavior can be successfully adopted; those involved must feel "psychologically safe from loss and humiliation" before they can accept a new approach.
- **Step 2: Moving:** Change is iterative and involves action research which enables people to move from one set of behaviors to another.
- **Step 3: Refreezing:** Now there is a new equilibrium, a new stability. "Lewin saw successful change as a group activity, because unless group norms and routines are also transformed, changes to individual behavior will not be sustained."

Schein argues that Lewin's unfreezing requires data-based dissatisfaction or frustration and that to overcome the natural tendencies to dismiss that data, blame it on others, ignore it, or deny it—all forms of human resistance to change—people must feel some sense of survival anxiety, that if they do not change, they will fail to meet goals or ideals they have set for themselves. He points out that there is also "learning anxiety," that "if we admit to ourselves and others that something is wrong or imperfect, we will lose our effectiveness, our self-esteem, and maybe even our identity."[30] Learning anxiety produces a defensive avoidance to change, which Lewin countered by engaging workers on the front lines in the change itself—what I have called ownership. This involvement, which happens in the moving phase, creates, according to Schein, the psychological safety people need to make the change:

> The key to effective change management, then, becomes the ability to balance the amount of threat produced by disconfirming data with enough psychological safety to allow the change target to accept the information, feel the survival anxiety, and become motivated to change.[31]

In the refreezing phase, Schein argues that teamwork gets redefined in a way that individualism, which the Power Paradigm rewards, does not just become "groupism," but that individual capabilities are expanded by their ability to work in groups and to be a good team player.[32] Reward structures can then be attached to group behavior as well as individual behavior, fostering collective responsibility and collaborative behavior once the change has happened.

Kurt Lewin could be considered the grandfather of the Collaborative Method on a number of dimensions:

- Teams are the unit of organizational change.
- There must be a burning platform or crisis that threatens the survival of the group or organization for people to be willing to move beyond their natural resistance to change.
- For the change to be successful, there must be psychological safety.
- Workforce ownership of the change produces that safety.
- Teams can refreeze around a set of norms for how they will work together.
- The reward system needs to focus on collective results of teams as well as individual results.

Finally, Lewin, as well as Schein's interpretation of his work, reinforces the point of this chapter: that organizational change is an intensely human endeavor, where there is anxiety, fear, guilt, resistance, blaming, denial, and avoidance behavior; that in order for a change to be successful, people must own the change. Human beings are complex and have needs, expectations, and hopes, and when thrown into the turmoil caused by rapid and volatile change, they will cling to whatever stabilizing forces exist in their lives. It is the change leader's responsibility to ensure that they feel safe during the change process, which is best created by giving them ownership of it.

David Cooperrider: Appreciative Inquiry, Positive Organizational Change[33]

David Cooperrider, a Professor of Social Entrepreneurship at the Weatherhead School of Management at Case Western Reserve University, is Faculty Director at the Center for Business and founder of the Taos Institute, an association of scholars and practitioners dedicated to exploring social constructionist ideas. Cooperrider is best known for what he calls appreciative inquiry, a theory of positive organizational behavior. An initial premise of this work is that many change theories start with the question "What is wrong?," in effect a deficiency approach to organizational change. Cooperrider does not believe that root cause analysis, "burning platforms," or remedial action planning is the way to change an organization. To the contrary, he believes appreciative inquiry is more effective as a positive approach to organizational change, a process of search and discovery designed to value, prize, and honor people in the organization. It assumes that organizations are networks and the goal of change is to "touch the positive core of organizational life."[34]

In his change model, you access the positive core by asking positive questions, which bring out the human spirit in the organization, and the organization, in a self-organizing way, begins to construct a more desirable future. There are four steps in this approach to change: 1) Discovery, which is a systematic inquiry; 2) Dream, a visioning process that attracts people; 3) Design, which focuses on how to redesign the organization to achieve the dream; and 4) Destiny, which is when the process is given away to others and self-organization occurs.[35]

In the spirit of appreciation, Cooperrider has given us a collaborative approach to change which relies on the principle of ownership and optimism. As a change management practitioner, though, I can personally testify to the reality that self-organization in a power-based leadership culture doesn't work. One Fortune 500 company I worked with conducted an experiment with self-directed teams, similar to the self-organization idea. It failed, not because of the good intentions of the managers who launched the effort, but because of the need for accountability and connectivity to the rest of the organization. The experiment was considered by senior leadership to be anarchy: "The inmates are running the asylum." With empowerment there has to be accountability.

The value of Cooperrider's work for the *Collaborative Method* is the following:

- The absolute critical role that ownership plays in ensuring the success of organizational change
- The importance of a positive vision that unifies the organization
- The value of building the internal capacity of the organization to facilitate the change process themselves
- The critical importance of empowerment plus accountability in the change process

Jim Collins: Strategy-Driven Change[36]

Jim Collins, a Professor at Stanford's Graduate School of Business, generated a massive amount of data on companies, which provided the basis for his books on what strategies enable a company to excel and sustain their growth and development. He focused on companies which made the leap from good to great business results that were sustained for at least 15 years. He compared these companies to a control group of similar companies that did not make that leap, analyzed the gap, and suggested seven elements of a strategy-driven approach for companies to go from good to great:[37]

1. **Level 5 Leadership:** Self-effacing and reserved; personal humility and professional will.
2. **First Who ... Then What:** Get the right people in the right seat on the bus; then they figure out where you're going.
3. **Confront the Brutal Facts:** Companies must confront the most brutal facts of their current reality.

4. **The Hedgehog Concept:** The core business must be based on the intersection of three factors: (1) Passion; (2) What it can be the best in the world at; and (3) What drives the economic engine.

5. **A Culture of Discipline:** Few have a culture of discipline; with disciplined people you don't need hierarchy; with disciplined thought, you don't need bureaucracy; with disciplined action, you don't need excessive controls.

6. **Technology Acceleration:** Good to great companies "never use technology as the primary means of igniting a transformation" yet are pioneers in applying carefully selected technologies.

7. **The Flywheel and the Doom Loop:** "Those who launch revolutions, dramatic change programs, and wrenching restructurings will almost certainly fail to make the leap from good to great"; this leap involves relentlessly pushing a giant flywheel in one direction, turn upon turn, building momentum until there is a breakthrough.

While Collins focuses on the strategic change process, there is no consideration of collaboration or collaborative change. Of great value, however, is the emphasis on a culture of discipline for implementation. He recognizes that leadership culture is a fundamental element of a change process (see Figure 8.2).

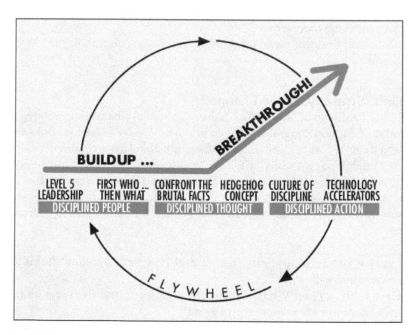

FIGURE 8.2 Going From Good to Great.[38]

John Kotter: Eight Steps of Change

Kotter, a Professor of Leadership at Harvard Business School, posits that there are eight steps in the change process. This method has been accepted as a way many companies have implemented organizational change. In *Leading Change,* he outlines each of these steps (see Figure 8.3):[39]

1. **Establish a Sense of Urgency:** Examine market and competitive realities; identify crises and opportunities.
2. **Create a Guiding Coalition:** Create a team with the power to lead the change; get them to work together as a team.
3. **Develop a Vision and Strategy:** Create a vision to direct the change effort; develop strategies to achieve it.
4. **Communicate the Vision:** Constantly communicate the vision and strategies.
5. **Empower Broad-Based Action:** Get rid of change systems or structures that undermine the vision; encourage risk-taking and action.
6. **Generate Short-Term Wins:** Create wins; recognize the people who made them.
7. **Consolidate Gains and Produce More Change:** Change all systems, structures, and policies that don't fit with the vision; hire and develop people who can implement the vision.
8. **Anchor New Approaches in the Culture:** Create better performance through customer- and productivity-oriented behavior, more and better leadership, and more effective management; develop means to ensure leadership development and succession.

Kotter goes on to say that you should not skip steps. The change process must be done in this sequence. Note that culture is last. In my experience, there is a logic to some of the steps and to the importance of a sequence, but Kotter's approach has four significant shortcomings that undercut its effectiveness:

How "Culture" is Defined: Kotter has defined culture rather narrowly—norms of group behavior and shared values.[40] He defines norms of group behavior as "common or pervasive ways of acting that are found in a group and that persist because group members tend to behave in ways that teach these practices to new members, rewarding those who fit in and sanctioning those who do not." Examples of norms are responding quickly to customer requests or managers staying an hour after closing time. He defines "shared values" as "important concerns and goals shared by most of the people in a group that tend to shape group behavior and that often persist over time even when group membership changes." Examples include executives who prefer long-term debt, and managers who care about customers.

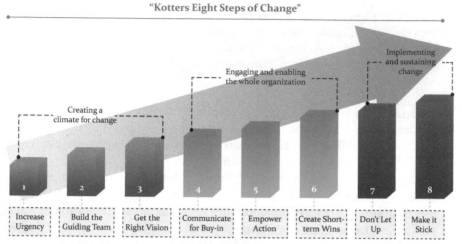

Kotter, John P. and Cohen, Dan S. **The Heart of Change.** Boston: Harvard Business School Press

FIGURE 8.3 Kotter's Eight steps of change.

In Chapter 2, organizational culture was defined as follows:

> *The shared assumptions and beliefs, principles, values, and ethics; and the history, language, and customs in the organization, all of which shape and drive the behaviors of people in the workforce, the workplace environment, work processes, and how the organization is designed and organized to produce results.*

Culture is norms and behaviors as well as shared values, but it is much more than that. It is also principles, ethics, history, language, customers, and the productive energy of the workforce. By having a narrow definition of culture, Kotter narrows the scope of his change methodology, and particularly the importance of the human side of change, ignoring the productive energy of the workforce.

<u>Putting Culture Last—Not Owning the Process:</u> Kotter puts culture last, rather than first. He argues that "culture changes only after you have successfully altered people's actions, after the new behavior produces some group benefit for a period of time, and after people see the connection between the new actions and the performance improvement." He goes on to warn his readers they should be "concerned" about change agents arguing that you need to put culture first.[41] He has not successfully argued his case by simply making assertions. As we will see in the next chapter, organizational change *must* start with culture first, because if leadership does not own how they are going to work together, the level of team trust, ownership and accountability for the change process will dissipate, one of the two main reasons change processes fail. Also, if they don't own a set of shared operating agreements, they will likely not model the behavior at the beginning of the process, putting their credibility and the change process at risk. Furthermore, if they don't own the change methodology from the very beginning, the change process becomes merely a transaction, a strategy, an event, or an activity. When there is another bright shiny object, the leaders will shift their attention—putting the initiative at risk.

Change That is Not Collaborative: There is a maxim in collaborative organizational change: *A change process can only create a collaborative outcome when the change process itself is collaborative.* Perhaps Kotter is not interested in collaborative outcomes or processes, which is entirely possible. But the failure to build ownership of the process on the front-end results in a lack of ownership throughout the process. This lack of ownership, particularly by those expected to implement it is the second reason why over 70+% of change processes fail.

The Human Dynamics of Change: Kotter's steps do not sufficiently recognize the critical role that human beings play in the process or the psychological dynamics of change processes. Recall the main proposition of this chapter: organizational change is an intensely human endeavor, where people's lives and relationships are thrown into chaos, jobs are lost, work habits are altered, and the stability required for productive effort is upended. Kotter has put culture last. In no other step does the workforce even show up, not even step 5, which is about changing structures and getting rid of obstacles. The bottom line of the eight-step method is that the workforce does not own the change and culture is put last. Psychological and human dynamics of change have simply been ignored. The failure to fully take the people into consideration as the most critical element in any change process calls into question the credibility of the entire method.

David A. Nadler: A Congruence Model

Nadler was an organizational theorist, consultant, and business executive who taught at Columbia and founded Delta Consulting Group. He is best known for his work in organizational design and architecture. In terms of organizational change, his most significant contribution was the idea of "congruence" or "fit":[42]

> *In systems, the interactions of the components are more important than the components themselves ... its overall effectiveness relies on the internal congruence, or fit, of its basic components. The tighter the fit the greater the effectiveness.*

Nadler saw organizations as systems, and his model of change considered elements such as the external environment; organizational resources; the organization's history, business strategy, strategic decisions made, and output/results; the operating organization. These are the heart of the congruence model, which converts strategy, resources, and other factors into performance as well as the formal and informal organization—culture, work practices, and leadership behaviors.[43]

Given all of these elements, Nadler argues that what is most important in terms of strategy and performance is the degree of "fit," or congruence, among them which affects the level of performance. The focus of the change strategy needs to be on the degree of fit, eliminating the gap between strategy and performance.

While all of the elements in Nadler's systems model are included in the Collaboration Paradigm, the difference is in the degree of emphasis in terms of what is most important. In the Collaborative Method of organizational change and transformation, it is the organization's leadership culture that drives the change. Nadler has minimized the importance of culture, placing it last, and subsuming it as merely one aspect of the informal organization. It is the organization's identity, its history, customs, principles, values, and the productive energy of the workforce. Culture is the engine for change. Culture informs and drives the behavior of leaders as well as the workforce, and shapes the degree to which the change process is owned by those who are implementing it.

While I appreciate Nadler's focus on a systems approach to change, his emphasis on structure, systems, strategy and performance limit the effectiveness of that change. You cannot achieve high performance, let alone successful organizational change, without the full engagement and ownership of the workforce. People are the engine of change and transformation. People implement strategy. People produce results.

THE ORIGINS OF ORGANIZATIONAL CHANGE: THREE TRADITIONAL APPROACHES

More than 70% of change processes fail.

—McKinsey & Company, 2019; *Harvard Business Review*, 2017[44]

The origins of organizational change management began with Kurt Lewin in 1948 with his three-stage model. It was based on the concepts and applications of what became known as organization development (OD). OD emerged in the 1950s from the work of the National Training Labs in group dynamics and leadership. Business schools and social psychology departments were finding that traditional industrial psychology no longer met the needs of organizations.[45] According to the American Psychological Association, another vector of organization development, industrial psychology, was defined as "the scientific study of human behavior in organizations and the workplace."[46] But the primary focus of industrial psychology was on diagnostic tools for individual rather than group behavior. Lewin helped us see that there was a new field of endeavor in organizations known today as organization development,[47] which focused on the behavior of groups.

By the mid-1960s, luminaries in the field like Beckhard, Bennis, and Schein designed an Addison-Wesley book series on different elements of OD. It was not a coherent theory at that time. Of particular note was Schein's work on process consultation.[48] Beckhard defined OD as follows:[49]

... an effort 1) Planned, (2) Organization-wide, (3) Managed from the top, to (4) Increase organization effectiveness and health through (5) Planned interventions in the organization's "processes," using behavioral-science knowledge.

He goes on to help us understand its goals, which were to (1) Develop a self-renewing, viable system that can respond to the work it has to do; (2) Optimize effectiveness by built-in continuous improvement mechanisms; (3) Address conflict in the organization; (4) Reach the point where decisions are made based on data rather than one's title; and (5) "[M]ove toward high collaboration and low competition between interdependent units."[50] These were the theoretical and behavioral science underpinnings for what we now call change management.

There are three basic types of change management that were used prior to the emergence of the Collaborative Method: structure-first, process-based, and digitally-driven. Each methodology has its own assumptions about how a business can best transform itself and achieve sustainable competitive advantage. Most approaches, however, were not systems oriented. They tended to focus on one dimension of how the organization works or on a technique. Some approaches even claimed to be revolutionary, enabling radical transformation and cost-cutting. Some claimed to be focused on quality or empowerment. Others made no claim at all. But when all the dust settled, few if any of them resulted in sustainable change. In fact, the 70+% failure rate in change management processes can largely be attributed to a failure to understand the significant role of the organization's culture, and the role of the workforce in owning and being responsible for the implementation of the change. They overlooked that fact that *organizational change is an intensely human endeavor and requires direct human ownership of that change if it is to succeed.*

Structure-First Change

A new CEO joins the company and wants to make his/her mark within the first 100 days. What is the easiest thing to demonstrate a bias for action? It is to reorganize the company. It's relatively easy to do, is quick, and enables the leader to demonstrate decisiveness. There's only one problem. Structural change produces fear in the workforce—"Will I lose my job? I better get my résumé out." This fear results in resistance to the change and an unwillingness to take a risk or to speak truth to power, and people go into a defensive crouch to protect their positions. The CEO gets the change but loses the people. Executives who thought that by using structural change they would gain control over the organization typically found the opposite results.

Let's take the change case of a Fortune 100 industrial company that decided to decentralize along product lines and formed five strategic business units. The rationale was to get closer to the customer. Each of the service functions—human resources, information technology, finance, and marketing—had what they called "liaisons" between headquarters and the business units. They were service partners with the heads of those units. With two bosses, this restructuring led to breakdowns in communications, the delivery of services, and the quality of the product delivered to the customer. After two years of pain, the CEO recentralized.

In effect, they compounded their problem. They consolidated service functions into what they called a shared service organization with the logic that centralized services would be more cost effective, could increase quality, and would streamline the organization. They believed the workforce would support this, that the business unit presidents would embrace the change, and they could become faster and more agile. This also failed. The workforce resisted the change, and the business unit presidents started voicing their concerns that the CEO did not know what he was doing and lobbied the board for a new CEO. When the new CEO arrived, the cycle started all over again.

At another Fortune 500 company, the workforce started hearing rumors of a major reorganization about six months ahead of when it actually happened. They immediately went into a defensive crouch, withheld information from each other, and refused to question decisions being made by executives or to take risks. They did not want to lose their jobs. The actual reorganization took a year to implement, during which time the workforce remained in their defensive position and got ready to reeducate their new bosses about how invaluable they were to the unit. The next six months were a time of readjustment as people were let go or moved to new business units. The culture of fear was palpable. Everything slowed down. For two full years, this megacorporation lost the productive energy of its people.

I've watched this same dynamic happen with mergers and acquisitions. The business model behind the deal is always to rationalize the two organizations, which is a fancy way of saying that a certain percentage of the workforce must be terminated in order to make the deal work. Structural change yet again, but what they fail to address is the cultural integration of the affected workforces. They have different ways of working, different leadership cultures, different goals and aspirations. Failure to effectively integrate the cultures results in a failure of the merger. I witnessed this when one Fortune 50 company bought a Fortune 200 company. During their 17 year alliance, the cultural differences between them were significant, impacting the results of both companies. They eventually split up.

This penchant to always start with a structural change, to reorganize, decentralize, or centralize got me to wondering—why do executives do this if the data show that these restructurings tend to fail at such a high rate? What I came to understand is there is a structure-first mind-set based on the following premises:

- There is a need for greater control over the organization.
- It is top-down and based on power.
- Leaders believe the workforce is not responsible and cannot be trusted with change.

- There is little to no ownership of the change by the workforce.
- The focus is on short-term gains.
- It ignores the cultural dimension of the organization's system.
- It disregards the human dynamic and impacts of the change.

The structure-first mindset may be able to produce short-term results, but it consistently sacrifices the human and cultural dynamics that are essential for any sustainable success.

Process-Based Change

A second commonly practiced approach to organizational change is focused on business processes, where they are realigned, strengthened, or rationalized to produce better financial, efficiency, or quality results. We will look briefly at total quality management, business process reengineering, and lean manufacturing and will assess their impact on the people in the workforce.

Dr. W. Edwards Deming and Total Quality Management: Deming was an engineer, professor, business consultant, and management theorist who lived from 1900 to 1993, and is best known for his work in making total quality a central focus for businesses. In his 1982 book *Out of Crisis*, Deming argues there is a crisis in management and that management must be totally transformed.[51] He had spent years working with the Japanese who were recovering from the devastation of World War II, and he sought to bring the principles of their amazing recovery to American industry, which was not competing effectively against the Japanese. I remember the debates in the boardrooms in the late 1980s about why the Japanese were doing so much better than US industry, and what they were going to do about it. Deming's approach to total quality was considered, at the time, to be a solution.

As a statistician, he was on a mission to seek sources of improvement, but knew that this could not happen without a fundamental transformation of management.[52] The way he sought to do this is by promoting a philosophy of total quality management, constant and continuous improvement of business processes, based on these principles for transforming business:[53]

1. Create constancy of purpose through continuous improvement.
2. Mistakes and negativism are unacceptable.
3. Cease dependence on mass inspection, which encourages defects; "With instruction, workers can be enlisted in this improvement."[54]
4. Seek the best quality.
5. Improve constantly and forever the system of production and service.
6. Institute training and retraining; help people do a better job.
7. Drive out fear; "It is necessary for better quality and productivity that people feel secure."[55]

8. Break down barriers between staff area; silos and competition have to be eliminated.
9. Eliminate slogans, exhortations, and targets for the workforce.
10. Eliminate numerical quotas.
11. Remove barriers to the pride of workmanship.
12. Institute a vigorous program of education and retraining.
13. Take action to accomplish the transformation.

As the founder of the total quality movement, Deming was a passionate and brilliant pioneer for radical transformation of industry. His work led to the famous Deming Prize, the highest award there is for total quality management, which originally focused on Japanese companies. In 1989 Florida Power and Light was the first American company to win.

In terms of the impact of process change on the workforce and our focus on the human dynamics of change, Deming's principles suggest that enlightened management would create some psychological safety for the workforce, and focus on training and helping them rather than punishing them. At the same time, Deming's approach was patriarchal, enhanced the dependence of the workforce on management, and did not challenge the hierarchical nature of power in the workplace. There was no consideration of the power of culture to transform an organization or of the power of ownership of the change by the workforce to transform processes.

Michael Hammer and Business Processes Reengineering: In 1993, Hammer and James Champy of CSC Index in Cambridge, Massachusetts, published their version of the need for revolutionary process change, entitled *Reengineering the Corporation: A Manifesto for Business Revolution.*[56] The central thesis of their work was that "corporations must undertake nothing less than a radical reinvention of how they do their work."[57] In 1990 Hammer argued, "It is time to stop paving the cow paths. Instead of embedding outdated processes in silicon and software, we should obliterate them and start over. We should 'reengineer' our businesses: use the power of modern information technology to radically redesign our business processes in order to achieve dramatic improvements in their performance."[58]

Hammer, like Deming, believed that the United States could not compete against Japan unless there was a revolutionary, versus evolutionary, change in how corporations were structured, processes designed, and led. "Most companies have no choice but to muster the courage to do it."[59] At the heart of Hammer's approach was the idea of discontinuous thinking; that is, "recognizing and breaking away from the outdated rules and fundamental assumptions that underlie operations."[60] Other theorists have defined reengineering as "the fundamental rethinking and radical redesign of business processes to achieve dramatic improvements in critical, contemporary measures of performance, such as cost, quality, service and speed."[61]

In Hammer's view, to achieve this rethinking, new rules had to be established and that the only way to break the hold of conventional business thinking was to tear everything apart, and to rebuild it from the ground up. To do this, he put forth seven principles:[62]

- Organize around outcomes, not tasks; responsibilities get compressed.
- Have those who use the output of the process perform the process; use technology and databases.
- Subsume information-process work into the real work that produces the information.
- Treat geographically dispersed resources as though they were centralized.
- Link parallel activities instead of integrating their results.
- Put the decision point where the work is performed and build control into the process; get rid of middle management.
- Capture information once and at the source.

In theory, Hammer's work reflects a response to both the increased global competition, the need to evolve corporate processes to compete, and the rise of information technology as a mediator of data and control. But there is absolutely no mention of the organization's culture as a component of the change process. In practice, however, reengineering wreaked havoc on American businesses. By Hammer's own words: "No one in an organization wants reengineering. It is confusing and disruptive and affects everything people have grown accustomed to."[63]

In one of his prescriptions, he showed great antipathy toward middle managers. In fact, he suggested that senior leadership should take the "bloody ax" to get rid of them. I saw the impact of this approach when consulting with the information technology group at a global corporation. A large reengineering consulting firm was brought in to redesign their business processes—or were they? Using Hammer's approach, the consultants asked every manager to identify the top 25% of their people they would eliminate as part of the process simplification effort. You can imagine the response—total resistance. My sponsor refused the consultant's demand and quickly found himself in front of the CIO, being told to comply. Command and control was the way reengineering would achieve the reduction in force. Given the overwhelming negative reaction to this strategy, within 15 months the consultants were asked to leave. Later it was discovered their contract incentivized them to eliminate people; they got an extra bonus for each person they removed from the headcount, which raised questions about their professional ethics. In effect, reengineering became a very expensive way to downsize a company. The promise of redesigned processes was lost in the maelstrom of disruption caused by radical change.

Reengineering was the rage fad during the early 1990s, but the reengineering gurus had forgotten the most critical resources for any change process—the people and the organization's culture. Reengineering had significant, intensely human impacts. As *Fast Company's* postmortem pointed out:[64]

> *The rock that reengineering has foundered on is simple: people. Reengineering treated the people inside companies as if they were just so many bits and bytes, interchangeable parts to be reengineered. But no one wants to "be reengineered." No one wants to hear dictums like, "Carry the wounded but shoot the stragglers"—language that makes workers feel like prisoners of war, not their company's most important assets. No one wants to see (them) putting the company's veterans through their paces like they're just another group of idiots who "can't think out of the box."*

Business leaders and their reengineering consultants actually talked this way. Faced with overwhelming negative reaction, CSC Index commissioned a "State of Reengineering Report" to find out why reengineering had gotten such a bad name. They found that half of the companies in their study said "the most difficult part of reengineering is dealing with fear and anxiety in their organizations."[65]

As the Executive Vice President for Human Resources of a Fortune 100 company said to me after his company had spent about $50 million on a reengineering effort, "Can we get our money back?" When you ignore the people and the culture in a change process, there are serious consequences.

Lean Manufacturing: Like Deming's total quality management, this business process improvement system actually began with the Industrial Revolution and Henry Ford's introduction of it in the automobile assembly line, but it was popularized about 80 years later in 1990, around the same time that Hammer was preaching the overthrow of the corporate order. Womack, in his book *The Machine That Changed the World,* defined *lean* as "proven tools and techniques that focus on minimizing wasteful activity and adding value to the end product to meet customer needs."[66] The ultimate objective of lean is "perfection: continually declining costs, zero defects, zero inventories, and endless product variety,"[67] a state which no one has yet achieved.

Lean production grew out of the Toyota Production System in the mid-20ᵗʰ Century as well as total quality management. It defines value from the customer's perspective and as eliminating waste. The ultimate goal is to provide "perfect value to the customer through a perfect value creation process that has zero waste."[68] The five core principles for lean manufacturing are to 1) Define value for the customer; 2) Identify things the customer considers to be waste and eliminate them; 3) Ensure the process runs without delays, including cross-functional work and training; 4) Limit inventory and work in progress while ensuring materials are available, or just in time; and 5) Pursue perfection by having lean thinking become part of the culture.[69]

From a collaborative perspective, similar to total quality management and reengineering, the methodology is implemented in a power-based format. There is no ownership of the change process by frontline workers. It is imposed from the top. Second, the focus is on rooting out inefficiencies and waste, with the only empowerment of the workforce being training them so they understand the importance of waste reduction. Third, Womack argues that "a key objective of production is to push responsibility far down the organizational ladder."[70] But with that additional responsibility there is no increased power, only more stress if mistakes are made. Lean essentially subordinates the individual to the machine and the customers' bottom line. It reflects more the dehumanization of Theory X than the value for people conferred by the people, principle, or Collaboration Paradigms.

Digitally-Driven Change

Gerd Leonhard's seven technological drivers require organizations to change the way they work, not the least of which are digitization, artificial intelligence and robotization.[71] The level of disruption caused by VUCA changes forces companies to consider how they will adjust, adapt, and respond, or face extinction. Large-scale digital transformations are a way in which companies can capture the benefits of digital technologies. But as McKinsey has pointed out in their 2018 global survey on digital transformations that there are 21 factors most responsible for success. They fall into five categories:[72]

- Having the right, digital-savvy leaders in place
- Building capabilities for the workforce of the future
- Empowering people to work in new ways
- Giving day-to-day tools a digital upgrade
- Communicating frequently via traditional and digital methods

Remember that at the beginning of this chapter, we pointed to the fact that 70+% of change processes fail. The failure rate of recent digital transformations exceeds that number:[73]

- Less than 30% succeed.
- Only 16% say their digital transformations have successfully improved performance and equipped them to sustain long term change.
- 7% said performance improved but were not sustained.
- Among digitally savvy industries, the success rate does not exceed 26%.
- For traditional industries, success is between 4 and 11%.

In terms of people and the human dynamics of change, McKinsey found that digital transformations require cultural and behavior changes like increased collaboration and customer centricity. But there were four ways companies with successful transformations empowered their employees: 1) Reinforcing new behaviors and ways of working through formal mechanisms; 2) Giving employees a say on where digitization could or should be adopted, increasing success by 1.4 times; 3) Ensuring that senior leaders and managers reinforce the change and are engaged in it, increasing success by 1.5 times; and 4) Leaders and managers having their units collaborate with others, increasing success by 1.6 times.[74]

As we prepare to look at the Collaborative Method's approach to organizational change in Chapter 9, McKinsey's 21 factors responsible for digital transformation

SIDE BOX 8.1: TEN MISTAKES ORGANIZATIONS MAKE IN IMPLEMENTING ORGANIZATIONAL CHANGE

The values, mind-sets, and biases of leadership cultures drive organizational change initiatives. But traditional change approaches have been a colossal failure, at a 70% rate. The mistakes of structural, process-based, and digital transformations are legend, and have been repeated at many companies. They fall into the ten categories:

1. **It's About Control, Not Ownership:** Traditional business leaders expect to retain control of the change process and use their positional power to do so. Change processes are top-down and do not give the people who are on the receiving end of the change any ownership over the process. It leads to fear, resistance, low morale, and a substantial loss of productive energy.

2. **The Search for the Silver Bullet:** Business leaders tend to look for a "silver bullet," that one technique, program, fad, or guru whom they believe holds the secret to success. These are rarely, if ever, systems oriented, or about behavior, beliefs, and the leadership culture. Consequently, these approaches have more transactional than transformative value.

success were evaluated.[75] None of them involved giving ownership over the change process to the people on the front line. Leadership did a lot of encouraging of the workforce, and people were engaged to do a job, but the prospect of full ownership did not exist beyond their ability to say yes or no to a change. Cultural change, while noted in this global survey, was not a driver for the change—digital changes and external market forces were the drivers.

THE HUMAN IMPACTS OF ORGANIZATIONAL CHANGE

At the beginning of this chapter, we noted that *organizational change is an intensely human endeavor.* It is not just about structure or process, value generation, efficiency, or headcount reduction. Organizational change is about the hopes and aspirations of the workforce, their professional careers, families, and communities. Any significant organizational change threatens the stability of their lives. The psychological contract with their employers that defines their mutual expectations gets upended when there is a fundamental change in the organization's structure, processes, or culture. Leaders tend to forget that their workforce consists of living, breathing human beings. Bridges, author of *Managing Transitions*, pointed to some of the human impacts of organizational change by saying it's about the following:[76]

- The loss of jobs, professional standing, self-confidence, and self-esteem
- Fear for their own futures, their families', and financial survival
- Anxiety about what happens next
- Their identity—who are they now?
- Feeling betrayed by the organization to which they gave of themselves

Even with increased awareness of the need for workforce involvement in early 21st Century change initiatives, leaders still implement approaches based on the power and control and have little regard for the impacts on the human beings who work there. There seems to be a blatant disregard for the psychological consequences of organizational change strategies on people. It should not come as a surprise, then, that there is a 70+% failure rate. Leaders cannot forget about the people.

How Organizational Changes Have Treated People

In this chapter we have documented the ways in which traditional organizational change approaches have treated the people factor. The bottom line is that the needs and interests of the workforce have been subordinated to the bottom line, short-term needs of the organization. In effect, as Davenport said about reengineering in his article "The Fad That Forgot People": "The rock that reengineering has foundered on is simple: people. Reengineering treated the people inside companies as if they were just so many bits and bytes, interchangeable parts."[77] Whether the change is structure first, process based, or digitally driven, leadership uses their power to control the change process, believing the "workers don't need to know." Fear is unleashed in the culture as people are terminated. There is a view that leaders do not need to give the workforce ownership of the change since they own the company and have the right to do with the workforce what they want. In some instances, leadership may encourage engagement, but it is a means to an end. Even the most enlightened leaders seem to defer to the Power Paradigm. I once heard a senior executive say in an executive team meeting of a global human resources company, "The workforce is just headcount; we need to move this process forward regardless of how they feel about it. It's *our* bottom line that is at risk."

As one of the final lines in the movie *Soylent Green* puts it, "It's the people."[78] Without them, change processes fail.

SIDE BOX 8.1: (CONTINUED)

3. **When in Doubt, Restructure:** Business leaders tend to have a structure-first mind-set, which, when combined with a short-term business mentality, leads to structural change as their default approach to organizational change. It is power based, ignores the organization's culture, does not involve workforce ownership, and results in fear, resistance, and a loss of trust.

4. **"Been There, Done That":** Cynicism, skepticism, and the not-invented-here syndrome play a major role in the failure of change initiatives. We have become jaded by all the promises leaders make, leading to a significant loss of their credibility. "We've tried all the programs. We have had it done to us or for us by outsiders, and none of it worked. There is no reason to believe that this next program will be any different."

5. **No Ownership:** People take care of what they own. If the workforce does not own the change, they will resist it. It's more than mere engagement. Own-

SIDE BOX 8.1: (CONTINUED)

ership is about opening up the process to the very people who will be affected by it, and must implement it if it is to be successful.

6. **Not Managing Expectations Effectively:** Change is often about hope, or even survival. Change can be about people, teams and organizations realizing their dreams. It is about people's expectations that things will get better after the change. Since an "upset" is an unfulfilled expectation, most change efforts do not meet them, leading to a loss of credibility for leadership, reduced change momentum, and probable failure.

7. **Impatience:** Because change initiatives are about control, quick fixes, and point solutions rather than fundamental behavioral or cultural changes, business leaders often get very impatient if there are not demonstrable results within 60 to 90 days. The notion that these types of changes take years in large companies, or that it is a journey not a destination, runs contrary to the leaders' expectations. This, in turn, leads to impatience, a shifting of priorities, and change failure.

8. **Bright Shiny Objects:** Business leaders tend to be fickle. They may like the idea of

The Human Impacts of Organizational Change

There is substantial research being done in other countries and regions on the human impacts of change, including South Africa, Tanzania, France, Pakistan, and the European Union. It is curious that very little research has been done in the United States, with one exception, the American Psychological Association. Its 2017 *Work and Well-Being Survey* looked specifically at the human impacts on people working in organizations going through organizational change and found that 50% of American workers were affected by them in these ways:[79]

- **Workforce Well-Being**

  - 71% reported lower levels of job satisfaction
  - 55% were more likely to report chronic work stress
  - 39% experienced work-family life conflicts

- **Workforce Issues With Management and Others**

  - 52% reported a lack of participation in decision-making
  - 49% had problems with their supervisors and 46% with their co-workers
  - 35% felt cynical and negative toward others during the workday
  - 34% didn't trust their employer
  - 34% felt there was more to the changes than management was admitting

- **Workforce Decisions**
  - 46% intend to seek employment elsewhere within the next year

The study went on to say that these negative human consequences of organizational change are system-wide in three areas: 1) Individual health and well-being like increased work stress and anxiety, illness, and absenteeism as stress affects the body; 2) Psychological impacts on individuals, like loss of a sense of identity, self-confidence and fear of job loss; and 3) Psychological impacts on the organization, like a culture of fear across the organization, distrust, dysfunctional behavior, tension, internal conflict, and increased gender and generational differences.

It is clear the human and organizational costs of the Power Paradigm's approach to organizational change are almost incalculable. It is unclear why leaders continue to promote the same old approaches. As the saying goes, "Insanity is continuing to do the same thing over and over, but expecting different results." There has to be a better way, and fortunately there is: The Collaborative Method, the 4th Evolution of organizational change, which is culture-driven.

CHAPTER CONCLUSION: HONOR THE HUMAN SIDE OF ORGANIZATIONAL CHANGE

A tsunami of change will continue to impact organizations—the velocity of technological change, the fundamental transformation of industry through artificial intelligence and robots, the increased volatility, uncertainty, complexity and ambiguity in markets, dramatic demographic changes, globalization, and existential threats like climate change and pandemics.

The central question we have been exploring is not about whether organizations need to change, but how traditional, power-based organizational change has been implemented, and its impact on the human beings who work there. We know that since the 1970s, more than 70+ percent of change processes have failed, due largely to two critical reasons: (1) The failure to give the workforce ownership of the change process and (2) The failure of leadership to sustain their commitment over time. Our central proposition, then, has been to focus on the human side of organizational change because it is an intensely human endeavor. It is not just about structure or process, value generation, efficiency, or headcount reduction. Organizational change is about the hopes and aspirations of the workforce, their professional careers, families, and communities.

SIDE BOX 8.1: (CONTINUED)

organizational change, but because they are impatient and have a short attention span, they get attracted to the next "bright shiny object," the next program, product, guru, or initiative that can keep their interest in growing the company.

9. **Default to the Negative:** One of the more interesting phenomena causing change failure is the apparent tendency we have to assume the worst about others, to believe that no matter what positive forces are at work, sooner or later it will go bad. In many instances, the cynicism is very justified. People have been disappointed so many times, they expect the change effort to be dropped or modified. Even when leadership speaks its commitment, distrust is high.

10. **We Don't Know How:** Business leaders either don't know about or don't know how to implement systemic or culture-driven change. Consequently, they default to change methods that are tangible—structure, process or digital.

In our journey in this chapter, we learned how five influential thinkers helped shape organization development, change management, and the cornerstones of what we will explore next, the *Collaborative Method*; namely the importance of the following:

- Culture as a driver of organizational behavior during a change process
- The people in any change process—forget them and it will fail
- Ownership as the core principle governing change success
- Understanding the psychology, human dynamics, and impacts of change processes
- Systems thinking in implementing any change

We explored the three traditional approaches most organizations have used to implement their change initiatives: (1) Structure-First, (2) Process-Based, and (3) Digitally-Driven. Our major finding on this journey through theory and practice has been that leaders either ignored the people and culture aspects of organizational change, or only gave them lip service, resulting in severe human impacts and a very high rate of change failure!

Let me conclude with a story about an alternative approach to change, the 4th Evolution—Collaboration. In the Gulf Coast of Texas, DuPont had a number of petro-chemical plants that made the raw material for plastics. At corporate headquarters in Wilmington, Delaware, senior executives were deciding the fate of the plants because of increasing competitive pressures from Dow Chemical. The word came down to the Information Systems Gulf Coast award-winning collaborative organization that they needed to reduce their workforce by one-third, and do so quickly. In the Power Paradigm, senior leadership would have drawn up a list of the people who were going to be terminated. In this collaborative organization, however, the largest team decided to do it themselves. They went away on a three-day retreat without any external advisors. They returned with the full one-third reduction in force. This was counterintuitive. How could they eliminate their own jobs? According to several team members, it wasn't easy. There were a lot of tears and angst, but they had a process that empowered members to make conscious choices about their next steps. Some chose to retire. Others decided it was time to try something else professionally. Still others decided to look for jobs elsewhere in the company. When asked why they made these decisions they said, "Because it's the right thing to do for the company." This team defied the senior leadership's view that the workers could not make tough decisions. They did. Even more stunning is that their rationale for this self-sacrifice was to do the right thing for the very company eliminating their jobs. I decided to try the same process at other companies and found the same commitment to do the right thing. The bottom line is that if you trust the people to own the change, even a reduction in force, they will do what is right for the company, not themselves.

In effect, in traditional organizational change initiatives since the 1970s, the workforce has been on the receiving end of the change, not the directing end. They are the

The Workers' Bill of Rights in Organizational Change

Because:

- Traditional organizational change processes have consistently demonstrated a disregard for the people who are directly affected by those change initiatives by not giving them direct ownership of the change initiatives,

- The workers are directly affected by the results of organizational change initiatives,

- The workers in any organization have a right to be respected and honored,

- The workers in any organization have a right to psychological safety, and

- They are responsible for ensuring that products and services are produced and

Therefore every worker affected by organizational change has these rights:

- To own the change process

- To be treated with respect

- To psychological safety throughout the change process

- To have a seat at the table where all change decisions are made

- To have a direct say in the goals of the change process

- To be fully engaged and involved in the implementation process

FIGURE 8.4   The Workers' Bill of Rights in Organizational Change.

objects, not subjects of the change process. People, however, are not headcount, objects, or bits and bytes in a machine. They are living, breathing human beings with dreams, goals, hopes, expectations, families, and community responsibilities. In organizational change initiatives their lives are upended by the chaos that follows terminations, restructurings, or process-based changes. The anomaly is that traditional leadership's profound disdain for their people's humanity actually results in the failure of their top-down change initiatives. Observing this failure to consider the workforce as full and coequal partners over several decades, in fact, is what fueled the development of a 21st Century approach to change, the Collaborative Method. In closing, to transform how we think about the role of the workforce in organizational change, I offer the workers bill of rights in organizational change (Figure 8.4).

CHAPTER REVIEW AND REFLECTIONS

Learning Objectives:

Let's reflect on the learning objectives for the chapter and summarize what we have learned:

- Understand that organizational change is an intensely human endeavor that involves the hopes, dreams, and aspirations of the workforce, that they are on the front lines of implementing the change, and that because they will be directly affected by the change, they have the right to own the change process.
- Understand the context for organizational change, its velocity, and its impact on organizations.

- Learn how key influential thinkers helped shape the field of organizational change and contributed to the development of the Collaborative Method.
- Discover the traditional approaches to organizational change—structure first, process based, and digitally driven—and why most initiatives fail.
- Understand the human impacts of these traditional approaches to organizational change.

Initial Questions Revisited, and for Reflection:

- *How do you now see organizational change as an intensely human endeavor and why?*
- *Now that you know the reasons why organizations have to change, as a leader, how should you respond so that the changes succeed?*
- *Given the five key thinkers who shaped how we have done change since the 1970s, what do you see as the rationale for the next evolution of organizational change, the 4th Evolution?*
- *Given the three traditional approaches to organizational change used in the past and even today, what do you see as the most critical elements that contributed to their high rate of failure for each type?*
- *What have been the human impacts of these change methods on the workforce? How would you, as an organizational leader, reduce the negative impacts so that the workers may feel psychologically safe, be their best selves, and do their best work?*

ADDITIONAL READINGS

- Bridges, William. *Managing Transitions: Making the Most of Change.* 4th ed. Philadelphia, PA: Perseus Books, 2016.
- Collins, Jim. *Good to Great.* New York: HarperBusiness, 2001.
- Edwards, Deming, W. *Out of the Crisis.* Cambridge, MA: MIT Press, 2018.
- Gallos, Joan V. ed. *Organization Development: A Jossey-Bass Reader.* San Francisco: Jossey-Bass, 2006.
- Leonhard, Gerd. *Technology vs. Humanity: The Coming Clash Between Man and Machine.* Zurich: Futures Agency, 2016.

ENDNOTES

1 Harry Robinson "Why Do Most Transformations Fail?," McKinsey & Company, July 2019; https://www.mckinsey.com/business-functions/transformation/our-insights/why-do-most-transformations-fail-a-conversation-with-harry-robinson

2   The Collaborative Method is a registered service mark of The Marshall Group, LLC, the result of 40 years of the development of a theory of collaboration and its application in consulting engagements in over 100 projects on five continents.

3   https://www.goodreads.com/quotes/898109-nothing-endures-but-change

4   Gerd Leonhard, *Technology vs. Humanity: The Coming Clash Between Man and Machine* (Zurich: Futures Agency, 2016), pp. iii–iv, 32–46.

5   Ibid., pp. 32–46.

6   Ibid., p. 32, 46.

7   http://theemergingfuture.com

8   Ibid.

9   Alec Ross, *The Industries of the Future* (New York: Simon & Schuster, 2016), pp. 12–14.

10   Deloitte, "Industry 4.0: Challenges and Solutions for the Digital Transformation and Use of Exponential Technologies," October 10, 2018, p. 3; https://www2.deloitte.com/content/dam/Deloitte/ch/Documents/manufacturing/ch-en-manufacturing-industry-4-0-24102014.pdf

11   Ibid., p. 1.

12   https://www.vuca-world.org/

13   Strategic Agility Institute, "The VUCA ReportTM," March 2016, p. 5, https://static1.squarespace.com/static/5579c941e4b00a23147233ce/t/56eff7f420c6474a7c-d617ab/1458567164889/The_VUCA_Report_1.1_March_2016.pdf

14   Ibid., p. 6.

15   Ezra Greenberg, Martin Hirt, and Sven Smit, "The Global Forces Inspiring a New Narrative of Progress," *McKinsey Quarterly: Trends and Global Forces*, April 2017, pp. 2–3.

16   Intergovernmental Panel on Climate Change, "Global Warming of 1.5°C, Summary for Policy Makers," United Nations, Zurich, January, 2019, pp. 6–7.

17   Aria Bendix, "Indonesia Is Spending $33 Billion to Move Its Capital," *Business Insider*, August 27, 2019.

18   William J. Ripple, Christopher Wolf, Thomas M. Newsome, Phoebe Barnard and William R. Moomaw, "World Scientists' Warning of a Climate Emergency," *Bioscience*, Vol. 70, No. 1, pp. 8-12.

19   Richard Fry, "Millennials Are the Largest Generation in the U.S. Labor Force," Pew Research Center, April 11, 2018; https://www.pewresearch.org/fact-tank/2018/04/11/millennials-largest-generation-us-labor-force/

20   Alastair Mitchell, "The Rise of the Millennial Workforce," *Wired*, August, 2013, https://www.wired.com/insights/2013/08/the-rise-of-the-millennial-workforce/

21   Ibid.

22   Deloitte Consulting, "The Deloitte Global Millennial Survey 2019." London.

23   Christie Smith and Stephanie Turner, "They Are Here! Meet the Current (and Rapidly Rising) Leaders of Our Workforce," Deloitte University, 2017, p. 1.

24   Edgar H. Schein, "Kurt Lewin's Change Theory in the Field and in the Classroom: Notes toward a Model of Managed Learning," *Reflections*, 1968, Vol. 1, No. 1, p. 60.

25 Bernard Burnes, "Kurt Lewin and the Planned Approach to Change: A Reappraisal," in *Organization Development,* ed. Joan V. Gallos (San Francisco: Wiley, 2006), pp. 133–137.

26 G. W. Allport, foreword to *Resolving Social Conflict,* ed. G. W. Lewin (London: Harper & Row, 1948), p. vii.

27 Burnes, op. cit., p. 137–38; Lewin used the male gender rather than gender-neutral terms that would be used today.

28 Ibid., p. 139.

29 Ibid., pp. 142–43.

30 Schein, op. cit., p. 60.

31 Ibid., p. 61.

32 Ibid.

33 David L. Cooperrider and Leslie E. Sekerka, "Toward a Theory of Positive Organizational Change," in *Organization Development,* ed. Joan V. Gallos (San Francisco: Wiley, 2006), pp. 223–238.

34 Ibid., pp. 224–227.

35 Ibid.

36 This section is based on Jim Collins, *Good to Great* (New York: HarperBusiness, 2001), pp. 3, 12–16, 142.

37 Ibid., pp. 12–16.

38 Ibid., p. 12.

39 John P. Kotter, *Leading Change* (Boston: Harvard Business Review Press, 2012), p. 22–27.

40 Ibid., pp. 156–159.

41 Op. cit., p. 164–166.

42 David A. Nadler, "The Congruence Model of Change," in *Organization Development,* ed. Joan V. Gallos, (San Francisco: Wiley, 2006), p. 259.

43 Ibid., pp. 253–262.

44 The failure rate of change processes has been consistently over 70 percent since the 1970s; two sources cited are: McKinsey & Company, "Why Do Most Change Processes Fail? A Conversation with Harry Robinson," July 2019, p. 1; https://www.mckinsey.com/business-functions/transformation/our-insights/why-do-most-transformations-fail-a-conversation-with-harry-robinson; N. Anand and Jean-Louis Barsoux, "What Everyone Gets Wrong about Change Management," *Harvard Business Review,* November–December 2017, p. 4.

45 Edgar H. Schein, "Foreword: Observations on the State of Organization Development," in *Organization Development,* ed. Joan V. Gallos (San Francisco: Wiley, 2006), p. xv.

46 American Psychological Association, "Industrial and Organizational Psychology, https://www.apa.org/ed/graduate/specialize/industrial

47 Schein, op. cit.

48 Edgar H. Schein, *Process Consultation: Its Role in Organization Development* (Boston, MA: Addison-Wesley, 1969).

49 Richard Beckhard, "What Is Organization Development?" in *Organization Development,* ed. Joan V. Gallos (San Francisco: Wiley, 2006), p. 3.

50 Ibid., p. 8.

51 W. Edwards Deming, *Out of the Crisis* (1982, Cambridge, MA: MIT Press, 2018), p. xiv.

52 Mary Walton, *The Deming Management Method* (New York: Berkley, 1986), p. 33.

53 These 14 principles are based on Deming, op. cit., pp. 17–82.

54 Walton, op. cit., p. 35.

55 Ibid.

56 Michael Hammer and James Champy, *Reengineering the Corporation: A Manifesto for Business Revolution* (New York: HarperCollins, 1993).

57 Ibid., p. vii.

58 Michael Hammer, "Reengineering Work: Don't Automate, Obliterate," *Harvard Business Review,* July–August, 1990, p. 1.

59 Ibid.

60 Ibid., p. 4.

61 US General Accounting Office, Accounting and Information Management Division, *Business Process Reengineering Assessment Guide,* GAO/AIMD-10.1.15, ver. 3 (Washington, DC: US General Accounting Office, Accounting and Information Management Division, 1997), p. 32.

62 Hammer, op. cit., pp. 5–8.

63 Ibid., p. 8.

64 Thomas H. Davenport, "The Fad That Forgot People," *Fast Company,* October 31, 1995; https://www.fastcompany.com/26310/fad-forgot-people

65 Ibid.

66 James Womack, Daniel T. Jones, and Daniel Roos, *The Machine That Changed the World* (New York: Free Press, 1990).

67 Ibid., pp. 11–12.

68 Ibid., p. 12.

69 This section is based on the work of theleanway.net/

70 Womack et al., *The Machine That Changed the World,* p. 12.

71 Gerd Leonhard, *Technology vs. Humanity: The Coming Clash between Man and Machine* (Zurich: Futures Agency, 2016), pp. iii–iv, 32–46.

72 Hortense de la Boutetière, Alberto Montagner, and Angelika Reich, "Unlocking Success in Digital Transformations," McKinsey & Company, 2018, p. 2; https://www.mckinsey.com/~/media/McKinsey/Business%20Functions/Organization/Our%20Insights/Unlocking%20success%20in%20digital%20transformations/Unlocking-success-in-digital-transformations.ashx

73 Ibid., p. 4.

74 Ibid., p. 8.

75 Ibid., p. 12.

76 William Bridges, *Managing Transitions: Making the Most of Change,* 4th ed. (Philadelphia, PA: Perseus Books, 2016).

77 Thomas H. Davenport, "The Fad That Forgot People" October 31, 1995, https://www.fastcompany.com/26310/fad-forgot-people

78 *Soylent Green,* https://www.youtube.com/watch?v=HpxS8oJ5S2M, Richard Fleischer, Director, May 9, 1973, MGM Studios, Beverly Hills, CA.

79 Center for Organizational Excellence, *2017 Work and Well-Being Survey* (Washington, DC: American Psychological Association, 2017), pp. 5–9, 38–44.

Figure Credits

Fig. 8.1: Source: http://theemergingfuture.com.
Fig. 8.2: Source: https://www.proinspire.org/book-review-good-to-great-by-jim-collins-2/.

CHAPTER NINE

The 4th Evolution of Organizational Change: The Collaborative Method

If you do not change direction, you may end up where you are heading.

—Lao Tzu, 6th Century BCE[1]

*L*INDA SHOWED UP *at the team's weekly meeting having done her homework on the human side of organizational change. She had done her reflections and was ready to move ahead but was frustrated that since the 1970s, the people who do all the work, make the products, deliver the services, ensure that quality is high, and engage with the customers have been on the receiving end of devastating change initiatives. "How can leadership do this? No wonder the change failure rate is over 70%." Priyanka was quite empathetic: "You're right. I know that business is not a democracy, but this is about workers' rights and the reality leadership must face that if they want change initiatives to succeed, they need to engage their workers. Force doesn't work and compliance doesn't motivate; they only create resistance and resignation." Morare was nodding his head and noted that Millennials will not stay in organizations that treat human beings like bits and bytes: "We need collaboration to animate any change process." Everyone acknowledged that given VUCA, technological acceleration, and climate change, it's no longer "business as usual." They were all eager to learn about the Collaborative Method. It gave them hope. They believed it was how change initiatives need to be done in the future. So, they opened up their books to find the following questions:*

- *What is the Collaborative Method? What makes it the 4th Evolution of organizational change?*
- *Who implements collaborative change, what do they do, and how do they do it?*
- *How is the Collaborative Method implemented? What are the major phases?*

- *What kinds of dynamics can change leaders expect, and how does the Collaborative Method address them?*

LEARNING OBJECTIVES

By the end of this chapter, you will:

- Understand what the 4th Evolution of organizational change, the Collaborative Method, is and what makes it significantly different from traditional approaches to implementing change
- Learn about the leadership infrastructure needed for collaborative change, who is involved, what they do, and guidelines for implementing it
- Learn about the phases involved in implementing the Collaborative Method
- Understand the human dynamics of collaborative change that leaders may encounter and how they are addressed

THE MAIN POINT OF THIS CHAPTER

The *Collaborative Method* is the 4th Evolution of organizational change, which is fundamentally about preserving the humanity of the change process by giving the workforce ownership of it. The role of leadership is to engage, facilitate, and support the workforce, not the other way around as we saw with traditional approaches to change. Collaborative organizational change is about the people, because it is through people that true, lasting, and successful change happens.

You may recall Ralph Stayer, CEO of Johnsonville Sausage, who built his family-owned company into a highly competitive, high-quality, global sausage brand. Stayer reflected, in his classic *Harvard Business Review* article, "How I Learned to Let My Workers Lead": "What worried me more than the competition ... was the gap between potential and performance. Our people didn't seem to care ... it was just that people took no responsibility for their work."[2] While collaboration was not yet seen as a way to lead in 1980, Stayer started his collaborative organizational change journey with research, where he learned that to transform his company, he would first have to transform himself, which he did.

Because of Stayer's high degree of self-awareness and empathy for his workers, he decided to transform the leadership culture of Johnsonville Sausage. He stopped expecting his people to be incapable. He gave them ownership of their jobs, the company's vision and mission, the making of sausage, and satisfying their customers. He flattened the pyramidal structure. He got rid of the human resources department and created coaching for all workers. He trusted his workforce, gave them responsibility, gave them a financial stake in the company, and let them hold each other accountable. Now any worker on the sausage line can "pull the chain" and stop it if they believe the quality of the sausage is not up to standard. They own this company at every level. In fact, Stayer mused, "For the last five years, my ambition has been to eliminate my job."3

Johnsonville Sausage's 10 year journey to a collaborative leadership culture is one of the earliest examples of successful collaborative change where he did what other leaders did not—he gave the workers ownership of the change and was consistent and persistent in his leadership commitment to that value.

My work in creating *the Collaborative Method* began in 1969 when I was working with the Ford Foundation in India. As I worked with the amazing people of this country, hundreds of millions of whom suffered from degrading poverty, I came to appreciate why they held their heads high in spite of it. It was their culture—thousands of years of history, their pride in having defeated the British colonialists, their deep religious faith, and their profound will to live. It was not about power or control, structure or process. It was about who they were, and are, as a people. They deeply inspired me to explore my own beliefs and values, and to understand the power of culture as a driver for human behavior. Over the next 20 years, I was able to formulate the cornerstones of what is now known as the Collaborative Method, the central focus of this chapter. Little did I know, at the time, that Ralph Stayer was already implementing it.

Fast-forward to the early 21st Century, where rapid and constant organizational change is a fact of life, and just as Linda has shared her frustration, I too have been frustrated, even horrified, by the impacts of structure-first, process-based, and digitally driven change initiatives on human beings. Yes, I understand the business rationale that organizations must survive. That is not the focus of my angst. It is *how* those change initiatives have been implemented, based on Power Paradigm assumptions that the people most affected by them are too incapable, ignorant, or don't have a right to be a direct part of the decision-making and implementation process. I have personally witnessed the arrogance of power-based leaders who treated people like interchangeable parts, bits and bytes, headcount not worthy of being directly involved. I have also seen how collaborative change processes, based on principle not power, and grounded in a deep respect for the culture of an engaged workforce, can fundamentally transform an organization's leadership culture, performance, and their own lives.

Ownership is the central principle governing the transformative power of the Collaborative Method: that people take care of what they own, have a right to own the change; and if they do own it, there will be success. In my consulting practice, the success rate was 80%. It took me years to understand why it was so high and why other leaders and consulting firms, including the largest ones in the world, continued to promote change approaches that didn't work. What I learned is that giving the workforce ownership over a change process has been anathema to those in power. Ralph Stayer had to confront this: "It's not always easy giving up control, even when it's what you've worked toward for ten years."4 At the end of the day, leaders cannot control change or force people to do what they want. Compliance is outdated and highly overrated as a way to motivate people. Their only hope is to give up control and empower the workforce so that those most directly affected by the change own it.

In this chapter we will first define what the Collaborative Method is and what governs its approach to organizational change, what collaborative change leadership looks like, the steps of the implementation process, the infrastructure needed to support it, and some of the dynamics that collaborative leaders may face in implementing culture-first change.

THE FOUNDATIONS OF THE COLLABORATIVE METHOD

It became increasingly clear to me that culture is not just about the soft stuff of communications, rewards, and morale. It is deeply connected to the fundamental issues of organizational goals and means ... the cultural DNA in that organization.

—Edgar Schein, 2006

Marriott International was facing a number of market challenges in its Lodging organization, and their leadership decided to launch a major transformation effort across the group. Eight change initiatives were created and launched simultaneously. I was asked to facilitate the information technology transformation initiative, which was later named Team Alpha by its members. There were three executive sponsors, suggesting the substantial impact this effort would have on the organization. The objective was to transform the back-room operations of Marriott's full service hotels from the "green eyeshade" manual billing process, where you received a paper bill under the door in the morning, to an automated system which eliminated the need for that process, and the people who did that work. In fact, fully 75% of the 1,800 people doing this work were slated to lose their jobs.

Team Alpha was responsible for designing and implementing this transformation process. Its members came from all levels of the organization and represented all regions of the country. The first step in their culture-first journey was to be formed as a collaborative team. They developed their operating agreements, built their charter, created a change strategy that would result in a transformed system while ameliorating the impact on the people who would lose their jobs. They chose a collaborative, direct engagement process that was fully transparent. Team members were trained to facilitate direct engagement work sessions, fanned out across the country, and held work sessions with all 1,800 people in two rounds. The first round was to define the current state of back-room financial operations. After processing what they learned and using the data to design the new system, there was a second round of direct engagement to get feedback on a proposed redesigned system. Fully 96% of the 1,800 people participated in the direct engagement events.

To ensure they were effectively listening to the workforce, the team created a feedback loop, which gave them weekly status reports on their effectiveness—a consistent 85% approval rating over a nine-month period. What was particularly rewarding was what some of the workers who were losing their jobs said about their participation. One worker's comments were illustrative: "No one ever asked me before about my work or where the problems were in the system. These have been driving me crazy for years, and I am very supportive of fixing them." Direct engagement honored every single worker, knowing that they had the most direct knowledge of where the issues were. What was counterintuitive, as with the DuPont example discussed previously, was that the people losing their jobs wanted to participate in creating the solution. This reinforced my belief that the workforce wants to do the right thing by the company. They just wanted to be asked, to be included, to own the change initiative.

Marriott took care of the nearly 1,400 workers who lost their jobs by transferring them to other parts of the company, retraining them, helping them find other jobs, or providing them excellent departure packages. Team Alpha finished its engagement a full two months ahead of the other change initiatives, and when they made their presentation to the executive team, it took about 30 seconds for them to give their unanimous approval for a significant investment in the new system.

Marriott's transformation, like Johnsonville Sausage's, reminds us that *organizational change is an intensely human endeavor, and to be successful, change processes must be culture-driven, people-centric, and owned by the workforce.* We have seen that traditional approaches to organizational change—structure first, process based, and digitally driven— have typically excluded the workforce from direct engagement in the decision-making and implementation processes. Instead, there has been resistance, fear, reduced morale, and a substantial loss of productive energy, all impacting the company's bottom line. We know that over 70% of these change processes failed, and yet senior leaders tried to defy the gravity of insanity by continuing to do the same thing over and over again.

There is another way—a way that is principled; honors the human spirit; is ethical, moral, and transparent; and engages the hearts, minds, and productive energy of the workforce so that the needed change can be achieved. The Collaboration Paradigm's approach to organizational is the Collaborative Method, the 4th Evolution of organizational change methodologies.

Defining the *Collaborative Method*

The 4th Evolution's definition of *collaboration* is:

> *Collaboration is a leadership culture paradigm, a comprehensive systems perspective on the culture, leadership, processes, and organization design of any organization. It is grounded in an explicit set of core beliefs and assumptions about people in organizations, and in the seven principles of collaboration that shape the culture. This paradigm informs every aspect of how an organization works.*

Let's apply this definition to the practice of designing and implementing a collaborative organizational change process. The *Collaborative Method* is defined as follows:

> *The Collaborative Method is a culture-first, principle-based, ownership-driven, and systems-oriented organizational change methodology which creates a psychologically safe environment where the workforce builds trust-based relationships, owns the design and implementation of change initiatives, and produces superior results.*

This method enables businesses and nonprofits to be responsive and adaptive to the rapid rate of VUCA, technological, global, demographic, and market changes coming at them daily. The speed of change becomes a critical variable in terms of their survival. Most importantly, they need the workforce engaged rather than resisting, and a process that leverages the productive energy of the workforce.

Guidelines for Implementing the Collaborative Method

Anyone considering an organizational change—whether it is a reorganization, business process redesign, digital transformation, or other significant change—can use the Collaborative Method. It ensures that *how* the change is implemented is collaborative, ensures that there is little/no resistance, and increases the prospects the change process will be successful. Here are some guidelines to help leaders and practitioners of collaborative change.

1. **A Compelling Need to Change:** There is a clear and compelling reason for change initiative. There may be a burning platform like a crisis in the market, a competitive disruptor, the loss of a major customer, merger/acquisition, or any number of reasons to initiate it. The need for the change must be clear and compelling to the workforce as well as leadership and middle management. The pain of not changing must be greater than the pain of changing. People are not going to be willing to invest in the change process, or to change their behavior unless it is absolutely clear to them *why* the change is necessary.

2. **Committed Leadership:** Senior leadership must be firmly committed not only to implementing the change, but to giving the workforce ownership of the process—that is, seats at the table where decisions are made about the initiative, and a direct role in its implementation. Leadership commits to staying the course. They review the progress of the initiative, learn lessons from their experience, and make adjustments to ensure its success. They honor the principles of collaboration, model collaborative behavior, and maintain their commitment in the face of adversity. During implementation, leadership is proactive, recognizes that change increases anxiety, and focuses on preventions as well as interventions to ensure success. At the end of the day, leadership is fully responsible and accountable for the change process and its outcomes.

3. **Culture-First and Front-Loaded:** This method puts the culture of building trust-based relationships first in the change process, rather than last. The people are not a means to an end, a bit or byte, or simply part of a transaction. This method recognizes that people are the heart of any change, need to be honored and respected, and that this will happen by building high-trust relationships as a first step in the change process. By taking this approach, the organization will tap into the productive energy of the workforce, mobilizing them to give their highest level of effort, and avoids people's natural resistance to change.

4. **Workforce Ownership:** Organizations don't cause change—people do. Ownership of the change process is essential for its success. Those people who are affected by an organizational change have a right to participate in and own it. By having a seat at the decision-making table, and being directly involved in managing the implementation process, psychological safety and trust are increased, while resistance is decreased.

5. **A Journey, Not a Destination:** Collaborative organizational change is a journey, not a destination. For Ralph Stayer, it was a ten-year process. Xerox's transformation occurred over a ten-year period.[5] Leaders and implementers of any significant organizational change understand that organizational systems and human behavior take time to change. Change is about evolution rather than revolution. Organizational change involves some level of struggle as people learn how to work together collaboratively and to transform their organization. This is to be expected. Anything worth having takes time, hard work, and the ability to persist.

6. **System-Wide Change:** Organizations are living organisms. A change in one part of the corporate body will affect every other part of the organization, as represented in the graphic below. Similarly, collaborative change is system-wide and comprehensive—culture, leadership, processes, and organization design. As Figure 9.1 shows, the Collaborative Method uses a Venn diagram to represent the various elements of the work environment, all of which are addressed in this approach to change. A full description of each component of this systems model may be found in Chapter 3. You will see that something has been added—a broken arrow, which represents the Culture-First guideline and is implemented through the Collaborative Team Governance Process. High trust relationships are built first before doing the team's change task.

7. **Teams as the Unit of Change:** The most efficient unit of change is the team, whether it is a departmental, management, executive, or project. The team is sponsored by a member of leadership, gets their task and deliverable from leadership, and then begin their work with the Collaborative Team Governance Process. Collaborative change happens one team at a time, and because they

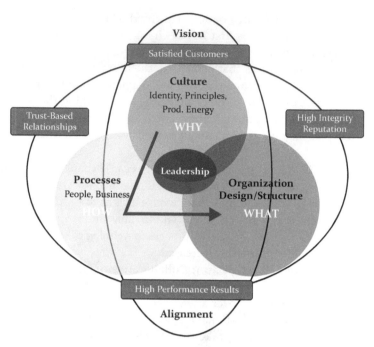

FIGURE 9.1 The Collaborative Method of Change.[6]

own the way they work together, and own the charter for their work. They become ambassadors for change, making collaborative cultural transformation possible through the implementation of many change projects. As organizations experience increasing levels of rapid change, the team becomes the unit for stability. Collaborative teams offer a safe harbor in the midst of the change storm. Trust and respect are the glue that holds them together.

8. **Real-Work-in-Real-Time and Results-Driven:** The common complaints I have heard from leadership about the front-loaded, culture-first approach to change are: (1) It's too process-oriented; (2) It takes too long; and (3) It will distract us from our core business. These are very real concerns, so I adapted the Collaborative Method to meet them by first, focusing on solving business issues in real time. Having a real-work task to do immediately on the other side of Collaborative Team Governance gives a team a level of comfort. Second, the length of the front-loaded process was obviated by the team realizing how much faster they could work as a result of governance. Third, the core business concern was addressed by creating two track system, one for the change process, and the other for the business: of the business.

9. **Ensure Transparency:** The entire change process is an open book and fully communicated with the workforce with periodic feedback. It is essential for the integrity and credibility of the change process that it be fully transparent to all members of the workforce. This means both successes and failures as well as lessons learned and changes to be made to address them.[7]

10. **Engage the Psychology of Change:** Leadership needs to be aware of and engage the psychology of the change process. As Figure 9.2 shows, any major organizational change has about 3 months to be able to tout some early visible successes. There should be "sure wins" with demonstrable results that teams can achieve and be broadcast widely. The objective is to generate momentum, and to convince the skeptical members of the workforce to get on board with the initiative. The best time to kill a collaborative change initiative is in the first 6 months. During that time, every single person in the organization needs to be touched either through a communication process, a survey, focus groups, all-hands meetings, or other direct connection. Within a year, everyone in the workforce needs to be involved in a team implementing some aspect of the change. There are ups and downs in the psychology of change. There are preventions that can reduce the down phases, and interventions that can be used once they happen. The overall goal is to achieve *critical mass*, the point of no return, which is about 25% of the workforce at a high level of commitment to the change.

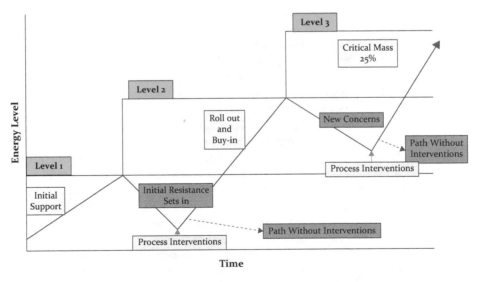

FIGURE 9.2 The Psychology of Change.

THE INFRASTRUCTURE FOR COLLABORATIVE CHANGE

*People acting together as a group can accomplish things which no
individual acting alone could ever hope to bring about.*

—President Franklin D. Roosevelt

Since rapid change is a constant reality for organizations in the 21st Century, they need to have the infrastructure in place to ensure that they are agile, adaptive and can respond, to disruptive forces. It is critical organizations have a collaborative change culture that ensures psychological safety, engagement, and ownership for the workforce. In the Collaborative Method, building this culture and infrastructure up-front will enable the organization to respond, adjust, and adapt. Without this infrastructure it may flounder. Based on several decades of designing and implementing change initiatives, there are eight functions that are essential to success.

1. **The Leadership Function:** There are two levels of leadership for collaborative change: The executive team level and the change leadership team.

   ○ **Executive Team:** This team has primary responsibility to ensure and protect the credibility, ethics, and integrity of the change process. It starts with the CEO, who sets the tone, establishes the urgency and rationale for the change, and is the Chief Cultural Officer for the entire process. The team members are champions and ambassadors for the change process, as well as sponsors of teams who will implement it. The team front-loads its own collaborative governance process and models the way for the workforce. They charter the Change Leadership Team and ensure there is alignment between that team and the overall strategy and vision of the organization. The Executive Team envisions the future for the organization and provides the resources necessary to get there.

   ○ **Change Leadership Team:** The Change Leadership Team is the backbone of a collaborative change process, an absolutely essential, small team whose primary responsibility is to keep their eye on the change ball. Typically, a change team has five to eight members, half of whom come from the workforce, who dedicate 100% of their time to this function. This role is *not* the responsibility of human resources; they focus on the personnel function. This team, at its core, focuses on the psychological safety, engagement, ownership, and integrity of the collaborative change process. In terms of its members, 50% are representatives of the workforce, while the other 50% are executives or line managers. They need to represent all levels of the organization, all departments or business units, and all geographic regions. People selected for this function should exhibit the attributes of collaborative leaders, including having ethics, the respect of the workforce, high emotional intelligence, self-awareness, and the ability to facilitate ownership of the change process by the workforce. Their responsibilities include protecting the integrity and credibility of the change process, developing the change strategy, ensuring the workforce owns the change, and implementing the communications strategy. They lead the implementation process, working with facilitators to ensure they are successful. They manage the psychology of the change process to build the momentum needed to reach critical mass. Finally, they help build the organization's internal collaborative change capability to sustain the culture long term.

2. **The Ownership Function:** Perhaps the most critical function of the Collaborative Method is ensuring the workforce owns the change, with a goal of 100%. In the Team Alpha example cited earlier, we achieved a 96% engagement and an 85% approval rating from 1,800 people, 75% of whom were going to lose their jobs. The Change Leadership Team, along with project team facilitators, ensure that the workforce understands the change initiative and its rationale, is aligned with its desired results, is engaged meaningfully and continuously in the change process, and has specific ownership over a part of the effort. Every team in the organization owns a part of implementing the change process in addition to the vision and strategy.

3. **The Facilitation Function:** The next most critical function is that of facilitation. There are three types of trained facilitators needed who become the backbone of the organization's change capability: (1) Collaborative team meeting

SIDE BOX 9.1: FULL OWNERSHIP

The former Captain of the USS *America*, one of the United States' super aircraft carriers based in Norfolk, Virginia, told me that every one of the 4,700 sailors on the ship owns a piece of it. They are given a specific location on the ship that is theirs to keep clean, painted, and clear of debris. They are periodically evaluated on their performance and are fully responsible and accountable for its condition. This is what full ownership looks like.

facilitators; (2) Collaborative team governance facilitators; and (3) Communications facilitators. All three types, with some overlaps, are on the front lines of collaborative change, working directly with the workforce on a daily basis. The change cannot be successfully implemented without this cadre of skilled, naturally facilitative individuals who spend 30 to 40% of their time working with teams. Their primary roles are to protect the integrity of the collaborative change process, ensure full ownership of the process, facilitate meetings, teams, communications, and be a good coach. In terms of attributes, facilitators are naturally that way—they are "people people" who are respected and naturally empathic; they are highly self-aware, reflective, humble, authentic, engaging, and self-accountable. They know how to help a team reach a true consensus decision, and how to have a difficult conversation with participants when warranted. They believe in creating a collaborative leadership culture and see themselves as agents for that change.

4. **The Communications Function:** Every collaborative change initiative has a communications strategy with its primary goal being transparency and inclusiveness. Communications are four-way, meaning that some come from senior leadership to the workforce, some come from the workforce to senior leadership, and there are cross-functional and cross-level communications as well. There is a free flow of information about the change process 24/7/365. Information is easy to access. Multiple media are used, and there is a feedback loop that enables the workforce to speak truth to power.

5. **The Implementation Function:** The implementation of the change strategy is led by the Change Leadership Team, and it engages the entire organization. Since teams are the unit of change, the change process is conducted by all kinds of teams. The Change Leadership Team monitors their progress to ensure they achieve the goals of the change initiative.

6. **Building Change Competence:** Rather than hire external consultants, the Change Leadership Team focuses on building the capabilities and skills of people inside the companies so that they can design, implement, and sustain the change process by themselves. The competencies required include facilitation, change process design and implementation, collaborative team development, change process preventions and interventions, interpersonal relations, and managing the psychology of change. There are five specific capabilities required for a collaborative change process: (1) Collaborative team meeting facilitators; (2) Collaborative Team Governance facilitators; (3) Communications facilitators; (4) Collaborative ChangeMasters; and (5) Collaborative coaches.

7. **The Recognition and Appreciation Function:** Most professionals do not know how to acknowledge, celebrate, or appreciate each other. They focus on

completing the task and then go on to the next one. Change initiatives require people to go the extra mile working long hours, be away from home and family, and still do their day job. In collaborative change initiatives, when the task is done there is a project-end celebration with recognition and appreciation. It's more than a party or a meal. It is people sharing from their hearts how they authentically feel about the process, their teammates, their own roles, and the differences they made in the organization. It is a joy to see how impactful their collaborative relationships are on them and to see how their work transforms more than the organization.

8. **The Evaluation Function:** One of my first clients asked me this question: "How will we know when we have gotten there? And where is 'there'?" Both are excellent questions. Most organizations have a measurement regimen with specific measures, surveys, after action reviews, and feedback loops. In a collaborative change initiative, in addition to the bottom-line measures, culture change is measured—is the culture more collaborative and more interdependent at the end of the change initiative than at the beginning? To be able to answer this question, and to address the "have we gotten there yet" questions, several colleagues of mine at DuPont and I spent two years developing what became known at the Collaborative Interdependence Index, which was administered at the beginning of a change process, and then every 12 months. We started out with over 300 variables tied to the seven principles of collaboration and narrowed the number of variables to 40 proxy measures, including questions on workforce productive energy. By comparing these two sets of numbers, we could determine, by business unit and department, where the organization's culture was in terms of the degree of collaboration and interdependence scale, and where interventions were needed.

THE 5 PHASES FOR IMPLEMENTING THE COLLABORATIVE METHOD

There are 5 phases in the implementation of the 4ᵗʰ Evolution of organizational change—the Collaborative Method. Collaborative organizational change is not a destination—it is a journey that involves continuous learning, growing, and evolving as a collaborative leadership culture. It is *how* the culture of an organization can shift from the power to the Collaboration Paradigm. Because the change process is collaborative, the end result will be collaborative. When the organization faces a change initiative like a new enterprise-wide technology, business process redesign, cultural

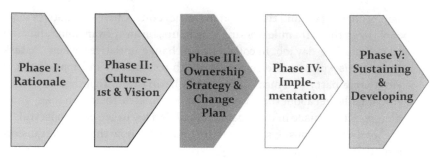

FIGURE 9.3 The 5 Phases of Collaborative Organizational Change.

transformation, merger or acquisition, or organization redesign, the executive team engages the change leadership team to design and implement the change process (see Figure 9.3).

Phase I: Rationale and Discovery

When a Fortune 500 high-tech company experienced the failure of a software update, the company knew it had a significant issue. Some of its biggest customers threatened to change operating systems and cancel their long-term contracts. Others threatened a lawsuit. Fully 40 million customers were impacted. In response to this crisis, the CIO launched a tiger team response, working 24 hours a day, until the fix was made. Meanwhile, the CEO hired an outside consulting firm to audit the incident and get to the root cause of the problem. They discovered that there was a breakdown between two silos in the IT organization, where engineers were not speaking with each other. The leadership of these silos was responsible for the competitive environment and conflict.

With the report in hand, the CIO decided to address this burning platform and begin a collaborative change process to break down the silo walls create a collaborative leadership culture. There are three steps in phase I:

- The rationale for the change initiative, or what is known as the "burning platform"
- Discovery and analysis of the problem
- Executive commitment to the change initiative

<u>**Step 1: Rationale for the Change Initiative:**</u> The high-tech company was facing a significant loss of business and even a potential lawsuit if they did not do something. That was their "burning platform." But what was the root cause of this issue? Discovery, in Step 2, is how it will be determined. There are all kinds of burning platforms organizations may face that are either internal or external threats to the business, to which they must react. For example, a new competitor enters the market with a disruptive technology, being acquired by, or merging with another organization, a

significant drop in profitability or stock value, a new CEO, or the loss of a major customer requiring the organization to restructure and lay people off.

These also be reasons to be proactive by launching a change initiative like the introduction of new enterprise software, anticipating a change in the market, or a cultural transformation to a collaborative leadership culture. No change process can be successful unless it is absolutely clear to everyone in the organization *why* the change is critical for organizational success and that there is a specific methodology for implementing it.

Step 2: The Discovery Process: In this step the root cause of the immediate crisis is discovered so that the change process actually addresses and resolves it. This involves data gathering of all types, from historical data to interviews and focus groups. The rule of five whys can be used to get to the root cause. In effect, you ask "why" five times to get beyond the description of the issue, denial, and defensiveness and get to the root cause(s) of the challenge. Only once you have gotten to the true root cause will you have the right solution.

A second part of this step is to document the *Current State* of the organization, using the collaboration systems model as a framework for collecting data from all dimensions of the organizational system: historical documents, strategic plans, financials, and qualitative data from interviews at every level of the organization. Market and competitor data may be helpful along with the degree of change readiness of the workforce. All the data get analyzed and assembled in a report that gets fed back to the executive team as part of leadership's commitment process.

Step 3: Gain Commitment to Act: One of the two main reasons change processes fail is because of a lack of sustained commitment on the part of senior leadership, who often get distracted by other priorities or lose interest. Because *every organizational change is a culture change*, it is critical when they make their commitment to the change process that they keep it as a top priority, remain engaged in its overall progress, and work with the Change Leadership Team to ensure the initiative is successful. A collaborative organizational change initiative is not a programmatic transaction that can be handed off to direct reports. It is a cultural transformation that impacts the lives of every single member of the workforce, and requires the direct engagement of senior leadership.

In addition, senior leadership needs to be committed to the collaborative change methodology. They are not bystanders who hope that the methodology will work. They must understand exactly what is involved, how it will be implemented, what the risks and rewards are, the potential barriers, and their roles and responsibilities. They help set the measures for success and work directly with the change leadership team.

The next level of commitment is at the Change Leadership Team level. These are seasoned and highly respected managers along with 50% of the team being respected members of the workforce from all levels and parts of the organization. Before they commit to the team, they also need to fully understand how the Collaborative Method works, the upsides and downsides of the change process, the psychology of change, the process of achieving critical mass, and what their roles and responsibilities are. Once they have committed to the process, senior leadership details them 100% of their time to design and implement this methodology, while working closely with senior leadership.

Phase II: Culture-First, Trust, and a Vision

At a major corporation, the Information Systems Leadership Team was invited to participate in Covey's *7 Habits of Highly Effective People* workshop. In the first week, there was an outdoor team exercise called "Stepping Stones". Seven teams of 10 members each had to walk across a "fiery gorge" without falling off nine stepping stones—one less than the number of team members. At one point, all 10 people had to be on the nine steps. If they "fell in," they would have to start all over. The winner was the first team that got all members safely across the gorge. Six teams did no planning—a just-do-it approach to leadership. They just started going across the gorge and did not do well. The 7th team spent about ten minutes doing up-front planning on how they were going to traverse the gorge. Then, they flawlessly executed their plan the first time. It is instructive that this was the only team with women members. It's all about relationship and front-loading the process.

NASA's space shuttle program was well known for its front-loaded planning of space missions. When they would send a shuttle to the International Space Station, they spent nine months planning and preparing for the launch. After liftoff from Cape Canaveral, Florida, it takes the shuttle about 12 minutes to reach deep space. That is a ratio of 99.97% planning to 0.03% doing. The point of these two stories is that when your life is on the line, or your organization's success is at stake, you take the time on the front end to build relationships, to leverage the culture of your organization, to plan and prepare. The motto of this approach is "just do it right."

The Collaborative Method's approach to organizational change is front loaded because the success of the change initiative depends on it. It is a culture-first approach to change, unlike Kotter's eight steps, which put culture last. This methodology has proven that leveraging the culture of the workforce to build high trust relationships first not only enables those teams to work faster and do higher quality work, but also transforms the culture of the organization, one team at a time.

There are three fundamental principles in the culture-first approach: (1) Build trust-based relationships first, using the Collaborative Team Governance Process; (2) Put relationships before task, as we saw with the 6 Conoco teams, when they went to task first; and (3) Make collaborative culture change a conscious choice and a conscious commitment to change how people work with each other on a sustained basis.

In Phase II, these principles are applied in 3 steps: (1) Create the Change Leadership Team, as already discussed; (2) Build collaborative change capability for facilitation of collaborative team meetings, governance, workforce engagement, communications, and coaching; and (3) Envision the future by having the Change Leadership Team work with the Executive Team to design a visioning process for the change initiative. This vision guides the change process.

Phase III: Ownership Strategy and the Change Plan

At Marriott, the Residence Inn story reflects the opposite result. To create the vision, every employee was invited to a weeklong event where they jointly created the vision statement. The level of excitement and energy was extremely high as they left the event. Not only did they own the vision, they owned the business. The ownership principle governing the development of the change plan is very simple: it's the people, and people take care of what they own. Recall the *Workers' Bill of Rights in Organizational Change* from Chapter 8. Workers have the right:

    I. To be treated with respect
   II. To psychological safety throughout the change process
  III. To have a seat at the table where all change decisions are made
  IV. To own the change process
   V. To have a direct say in the goals of the change process
  VI. To be fully engaged and involved every step of the implementation process
 VII. To full transparency from senior management

The Residence Inn example reflects the ownership principle at work, as did Stayer's approach at Johnsonville Sausage. There are three steps that will bring ownership to life:

    Step 1: Conduct a Current to Future State Analysis: Using the Collaboration Systems Model, and the discovery report results, to create the Current State analysis of the organization. Then use the vision to create the Future State, the goal of the initiative. Then complete a gap analysis to identify what needs to change. This provides the data needed to create the change process interventions to reach the future state (Figure 9.4).

    Step 2: Manage the Psychology of Change: Change initiatives are all about positive, human momentum and increasing workforce commitment to the change. Momentum is built by full engagement and giving ownership of the vision and implementation strategy to project teams.

    The goal is to get to 25% of the workforce at a high level of commitment to the change process within the first year, which is the "tipping point" where the change cannot be reversed. Pilot projects, in the first 90 days, generate early successes that are evidence the strategy is working. The number of project teams working on the change strategy is then expanded. People are trained as facilitators and coaches. With more success, the skeptics are convinced and the change process becomes self-sustaining.

    Step 3: The Change Plan: The change plan spells out how the goals and objectives will be achieved, and the specific steps that will be taken to get from the current to

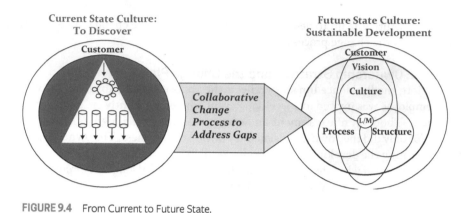

FIGURE 9.4 From Current to Future State.

the future state. It applies the real-work-in-real-time principle, clarifies how the work-force will own the process, ensures four-way communications and transparency, sets up a two-track system, one for the change process, and the second for the ongoing business. Evaluation metrics and a measurement process are established, along with a way to codify lessons learned. Finally, it spells out how the change capability will be trained and deployed so that the organization can sustain the new collaborative leadership culture.

Phase IV: Implementation and Building Value

As the change process moves through the first year of implementation, the focus needs to be on building value and producing results. Continuing to build momentum is essential, even though there will be both successes and some level of failure. The focus is always on learning, growing, and evolving. Here are eight guidelines for the implementation process:

1. **Build Value Continuously:** A collaborative change process requires continuous care and feeding by engaging others in projects and capability development.
2. **Emphasize Benefits and Results:** Value can be built, along with momentum, if people see the benefits and results of the process that impact them directly.
3. **Continue to Manage the Psychology of Change:** The management of the psychology of change is about managing momentum, instilling confidence in the workforce, demonstrating the benefits of the process, continuing to deepen their ownership of the change and their work, and honoring their achievements.
4. **Expand Facilitation Capability:** As the initial phase of the change process is completed, the Change Leadership Team needs to expand the number of

facilitators, communicators, and coaches. By creating a trained change cadre, the process can be accelerated.

5. **Expand Communications:** People need information to function effectively. Without it they will do what comes naturally—make it up based on the best information available. This dynamic is called the mystery house effect. The Change Leadership Team creates an ongoing dialogue with the workforce that is frequent, universal, and contains a feedback loop.

6. **Manage Disconnects:** There will be disconnects in the change process. The Change Leadership Team listens for them and is prepared to make the necessary interventions.

7. **Achieve Critical Mass:** As noted earlier, a key goal for any organizational change process is to achieve critical mass, the point where the change is self-sustaining and cannot be reversed by the skeptics and resisters.

8. **Celebrate Successes:** As change projects begin to demonstrate results, it is important to acknowledge their successes and give teams credit for the results they have produced. It is important to leverage these successes into other projects. The lessons learned, team dynamics that have worked, and the team leadership that has emerged can all brought to bear on the new projects.

Phase V: Sustaining and Developing an Evolving Collaborative Organization

A major Mid-Western company had completed its third year of the transformation process and had become a collaborative leadership culture. The Senior Leadership Team had come many miles from the original meeting with the CEO, who declared that to grow the company he needed the help of all of his team members. They had completed all of the phases of the collaborative change process and confronted significant business and financial challenges, in a constructive way. Their biggest business challenge came after the 9/11 terrorist attacks, which negatively affected their bottom line. They had transformed the performance management process based on feedback from the entire workforce, and had created a team-based organization that was growing in its ability to work together collaboratively. Now what?

They had taken to heart the idea that collaborative change is a journey, not a destination. So now it was time for them to put together their strategy for sustaining the change so that they could deepen and broaden their practice of collaborative behaviors, while expanding their business. They had developed a small cadre of facilitators for meetings, teams, and communications, but now it was time to expand that. There were organization development and structural challenges they needed to address, including going from a holding company structure of seven companies to a single integrated company. There were managers who needed to be replaced. A succession plan for the CEO needed to be put in place, and they needed to continue to expand the level of ownership of the ongoing change process.

When companies get to the "Now what do we do?" stage in their change initiative, they face a critical choice—whether to abandon the journey now that the main change objective has been reached, or to continue with the development and evolution of the organization. Most traditional change projects are transactional, and once the restructuring, process redesign, or digital change has been completed, they go back to the old way of working. This happens largely because they do not see organizational changes as cultural transformation processes.

The 4th Evolution of organizational change, the Collaborative Method, on the other hand, recognizes that the change is a journey, that the people must own it on a sustained basis if it's going to be successful, and that every organizational change is a culture change. It recognizes that organizations are living, breathing, dynamic, human organisms that are constantly changing in response to internal and external events. There are five guidelines for the organization to consider as they make this critical choice:

1. **<u>Nurture the Culture:</u>** Building and sustaining a collaborative leadership culture which empowers the workforce to be their best selves so they can do their best work is about continuing to build the trust and credibility of the process and in the work of the organization. Evaluate from time to time whether the organization is living up to the principles of collaboration. Be brutally honest about where the culture is, identify areas where it needs to be strengthened, and make the organization development and leadership interventions necessary. Introduce a coaching culture to support leaders and teams to maintain their commitment to collaborative principles. There is an accountability process to address situations that are intractable. The net result of this nurturing work is measured by the productive energy of the workforce. The goal is 80% of the workforce at 80% of their productive energy (Figure 9.5).

2. **<u>Reflect and Renew:</u>** Human beings, especially in the digital and sound-bite era, have very short memories. So, over 6 to 12 months, and certainly after a couple

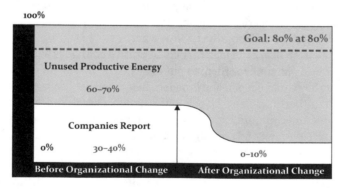

FIGURE 9.5   Increasing Productive Energy.

of years, leadership and the workforce will begin to take the change process for granted; it will simply have become the way they work. They are also likely to forget their team operating agreements. They may lose perspective or value for the power of their ownership role. So, a reflection and renewal process become a critical component of the change journey. This means each team reflects on their own performance, both in terms of how they work with each other, and how well they have executed their tasks. It means every team reviews and upgrades its operating agreements periodically. It means the annual culture survey of the workforce generates data to help the leadership make the appropriate interventions.

3. **Invest in the People:** Invest in the people in terms of capability development, collaborative skills, technical training, coaching, and support. Create a formal feedback process that enables them to grow and develop as professionals and humans, and support them with system-wide coaching. Develop a celebration and acknowledgements process that authentically recognizes the teams who have excelled. Build a professional development process that ensures a pathway of progress for each member of the workforce.

4. **Develop the Organization:** As the business and people evolve and grow, so does the organization itself. In a collaborative leadership culture, the organization design is very flat. Acxiom, a data management company, chose to have a two-level organization for its then 1,000 employees. There was management and the associates, with associates being tied to functions (e.g., associate in data management). They experimented with this for a year. The idea was to shift from a focus on upward progression to serving the customer and getting work done. It was a big shift for people in terms of their identity and perceived value to the company. After a year, it was put to a vote whether to keep the two-tier structure. It was nearly unanimous to keep it.

5. **Evaluate Impact:** Periodic evaluation and measurement of the impact of the change process is organization-wide as well as department/business unit-specific. Every project should have an after action review process for lessons learned. The lessons learned are assessed by the change leadership team for any adjustments to be made. At the organizational level, the evaluation is annual project assessments are done at their conclusion. Departmental and business unit assessments can be done at least once a year, possible twice.

THE HUMAN DYNAMICS OF COLLABORATIVE CHANGE

Organizational change processes are complex. There are many moving pieces, and at any point along the journey, just like a cross-country trip in a car, there can be a breakdown. In fact, there may be detours due to road damage, barriers like ice storms in mountain passes, and potholes along the way that can damage the tires and alignment. Organizational change processes face serious hurdles before they even get off the ground. What if members of the leadership team don't agree or think the change is ill timed? What if the company decides to hire an external consulting firm and they are incompetent in the implementation process? What if the change methodology is so disruptive to the organization's culture there is more damage done to workforce morale? All of these things can happen. There are at least three categories of things that can go wrong, with collaborative solutions for each one. They are 1) Leadership dynamics and breakdowns; 2) Workforce dynamics; and 3) Change process breakdowns.

Leadership Dynamics and Breakdowns: We know that one of the primary reasons for the failure of change processes is leadership at the executive or senior level of the organization. They may fail for any number of reasons:

- **Bright Shiny Objects:** This syndrome has already been noted, but it can be lethal for a change process. If they see the process as an event or transaction that can be handed off to a consulting firm or human resources, they will undermine its credibility and it may die. Or they may get tired of the process and chase any number of bright shiny objects that distracts their focus. Again, the process could be derailed.

  - *The Collaborative Solution: There must be a sufficiently critical burning platform for executive leadership to firmly commit their energy to resolve it. The commitment is about their integrity and discipline, and it is agreed to by the executive team at 100% true consensus. If a leader gets distracted, the other team members hold them accountable. In addition, a failed change could result in financial, professional or reputational consequences.*

- **Integrity Breakdowns:** There is a global epidemic of ethical breaches by leaders in organizations worldwide. When there is a breach of integrity, leaders lose all credibility, the trust is broken with the workforce, and any change process they are implementing gets undercut. It might as well be shut down.

  - *The Collaborative Solution: Unethical leaders should be removed from the organization—period.*

- **Executives Leaving:** Florida Power & Light, before it was acquired, was the first US company to win the prestigious Deming Award for quality. The CEO had been the primary champion of this multiyear effort. When he left Florida Power & Light (FP&L), the company's quality left with him, and it was soon purchased by Carolina Power & Light. Sometimes a leader is a champion for the change leaves before critical mass is achieved or the change infrastructure is built. Organizations that put all their eggs in one basket, a single executive, will find themselves facing a failed change process when that person leaves.

- ○ *The Collaborative Solution: The key to addressing this challenge is to create the Change Leadership Team at the beginning of the change process, with formal executive team support so that the change process has several levels of leadership support, so that should one leader leave, there are others who will fill the gap.*
- **New Executive:** Just as there are executives leaving, there may be new ones who arrive. They may come from another company that has a different culture or does not agree with a collaborative leadership culture. The new leader may also come from another part of the organization or another position on the executive team, and have resentments about the collaborative process. The emergence of a new leader creates uncertainty. In most instances, existing leadership may take a wait-and-see attitude, looking to where the new leader is taking the organization. By the end of the first 100 days, the leader may choose to take the organization in a different cultural direction, resulting in serious disruption to the organization.

  - ○ *The Collaborative Solution: If the leader who left has done his or her job in the first phase of the collaborative change process, there is a wide and deep consensus among the other members of the executive team, which the new leader is not going to want to contravene without alienating themselves. Another approach is in the recruitment process for a new leader. The executive team establishes, as a primary criterion for getting hired, that the individual be collaborative. There is really no sense in trying to fight a values battle by hoping you get a leader who is collaborative, or by taking the person's word for it. He or she must be vetted.*

- **Workforce Dynamics:** In nearly all change processes where the leadership culture is based on the Power Paradigm, the workforce becomes the *object* of the change process, not the *subject*. They have no say, no power, and are left to react to decisions over which they have no control, but which will significantly impact their professional and personal lives. The primary response to traditional change initiative is fear and resistance. But there are many other human consequences as we discussed in Chapter 8, like fear of job loss and low morale.

  - ○ *The Collaborative Solution: In a collaborative change process, fear and resistance are replaced by trust and ownership, because the workforce is engaged and owns it. There is a fundamental belief in the goodness, loyalty, and commitment of the workforce, their intellect and capabilities, and leadership is not afraid to engage them in direct ownership of the change process. Even if there is disruption, as we have shown at Marriott or DuPont, the workforce is eager to do what is best for the company, even if it means they may lose their jobs. They just want to be asked, to be engaged, to be a part of the decision. In culture-first collaborative changes, psychological safety and trust are created through the Collaborative Team Governance Process, so that when any change challenge or crisis occurs, they are ready to meet it head on, with firm resolve. It's what Lao Tzu said of collaboration, that we will say "We did it ourselves."*

- **Change Process Breakdowns:** There are many moving pieces in a change process and many points along the journey where the process can break down. These breakdowns can occur without any of the leadership, organizational, or workforce dynamics issues already discussed. The focus here is specifically on the implementation of the various phases of the process. Process breakdowns can shake the confidence of leadership and the workforce, calling into question the competence of the change leadership team, or the effectiveness of the methodology. Skeptical leaders and managers may seize on these breakdowns as evidence the process is not working and should be shut down, the "I told you so" objection. Unfortunately, at least in my experience, there is a presumption of perfection that is applied to those implementing the change, that they should never make any mistakes. This presumption is totally unrealistic. Change processes are led by human beings, and they are going to make mistakes. The focus should really be on what people learn from their mistakes and how they will adapt and make adjustments.

  The types of breakdowns that could occur include disagreements among leadership about the methodology after the change process has already begun; the initiative lacks sufficient front loading or effective communications; there is a lack of urgency or executive support; the change cadre may lack the necessary facilitation skills; an early project that is visible fails, which is used as "evidence" by skeptics that the change process is a failure; or there is the "reversion effect," where the champion leader leaves the company and the leadership culture reverts back to power, politics, and fear.

  o *The Collaborative Solution: Rigorous adherence to the Collaborative Method's principles and guidance—particularly front-end commitment from leader, creating alignment between leadership and the workforce, creating the Change Leadership Team, front-loading the collaborative governance process, and building high levels of ownership among the workforce—are critical to prevent change process breakdowns.*

CHAPTER CONCLUSION: COLLABORATION IS THE 4TH EVOLUTION OF ORGANIZATIONAL CHANGE

As has been said many times, *organizational change initiatives are intensely human endeavors.* They involve human beings who have hopes and dreams, expectations and aspirations. They also have personal and professional challenges, styles that may be in conflict with the existing culture, have interpersonal or relationship challenges, and even come from toxic or dysfunctional families. All of the positives and negatives play out in an organizational change process. In fact, they can be amplified because of the tenuousness and complexity of the process.

The *Collaborative Method* is the 4th Evolution of Organizational Change, which is fundamentally about preserving the humanity of the change process by giving the workforce ownership of it. The role of leadership is to engage, facilitate, and support the workforce, not the other way around, as we saw with power-based traditional approaches to change. Collaborative organizational change is about the people, because it is through people that true, lasting, and successful change happens. By honoring the people and giving them a direct say in changes that impact their lives and futures, this methodology honors Douglas McGregor's prescient prediction in 1960 that collaboration would eventually be the way we worked. That day has arrived and we now have the detailed change methodology that will enable us to realize that vision.

CHAPTER REVIEW AND REFLECTIONS

Learning Objectives:
Let's reflect on the learning objectives for the chapter and summarize what we have learned:

- Understand what the 4th Evolution of organizational change, the Collaborative Method, is and what makes it significantly different from traditional approaches to implementing change.
- Learn about the leadership infrastructure needed for collaborative change, who is involved, what they do, and guidelines for implementing it.
- Learn about the phases involved in implementing the Collaborative Method.
- Understand the human dynamics of collaborative change that leaders may encounter and how they are addressed.

Initial Questions Revisited, and For Reflection:

- *Now that you understand the foundations of the Collaborative Method, the 4th Evolution of organizational change methods, how and where could you see it being applied?*
- *Are you interested in becoming a leader or facilitator of collaborative change? What steps will you take to get yourself trained and ready to participate?*
- *Do you know of change situations where the Collaborative Method of change could be applied? How would you apply this five-phase methodology to achieve success?*

- *If you encountered any of the change dynamics just discussed, how would you lead your team or organization through it while honoring the principles of collaboration?*

ADDITIONAL READINGS

- Marshall, Edward. *Building Trust at the Speed of Change.* New York: AMACOM Books, 2000.
- Marshall, Edward. *Transforming the Way We Work: The Power of the Collaborative Workplace.* New York: AMACOM Books, 1995.
- Stayer, Ralph. "How I Learned to Let My Workers Lead." *Harvard Business Review,* November–December, 1990, pp. 1-11. This is a classic and one of the first collaborative change initiatives that was company-wide.

ENDNOTES

1 Lao Tzu, the *Tao Te Ching,* 6th Century BCE.
2 This quote and opening section of the Main Point, are based on Ralph Stayer, "How I Learned to Let My Workers Lead," *Harvard Business Review,* November–December, 1990, p. 1–11.
3 Ibid., p. 11.
4 Ibid.
5 Xerox Quality Services, *A World of Quality: Business Transformation at Xerox* (Norwalk, C3T: Xerox Quality Services, 1996).
6 This model was developed by Dr. Edward Marshall over 40 years of research and practice in organizations of all types on five continents, and has been validated by several hundred managers and leaders. It is more fully elaborated in Edward M. Marshall, *Transforming the Way We Work: The Power of the Collaborative Workplace* (New York: AMACOM Books, 1995).
7 Adam Werbach, *Using Transparency to Execute Your Strategy* (Boston, MA: Harvard Business Press, 2009).

Figure Credits
Fig. 9.4: Edward M. Marshall, "From Current State to Future State," Transforming the Way We Work: The Power of the Collaborative Workplace, AMACOM Books, 1994.

PART V

Global Collaborative Leadership

CHAPTER TEN

Collaborative Leadership in a World at Risk

Nero fiddled while Rome burned.[1]

THE TEAM came together for their final meeting, but it was a virtual meeting since the COVID-19 virus was spreading around the world and the university was shut down. Everyone was working remotely from their apartments near campus. The team reminded themselves that they would likely work virtually the rest of their professional lives, and they welcomed the opportunity to practice, but the circumstances were incredibly stressful. Morare was deeply upset because the President of South Africa had just shut his country down due to the rapid increase of infections, and his family was at risk. Priyanka nodded, since the President of India had just put India's 1.3 billion people on lockdown. Linda lamented the fact that the US President seemed not to care that the country had the highest number of infections and deaths in the world. Hanyue was cautiously optimistic because his President had locked down China early, and the cases of COVID-19 had drastically fallen off. Ana commiserated with Linda because her nationalist President also was in denial, encouraging people to go back to work in spite of thousands of cases across Brazil.

Morare made an observation. "Perhaps this is a dress rehearsal for a far more pressing problem the world faces, climate change. Perhaps this is a warning to the world's leaders that we must all come together if the peoples of the planet are to survive. Africa is experiencing drought, once-in-500-year hurricanes, and now locusts consuming crops. And our leaders are still not working together."

Hanyue agreed and talked about the monster cyclones that have hit China more frequently in the past few years. Linda pointed to the recent fires in Australia that devastated the bush country and killed over 1 million animals, and to the fact that Australia is already at 3.5°C, well above the United Nations' 2030 target of 1.5°C. Ana noted that Antarctica is melting, which will add many inches of sea level rise around the world. At the same time, Brazil's new leadership was allowing the Amazon rain forests, the greatest resource for carbon capture on Earth, to be burned down for farmland. The entire planet is being impacted, and global leaders,

who met in Spain for their annual climate change meeting, did nothing. What needs to be done? How can collaborative leadership help the world's leaders tackle both the pandemic and global climate change? They opened their assignment to see these initial study guide questions for this chapter:
- *What are the dimensions of the existential threat known as climate change?*
- *What are the consequences for the planet and its people?*
- *What have world leaders done so far to tackle it?*
- *What can you do as a collaborative leader to address the climate emergency? What are your responsibilities to the peoples of the planet as we all face the consequences of global warming?*

LEARNING OBJECTIVES

By the end of this chapter, you will:
- Understand what it means for the world to be at risk as a result of the existential threat of climate change, and the multiple dimensions of the climate emergency
- Understand the many interconnected and horrific consequences of global warming for plants, animals, fish and sea creatures, oceans and the cryosphere, and human beings
- Provide a brief review of what global leaders have done to date to address the climate emergency
- Provide a framework for you to reflect on what your responsibilities and commitments are as a collaborative leader for addressing this existential threat

THE MAIN POINT OF THIS CHAPTER

It is 100 seconds to midnight.

—The 2020 Doomsday Clock, January 23, 2020

Humanity continues to face two simultaneous existential threats—nuclear war and climate change—that are compounded by a threat multiplier, cyber-enabled information warfare, that undercuts society's ability to respond.[2]

What kind of planet will the children of the 21st Century inherit? And their children? Beyond the threats of global pandemics like Covid-19 and nuclear proliferation, we appear, based on overwhelming scientific data, to be on a collision course with a mass extinction event at some point in the next century. Even terrorist attacks and warfare, cyberwarfare, and bioterrorism seem imminently more controllable by global leaders than the cataclysmic force of climate change. The rippling and interconnected consequences of global warming due to dramatically increased, fossil fuel–caused carbon dioxide emissions. Are seismographic and feel totally out of our control. And yet they will determine whether the human race will have plants, animals, and fish to eat; whether hundreds of millions of city dwellers on coasts on every continent will find their cities underwater; and whether the billions of people on this overpopulated planet will avoid starvation, plagues, mass migrations, and conflict.

We are indeed living in a world at risk! But why should climate change be at the center of this final chapter? Our journey has been one from the "inside out," starting with you as a leader in an organization, and the journey you have gone on to become a collaborative leader who is prepared to meet the challenges of the 21st Century. Then you learned how to help a team work together collaboratively so that you could, with trust and mutual respect, tackle projects and processes together more effectively. The third level of collaborative competence was how to design and implement collaborative organizational change in such a way that everyone affected owns the change initiative. We are now at the 4th level of collaborative development, where you are focused on your role and responsibilities for our planet. You have, unfortunately, arrived at this level at the precise time that the global conversation is about whether the peoples on Earth will be able to survive its warming over the next 80 to 100 years. As the new year and decade began (2020), this reality was punctuated by the head of the Bank of England, who on January 2 warned that we are headed toward an unsustainable world of 4°C of global warming above preindustrial levels, when the planet cannot tolerate much more than 1.5°C.[3] It is increasingly clear that climate change is the most critical global challenge we face. As we will see in this chapter, it impacts every person on the planet, every facet of our lives, and requires collaborative leadership to be able to confront it, leadership in all aspects of our collective life—public policy, business, government, economic development, engineering, technology, biodiversity, and many more. Everything in our lives is now, and will increasingly be, impacted by climate change. The question then is, what will you do? How will you bring your collaborative leadership skills and capabilities to bear on the most pressing issue in our history as a species?

Global leaders, to date (2020), have failed spectacularly to come together and act on the commitments that were made in the 2015 Paris Climate Agreement. We need go no further than the December 2019 United Nations Conference of Parties (COP)25 climate conference in Madrid, Spain, which, even in the face of new harsh realities about continued increases in CO_2 emissions, chose compromise, not transformational action.[4] For many, especially the thousands of protestors outside the meeting halls, COP25 was a colossal failure of leadership and inaction.

Climate change has exposed some of the deepest vulnerabilities in our economic, political, government, and civic systems, no matter where you live. These systems must be transformed into something we have not yet considered as one global population—and the scientists at the United Nations Intergovernmental Panel on Climate Change have given us until 2030 to do it before we reach the "point of no return"—where the chaos of CO_2-fueled global warming is irreversible.[5]

I remain optimistic. I believe that if our global leaders can see the collective horror of the death, pain, and suffering that has just begun to be witnessed, just as they saw the horrors of nuclear war, and are seeing the devastation of the COVID-19 epidemic around the world, they will collaborate rather than compete, act rather than talk, and mobilize the resources needed to transform how we live on this blue and green jewel in the middle of the universe. But if the global Covid-19 response so far and the Madrid climate conference are any indication, we have an extraordinarily long way to go. We may have to abandon what has not worked. Global leaders need to choose to transform global political and economic systems and mobilize the citizens of the planet in collective action if we are to get to net-zero CO_2 emissions by 2030.

I believe that you are the primary solution, by how you consciously choose to lead your personal and professional life, lead and inspire others, and bring your collaborative leadership to bear on the great issues of the day. Just like Greta Thunberg, the young Swedish climate activist, who in three years went from demonstrating alone every Friday at her high school, to over 10 million students on "strike" in countries all over the world three years later, it is the power of one that can lead to the collective power of all. Through true collaborative leadership we can together save the peoples of planet Earth from mass extinction.

A WORLD AT RISK OF MASS EXTINCTION

We are the first generation to feel the impacts of climate change, the last with the chance to do something about it ... we only have one planet ... there is no Plan B.

—President Barack Obama, August 3, 2015[6]

There have always been significant challenges facing the planet, but the 21st Century is facing an existential threat to the human race, the very real prospect that by the end of the century human life, as we know it, could either be extinct or our existence extremely difficult. The next mass extinction, according to global climate scientists, could occur within the next 80 to 100 years. The expanding threats of nuclear proliferation and war, global pandemics, the rise (again) of authoritarian regimes around the world, and cyber warfare[7] have faded in comparison to the goliath that is the climate emergency now upon us. Global leaders, in the past have come together to sign treaties, form alliances, and reduce nuclear stockpiles. That these threats are reemerging certainly adds to our anxiety about the future of the human race. What will global leaders do now that the world is 100 seconds before midnight?

The history of mass extinctions is instructive, and gives us context for what we're experiencing now. Nesbit has summarized the five mass extinctions so far this way:[8]

- 1st: 450 million years ago, 86% of all species dead
- 2nd: 380 million years ago, 75% of all species dead
- 3rd: 255 million years ago, 96% of all species dead
- 4th: 205 million years ago, 80% of all species dead
- 5th: 70 million years ago, 70% of all species dead

All but the mass extinction that killed the dinosaurs involved climate change produced by greenhouse gases. The most notorious and instructive for today's emergency, according to Nesbit, was 255 million years ago, which began when CO_2 warmed the planet by 5°C. Nesbit continues: "We are currently adding carbon to the atmosphere at a considerably faster rate; by most estimates, at least 10 times faster. The rate is one hundred times faster than at any point in human history before the beginning of industrialization. And there is already, right now, fully a third more carbon in the atmosphere than at any point in the last 800,000 years—perhaps in as long as 15 million years."

We have not been successful at all, however, in defusing the ticking 2030 climate time bomb as global leaders fail to act collaboratively and decisively to implement the political, economic, social, and infrastructure transformations required to get to net-zero carbon emissions by the end of the current decade. There is a very real prospect that global leaders will continue to fail the peoples of the planet as they continue to deny the scientific reality of the emergency, do a lot of talking, make paper commitments, but do not act collectively to achieve the 1.5°C goal of global warming.

First, we will look at the scientific data-based realities of where we are as a human race with carbon-fueled global warming. Second, we will briefly explore the interconnected web of consequences that threaten our very existence. Third, we will consider the failures of global leadership to act decisively in what was once a hopeful framework for global action—the United Nations Framework Convention on Climate Change. Finally, we will briefly consider what the experts are telling us must happen if we are to save the human race.

We will discover a number of phenomena that frame at least our near-term future:

- That there is overwhelming scientific data describing the enormity and complexity of the climate emergency and its web of interconnected consequences
- The good intentions of the United Nations in its efforts to realize global action
- The undermining of global, collaborative, and collective action by corporate greed, nation-state based self-interest
- The near total lack of focus on the type of collaborative leadership needed to transform global political, economic, and infrastructure institutions and to mobilize the peoples of the planet for concerted, immediate behavior change

We will then turn to two questions: (1) What type of collaborative leadership is required to transform systems and mobilize a global citizen campaign to save the species? and (2) What does this mean for you as a 21st Century collaborative leader?

The Climate Change Emergency

The point of no return is no longer over the horizon. It is in sight and hurtling towards us.

—António Guterres, Secretary-General of the United
Nations, December 2, 2019, Madrid COP25[9]

The Secretary-General issued this stark warning based on a wide range of scientific facts that have been generated by thousands of climate scientists around the world. He was exhorting the delegates to the Madrid COP25, the global leadership group that meets annually to find a global consensus on actions nations will take to reduce carbon emissions. A mere two weeks later, Secretary-General Guterres and the rest of the world were sorely disappointed with the results:

I am disappointed with the results of COP25. The international community lost an important opportunity to show increased ambition on mitigation, adaptation & finance to tackle the climate crisis. But we must not give up, and I will not give up.[10]

This was certainly not our first warning, and unfortunately not the first disappointment. In November 2018 the United Nations' scientific panel of global climate scientists, known as the Intergovernmental Panel on Climate Change (IPCC), issued a very stark warning to all of us—it gave world leaders until 2030 to reverse the trajectory of carbon dioxide levels in the atmosphere and keep global warming to 1.5° Celsius below preindustrial levels of CO_2 in the atmosphere or face catastrophic consequences as we pass the point of no return.[11] In 2019, 11,000 climate scientists gave us another warning that the peoples of the world are now in a climate emergency and that our lifestyles are going to have to dramatically change if we are to survive.[12]

The Scope and Complexity of the Climate Emergency

It is worse, much worse, than you think.

—David Wallace-Wells, *The Uninhabitable Earth: Life after Warming*

Let's consider the scope and complexity of the climate emergency based on scientific data accumulated over close to 50 years by climate scientists around the world. The IPCC says our planet is on a carbon path that human activities, which have caused us to get to 1°C in 2018, will take us to 1.5° between 2030 and 2052 "if it continues at to increase at the current rate." The IPCC goes on to say that the impacts of global warming at 2°C will be very significant, including increases in mean temperatures, hot extremes in most inhabited regions, extreme precipitation in several regions, sea level rise, and risks to health, food security, water supply, and human security.[13] According to David Wallace-Wells, in his book *The Uninhabitable Earth: Life after Warming,* while the landmark Paris Agreement of 2015 had 192 nations commit to a 1.5°C goal by 2030, 2° now looks like the best case scenario. Wallace-Wells cites the 2018 IPCC report:[14]

> *If we take action on emissions soon, instituting immediately all of the commitments made in the Paris accords but nowhere yet actually implemented, we are likely to get about 3.2 degrees of warming, or about three times as much warming as the planet has since the beginning of industrialization—bringing the unthinkable collapse of the planet's ice sheets not just into the realm of the real but into the present.*

Wallace-Wells goes on to summarize some examples of the impacts of each degree of global warming above 1.5°C:[15]

- At 2 degrees, the current best-case scenario:
  - Ice sheets will begin to collapse
  - More people will suffer from water scarcity
  - Major cities in the equatorial band will become unlivable, and in northern latitudes, heat waves will kill thousands each summer
- At 3 degrees:
  - Southern Europe in permanent drought
  - Average drought in Central America would last 19 months longer
  - Northern African droughts are 60 months longer
  - 6 times more land burned in fires in the US
- At 4 degrees:
  - 8M more cases of dengue fever each year
  - 9% more heat related deaths
  - Damages from river flooding would grow 30-fold in Bangladesh, 20x in India, 60x in UK
  - Damages about $600 trillion, more than twice the wealth that exists in world today
  - Conflict and warfare could double

The cost of global warming is equally overwhelming: Every degree of warming costs a temperate country like the United States about 1% GDP; at 1.5° the world would be $20 trillion richer than at 2°; at 3.7°, cost would be $551 trillion; total worldwide wealth in 2019 is $280 trillion. Wallace-Wells' assessment is: "Some of these processes take thousands of years to unfold, but they are also irreversible, and therefore effectively permanent. You might hope to simply reverse climate change; you can't. It will outrun all of us." [16]

The Climate Emergency by the Numbers

The scientific and practical reality of where we are with the climate as of 2020 helps us understand the dimensions of the climate emergency, why the fuse on the climate time bomb has been lit—by us, and provides insight into what must be done to save the human species:

- **800,000 Years:**[17] Over 800,000 years, records show the average global CO_2 levels fluctuated between about 170 ppm and 280 ppm. Once humans started to burn fossil fuels in the industrial era, things changed rapidly, rising above 300 ppm, and by 2013 above 400 ppm. The last time carbon dioxide levels were this high was likely in the Pliocene era, between 2 and 4.6 million years ago, when sea levels were 60 to 80 feet higher than they are today. It took 1,000 years for CO_2 to increase by 35 ppm; now it's 2 ppm/year, which means that by 2063 or sooner, it could be 500 ppm.
- **Global Temperatures and CO_2 Levels:** According to US government data, since 1880 until about 2020, there is a direct correlation between the amount of CO_2 in the atmosphere and the increase in global temperatures (See Figure 10.1).
- **CO_2 Levels in 2020:** As of November 2019, the Scripps Observatory at Mauna Loa in Hawaii, where CO_2 has been measured since 1958, the level was 410.27 ppm, over 2 ppm from the November 2018 level of 208.02 ppm (See Figure 10.2).[19]

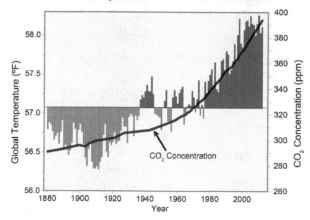

FIGURE 10.1   CO2 Concentrations and Global Temperature Increases, 1880–2020.[18]

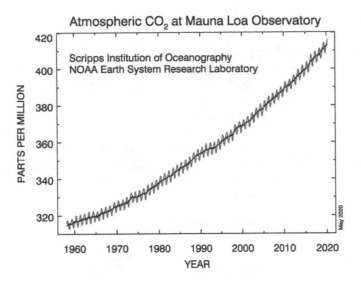

FIGURE 10.2   Atmospheric CO2 at Mauna Loa Observatory, 1960–2020.

- **2015 Paris Agreement 1.5°C Threshold:** The 2015 Paris Agreement, signed by 192 nations—the only global, collaborative, signed agreement on climate change—said that the global temperature was to be kept well below 2°C, and closer to 1.5°C to prevent dire consequences for the peoples of planet Earth.[20]
- **1°+ C Above Pre-Industrial Levels:** The global mean temperature in January–October 2019 was 1.1°C above preindustrial levels, with 2019 likely to be the second- or third-hottest year on record; as of late 2018, the planet was on the way to 1.5°C between 2030 and 2052, and, without the drastic transformation of current behaviors by nations around the world, we are on a path to 7°C by 2100, a catastrophic number.[21]
- **Status of the Carbon "Budget":** How much carbon is left in the global carbon budget, which if used up, would result in catastrophic climate change? In December 2019, just before the United Nations COP25 meeting in Madrid, a highly scientific report was released on the global carbon budget, reporting that as of the end of December 2019, only 23.3% remains, projected to last until 2036.[22]
- **4 Largest CO$_2$ Emitting Nations:** China, the United States, the European Union, and India account for 59% of the world's CO$_2$ emissions.[23]
- **The Tipping Point, or Point of No Return:** This leads us to the obvious question of how much longer we really have before it's too late, where the effects of global warming are irreversible. Assuming a moderate mitigation strategy, a 2° warming threshold, and accepting a 67% likelihood of remaining below the

threshold, the point of no return will arrive around the year 2035. If we aggressively reduce greenhouse gas emissions, it could be delayed until 2042. Some believe we have already passed this threshold.

- **Global Temperature and Precipitation Projections:**[24] The IPCC scientists have made these heat and precipitation projections: surface temperature is expected to rise by an average of up to 12°C above preindustrial levels by 2100, and precipitation is expected to increase an average of 60% in some places on the planet.

- **CO_2 Emissions Gap Increasing:** The United Nations Environment Programme released its 2019 *Emissions Gap Report* in November 2019, just prior to the Madrid COP25 global leadership meeting. Its summary findings are at best disturbing (See Figure 10.3):[25]

  o Green House Gas emissions continue to rise, despite scientific warnings and political commitments; China's emissions have increased 400%; the US is flat; the EU declined; India is up 200%
  o G20 members account for 78% of global GHG emissions
  o The emissions gap is large, a 32 gigaton gap between where we are and where we need to be (15 gigaton) to achieve the 1.5°C goal
  o Decarbonizing the global economy will require fundamental structural changes

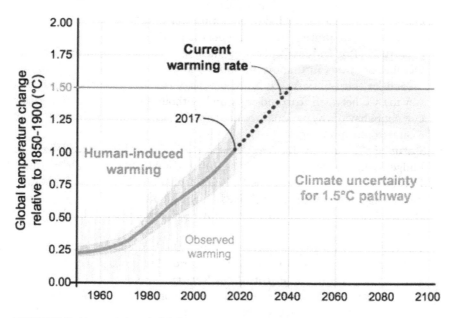

FIGURE 10.3   Human-Induced Global Warming, 1960–2100.

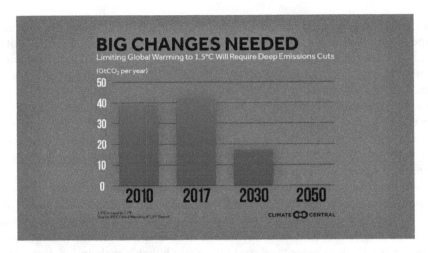

FIGURE 10.4   Deep Emissions Cuts Required to Meet 1.5°C Goal.

○ Renewables and energy efficiency, in combination with electrification of end uses are key to a successful energy transition and to driving down emissions

· **Much global warming is "baked in" from past CO_2:**[26] Professor Drew Shindell of Duke University's Nicholas School of Environment and a coordinating lead author of the IPCC 2018 1.5° global warming report, said that the global warming already "baked in" to the current trajectory is not by itself enough to cause further long-term changes in our climate. On the other hand, what we as a society do now matters. The urgency with which the world addresses greenhouse gas emission reductions now will help determine the degree of future warming (See Figure 10.4).

· **CO_2 Emissions Cuts Required to Meet Well Below 2° Celsius (Paris Agreement):**[27] Net CO_2 emissions need to drop 45% from their 2010 levels by 2030 and reach net-zero by 2050.

THE CONSEQUENCES OF THE CLIMATE EMERGENCY ON OUR PLANET AND PEOPLE

All of these seemingly random events are connected. The small changes happening are harbingers for something bigger. More consequential changes are coming much sooner than we know. ... We are living under a black sky, in a time of uncertainty.

—Jeff Nesbit, *This Is the Way the World Ends*[28]

The climate emergency is here now. This year. Today! It is not something that is off in the future. Mother Earth is fighting back against a century of industrial pollution, greed, and government inaction as the developed countries exploited natural resources all over the world, particularly fossil fuels, belched carbon into the atmosphere and pumped toxic pollutants into our oceans and streams with reckless disregard. Now we are paying the price for that neglect and disrespect, and our economic, political, and global institutional systems are still hamstrung by the incentives of wealth, power, and national self-interest. It will be extraordinarily difficult to shift gears and transform these systems, values, and behaviors of an entire planet in less than a decade. As Nesbit warns us, "Our world is in trouble."[29]

In California's San Joaquin Valley, America's fruit basket, "thousands of itinerant migrant workers have to walk miles just to get fresh water, while almonds grown there get it from the drying up aquifer."[30] Nesbit goes on to describe other consequences such as farmers abandoning their farms in the African Sahel as drought and desert consume them, forcing them to become climate refugees; a billion people in India wondering if the monsoon season that provides their fresh water is in trouble; tens of thousands of species under severe pressure, leading to local extinctions; extreme weather events affecting 10% of the Northern Hemisphere versus 0.5% two decades ago; and temperatures in 2014–17 being the hottest in human history, causing ice sheets to melt and sea levels to rise. James Blalog, in his 2012 Emmy-winning film *Chasing Ice*, over several years recorded the receding of glaciers in Alaska and Greenland. He ends the film with a haunting warning to us all. When asked whether he thought his movie was going to wake up the world to the catastrophic consequences of climate change, he said, and I will paraphrase, "Only when it hits them in their own backyards."[31]

Human beings, and our leaders in particular, seem incapable of doing anything that is transformative unless it is in their backyard, and even then, many remain in denial. It took the Japanese attacks on Pearl Harbor in 1941 for President Franklin D. Roosevelt to declare war. It took two atomic bombs dropped on Japan in 1945 for the Japanese to surrender. Given the anemic results coming from global leaders to act on climate change, what must happen before they do? Will it be the extinction of honeybees and other pollinators resulting in the end of food as we know it? Will it be the elimination of plankton on the Great Barrier Reef due to acidification? Or will it be the melting of West Antarctica's ice shelf unleashing up to 11 feet of sea level rise worldwide?

Let's take a brief look at the interconnected web of consequences coming from global warming, many of them right now, which, when taken together, present leadership at all levels of society with an urgent and critical call to immediate action. Our focus is on three interconnected dimensions of the emergency: (1) The extinction of animal and plant species; (2) The heating of our oceans and melting of our glaciers; and (3) The consequences and unequal impacts on the human species around the world. An overview is provided here. If you are interested in the research, you will find these sources in the footnotes most credible.

Extinction of Species

The health of ecosystems on which we and all other species depend is deteriorating more rapidly than ever. We are eroding the very foundations of our economies, livelihoods, food security, health and quality of life worldwide.

—Sir Robert Watson, chair, UN Intergovernmental Science-Policy Platform on Biodiversity and Ecosystem Services, May 2019[32]

Watson's UN panel released a report in May 2019 that said of the 8 million animal and plant species on Earth, fully 12.5%, or 1 million of them, are now threatened with extinction as a result of climate change: "Ecosystems, species, wild populations, local varieties and breeds of domesticated plants and animals are shrinking, deteriorating or vanishing. The essential, interconnected web of life on Earth is getting smaller and increasingly frayed. This loss is a direct result of human activity."[33]

A total of 145 experts from 50 countries, with 310 contributing authors, 15,000 documents, and an 1,800-page report that covers 50 years of research, present a powerful, rigorous, scientifically proven "burning platform," where *climate change is a crucial underlying factor that is helping to drive destruction around the world ... while the Earth has always suffered from the actions of humans through history, over the past 50 years, these scratches have become deep scars."*[34] Here are several additional, disturbing data points from the report: Forests have been cleared at astonishing rates, especially in tropical areas; only 13% of wetlands that existed in 1700 were still in existence in 2000; the rate of species destruction is tens to hundreds of times higher than the average over the past 10 million years; every year, 300–400 million tons of heavy metals, solvents, toxic sludge go into our waters;[35] and bees and pollinators, essential to our food supply, are going extinct.[36] Dr. Kate Brauman, who was a coordinating lead author of the UN biodiversity report, leaves us with this chilling warning: *"We have documented a really unprecedented decline in biodiversity and nature; this is completely different than anything we've seen in human history in terms of the rate of decline and the scale of the threat."*[37]

The Oceans and Cryosphere

A complete collapse of West Antarctica would push sea levels up 10 to 11 feet. ... That would likely take centuries but it could happen more rapidly.

—Ted Scambos, coleader, International Thwaites Glacier Collaboration, 2019[38]

The five-year research project at the bottom of the planet on an endangered glacier the size of Great Britain, in remote West Antarctica, is designed to develop more accurate global sea level rise models so coastal residents and governments around the world have enough time to plan. If this huge, unstable glacier continues to melt, it could change the coastlines of the world's cities, raising global sea levels 1 to 2 feet within decades. The melting of Thwaites could unleash an additional 8 to 10 feet or more of global sea level rise, putting hundreds of millions of people in coastal cities worldwide at risk, while disappearing many island nations.[39] Thwaites, is, please excuse the pun, merely the tip of the iceberg. There are a number of scientifically documented phenomena by the IPCC in a September 25, 2019, report entitled *Special Report on the Ocean and Cryosphere in a Change Climate, Summary for Policymakers.*[40] The bottom line of this report was summarized by Dr. Jean-Pierre Gattuso, the coordinating lead author: "The blue planet is in serious danger right now, suffering many insults from many different directions and it's our fault."[41]

There are five impacts of global warming on our oceans and cryosphere: (1) Warming seas, (2) Melting glaciers and frozen places, (3) Sea level rise, (4) Acidification, and (5) Deoxygenation, which together put our greatest resource for life itself on the verge of extinction.

- **Warming Seas:** According to the IPCC scientists who wrote the *Special Report*, the oceans have been warming since 1970, soaking up more than 90% of the extra heat generated by humans, a rate that has doubled since 1993.[42] A new NASA study, based on 15 years of data from NASA's Atmospheric Infrared Sounder instrument, found that warming seas contribute to the frequency of extreme rain storms; 21% more storms form for every 1.8° Fahrenheit that ocean surface temperatures rise in tropical oceans. Current climate models project that increased CO_2 in the atmosphere will result in 4.8° Fahrenheit by 2100. *"The study team concludes that if this were to happen, we could expect the frequency of extreme storms to increase by as much as 60% by that time. … More storms mean more flooding, more structure damage, more crop damage and so on, unless mitigating measures are implemented."*[43]

- **Melting Glaciers:** Glaciers are melting on both poles, in Greenland, and in the tallest mountain ranges around the world. It is estimated that 80% of all glaciers will be gone by 2100.[44] The bellwether for ice melting is Antarctica, and specifically the West Antarctic ice sheet, whose fate will determine whether we have a global flood.[45] The last time this ice sheet underwent a major retreat was 10,000 to 12,000 years ago, when the world was actually cooler than it is today. But now West Antarctica is facing collapse. It has lost more than 3 trillion tons of ice between 1992 and 2017.[46]

- **Sea Level Rise:**[47] The UN's *Special Report* has confirmed what we have just learned about the West Antarctic ice shelf: "Global mean sea level (GMSL) is rising, with acceleration in recent decades due to increasing rates of ice loss from the Greenland and Antarctic ice sheets as well as continued glacier mass loss and ocean thermal expansion." This results in increased tropical cyclones, rainfall, and extreme waves, putting people at risk from extreme weather events.

- **Ocean Acidification:** Scientists estimate that one-third of all the CO_2 humans produce is going into our oceans, "which is changing their chemistry by triggering reactions that make seawater more acidic, a phenomenon called ocean acidification."[48] There is more acid now than at the beginning of the industrial era over 100 years ago, "a change larger and more rapid than seen in the fossil record going back at least 800,000 years, before the appearance of vertebrates and plants in the fossil record."[49] The IPCC predicts that when we reach 1.5°C from global warming, 90% of the coral reefs will disappear.[50]

- **Ocean Deoxygenation:**[51] "The world's oceans are gasping for breath," according to a 2019, highly researched, 588-page scientific report from 67 scientists in 17 countries, who are in the International Union for the Conservation of Nature. Fish and sea creatures require oxygen to breath. The loss of oxygen is due to climate change and agricultural nutrient run off into our waters. The journal *Science* reports that in some parts of the tropics, there has been a 40 to 50% reduction in oxygen, which can lead to dead zones in our oceans where nothing lives.[52] The International Union Scientists consider this loss of ocean oxygen "the ultimate wake-up call needed to dramatically raise our ambitions to tackle and immediately curb our emissions of carbon dioxide and other powerful greenhouse gases such as methane."[53]

The Human Consequences of the Climate Emergency

Carbon dioxide levels continue to be emitted at unsustainable levels, pushing the planet ever closer to the point of no return, projected to be 2030 or sooner. More than 1 million plant and animal species, or 12.5% of all species on Earth, are going extinct. The oceans are warming, the glaciers are melting, sea levels are rising, and fish and sea creatures are struggling to breath. No, this is not the famed Chicken Little saying that "the sky is falling, the sky is falling." This is scientifically proven fact, with all of the inevitable consequences for the human race, especially for those living in the Southern Hemisphere and on island nations.

In his sobering and scary book, *The Uninhabitable Earth,* David Wallace-Wells cites research on what he calls the 12 elements of chaos for the human race: heat death, hunger, drowning, wildfire, climate disasters, a drain on freshwater, dying oceans, unbreathable air, plagues of warming, economic collapse, climate conflict, and climate refugees.[54] Indeed, the World Meteorological Organization's *Provisional Statement on the State of the Global Climate in 2019* pointed to these examples of the human consequences of global warming:[55] Cyclone Idai, one of strongest-known cyclones to make landfall on east coast of Africa, devastating farmlands and forcing hundreds of thousands of people from their homes in three countries in Eastern Africa; extreme heat conditions taking their toll on human health and health systems;

conflicts, insecurity and economic slowdowns; and a rise in global hunger with 820 million people suffering in 2018.

In addition, there are four critical human consequences that require special attention, global leadership, and investment: 1) Hunger and malnutrition, 2) Climate migration, 3) Climate inequality, and 4) Disappearing island nations, which have the severest consequences for the poorest among us, a moral challenge for global leaders. The focus on these four dimensions is a call for climate justice and global collaborative leadership:

- **Hunger and Malnutrition:**[56] In its 2017 report on world hunger, the UN Food and Agriculture Organization found that hunger affected 815 million people in 2016, 11% of the global population, and malnutrition affected 155 million children under age five.

- **Climate Refugees:** In a microcosm of the climate refugee crisis that is already upon us, Bangladesh, on the eastern edge of India, has experienced 700,000 Bangladeshi refugees who were displaced 2009–19 every year due to natural disasters fueled by climate change; for example catastrophic Cyclone Aila in 2009 in which millions were displaced, sea levels rose, land eroded, and farmland was destroyed by salt water. The World Bank is anticipating as many as 13.3 million climate refugees by 2050. The World Bank estimates that by 2050, sub-Saharan Africa, South Asia, and Latin America, which represent 55% of the developing world, climate change could force more than 143 million people to move within their countries, with 86 million of them in sub-Saharan Africa. Its 2018 report, *Groundswell*, has four messages for global leaders:[57]

  1. The scale of internal climate migration will ramp up by 2050 and then accelerate unless concerted climate and development action is taken.
  2. Countries can expect to see "hotspots" of climate-induced in-and out-migration.
  3. Migration can be a sensible climate change adaptation strategy if managed carefully and supported by good development policies and targeted investments.
  4. Internal climate migration may be a reality but it doesn't have to be a crisis.

  The United Nations has significantly higher estimates of climate refugees, ranging from 200 million to 1 billion or more "vulnerable poor people with no choice but to fight or flee."[58]

- **Climate Inequality:** Climate inequality starts with the overpopulation of the planet. In 2019 there were 7.7 billion people on a planet that can only support 1.5 billion at the United States' standard of living. The United Nations estimates that there will be 8.5 billion on Earth in 2030 and 9.7 billion in 2050, when we are supposed to be at net-zero carbon emissions.[59] Overpopulation leads to resource scarcity, starvation, diseases and pandemics, and enormous wealth disparities. Those who are least able to fend for themselves, mostly in the Southern Hemisphere, are the ones most negatively affected by inequality and climate change, and are the first ones to suffer.[60] This gross level of inequality, driven by overpopulation and the egregious maldistribution of wealth, income, and resources, extends to the global climate emergency debate, where the developing world has consistently complained that the developed countries created the climate emergency, but now those same countries expect the developing world to curtail theirs, and they should.

- **Disappearing Island Nations:** Nowhere is this inequality more evident than with the island nations of the South Pacific, Indian Ocean, and other seas around the world, where they are on the edge of disappearing underwater as the sea levels rise. The island of Tuvalu in Oceana is the 4th smallest nation on the planet at 26 square kilometers and has already started to disappear due to sea level rise.[61] Two of its nine islands are on the verge of submerging as a result of sea level rise. In 2012 the United Nations Development Programme predicted this probability in its report *Climate Change and Pacific Island Countries*: "Over the next few decades, it seems unavoidable that large numbers of people will be displaced from their present homes and livelihood bases by sea-level rise and forced to relocate these in less vulnerable locations elsewhere."[62]

What we're seeing with human consequences of global warming is an inversion effect, where those least able to fend for themselves, the poorest, the weakest, and the smallest, are the most dramatically and significantly impacted—by starvation, disease, forced migrations, droughts, intense poverty, and even submersion underwater—and most of these fellow human beings are in the Southern Hemisphere of planet Earth.

THE GLOBAL LEADERSHIP LEDGER

As countries usually scope out their plans over five and 10 year timeframes, if the 45% carbon cut target by 2030 is to be met then the plans really need to be on the table by the end of 2020.[63]

While global leaderships' actual CO_2 emissions reductions to date have been a colossal failure, with emissions actually going up since the 2015 Paris Agreement, it has not been without heroic efforts by some international, city, state, and youth leaders. Let's look at what has been attempted so that we can understand what must happen next in the next decade to get to net-zero carbon emissions. It is not our intention to review the entire history of what the United Nations and its many agencies have done on the climate emergency, but it is clear, whether it was the failure of the Kyoto Protocol in 1997, all the way to the anemic compromises at the 2019 Madrid Conference of Parties, that UN leadership has done heroic work to foster global collaboration on this crisis, but national self-interest and corporate greed undermined these efforts. As Laurence Tubiana from the European Climate Foundation, an architect of the Paris Climate agreement, said: "Major players who needed to deliver in Madrid did not live up to expectations."[64] A new leadership construct is required if the human race is to survive.

Global Goals

In 2015, 197 nations signed the landmark Paris Climate Agreement, in which Article II stated the global goal was "holding the increase in the global average temperature to well below 2°C above pre-industrial levels and pursuing efforts to limit the temperature increase to 1.5°C above pre-industrial levels, recognizing that this would significantly reduce the risks and impacts of climate change."[65] To meet this goal, the 2018 IPCC report indicated a number of significant areas where global collaboration is required:[66]

- Limiting the risks from global warming of 1.5°C in the context of sustainable development and
- poverty eradication implies system transitions that can be enabled by an increase of adaptation and mitigation investments, policy instruments, the acceleration of technological innovation and behavior changes
- Strengthening the capacity for climate action of national and subnational authorities, civil society, the private sector, indigenous peoples and local communities to support the implementation of ambitious actions
- International cooperation for developing countries and vulnerable regions

What Is Required to Achieve 1.5–2°C, a Sustainably Developed World for All

As President Obama said, "There is no Plan B."[67] Time has run out—less than ten years as of this writing (2020). The failure of the Madrid COP25 climate talks in December 2019 speaks volumes to how little time is left. It took the human race several hundred years of burning carbon to get us into this quagmire; it is not likely we will reverse that trend any time soon. What is needed?

- **Change How We Live:**[68] In November 2019, 11,000 climate scientists threw down the gauntlet and told us we were in a climate emergency. They also gave us a blueprint for what we must do to escape it—we must do nothing less than change how we live:

  - **Energy:** Massive energy efficiency and conservation practices; replace fossil fuels with renewables; leave the rest of fossil fuels in the ground; carbon capture and extraction

- ○ **Short-Lived Pollutants:** Promptly reduce emissions of short-lived climate pollutants like methane, black carbon, and HFCs
- ○ **Nature:** Protect and restore Earth's ecosystems—coral reefs, phytoplankton, forests, grasslands, wetlands, soils, mangroves, sea grasses; curb habitat and biodiversity loss; reforestation
- ○ **Food:** Eat mostly plant-based foods; reduce global consumption of animal products
- ○ **Economy:** Carbon-free economy; sustain ecosystems and biosphere; reduce inequality, improve human well-being
- ○ **Population:** Still increasing at 80 million people per year, 200,000/day; it must be stabilized and reduced in a way that protects social integrity

- **<u>Achieve the 17 UN Sustainable Development Goals by 2030:</u>** Limiting global warming to 1.5°C must—as we have seen by the interconnected web of impacts on people, plants, animals, fish and sea creatures, oceans, and the cryosphere—be achieved in the context of a broader set of development goals that benefit humankind. The United Nations Development Programme has established 17 Sustainable Development Goals, which were adopted by all UN member states in 2015 "as a universal call to action to end poverty, protect the planet, and ensure that all people enjoy peace and prosperity by 2030."[69] The goals are integrated because the problems we face are interconnected and because development must balance social, economic, and environmental sustainability.

- **<u>Maintain Optimism:</u>** Even David Wallace-Wells has left room for optimism. He concluded that with the human race headed for 6–8° C, the prospect of 3–3.5°, even with untold suffering, is better than the where we're going now. He also doesn't believe in surrender or withdrawal.[70] The 11,000 scientists who issued the "climate emergency" notice on November 5, 2019, even said that there were a few encouraging signs, like decreases in global fertility rates, reduced deforestation in the Amazon, increases in wind and solar fossil fuels consumption, and divestment of $7 trillion from fossil fuels.[71] A healthy and resilient sense of optimism, being innovative and creative, inspiring others, and creating shared purpose, respect, and collective responsibility must be at the center of the mobilization for *action*. Never ever quit!

- **<u>Implement Transformative Change:</u>**[72]

  Mitigating and adapting to climate change while honoring the diversity of humans entails major transformations in ... our global society.

  — "World Scientists Warning of a Climate Emergency," *Bioscience*, November 5, 2019

Because the projected negative trends discussed here have already been set in motion, the momentum will carry the human into 2050 and beyond. The only climate projection that scientists have found that does not continue toward ecological disaster involves "transformative change": limited economic growth, keeping all fossil fuels in the ground immediately, measuring quality of life, not gross domestic product, and eliminating subsidies for fossil fuels, industrial fishing, and agriculture. In addition, transformative change involves infrastructure investment in the trillions of dollars as we transform the capitalist economic system that got us to this point in the first place. As Jonathan Baillie of the National Geographic Society said, "We need to secure half of the planet by 2050 with an interim target of 30% by 2030. Then we must restore nature and drive innovation. Only then will we leave future generations a healthy and sustainable planet."[73] There are three key focus points for this transformation:

- **Global Interest, Not National Self-Interest:** A relic of the 20ᵗʰ Century is the construct in international relations known as "national self-interest." It has its place in certain affairs of state, such as negotiating trade relationships and certain military alliances, but when it comes to the existential threat of a mass extinction due to global warming, national governments must first put global interests first. When discussing ambition and actions to be taken at any global meeting, like COP25, national governments must park their national self-interest at the door and make decisions for the good of all.
- **An End to Greed and Inequality:** Corporate and individual greed, grounded in an economic system based on consumption, capital, and the exploitation of natural resources for the good of the few, must be transformed into a global economic system grounded in equity, the end to inequality, fairness, and the economic survival of all. Sacrificing the well-being of 3.5 billion people so that 8 people can own most of the global wealth is an unsustainable and unacceptable future.
- **Leading Collaboratively:** While leaders like Secretary-General of the United Nations António Guterres have distinguished themselves as global collaborative leaders, if the Madrid conference is any indication, that is where global collaborative leadership ends. There is, in all the literature covered so far, a dearth of research on what it takes for there to be collaborative leadership to address the climate emergency. It is rather the politics of exhortation, increased awareness based on the most recent scientific data, and political manipulation, undermining, and compromises that go nowhere. There *must* be a laser-like focus on building a global cadre of collaborative leaders who will be mobilized to facilitate the implementation of *action plans* that will achieve the 1.5–2° global warming threshold goal.

Constituencies for Transformation and Action

We have no choice now. We have to work together on real-world solutions. After decades of failure to act at a global level ... a blueprint is emerging—one that shows what we need to do to literally save the planet and its species, including human beings. We just need to learn how to follow the directions over the next ten to fifteen years to prevent this slow-moving catastrophe from altering life as we know it.

—Jeff Nesbit, *This Is the Way the World Ends*

Here are three examples of global collaborative leadership that can inspire us all:

- **Youth Activism:** Since 2016 the world has watched in awe of a young Swedish climate activist, Greta Thunberg, who began her collaborative leadership journey outdoors on the steps of her high school every Friday, and three years later mobilized over 10 million young people in countries around the world in a Friday strike for climate action. Her activism, inspiration, humility, and plain-spoken messages have shown us what moral authority looks like—the older generation is stealing the future of her generation, and it is unacceptable to not act. Her activism gave rise to the Sunrise Movement of youth around the world, Extinction Rebellion, and to many acts of courage and conviction by citizens around the world. The Power of One—she moved the young people of the world to act and was nominated for the Nobel Peace Prize. One person can indeed transform the world.

- **Global Large City Mayors:** The mayors of some of the world's largest cities are another critical constituency for climate change transformation and action. They are over 90 megacities with more than 650 million people that are delivering 30% of all climate actions through city-to-city collaboration. They are taking actions to take 2.4 gigatons of CO_2 out of the atmosphere.[74]

- **US State Governors:** The United States Climate Alliance is a bipartisan group of 24 states committed to meeting the goals of the Paris Agreement. It represents 55% of the US population and an $11.7 trillion economy, which is larger than all countries except the United States and China:[75]

  o Their climate and clean energy policies have attracted billions of dollars of new investment and helped create more than 1.7 million clean energy jobs, over half the US total.

  o Between 2005 and 2016, alliance states reduced their emissions by 14% compared to the national average of 11%.

  o In that same time period, the combined economic output of alliance states grew by 16%, while the rest of the country grew by only 14%.

YOUR COLLABORATIVE LEADERSHIP IN A WORLD AT RISK

... the question before us ... is whether we can save ourselves a as a vanquished earth begins to turn against us. In the end, the planet will be fine. We might not be.[76]

—Jeff Nesbit, *This is the Way the World Ends*

You have been on a long journey to get here, to this place where you are now facing your own demise, and that of the people you love, as well as the other peoples on the planet. It is a difficult place to be, but as you have discovered in this chapter, it is the hard reality we have no choice but to face. Each of us now has a choice to make. We can deny the existence of the scientific data. We can rationalize away extreme weather events as mere episodes. We can become very fearful or depressed and bury ourselves in our work, hoping that what is happening is not really happening. Or we can make a conscious choice to embrace these hard facts and commit ourselves to saving humanity from itself.

The Ten Attributes of a Collaborative Leader

What does it mean to be a collaborative leader in a world at this level of risk? It is my profound belief that each one of us has a moral obligation and ethical responsibility to do whatever we can, in whatever capacity and sphere, to address the existential threat of climate change by bringing our values, intention, intellect, skills, and productive energy to bear. A way to frame our conscious choice to *act* is to put it in the context of the ten attributes of collaborative leaders:

- **Ethical Above Reproach:** The highest integrity and ethically are above reproach
- **Principle-Based:** Practice the seven principles of collaboration
- **A Clear Purpose:** Complete their journey work
- **Credible and Trustworthy:** Are credible and trustworthy
- **Collaborative Mind-Set:** Focus on relationships first, the leadership culture, and building ownership and trust through full engagement
- **Emotionally Intelligent:** Are self-aware about their behavior and its impacts on others; self-reflective
- **Facilitative and Builds Ownership:** Are facilitators of relationships and processes for ownership
- **Optimistic and Inspiring:** Maintain a high level of optimism
- **Leadership Will:** Have a deep reservoir of willpower and persistence; they never ever give up
- **Leadership Discipline:** Stay on track, grow trust, respect and ownership, and produce results

These attributes are the foundation of who you are as a collaborative leader. You've been on your journey and are continuing to learn and grow. The question is: Now that you know who you are, know how to work with collaborative teams, and how to transform a leadership culture into a 4th Evolution collaborative organization, what is your responsibility to the peoples of the planet, and how will you show up?

A Creed for Leading in a 21st Century World at Risk

> *Never doubt that a small group of thoughtful citizens can change the world. Indeed, it is the only thing that ever has.*

—Margaret Mead

Are you a Greta Thunberg, who is mobilizing the youth of the world to combat climate change? Are you a Nelson Mandela, who freed the peoples of South Africa by his commitment to freedom and love? Are you a Mahatma Gandhi, who freed the peoples of India from British colonial rule through nonviolent protest? You are a citizen of the world, by definition. And as a collaborative leader, you have a special role to play, a

A Collaborative Leader's Creed

As a collaborative leader, I am aware that the world as I know it, and the peoples of this planet, are facing an existential threat of mass extinction. It is my ethic responsibility to do everything in my power to mitigate this threat and to help save the peoples of the Earth. I will honor the following 7 commitments as I make personal and professional choices:

· **I Am a Global Citizen:** I am first a citizen of the world who is committed to doing whatever I can to maintain global temperatures at or below 1.5°C and to serve the peoples of the planet in a manner consistent with the United Nations' goals for sustainable development

· **I Am Morally Committed:** I understand and accept the moral imperative to redress the economic, social, and political inequalities that are impacting poor and indigenous peoples around the world

· **I Am Fully Responsible:** I accept full responsibility for the health and well-being of the planet, and affirm that I will apply my talents, skills, and intellect to help protect the Earth from further degradation

· **I Promote Ownership:** I understand that in order to ensure the sustainability of the planet, everyone must own their part of the solution. I commit to raising awareness and facilitating ownership of the climate emergency, and to engaging others in creating solutions

· **I Will Act:** I understand and accept the urgency of the climate emergency, and will take immediate and persistent actions to address this existential threat

· **I Am Optimistic:** I believe in that the power of one person can lead to the empowerment of all, and that collectively we can save our planet and the peoples who live here

· **I Will Never Ever Give Up:** In the face of the horrific consequences of global warming for all peoples and creatures on the planet, I will persist in my efforts to save the planet utilizing my fully capability

FIGURE 10.5 A Collaborative Leader's Creed.

special responsibility to serve others, facilitate transformation, and to help the peoples of the planet survive. On a very personal note, there really is no choice but to act, or you, your children, and grandchildren will all suffer the consequences.

This is a moment of deep reflection, a time to consider what is truly meaningful in your life, what type of legacy you will leave, and how you will take a stand to serve others, to engage them, to mobilize with them, and to *act*. A part of this reflection is to consider the following *Collaborative Leader's Creed*. A creed provides an ethical framework for the conscious choices you will make to shape how you will live and work in the global space.

Given the realities of global warming, will you lead? Will you step up? Will you accept the moral responsibility of this Creed to help us save the planet?

CHAPTER CONCLUSION: COLLABORATIVE LEADERSHIP CAN SOLVE GLOBAL CLIMATE CHANGE

We are living in extraordinary times that require extraordinary, almost superhuman efforts to address the most serious existential threat ever to face the peoples of Earth in the past 800,000 years. The scientific data leave no doubt that if collective actions are not taken *now*, the human race is likely to face a mass extinction event at some point in the next century. Life, as we have known it to this point, will evaporate in the heat of a warming planet. As the CO_2 emissions continue to increase; the water continues to warm; the glaciers continue to melt; and plant, animal, fish, and sea creatures continue to go extinct, the human consequences will be horrific and disproportionately allocated. Those who are already poor, hungry, diseased, suffering drought or floods, and living mostly in the Southern Hemisphere are the first to suffer now, and this suffering will only increase exponentially as we pass the point of no return. We have until 2030 to achieve net-zero carbon emissions.

It is up to the leaders of the world, in governments, businesses, civil society, and international organizations, to transform our economic, social, and political systems so that greed, corruption, national self-interest, and political short-sightedness are no longer the drivers of the future. To date, even with the formidable efforts of the United Nations, these leaders have failed us. At the glacial rate at which they are moving, mostly backwards, it is now crystal clear that there is not yet the will to take the actions required to save the planet and the peoples who live here.

Greta Thunberg has given us an alternative way to save ourselves from the horrific consequences of global warming—the power of one that leads to the collective power of all. In Zulu culture, the word *ubuntu* means, in effect, "I am because we are." I am connected to each and every human being on this planet. I am responsible to them and for them. I am responsible for what happens next. We have until 2030 to act. I believe that collaborative leaders can be the Power of One, who facilitate the collective Power of All. No matter who we are, where we live, and what we do, as collaborative leaders we can work with others to save the planet, transform systems, and serve all peoples so that there is peace, security, sustainability, and prosperity for all.

You are now at the end of this part of your collaborative leadership journey. You have traveled quite a long distance, first understanding the 4th Evolution of leadership cultures, the Collaboration Paradigm of leadership, what collaborative leadership is and how to become one, what collaborative teams are and how to form them, and then the 4th Evolution of organizational change through the Collaborative Method. We then realized that we have a global responsibility as collaborative leaders as well and tackled the most serious issue facing the human race. You have been an excellent partner on this journey. I salute you, and wish you the very best as you continue. I know you will be an exceptional collaborative leader.

Let us end this journey with a quote from Albert Einstein:

> Strange is our situation here upon earth. Each of us comes for a short visit, not knowing why, yet sometimes seeming to divine a purpose. From the standpoint of daily life, however, there is one thing we do know: that we are here for the sake of each other, above all, for those upon whose smile and well-being our own happiness depends, and also for the countless unknown souls with whose fate we are connected by a bond of sympathy.[77]

CHAPTER REVIEW AND REFLECTIONS

Learning Objectives:

Let's reflect on the learning objectives for the chapter and summarize what we have learned:

- Understand what it means for the world to be at risk as a result of the existential threat of climate change, and the multiple dimensions of the climate emergency.
- Understand the many interconnected and horrific consequences of global warming for plants, animals, fish and sea creatures, oceans and the cryosphere, and human beings.
- Provide a brief review of what global leaders have done to date to address the climate emergency.
- Provide a framework for you to reflect on what your responsibilities and commitments are as a collaborative leader for addressing this existential threat.

Initial Questions Revisited, and For Reflection:

- *Now that you understand the level of threat posed by the climate emergency, the horrific impacts it is now having on the planet and the people who live here, and that the crisis is accelerating, how is this affecting you emotionally and intellectually?*

- *Given global leaders' anemic response to the climate emergency, what would true global collaborative leadership look like to solve this threat to the planet?*
- *In reflecting on the collaborative leader's creed, how do you see your responsibilities as a global citizen and leader to make conscious choices to act to save the planet and the peoples who live here?*

RECOMMENDED VIDEO AND READINGS

- Goldstein, Joshua S., and Staffan A. Qvist, *A Bright Future: How Some Countries Have Solved Climate Change and the Rest Can Follow.* New York: Hachette Book Group, 2019.
- Hawken, Paul, ed. *Drawdown: The Most Comprehensive Plan Ever Proposed to Reverse Global Warming,* New York: Penguin Books, 2017.
- Intergovernmental Panel on Climate Change. *Global Warming of 1.5 °C.* Geneva: IPCC, 2018.
- Nesbit, Jeff. *This Is the Way the World Ends.* New York: St. Martin's Press, 2018.
- Sachs, Jeffrey D. *Common Wealth: Economics for a Crowded Planet.* New York: Penguin Books, 2008.
- Thunberg, Greta. *Speech to the United Nations on Climate Change.* YouTube, September 23, 2019. https://www.youtube.com/watch?v=KAJsdgTPJpU
- United Nations. *Paris Agreement.* Paris: United Nations, 2015.
- Wallace-Wells, David. *The Uninhabitable Earth: Life after Warming.* New York: Tim Duggan Books, 2019.

ENDNOTES

1 *History,* "Did Nero Really Fiddle while Rome Burned?," August 31, 2018, https://www.history.com/news/did-nero-really-fiddle-while-rome-burned
2 John Mecklin, ed., "It Is 100 Seconds to Midnight, 2020 Doomsday Clock Statement," *Bulletin of the Atomic Scientists,* January 23, 2020, p. 1.
3 Andy Bruce, "Bank of England Boss Warns Climate Change Will Wipe Out Assets," *Independent* (London), December 31, 2019.
4 Matt McGrath, "COP25: Longest Climate Talks End with Compromise Deal," BBC, December 15, 2019, https://www.bbc.com/news/science-environment-50799905
5 Intergovernmental Panel on Climate Change, "Global Warming of 1.5°C, Summary for Policy Makers," United Nations, October, 6, 2018.
6 Barack Obama, "Remarks by the President in Announcing the Clean Power Plan," White House, August 3, 2015, https://obamawhitehouse.archives.gov/the-press-office/2015/08/03/remarks-president-announcing-clean-power-plan

7   Union of Concerned Scientists, "Nuclear Weapons Worldwide," January, 2019, https://www.ucsusa.org/nuclear-weapons; Ankit Panda, "New U.S. Missiles in Asia Could Increase the North Korean Nuclear Threat," *Foreign Policy,* November 14, 2019, https://foreignpolicy.com/2019/11/14/us-missiles-asia-inf-north-korea-nuclear-threat-grow/; Gregory Kulacki, "The Risk of Nuclear War with China: A Troubling Lack of Urgency," Union of Concerned Scientists, May 2016, https://www.ucsusa.org/sites/default/files/attach/2016/05/Nuclear-War-with-China.pdf; Crowdstrike, "2018 Global Threat Report: Blurring the Lines between Statecraft and Tradecraft," https://www.crowdstrike.com/resources/reports/2018-crowdstrike-global-threat-report-blurring-the-lines-between-statecraft-and-tradecraft/

8   Jeff Nesbit, *This Is the Way the World Ends* (New York: St. Martin's Press, 2018), pp. 3–4.

9   Andy Gregory, "COP25: Climate Change Close to 'Point of No Return', UN Secretary General Warns ahead of Key International Talks," *Independent (London),* December 2, 2019, https://www.independent.co.uk/environment/cop25-climate-change-un-greta-thunberg-antonio-guterres-madrid-a9228851.html

10 United Nations, "Statement by the UN Secretary-General António Guterres on the Outcome of COP25," United Nations Climate Statement, New York, December 15, 2019, *Economic Times, December 16, 2019,* https://economictimes.indiatimes.com/news/politics-and-nation/disappointed-with-cop25-results-says-un-secretary-general/articleshow/72702378.cms#:~:text=UN%20Secretary%20General%20Antonio%20Guterres,climate%20crisis%2C%E2%80%9D%20he%20said

11 Intergovernmental Panel on Climate Change, "Global Warming of 1.5°C, Summary for Policy Makers."

12 William J. Ripple, Christopher Wolf, Thomas M. Newsome, Phoebe Barnard, and William R. Moomaw, "World Scientists' Warning of a Climate Emergency," *Bioscience,* Vol. 70, No. 1, (November 5, 2019): pp. 8–12.

13 Intergovernmental Panel on Climate Change, op. cit.

14 David Wallace-Wells, *The Uninhabitable Earth: Life after Warming* (New York: St. Martin's Press, 2019), p. 1.

15 Ibid., pp. 12, 13, 27.

16 Ibid., p. 27.

17 Kevin Loria, "CO_2 Levels Are at Their Highest in 800,000 Years," World Economic Forum, in partnership with *Business Insider,* May 9, 2018, https://www.weforum.org/agenda/2018/05/earth-just-hit-a-terrifying-milestone-for-the-first-time-in-more-than-800-000-years

18 Climate Change Impacts in the United States: The Third National Climate Assessment, Globalchange.gov, https://www.globalchange.gov/browse/multimedia/global-temperature-and-carbon-dioxide

19 Monthly Average Mauna Loa CO_2, Earth System Research Laboratory, Global Monitoring Division, National Oceanic and Atmospheric Administration, November 2019, https://www.esrl.noaa.gov/gmd/ccgg/trends/

20 United Nations, *Paris Agreement* (Paris: United Nations, 2015), article II; signed by 192 nations, including the United States, China, and India.

21 Climate Central, "The Globe Is Already above 1°C, on Its Way to 1.5°C," October 9, 2018, https://www.climatecentral.org/gallery/graphics/the-globe-is-already-above-1c

22 Nick Evershed, "Carbon Countdown Clock: How Much of the World's Carbon Budget Have We Spent?," *Guardian* (Manchester), January 19, 2017; the countdown clock's 23.3% figure was accurate as of December 29, 2019, https://www.theguardian.com/environment/datablog/2017/jan/19/carbon-countdown-clock-how-much-of-the-worlds-carbon-budget-have-we-spent

23 Emma Newburger, CNBC, "'Any Growth Is More than We Can Afford': Carbon Dioxide Pollution Hits Record High as Planet Warms," NBC News, December 15, 2019.

24 IPCC AR5 Simulations, as reported by SERC Media, https://serc.carleton.edu/details/images/58499.html

25 United Nations Environment Programme, *Emissions Gap Report 2019, Executive Summary* (Nairobi, Kenya, United Nations Environment Programme, 2019), pp. 4–12

26 Alan Buis, "A Degree of Concern: Why Global Temperatures Matter," Global Climate Change, Vital Signs of the Planet, NASA, June 19, 2019.

27 United Nations Environment Programme, op.cit.

28 Jeff Nesbit, *This Is the Way the World Ends* (New York: St. Martin's Press, 2018), p. xiv.

29 Ibid., p. ix.

30 Ibid., pp. ix–xiv, 233–234; the following data points come from Nesbit's narrative description of selected data points, many of which will be discussed in more detail in this section; also this data is supported by the 11,000 climate scientists cited in Ripple et al., "World Scientists' Warning of a Climate Emergency."

31 James Blalog, *Chasing Ice*, 2012, https://chasingice.com/, Jeff Orlowski, Director, Exposure Studios, Nashville, TN; it won the Emmy in 2014 along with many other film awards.

32 "UN Report: Nature's Dangerous Decline 'Unprecedented'; Species Extinction Rates 'Accelerating,'" United Nations Intergovernmental Science-Policy Platform on Biodiversity and Ecosystem Services, May 6, 2019, https://www.un.org/sustainabledevelopment/blog/2019/05/nature-decline-unprecedented-report/

33 Ibid.

34 Matt McGrath, "Nature Crisis: Humans 'Threaten 1m Species with Extinction,'" BBC, May 6, 2019, https://www.bbc.com/news/science-environment-48169783

35 Ibid.

36 World Wildlife Fund and Buglife, *Bees under Siege from Habitat Loss, Climate Change and Pesticides* (Peterborough, United Kingdom: Buglife, 2019), pp. 6.

37 McGrath, op. cit.

38 Carolyn Beeler, "What Thwaites Glacier Can Tell Us about the Future of West Antarctica," *The World*, January 23, 2019, Public Radio International, https://www.pri.org/stories/2019-01-23/what-thwaites-glacier-can-tell-us-about-future-west-antarctica

39 Ibid.

40 United Nations, *Special Report on the Ocean and Cryosphere in a Changing Climate: Summary for Policymakers* (Geneva: IPCC, 2019).

41 Matt McGrath, "Climate Change: UN Panel Signals Red Alert on 'Blue Planet,'" BBC, September 25, 2019; United Nations, *Special Report,* https://www.bbc.com/news/science-environment-49817804

42 Ibid.

43 Esprit Smith, "Warming Seas May Increase Frequency of Extreme Storms," NASA Global Climate Change, Jet Propulsion Lab, Pasadena, CA, January 29, 2019.

44 McGrath, "Climate Change."

45 Douglas Fox, "The West Antarctic Ice Sheet Seems to Be Good at Collapsing," *National Geographic,* June 13, 2018, https://www.nationalgeographic.com/news/2018/06/west-antarctic-ice-sheet-collapse-climate-change/

46 IMBIE Team, "Mass Balance of the Antarctic Ice Sheet from 1992 to 2017," *Nature,* June 13, 2018, http://eprints.whiterose.ac.uk/132373/8/IMBIE2_accepted_v16.pdf; Fox, op. cit.

47 United Nations, *Special Report,* p. 10.

48 National Research Council, *Ocean Acidification: Starting with the Science* (Washington, DC: National Research Council, 2013), pp. 2.

49 Ibid.

50 United Nations, *Special Report.*

51 D. Laffoley and J. M. Baxter, ed., "Ocean Deoxygenation: Everyone's Problem," International Union for the Conservation of Nature, Switzerland, 2019, https://portals.iucn.org/library/sites/library/files/documents/2019-048-En.pdf

52 Kendra Pierre-Louis, "World's Oceans Are Losing Oxygen Rapidly, Study Finds," *New York Times,* December 7, 2019.

53 D. Laffoley, op. cit., p. xiii; Kendra Pierre-Louis, op. cit.

54 David Wallace-Wells, *The Uninhabitable Earth: Life after Warming* (New York: St. Martin's Press, 2019), pp. 37–140.

55 World Meteorological Organization, *Provisional Statement on the State of the Global Climate in 2019; World Meteorological Organization, Impacts of Climate Change throughout the World as of 12/3/19* (Geneva: World Meteorological Organization, 2019).

56 Food and Agriculture Organization, "Sharing the World's Resources," http://www.fao.org/3/u8480e/U8480Eox.htm; OXFAM, "An Economy for the 99%," Oxfam Briefing Paper, January 2017, pp. 3–7; Worldwatch Institute, https://securesustain.org/job/worldwatch-institute/; Tim McDonnell, "Climate Change Creates a New Migration Crisis for Bangladesh," *National Geographic,* January 24, 2019.

57 World Bank, *Groundswell* Washington, DC: World Bank, 2018), pp. xxi–xxv.

58 United Nations, "World Population Prospects 2019," Department of Economic and Social Affairs, Population Division, New York, 2019, https://www.un.org/development/desa/publications/world-population-prospects-2019-highlights.html#:~:text=World%20Population%20Prospects%202019%3A%20Highlights,-17%20June%202019&text=The%20world's%20population%20is%20expected,United%20Nations%20report%20launched%20today

59 Ibid.

60   OXFAM, *"An Economy for the 99%," January, 2017,* https://oi-files-d8-prod.s3.eu-west-2. amazonaws.com/s3fs-public/file_attachments/bp-economy-for-99-percent-160117-summ-en.pdf

61   Eleanor Ainge Roy, "'One Day We'll Disappear': Tuvalu's Sinking Islands," *Guardian* (Manchester), May 16, 2019, https://www.openteam.co/2019/05/16/0390ne-day-we039ll-disappear039-tuvalu039s-sinking-islands-eleanor-ainge-roy/

62   Patrick D. Nunn, *Climate Change and Pacific Island Countries (New York:* United Nations Development Programme, 2012), pp. 1–2.

63   McGrath, "Climate Change."

64   McGrath, "COP25."

65   United Nations, *Paris* Agreement, p. 3.

66   United Nations, "Global Warming of 1.5°C, Summary for Policy Makers," Intergovernmental Panel on Climate Change, United Nations, Geneva, October 6, 2018, pp. 29–30.

67   Barack Obama, "Remarks by the President in Announcing the Clean Power Plan," White House, August 3, 2015, https://obamawhitehouse.archives.gov/the-press-office/2015/08/03/remarks-president-announcing-clean-power-plan

68   William J. Ripple, Christopher Wolf, Thomas M. Newsome, Phoebe Barnard, and William R. Moomaw, "World Scientists' Warning of a Climate Emergency," *Bioscience* (November 5, 2019): Vol. 70, No. 1, p. 4.

69   United Nations Development Programme, "Deadline 2030: Sustainable Development Goals," January 1, 2016, https://www.undp.org/content/undp/en/home/sustainable-development-goals.html

70   Wallace-Wells, op. cit. p. 31.

71   Ripple et al., "World Scientists' Warning of a Climate Emergency."

72   This section is based on McGrath, "Nature Crisis."

73   Erin Waite, "Many people want to set aside half of Earth as nature," *National Geographic*, September 17, 2017, https://www.nationalgeographic.com/animals/2019/09/poll-extinction-public-slow-extinction/

74   C-40 Cities, "About," 2020, https://www.c40.org/about

75   United States Climate Alliance, "2019 Fact Sheet," 2019, http://www.usclimatealliance.org/

76   Nesbit, *This Is the Way the World Ends*, p. 273.

77   https://www.goodreads.com/quotes/762976-strange-is-our-situation-here-upon-earth-each-of-us

Figure Credits

Fig. 10.1: Source: https://www.globalchange.gov/browse/multimedia/global-temperature-and-carbon-dioxide.
Fig. 10.2: Source: National Oceanic and Atmospheric Administration.
Fig. 10.3: Source: climate.nasa.gov.
Fig. 10.4: Source: climatecentral.org.

Epilogue: The Urgency of Now— A Call to Action

IT'S NO LONGER business as usual! We can no longer afford to use 20th Century leadership paradigms that do not and cannot address the crises facing us in the 21st Century. Those days are over. It is time to act—and to act now, to transform how we lead our teams and organizations from hierarchy, power, and control to collaboration, ownership and trust. Only then will we be able to meet the complex challenges of a digital, technologically accelerating, VUCA world—one that is racing toward the cliff of mass extinction due to climate change.

This book is a call to action. The time for debate has passed. If we do not mobilize to do everything in our collective power to get to net-zero carbon emissions by 2030, by 2050 it will not matter what type of leadership culture you have in your organization. The peoples of the planet will experience the same kind of panic, chaos, and destruction that Australia faced in 2019–20 as their 3.5°C climate resulted in fires that could not be contained, destroyed homes, and killed dozens of people and over 1 billion animals. Or the peoples of Jakarta, Indonesia, who must move their capital to Borneo because it is sinking. Or the peoples of southern Bangladesh, who had to flee to Dacca as sea level rise consumed their farmland. Or the peoples of East Africa, who suffered the worst of Cyclone Idai in 2019, only to be followed by drought and the devastation of two separate hordes of locusts that consumed their only source of food.

It has been the intention of this book to provide the theoretical foundation and practical applications for collective action—a theory of collaboration that has been developed, tested, and proven to work over 40 years—and a methodology that can be implemented at the individual, team, organizational, and global levels. It is only through collective, collaborative action, putting the interests of the many ahead of the interests of the few, that will enable the human race to survive.

Every one of us can take action on any number of fronts. As individuals, we can go on the collaborative leadership journey, go through the steps, and reflect on what type of leader we want to be. You can develop your own personal moral code of ethics, and make a commitment to be an ethical leader above reproach. You can take workshops on collaborative leadership skills, particularly facilitation. In terms of global warming, you can evaluate your own carbon footprint and commit to getting to net-zero carbon emissions in your own household, and in the households of your friends. You can use Chapter 10 as a way to increase shared understanding about the scientific realities of global warming, as well as the consequences of inaction.

At the team level, you can facilitate yours through the collaborative team governance process, even if the team has been underway for a while. It's part of learning and growing as a team and strengthening levels of trust and ownership. You can urge your organization to commit to net zero carbon emissions by a date before 2030 and take on extracurricular projects in your communities to achieve that goal.

At the organizational level, you can engage senior leadership in a conversation about giving the workforce ownership, as a partner, in any change initiative being undertaken. If you're a senior leader, you can engage the executive team in making this principle a priority and adopt the workforce bill of rights as part of corporate policy. You can commit to, and work toward, the transformation of the leadership culture to one that is collaborative and psychologically safe, one that empowers the workforce to be their best selves so they can do their best work and produce sustainable results. In terms of climate change, you can work to have your organization commit to net zero carbon emissions by a date before 2030 and sponsor project teams to evaluate every business process so that it meets that objective. Organizational leadership can lobby national leaders to take collective action to address the climate emergency and confront climate deniers with the scientific evidence.

At the global level, we only have one planet. There is no Plan B. You can be Greta Thunberg, where the power of one mobilizes the power of all in your area of expertise or concern. You can act as a citizen of your country to get your leadership to put the interests of the many ahead of national self-interest. You can join civic organizations or global networks of citizens who are taking positive, constructive, and collective action to keep fossil fuels in the ground. You can engage with international organizations to work on research, development, or community action projects focused on getting to net zero carbon emissions.

We are not powerless. We do not have to be victims of circumstances we have talked ourselves into thinking are beyond our control. They are not. It starts inside each of us, with our values, mission, and vision and how we consciously choose to lead our lives. We can watch life as it passes us by, or we can seize the moment and lead. It's up to each of us, and it's up to all of us to make the conscious decisions about what type of world we want to live in, and what kind of world we want to leave our children and future generations.

You now have a new theory of collaboration, leadership's 4ᵗʰ Evolution, leadership fit for the challenges of the 21ˢᵗ Century. You also have a methodology that will empower you to implement the transformation at all levels. Start your journey from the inside-out. Own your leadership. Empower those you work with. Take a stand for what you believe in. Help us save the peoples of the planet from mass extinction. *Carpe diem.* The time to lead collaboratively is now. As the father of collaborative leadership told us over 26 centuries ago:

> *A leader is best when people barely know he/she exists, when his/her work*
> *is done, his/her aim fulfilled, they will say: we did it ourselves.*

—Lao Tzu, 6ᵗʰ Century BCE

Bibliography

Allport, G. W. Foreword to *Resolving Social Conflict,* ed. G. W. Lewin. London: Harper & Row, 1948.

Anand, N., and Jean-Louis Barsoux. "What Everyone Gets Wrong about Change Management." *Harvard Business Review,* November–December, 2017.

Archer, David, and Alex Cameron. *Collaborative Leadership.* Boston, MA: Elsevier, 2009.

Argyris, Chris. "The Individual and the Organization." *Administrative Science Quarterly* 2, no. 1 (June 1957).

Argyris, Chris. *Integrating the Individual and the Organization.* New York: Wiley, 1964.

Armstrong, Michael. "The Psychological Contract." Chap. 16 in *A Handbook of Human Resource Management Practice.* 10th ed. New York: Kogan Page, 2006.

Ashkenas, Ron. "Change Management Needs to Change." *Harvard Business Review,* April 16, 2013. https://hbsp.harvard.edu/product/H00AHI-PDF-ENG?Ntt=Ashkenas%2C+Ron.+%E2%80%9CChange+Management+Needs+to+Change.%E2%80%9D+Harvard+Business+Review%2C+April+16%2C+2013&itemFindingMethod=Search

Barrett, Morag. "What Exactly Is the Mentor's Role? What Is the Mentee's?" Association for Training and Development, Alexandria, VA, January 21, 2014. https://www.td.org/insights/what-exactly-is-the- mentors-role-what-is-the-mentees

Beckhard, Richard. "What Is Organization Development?" In *Organization Development,* edited by Joan V. Gallos. San Francisco: Wiley, 2006.

Beeler, Carolyn. "What Thwaites Glacier Can Tell Us about the Future of West Antarctica." *The World,* Public Radio International, January 23, 2019. https://www.pri.org/stories/2019-01-23/what-thwaites-glacier-can-tell-us-about-future-west-antarctica

Bendix, Aria. "Indonesia Is Spending $33 Billion to Move Its Capital." *Business Insider,* August 27, 2019.

Benko, Cathleen, and Molly Anderson. "Lattice Ways to Participate." Chap. 5 in *Creating a Company Culture of Collaboration and Transparency.* Boston, MA: Harvard Business Review Press, 2010.

Bennis, Warren. *On Becoming a Leader.* Philadelphia, PA: Basic Books, 1989.

Bennis, Warren, and James O'Toole. "How Business Schools Lost Their Way." *Harvard Business Review,* May 2005, 10 pages.

Blake, Robert, and Jane Mouton. *The Managerial Grid: The Key to Leadership Excellence.* Houston, TX: Gulf, 1964.

Blalog, James. *Chasing Ice* James Blalog, *Chasing Ice,* Jeff Orlowski, Director, Exposure Studios, Nashville, TN. 2012. https://chasingice.com/

Bridges, William. *Managing Transitions: Making the Most of Change.* 4th ed. Philadelphia, PA: Perseus Books, 2016.

Burnes, Bernard. "Kurt Lewin and the Planned Approach to Change: A Reappraisal." In *Organization Development,* edited by Joan V. Gallos. San Francisco: Wiley, 2006.

Burns, James MacGregor. "The Power of Leadership." In *Leadership.* New York: Harper Collins, 1978.

Boutetière, Hortense de la, Alberto Montagner, and Angelika Reich. "Unlocking Success in Digital Transformations." McKinsey, 2018. https://www.mckinsey.com/~/media/McKinsey/Business%20Functions/Organization/Our%20Insights/Unlocking%20success%20in%20digital%20transformations/Unlocking-success-in-digital-transformations.ashx

Buis, Alan. "A Degree of Concern: Why Global Temperatures Matter." Global Climate Change, Vital Signs of the Planet, NASA, June 19, 2019. https://climate.nasa.gov/news/2865/a-degree-of-concern-why-global-temperatures-matter/

Burns, Tom, and G. M. Stalker. "Mechanistic and Organic Systems." *The Management of Innovation,* Oxford University Press, Oxford, England, 1961.

Cashman, Kevin. "Remembering Warren Bennis: The Father of Leadership Development." *Forbes,* August 5, 2014. https://www.forbes.com/sites/kevincashman/2014/08/05/350/#11f49661300d

Center for Organizational Excellence. *2017 Work and Well-Being Survey.* Washington, DC: American Psychological Association, 2017.

C-40 Cities. "About." 2020. https://www.c40.org/about

Chang, Emily. *Brotopia.* New York: Penguin Random House, 2018.

Chrislip, David D. *The Collaborative Leadership Fieldbook.* San Francisco: Jossey-Bass, 2002.

Clawson, James. "Active Listening." *Harvard Business Review,* March 28, 2018.

Climate Central. "The Globe Is Already Above 1°C, on Its Way to 1.5°C." October 9, 2018. https://www.climatecentral.org/gallery/graphics/the-globe-is-already-above-1c

Collins, Jim. *Built to Last: Successful Habits of Visionary Companies.* New York: HarperCollins, 1994.

Collins, Jim. *Good to Great.* New York: HarperCollins, 2001.

Cooke, Robert A. Interview by Dr. Edward Marshall. March 25, 2019, and May 27, 2019.

Cooke, Robert A., and Janet L. Szumal. "The Impact of Group Interaction Styles on Problem-Solving Effectiveness." *Journal of Applied Behavioral Science* 15 (December 1994): 415–437.

Cooke, Robert A., and Janet L. Szumal. "Using the *Organizational Culture Inventory®* to Understand the Operating Cultures of Organizations." In *Handbook of Organizational Culture & Climate,* edited by Neal M. Ashkanasy, Celeste P. M. Wilderom, and Mark F. Peterson. Thousand Oaks, CA: Sage, 2011.

Cooperrider, David L., and Leslie E. Sekerka. "Toward a Theory of Positive Organizational Change." In *Organization Development,* edited by Joan V. Gallos. San Francisco: Wiley, 2006.

Covey, Stephen M. R. *The Speed of Trust.* New York: Free Press, 2006.

Covey, Stephen R. *Principle-Centered Leadership.* New York: Free Press, 1990.

Covey, Stephen R. *The Seven Habits of Highly Effective People.* New York: Free Press, 1989.

Crowdstrike. "2018 Global Threat Report: Blurring the Lines between Statecraft and Tradecraft." 2018. https://www.crowdstrike.com/resources/reports/2018-crowdstrike-global-threat-report-blurring-the-lines-between-statecraft-and-tradecraft/

Davenport, Thomas H. "The Fad That Forgot People." *Fast Company,* October 31, 1995. https://www.fastcompany.com/26310/fad-forgot-people

Davis, Keith. *Human Relations at Work.* 3rd ed. New York: McGraw-Hill, 1969.

Deloitte Consulting. "The Deloitte Global Millennial Survey 2019." London, England. https://www2.deloitte.com/global/en/pages/about-deloitte/articles/millennialsurvey.html

Deloitte Consulting. "Industry 4.0: Challenges and Solutions for the Digital Transformation and Use of Exponential Technologies." October 10, 2018. https://www2.deloitte.com/content/dam/Deloitte/ch/Documents/manufacturing/ch-en-manufacturing-industry-4-0-24102014.pdf

Deloitte Consulting. "Trust in the Workplace: 2010 Ethics and Workplace Survey." 2010. https://docplayer.net/13107004-Trust-in-the-workplace-2010-ethics-workplace-survey.html

Deming, W. Edwards. *Out of the Crisis.* Cambridge, MA: MIT Press, 2018.

Denning, Steve. "Why Today's Business Schools Teach Yesterday's Expertise." *Forbes,* May 27, 2018. https://www.forbes.com/sites/stevedenning/2018/05/27/why-todays-business-schools-teach-yesterdays-expertise/#26310793488b

DePree, Max. *Leadership Is an Art.* New York: Dell, 1989.

Dhawan, Erica, and Tomas Chamorro-Premuzic. "How to Collaborate Effectively If Your Team Is Remote." *Harvard Business Review,* February 27, 2018. https://hbr.org/2018/02/how-to-collaborate-effectively-if-your-team-is-remote

Drucker, Peter. *What Makes an Effective Executive, Harvard Business Review Press,* June, 2004.

Dubash, Navroz, and Ankit Bhardwag. "Guest Post: India's Emissions Will Double at Most by 2030." *Carbon Brief,* August 22, 2018. https://www.carbonbrief.org/guest-post-indias-emissions-will-double-at-most-by-2030

DuBois, Shelley. "The Rise of the Chief Culture Officer." *Fortune,* July 30, 2012. https://fortune.com/2012/07/30/the-rise-of-the-chief-culture-officer/

Duffy, Jim. "Cisco Restructures, Streamlines Operations." *Network World*, May 5, 2011. https://www.networkworld.com/article/2202930/cisco-restructures--streamlines-operations.html

Economist. "The Hawthorne Effect." November 3, 2008. https://www.economist.com/news/2008/11/03/the-hawthorne-effect

Economy, Peter. "The (Millennial) Workplace of the Future Is Almost Here—These 3 Things Are about to Change Big Time." *Inc.*, January, 15, 2019. https://www.inc.com/peter-economy/the-millennial-workplace-of-future-is-almost-here-these-3-things-are-about-to-change-big-time.html

Edmundson, Amy C. *The Fearless Organization*. Hoboken, NJ: Wiley, 2019.

Edmundson, Amy C. "The Importance of Psychological Safety." *Human Resources*, December 4, 2018.

Etzioni, Amitai. "Position Power and Personal Power." Adapted from *A Comparative Analysis of Complex Organizations*. Glencoe, IL: Free Press, 1961.

Evershed, Nick. "Carbon Countdown Clock: How Much of the World's Carbon Budget Have We Spent?" *Guardian* (Manchester), January 19, 2017. https://www.theguardian.com/environment/datablog/2017/jan/19/carbon-countdown-clock-how-much-of-the-worlds-carbon-budget-have-we-spent

Fox, Douglas. "The West Antarctic Ice Sheet Seems to Be Good at Collapsing." *National Geographic*, June 13, 2018. https://www.nationalgeographic.com/news/2018/06/west-antarctic-ice-sheet-collapse-climate-change/

Frankl, Viktor E. *Man's Search for Meaning*. Boston, MA: Beacon Press, 2006.

Fry, Richard. "Millennials Are the Largest Generation in the U.S. Labor Force." Pew Research Center, April 11, 2018. https://www.pewresearch.org/fact-tank/2018/04/11/millennials-largest-generation-us-labor-force/

George, Bill, Peter Sims, Andrew N. McLean, and Diana Mayer. "Discovering Your Authentic Leadership." *Harvard Business Review*, February 2007, 10 pages

Gerstner, Louis. *Who Says Elephants Can't Dance?* New York: HarperBusiness, 2002.

Gianniris, Demetrios. "The Millennial Arrival and the Evolution of the Modern Workplace." *Forbes*, January 25, 2018. https://www.forbes.com/sites/forbestechcouncil/2018/01/25/the-millennial-arrival-and-the-evolution-of-the-modern-workplace/#59e6e0045a73

Giberson, Tomas, Christian Resick, Marcus W. Dickson, Jacqueline K. Deuling. "Leadership and Organizational Culture: Linking CEO Characteristics to Cultural Values." Springer Science+Business Media, LLC, (April 26, 2009).

Goldsmith, Marshall. *What Got You Here Won't Get You There*. White Plains, NY: Disney Hyperion, 2007.

Goldsmith, Marshall, and Laurence S. Lyons, eds. *Coaching for Leadership*. 2nd ed. San Francisco: Pfeiffer, 2006.

Goleman, Daniel. *Emotional Intelligence*, New York: Bantam Books, 1995.

Goleman, Daniel. "What Is Empathy?" *Harvard Business Review*, December 2013, 160.

Goleman, Daniel. "What Makes a Leader?" *Harvard Business Review*, January 2004, 1–10.

Gratton, Lynda, and Tamara J. Erickson. "Eight Ways to Build Collaborative Teams." In *On Teams*. Boston, MA: Harvard Business Publishing, 2013.

Greenberg, Ezra, Martin Hirt, and Sven Smit. "The Global Forces Inspiring a New Narrative of Progress." *McKinsey Quarterly: Trends and Global Forces*, April 2017. https://www.mckinsey.com/business-functions/strategy-and-corporate-finance/our-insights/the-global-forces-inspiring-a-new-narrative-of-progress

Greenleaf, Robert. *Part I: The Servant Leader Within*. Atlanta, GA: Greenleaf Center for Servant-Leadership, 1970.

Gregory, Andy. "COP25: Climate Change Close to 'Point of No Return', UN Secretary General Warns Ahead of Key International Talks." Independent (London), December 2, 2019. https://www.independent.co.uk/environment/cop25-climate-change-un-greta-thunberg-antonio-guterres-madrid-a9228851.html

Groysberg, Boris, Jeremiah Lee, Jesse Price, and J. Yo-Jud Cheng. "The Leaders Guide to Corporate Culture: How to Manage the Eight Critical Elements of Organizational Life." *Harvard Business Review*, January–February 2018, 15 pages.

Hamel, Gary. "W.L. Gore: An Innovation Democracy." In *The Future of Management.* Boston, MA: Harvard Business School Press, 2007, 21 pages.

Hammer, Michael, and James Champy. *Reengineering the Corporation.* New York: HarperCollins, 2001.

Hammer, Michael, and James Champy. *Reengineering the Corporation: A Manifesto for Business Revolution.* New York: HarperCollins, 1993.

Hansen, Morten T. *Collaboration: How Leaders Avoid the Traps, Create Unity, and Reap Big Results.* Boston, MA: Harvard Business Publishing, 2009.

Hanson, Rick. *Resilient.* New York: Harmony Books, 2018.

Heider, John. *The Tao of Leadership.* Atlanta, GA: Humanics New Age, 1985.

Hersey, Paul, and Walter Natemeyer. "Situational Leadership and Power." In *Classics of Organizational Behavior,* 4th ed., edited by Walter Natemeyer and Paul Hersey. Long Grove, IL: Waveland Press, 2011.

Herzberg, Frederick. "One More Time, How Do You Motivate Employees?" *Harvard Business Review,* January 2003, 14 pages.

Hofstede, Geert, and Gert Jan Hofstede. *Cultures and Organizations: Software of the Mind.* New York: McGraw-Hill, 2005.

Human Synergistics and Center for Applied Research. *Organizational Culture Inventory. OCI®: Interpretation and Development Guide.* Plymouth, MI: Human Synergistics/Center for Applied Research, 2009.

Human Synergistics International. *Organizational Culture Inventory, OCI®: Interpretation and Development Guide.* Plymouth, MI: Center for Applied Research, 2009.

IMBIE Team. "Mass Balance of the Antarctic Ice Sheet from 1992 to 2017." *Nature,* June 13, 2018. https://www.nature.com/articles/s41586-018-0179-y

Intergovernmental Panel on Climate Change. "Global Warming of 1.5°C, Summary for Policy Makers." United Nations, October, 6, 2018. https://www.ipcc.ch/sr15/chapter/spm/

Intergovernmental Panel on Climate Change. "Global Warming of 1.5°C, Summary for Policy Makers." United Nations, Zurich, January 2019. https://www.ipcc.ch/sr15/chapter/spm/

Jung, Carl. *The Collected Works of C.G. Jung, V. 6, Personality Types.* Revision by R. F. C. Hull. Princeton, NJ: Princeton University Press, 1971.

Kahn, William A. "Psychological Conditions of Personal Engagement and Disengagement at Work." *Academy of Management Journal* 33, no. 4, 692-724, 1990.

Katzenbach, Jon R., and Douglas K. Smith. *The Wisdom of Teams. Boston, MA:* Harvard Business Review Press, 1993.

Kotter, John P. *Leading Change.* Boston, MA: Harvard Business Review Press, 2012.

Kotter, John P., and Dan S. Cohen. *The Heart of Change.* Boston, MA: Harvard Business Review Press, 2002.

Kouzes, James, and Barry Posner. *The Leadership Challenge.* 4th ed. San Francisco: Jossey Bass, 2007.

Kouzes, James, and Barry Posner. *The Leadership Challenge.* 6th ed. Hoboken, NJ: Wiley, 2017.

Krippendorf, Klaus. *Content Analysis: An Introduction to Its Methodology.* Thousand Oaks, CA: Sage, 2004.

Kuhn, Thomas. *The Structure of Scientific Revolutions.* 3rd ed. Chicago, IL: University of Chicago Press, 1996.

Kulacki, Gregory. "The Risk of Nuclear War with China: A Troubling Lack of Urgency." Union of Concerned Scientists, May, 2016. https://www.ucsusa.org/sites/default/files/attach/2016/05/Nuclear-War-with-China.pdf

Laffoley, D., and J. M. Baxter, eds. "Ocean Deoxygenation: Everyone's Problem." International Union for the Conservation of Nature, Switzerland, 2019. https://portals.iucn.org/library/sites/library/files/documents/2019-048-En.pdf

Lagace, Martha. "Gerstner: Changing Culture at IBM." Harvard Business School, December 9, 2002. https://hbswk.hbs.edu/archive/gerstner-changing-culture-at-ibm-lou-gerstner-discusses-changing-the-culture-at-ibm

Lao Tzu. *Tao Te Ching.* 6th Century BCE, Stephen Mitchell, Translator, Perennial Classics, New York, 2006.

Leigh, Andrew. *Ethical Leadership.* London: Kogan Page, 2013.

Lencioni, Patrick. *The Five Dysfunctions of a Team.* San Francisco: Jossey-Bass, 2002.

Leonhard, Gerd. *Technology vs. Humanity: The Coming Clash between Man and Machine.* Zurich: Futures Agency, 2016.

Likert, Rensis. "Management Systems 1–4." In *The Human Organization: Its Management and Value,* 3–12. New York: McGraw-Hill, 1967.

Loria, Kevin. "CO_2 Levels Are at Their Highest in 800,000 Years." World Economic Forum, in partnership with Business Insider, May 9, 2018. https://www.weforum.org/agenda/2018/05/earth-just-hit-a-terrifying-milestone-for-the-first-time-in-more-than-800-000-years

Marshall, Edward M. *Building Trust at the Speed of Change: The Power of the Relationship-Based Corporation.* New York: AMACOM Books, 2000.

Marshall, Edward M. *Transforming the Way We Work: The Power of the Collaborative Workplace.* New York: AMACOM Books, 1995.

Maslow, Abraham H. "A Theory of Human Motivation." *Psychological Review* 50 (July 1943), pp. 370–396.

Maslow, Abraham H. *Motivation and Personality.* New York: Harper, 1954.

Maxwell, John C. *The 17 Essential Qualities of a Team Player.* Nashville, TN: Thomas Nelson, 2002.

Mayer, John D., Peter Salovey, and David R. Caruso. "Emotional Intelligence: New Ability or Eclectic Traits?" *American Psychologist* 63, no. 6 (September 2008): 503–517.

McDermott, Ian, and L. Michael Hall. *The Collaborative Leader.* Williston, VT: Crown House, 2016.

McDonnell, Tim. "Climate Change Creates a New Migration Crisis for Bangladesh." *National Geographic,* January 24, 2019. https://www.nationalgeographic.com/environment/2019/01/climate-change-drives-migration-crisis-in-bangladesh-from-dhaka-sundabans/

McGrath, Matt. "COP25: Longest Climate Talks End with Compromise Deal." BBC, December 15, 2019. https://www.bbc.com/news/science-environment-50799905

McGregor, Douglas. *The Human Side of Enterprise.* New York: McGraw-Hill, 1960.

McKinsey & Company. "Why Do Most Change Processes Fail? A Conversation with Harry Robinson." July 2019.https://www.mckinsey.com/business-functions/transformation/our-insights/why-do-most-transformations-fail-a-conversation-with-harry-robinson

McNeish, Dr. Robert. "Lessons From The Geese," Baltimore, MD, 1972. https://transformation-center.org/wp-content/uploads/2015/03/Lessons_From_The_Geese1.pdf

Mecklin, John, ed. "A New Abnormal: It Is Still 2 Minutes to Midnight, 2019 Doomsday Clock Statement." *Bulletin of the Atomic Scientists,* January 24, 2019. https://www.cndpindia.org/a-new-abnormal-it-is-still-2-minutes-to-midnight/

Moldoveanu, Mihnea, and Das Narayandas. "Educating the Next Generation of Leaders." Harvard Business Review, March–April 2019.

Morgan, Blake. "Chief Culture Officer and Chief Customer Officer: A Winning Combination." *Forbes,* January 16, 2018. https://www.forbes.com/sites/blakemorgan/2018/01/16/chief-culture-officer-and-chief-customer-officer-a-winning-combination/#371816973ab1

Morris, Desmond. *The Naked Ape,* New York: Dell, 1967.

Myers & Briggs Foundation. MBTI® Manual: A Guide to the Development and Use of the Myers-Briggs Type Indicator®. https://www.myersbriggs.org/my-mbti-personality-type/mbti-basics/

Nadler, David A. "The Congruence Model of Change." In *Organization Development,* edited by Joan V. Gallos. San Francisco: Wiley, 2006.

Natemeyer, Walter, and Paul Hersey, eds. *Classics of Organizational Behavior.* 4th ed. Long Grove, IL: Waveland Press, 2011.

National Research Council. *Ocean Acidification: Starting with the Science.* Washington, DC: National Research Council, 2013.

Neeley, Tsedal. "Global Teams That Work." *Harvard Business Review,* October 2015. https://hbr.org/2015/10/global-teams-that-work

Nesbit, Jeff. *This Is the Way the World Ends.* New York: St. Martin's Press, 2018.

Nunn, Patrick D. *Climate Change and Pacific Island Countries.* New York: United Nations Development Programme, 2012.

Obama, Barack. "Remarks by the President in Announcing the Clean Power Plan." White House, August 3, 2015. https://obamawhitehouse.archives.gov/the-press-office/2015/08/03/remarks-president-announcing-clean-power-plan

O. C. Tanner Institute. *2020 Global Culture Report.* Salt Lake City, UT: O. C. Tanner Institute.

OXFAM. "An Economy for the 99%." Oxfam Briefing Paper, January 2017. https://www.oxfam.org/en/research/economy-99

Panda, Ankit. "New U.S. Missiles in Asia Could Increase the North Korean Nuclear Threat." *Foreign Policy,* November 14, 2019. https://foreignpolicy.com/2019/11/14/us-missiles-asia-inf-north-korea-nuclear-threat-grow/

Parsons, Talcott. *The Social System.* London: Routledge & Kegan Paul, 1951.

Parsons, Talcott. *Structure and Process in Modern Societies.* New York: Free Press, 2006.

Pierre-Louis, Kendra. "World's Oceans Are Losing Oxygen Rapidly, Study Finds." *New York Times,* December 7, 2019. https://www.nytimes.com/2019/12/07/climate/ocean-acidification-climate-change.html

Reese, Brad. "Management Vision of Cisco CEO John Chambers under Fire." *Network World,* August 7, 2009. https://www.networkworld.com/article/2236730/management-vision-of-cisco-ceo-john-chambers-under-fire.html

Reina, Dennis, and Michelle Reina. *Trust and Betrayal in the Workplace.* Oakland, CA: Barrett-Kohler, 2015.

Ricci, Ron, and Carol Wiese. *The Collaborative Imperative: Executive Strategies for Unlocking Your Organization's True Potential.* Cary, NC: Cisco Systems, 2012.

Ripple, William J., Christopher Wolf, Thomas M. Newsome, Phoebe Barnard, and William R. Moomaw. "World Scientists' Warning of a Climate Emergency." *Bioscience* 70, no. 1, pp. 8-12

Riso, Don Richard. *Personality Types.* New York: Houghton Mifflin Harcourt, 1996.

Robinson, Harry. "Why Do Most Transformations Fail?" McKinsey & Company, July, 2019. https://www.mckinsey.com/business-functions/transformation/our-insights/why-do-most-transformations-fail-a-conversation-with-harry-robinson

Roethlisberger, Fritz J. "The Road Back to Sanity." In *Management and Morale.* Boston, MA: Harvard University Press, 1941.

Ross, Alec. *The Industries of the Future.* New York: Simon & Schuster, 2016.

Rousseau, Denise, *Psychological Contracts in Organizations: Understanding Written and Unwritten Agreements.* Thousand Oaks, CA: Sage, 1994.

Roy, Eleanor Ainge. "'One Day We'll Disappear': Tuvalu's Sinking Islands." *Guardian* (Manchester), May 16, 2019. https://www.theguardian.com/global-development/2019/may/16/one-day-disappear-tuvalu-sinking-islands-rising-seas-climate-change

Salovey, Peter, and John D. Mayer. "Emotional Intelligence." *Imagination, Cognition, and Personality* 9, 1990, pp. 185–211.

Salovey, Peter, and John D. Mayer. *Emotional Intelligence.* Amityville, NY: Baywood, 1990.

Satir, Virginia. *The New People Making.* Atlanta, GA: Atlanta Book Company, 2009.

Schein, Edgar H. "Cultural DNA Workshop." Presentation at Human Synergistics International, Berkeley, CA, April 13–14, 2016.

Schein, Edgar H. "Foreword: Observations on the State of Organization Development." In *Organization Development,* edited by Joan V. Gallos. San Francisco: Wiley, 2006.

Schein, Edgar H. Humble Consulting. Oakland, CA: Barrett-Koehler, 2016.

Schein, Edgar H. "Kurt Lewin's Change Theory in the Field and in the Classroom: Notes toward a Model of Managed Learning." *Reflections* 1, no. 1. http://citeseerx.ist.psu.edu/viewdoc/download?doi=10.1.1.475.3285&rep=rep1&type=pdf

Schein, Edgar H. *Process Consultation: Its Role in Organization Development.* Boston, MA: Addison-Wesley, 1969.

Schein, Edgar H., with Peter Schein. *Organizational Culture and Leadership.* 5th ed. Hoboken, NJ: Wiley, 2017.

Schuman, Sandor P. "The Role of Facilitation in Collaborative Groups." Executive Decision Services, 1996, 1999.

Seashore, Charles N., Edith W. Seashore, and Gerald M. Weinberg. *What Did You Say? The Art of Giving and Receiving Feedback.* Columbia, MD: Bingham House Books, 2003.

Senge, Peter M. *The Fifth Discipline.* New York: Crown, 2006.

Senge, Peter. "The Learning Organization." In *Classics of Organizational Behavior,* 4th ed., edited by Walter Natemeyer and Paul Hersey. Long Grove, IL: Waveland Press, 2011.

Smith, Christie, and Stephanie Turner. "They Are Here! Meet the Current (and Rapidly Rising) Leaders of Our Workforce." Deloitte University, 2017. https://www2.deloitte.com/content/dam/Deloitte/us/Documents/about-deloitte/us-millennial-majority-will-transform-your-culture.pdf

Smith, Esprit. "Warming Seas May Increase Frequency of Extreme Storms." NASA Global Climate Change, Jet Propulsion Lab, Pasadena, CA, January 29, 2019. https://climaticwatch.com/post/-LXPsfckatzG7YZ1N1f1

Spears, Larry. "The Understanding and Practices of Servant Leadership." Presentation at Servant Leadership Research Roundtable, Greenleaf Center for Servant-Leadership, Regent University School of Leadership Studies, August 2005.

Stayer, Ralph. "How I Learned to Let My Workers Lead." *Harvard Business Review,* November–December, 1990, 14 pages.

Stone, Douglas, Bruce Patton, and Sheila Heen. *Conducting Difficult Conversations: How to Discuss What Matters Most.* New York: Penguin Books, 2010.

Strategic Agility Institute. "The VUCA ReportTM." March 2016. https://static1.squarespace.com/static/5579c941e4b00a23147233ce/t/56eff7f420c6474a7cd617ab/1458567164889/The_VUCA_Report_1.1_March_2016.pdf

Susskind, Lawrence. "Breaking Robert's Rules: Consensus-Building Techniques for Group Decision-Making." *Negotiation,* May 1, 2005, 3 pages.

Szumal, Janet L., with Robert A. Cooke. *Creating Constructive Cultures.* Plymouth, MI: Human Synergistics International, 2019.

Tamm, James W., and Ronald J. Luyet. *Radical Collaboration.* New York: HarperCollins, 2004.

Taylor, Frederick Winslow. "The Principles of Scientific Management." In *Classics of Organizational Behavior,* 4th ed., edited by Walter Natemeyer and Paul Hersey. Long Grove, IL: Waveland Press, 2011.

Thomas, Kenneth. "Four Intrinsic Rewards." Chap. 4 in *Intrinsic Motivation at Work.* 2nd ed. Oakland, CA: Barrett-Koehler.

Tuckman, Bruce W., "Developmental Sequence in Small Groups," *Psychological Bulletin* 1965, Vol. 63, No. 6, pp. 384-399.

Tuckman, Bruce, and Mary Ann Jensen. "Stages of Small-Group Development Revisited." *Organization and Management,* Sage Publications, Inc. *Journals,* December 1977.

Union of Concerned Scientists. "Nuclear Weapons Worldwide." January 2019. https://www.ucsusa.org/nuclear-weapons/worldwide

United Nations. "Global Warming of 1.5°C, Summary for Policy Makers." Intergovernmental Panel on Climate Change, Zurich, January, 2019. https://www.ipcc.ch/sr15/chapter/spm/

United Nations. "Only 11 Years Left to Prevent Irreversible Damage from Climate Change, Speakers Warn during General Assembly High-Level Meeting." March 28, 2019. https://www.un.org/press/en/2019/ga12131.doc.htm

United Nations. *Paris Agreement. Paris:* United Nations, 2015. Signed by 192 nations, including the United States, China, and India.

"UN Report: Nature's Dangerous Decline 'Unprecedented'; Species Extinction Rates 'Accelerating.'" United Nations Intergovernmental Science-Policy Platform on Biodiversity and Ecosystem Services, May 6, 2019. https://www.un.org/sustainabledevelopment/blog/2019/05/nature-decline-unprecedented-report/

United Nations. *Special Report on the Ocean and Cryosphere in a Changing Climate: Summary for Policymakers*. Geneva: IPCC, 2019.

United Nations. "Statement by the UN Secretary-General António Guterres on the Outcome of COP25." New York: United Nations Climate Statement, December 15, 2019. https://blogs.un.org/blog/2020/01/07/key-takeaways-from-the-un-climate-conference/

United Nations. "World Population Prospects 2019." Department of Economic and Social Affairs, Population Division, New York, 2019. https://www.un.org/development/desa/publications/world-population-prospects-2019-highlights.html#:~:text=World%20Population%20Prospects%202019%3A%20Highlights,-17%20June%202019&text=The%20world's%20population%20is%20expected,United%20Nations%20report%20launched%20today

United Nations Development Programme. "Deadline 2030: Sustainable Development Goals." 2018. https://www.undp.org/content/undp/en/home/sustainable-development-goals.html

United Nations Environment Programme. *Emissions Gap Report 2019, Executive Summary*. Nairobi, Kenya: United Nations Environment Programme, 2019.

Wallace-Wells, David. *The Uninhabitable Earth: Life after Warming*. New York: St. Martin's Press, 2019.

Walton, Mary. *The Deming Management Method*. New York: Berkley, 1986.

Weber, Max. *Essays in Sociology*. New York: Oxford University Press, 1958.

Werbach, Adam. *Using Transparency to Execute Your Strategy*. Boston, MA: Harvard Business Publishing, 2009.

Whitehurst, Jim. "Leadership Can Shape Company Culture through Their Behaviors." *Harvard Business Review*, October 13, 2016. https://hbsp.harvard.edu/product/H036W0-PDF-ENG?Ntt=Whitehurst%2C+Jim.+%E2%80%9CLeadership+Can+Shape+Company+Culture+through+Their+Behaviors.%E2%80%9D+Harvard+Business+Review%2C+October+13%2C+2016&itemFindingMethod=-Search

Womack, James, Daniel T. Jones, and Daniel Roos. *The Machine That Changed the World*. New York: Free Press, 1990.

Wong, Zachary. *The Eight Essential People Skills for Project Management*. Oakland, CA: Barrett-Koehler, 2018.

World Bank. *Groundswell*. Washington, DC: World Bank, 2018.

World Meteorological Organization. *Provisional Statement on the State of the Global Climate in 2019; World Meteorological Organization, Impacts of Climate Change throughout the World as of 12/3/19*. Geneva: World Meteorological Organization, 2019.

World Wildlife Fund and Buglife. *Bees under Siege from Habitat Loss, Climate Change and Pesticides*. Peterborough, United Kingdom: Buglife, 2019.

Wyatt, Watson. *Driving Business Results through Continuous Engagement*. Watson Wyatt, Arlington, VA, 2009.

Xerox Quality Services. *A World of Quality: Business Transformation at Xerox*. Norwalk, CT: Xerox Quality Services, 1996.

Index

CPSIA information can be obtained
at www.ICGtesting.com
Printed in the USA
LVHW060925020822
724902LV00003B/8

9 781516 598465